Tikanga Māori

Tikanga Māori

Living by Māori Values

Hirini Moko Mead

HUIA

TE WHARE WĀNANGA O
AWANUIĀRANGI

Ki taku hoa rangatira ki a June Te Rina Walker-Mead.

First published in 2003 by Huia Publishers,
39 Pipitea Street, PO Box 17–335,
Wellington, Aotearoa New Zealand.
www.huia.co.nz
ISBN: 1-877283-88-6

National Library of New Zealand Cataloguing-in-Publication Data
Mead, Sidney M. Tikanga Māori : living by Māori values / Hirini Moko Mead.
Includes bibliographical references and index.
ISBN 1-877283-88-6
1. Māori (New Zealand people)—Social life and customs.
2. Māori (New Zealand people)—Rites and ceremonies. I. Title.
390.008999442—dc 21
Published with the assistance of Creative New Zealand
Index prepared by Elaine N. Hall

A note on style

Macrons to indicate the long vowel have not been used for personal pronouns nor for place names, and quoted material remains unaltered.

Contents

Acknowledgements

This book began as a workbook which was a collection of articles and quotes from various sources and became the major source book for a course on tikanga Māori at Victoria University of Wellington. Many years have passed since then and many students have looked to the workbook for some knowledge. The workbook has been reshaped, recast, extended and delivered in a new and hopefully more useful form.

Many people assisted me in various ways, big and small but necessary in the reshaping of this book. Phone calls, emails, discussions and seminars all helped, as did various groups who came to hear me talk about tikanga Māori and ask questions. The questions helped. I acknowledge my whānau who have witnessed my efforts to find sources, identify references, search the internet, write and write again. The Whare Wānanga o Awanuiārangi has been a testing ground for many parts of this book. I acknowledge the assistance of Awanuiārangi in making it possible to publish this book and agreeing to make this the beginning of a Whare Wānanga o Awanuiārangi series. I acknowledge also the help of my larger whānau of Ngāti Awa at various tikanga hui we held and especially of Te Hau Tutua, Hohepa Mason and Pouroto Ngaropo. Enlightenment comes at different times and with different discussion groups. Pouroto Ngaropo and I ran many hui at which the main topic was tikanga.

Grateful thanks are extended to the Māori Purposes Fund Board and Creative New Zealand for their financial support. I wish also to thank the Honourable Justice E. Taihakurei Durie for providing the foreword to this publication. Huia Publishers provided the technical support and offered a helping hand in typing drafts of chapters. I acknowledge especially the assistance of John Huria of Huia Publishers and appreciate his sharp editor's eye for detail and for gaps that needed to be filled.

Finally I acknowledge my wife June Te Rina who has, in a sense, mothered another book, and this time on tikanga Māori.

Many minds have contributed to the unfolding story of tikanga Māori and many more are required to fully explore the complexities of this part of our culture. The story which is represented here is but an introduction to the topic. It might appear to be comprehensive in its coverage but in fact there is more to unfold and discover.

– **Sidney (Hirini) Moko Mead**

Foreword

This book provides a scholarly background to practices and values that many Māori, a growing number, see as necessary for good relations with people and with the land on which they live. These practices and values make up tikanga Māori, or that which exemplifies proper or meritorious conduct according to ancestral law.

While detailing ancient practices, this book is fundamentally about the future. Professor Hirini Mead promotes the principled application of traditional practices in modern situations. He does so not merely to secure tikanga for coming generations of Māori. He also contributes a Māori perspective to the developing world order.

In this work Professor Mead follows a line of action that he started long ago. He is well known in the Māori world for his respected family lines and academic achievements, but equally he is known for his capacity to make pragmatic changes. He has challenged universities to promote Māori studies as a separate and dynamic discipline. He has challenged museums to call in aid the living culture behind ancient artefacts. Most of all, for many years he has challenged Māori to develop traditional protocols in new ways that keep pace with world changes.

Professor Mead is especially noted for his role in organising the highly successful and innovative Te Māori exhibition in New Zealand and the United States. The trust reposed in him by diverse Māori groups and museum authorities is a tribute to his standing in both communities. More recently he has transposed his many years of academic teaching to the demanding task of managing the social and economic advancement of his own Ngāti Awa hapū. There he has promoted land management, traditional education and redress for the historic confiscation of Ngāti Awa land before the Waitangi Tribunal and with the Government.

Accordingly this book is more than an academic work. It reflects the author's personal experience, from his upbringing firmly rooted in the tikanga of his people to his role as a tribal leader. As an introduction to tikanga Māori it covers a wide range of the life experiences of a Māori, but its validity lies most especially in the fact that it reflects the life experience of its author.

The Honourable Justice E. Taihakurei Durie
High Court
Wellington

1
He Tīmatanga Kōrero
Introduction to Tikanga Māori

My interest in tikanga began unexpectedly in 1979 when I suggested that a rāhui be placed on playing rugby with South Africa as a way of preventing Māori from going to that country. The notion of rāhui comes out of tikanga Māori and to most people it was a strange word. It has to do with placing a ritual prohibition on a place, part of a river, part of the foreshore and on certain resources. The idea was either to place a rāhui on the playing fields of South Africa – and that was a preposterous idea – or to place it on the Māori players chosen to go on a rugby tour to that country – and that was a difficulty as well. This was at a time when South Africa followed a policy of apartheid that discriminated against its black population. Opposition to rugby relationships between South Africa and New Zealand was becoming more vocal. The very idea of applying a Māori concept to a highly political issue raised hackles around the country and caused some furious debate on marae and in the pubs of the land. I took part in several marae discussions and talked to my elders at several meetings. They were sympathetic about the cause, but saw difficulties in applying a tikanga such as the rāhui.

It was as a result of the debate, however, that the idea developed of introducing a course on customary concepts at Victoria University of Wellington. It was very obvious in 1979 that few people really under-stood our tikanga, and this included our own people. So was born in 1980 a third-year-level Māori studies course on Māori concepts and ethics, tikanga tuku iho, customs and modes of behaviour handed down to the present generations. That was a revolutionary idea at the time because no university or polytechnic or high school in the country offered, as part of a Māori studies programme, a course on tikanga. Now tikanga Māori has seen the light of day and there are courses and discussions on this subject everywhere, and not before time.

Tikanga Māori is thus a relatively new subject for teaching institutions, a new field of study for researchers, but an old one for Māori who wish to recover knowledge that we had lost. In this book tikanga Māori is explored in some depth and its many faces are looked at. An attempt is made to understand a particular tikanga in its traditional setting and then examine how it is being put into practice today. It is a fascinating subject of study, but what is set out in this book is but a preliminary exploration of tikanga Maori, an introduction. It extends the work of other thinkers such as Cleve Barlow (2001), E. Taihakurei Durie (1994), Joseph Williams (1996) and Anne Salmond (1975, 1976, 1980). Salmond's book *Hui* is all about tikanga. In addition there are numerous references to tikanga in her biographies of 1976 and 1980.

A great deal more research is required in order to expand our understanding of the different aspects of tikanga Māori. The content of the book is supported by several years of teaching the subject at university level, by the presentation of seminars to various groups, and by holding weekend seminars in te reo Māori with members of my iwi.

It is worth noting that one's understanding of tikanga Māori is informed and mediated by the language of communication. One's understanding through te reo Māori is different from one obtained through the English language. Reo Māori participants usually have the advantage of prior knowledge and prior experience. This is not necessarily the case for others. It is to be expected therefore that readers of this book begin with different degrees of preparation and readiness.

The suppression of knowledge

Tikanga Māori has become a common term in our world today, but understandings of what it means vary considerably. Though a few people are quite knowledgeable, the vast majority know little about the subject, and there are reasons why this is so. Active suppression by agencies of the Crown over the last century is one reason. Another is the conversion of Māori to Christianity and its accompanying repudiation of culture.

Another more obvious one was the general belief among both politicians and educationists that progress and development meant turning away from Māori culture and accepting only 'proper knowledge' from the western world. Some of that sort of negative thinking is still present today.

Mātauranga Māori (Māori knowledge) and tikanga Māori remained very much out of sight and absent from school curricula for over a century. There have been some exceptions: in the 1930s, for example, Māori arts and crafts and some music and dance were allowed by the Government to be introduced into Māori schools. The rest of the country, however, remained aloof and blissfully unaware of tikanga Māori. What this indicated, of course, was that the Government, through its Department of Education, determined the curriculum and what knowledge could be made available to Māori in the education system. Suppression of tikanga Māori and mātauranga Māori was thought to be necessary in order to speed the process of assimilation into western ways. A recent book entitled *A Civilising Mission* (Simon & Smith 2001) explores the role of schools in achieving Government policies.

Landmark events

From the 1960s onwards there has been a steady movement towards a greater acceptance of aspects of Māori culture in New Zealand. There were two very important cultural events which dramatically changed the attitudes of many Māori towards our culture and of the general public to our arts. The events were the international exhibition of Māori art, Te Māori (1984–1987), and the waka taua (war canoes) revival for New Zealand's sesquicentennial celebrations at Waitangi in 1990.

Te Māori introduced into the museum world the idea of Māori presenting our own culture and knowledge to the general public rather than have someone else do it for us. It also reinforced the idea of training our guides so that they would know what to say. This involved research into the histories of valuable art objects which inevitably led to the investigation of Māori knowledge and Māori customs. Because iwi were directly involved in Te Māori by being asked to welcome groups to the exhibition, many people had to learn tikanga Māori – by direct research, by witnessing what their iwi did, and especially by being active participants in the activities of their own iwi. This event was instrumental in encouraging iwi to re-examine their tikanga and, in many cases, to rediscover much of it.

The 1990 waka taua revival aroused interest in waka building and the associated customs and practices of the ancestors – navigating, steering, paddling and learning the rituals. The revival also required a large number of youth to learn, research and practise so that they knew the tikanga of their iwi. It was an unforgettable sight to see the waka at Waitangi in 1990 and to witness the activities of their crews, leaders and supporters. Hundreds of people were involved and there were a variety of waka: some small, some high in the water, some low in the water and some very large; some made of fibreglass, some of laminated wood and a few made of solid logs of tōtara, the favoured wood for canoe-building.

These two well-publicised and very popular events helped focus attention upon Māori knowledge, Māori customs and ceremonials, and upon Māori control over our own knowledge, history, traditions and customs. This is not to deny other influences, however, such as the establishment of the Waitangi Tribunal and the success of the reo Māori case (WAI 11) in 1986 (Waitangi Tribunal 1986). Nationwide movements such as the kōhanga reo (language nest) movement for pre-school education in the Māori language, the development of kura kaupapa Māori (Maori-medium primary and secondary schools) and wānanga (tertiary institutions) have also played a very important role in increasing the number of people playing active roles in the Māori world, ensuring that Māori knowledge and tikanga Māori will be pursued with some vigour and will be studied for years to come. There is no turning back.

Tikanga Māori in law

By the final two decades of the twentieth century tikanga Māori had become more widely known and accepted. The term now appears in legislation. The Education Act of 1989 is an example. Tikanga Māori is mentioned in describing the characteristics of a wānanga. Section 162(b) (iv) states that 'a wananga is characterised by teaching and research that maintains, advances, and disseminates knowledge and develops intellectual independence, and assists the application of knowledge regarding ahuatanga Maori (Maori tradition) according to tikanga Maori (Maori custom)'.

The term also appears in the Resource Management Act 1991. In part 1, section 2 tikanga Māori is defined thus: ' "Tikanga Maori" means Maori customary values and practices'.

This Act is also remarkable in the number of Māori terms used and defined in it. Examples are: kaitiakitanga ('the exercise of guardianship'); maataitai ('food resources from the sea'); mahinga maataitai ('area from which these resources are gathered'); tangata whenua ('iwi or hapū that holds mana whenua over that area'); taonga raranga ('plants which produce material highly prized for weaving'); tauranga waka ('canoe landing site').

The term tikanga Māori also appears in the Te Ture Whenua Maori Land Act 1993. In this Act meanings are given for several Māori terms. The following are listed under section 3: ahi kā ('fires of occupation'); kai tiaki ('guardian'); tikanga Māori ('Maori customary values and practices'); tipuna ('ancestor'); whanaunga ('person related by blood'); whāngai ('person adopted in accordance with tikanga Maori').

Section 62 of the Act deals with appointing additional members with knowledge and experience in tikanga Māori. In section 61 tikanga Māori is an issue as between the High Court and the Māori Appellate Court. An opinion of the Appellate Court on an issue of tikanga Māori 'shall be binding on the High Court'. Thus there is clear evidence of increasing awareness of tikanga Māori and its importance in the laws of the land.

Approaches to tikanga Māori

There are several ways of looking at tikanga Māori. These ways are discussed in the following chapters, some briefly and others in more detail. An obvious way is to consider tikanga Māori as a means of social control. Looked at from this point of view, tikanga Māori controls interpersonal relationships, provides ways for groups to meet and interact, and even determines how individuals identify themselves. It is difficult to imagine any social situation where tikanga Māori has no place. Ceremonies relating to life itself – birth, marriage, sickness and death – are firmly embedded in tikanga Māori.

One may choose to look at tikanga Māori from the point of view of ethics. Tikanga Māori might be described as the Māori ethic, referring in particular to a 'system or philosophy of conduct and principles practised by a person or group' (*Living Webster* 1973, 337). The word 'tikanga' itself provides the clue that tikanga Māori deals with right and wrong. 'Tika' means 'to be right' and thus tikanga Māori focuses on the correct way of doing something. This involves moral judgements about appropriate ways of behaving and acting in everyday life.

From this standpoint it is but a short step to seeing tikanga Māori generally as a normative system. A normative system deals with the norms of society, with what is considered to be normal and right. Tikanga Māori was an essential part of the traditional Māori normative system since it dealt with moral behaviour, with correct ways of behaving and with processes for correcting and compensating for bad behaviour. When ceremonies are performed this is still the case today. It is interesting to note that the late Eruera Stirling of Te Whānau-a-Apanui, in discussing mātauranga Māori at an interview with the scholar Dame Anne Salmond in 1979, said, 'Knowledge and matauranga is a blessing on your mind, it makes everything clear and guides you to do things in the right way ... and not a word will be thrown at you by the people' (Salmond 1980:247). He was in effect talking about the normative aspect of tikanga Māori and its knowledge base. Respect the general guidelines of acceptable behaviour as encapsulated in tikanga Māori, is the general message.

By contrast, lawyers tend to view tikanga Māori as customary law or as the 'body of rules or principles, prescribed by authority or established by custom, which a state, community, society, or the like recognises as binding on its members' (*Living Webster* 1973:541).

There was a time when tikanga Māori was followed by a majority of the Māori population and was binding. That is plainly not the case today because there are choices for people to make about how they conduct their lives, and tikanga Māori is being revisited. Although it is better known than thirty years ago, there is still a long way to go to reach a time when tikanga Māori might be adopted as customary law, binding upon a majority of the Māori population.

There are discussions about whether tikanga Māori can be regarded as a system of rules which is produced by agents of the community and which could have courts where offenders could be formally tried. Obviously tikanga Māori has not worked this way in the past. But there is some force and power in tikanga Māori. Transgressions can hurt the offenders and result in some punishment. Tikanga Māori is supported by a social and ritual force which does not need to be monitored by a police force. People who are committed to being Māori generally regard themselves as being bound to uphold tikanga Māori. For them, tikanga Māori definitely has a bite to it.

Economists look at tikanga Māori as an element of economic activity. Firth's 1959 book *Economics of the New Zealand Maori* is a good example of this approach. Another perspective is adopted by prison workers, who see tikanga Māori as a means of rehabilitation and re-education of those Māori prisoners who are willing to commit to acquiring Māori knowledge and live their lives according to Māori customs. Rehabilitation programmes based on tikanga Māori and Māori knowledge are seen to be useful and effective for prisoners who choose to join them.

A different approach is to look at tikanga Māori as an essential part of mātauranga Māori, or Māori knowledge. In point of fact tikanga Māori cannot be understood without making use of mātauranga Māori. All tikanga Māori are firmly embedded in mātauranga Māori, which might be seen as Māori philosophy as well as Māori knowledge. While mātauranga Māori might be carried in the minds, tikanga Māori puts that knowledge into practice and adds the aspects of correctness and ritual support. People then see tikanga in action, and they do it, feel it, understand it, accept it and feel empowered through experience. Tikanga Māori might be described as Māori philosophy in practice and as the practical face of Māori knowledge. In this book an attempt has been made to focus upon tikanga Māori and how it is applied in a variety of situations and expressed through many different ceremonies. Some concepts such as mana whenua and mana moana are avoided because these are political ideas which are used especially in laying claims to resources. Other scholars may choose to explore these terms. The aim here has been to limit the scope of the book because the author is not proposing to write an encyclopaedia. This is an introduction to tikanga Māori, a beginning of serious study of the subject in order to meet a need for information. There is far more to tikanga Māori than is covered in this book.

It is clear from the range of chapters offered in this book that tikanga Māori reaches out to many different aspects of life, that it pervades and informs whatever we do, and that its tentacles reach far and wide. After each chapter there is a perspectives section which provides other views and/or additional information either from early contact times or from the contemporary period. The aim here is to provide, as the heading suggests, other perspectives from those covered in the chapter, or to provide examples that stimulate debate.

Regional variations

It is important to stress that ideas and practices relating to tikanga Māori differ from one tribal region to another. While there are some constants throughout the land, the details of performance are different and the explanations provided may differ as well. There is always a need to refer to the tikanga of the local people. The author's tribal base is Mātaatua in the Bay of Plenty. My experiences in tikanga Māori are based largely upon the region from Lake Taupo, around the eastern seaboard and as far as Hawkes Bay. Within this vast area differences are to be expected.

Kawa and tikanga

Discussions of tikanga Māori generate some debate among tribal groups. In this book a distinction is made within the term tikanga Māori between 1) mātauranga Māori (the knowledge base and ideas associated with a particular tikanga), and 2) the protocols associated with the correct practice of a tikanga. Broadly speaking, tikanga Māori includes both aspects. But in addition, some practices or protocols may be called kawa. When this occurs the knowledge base is the tikanga Māori aspect and the practice of it is the kawa. For example the kawa of the marae is all about protocols. Te Arawa scholars would not agree with this position. To them the kawa is the major term that deals with the knowledge base and tikanga Māori is the practice of that knowledge. Readers need to be aware of this difference of opinion and the position taken in this book.

Perspectives

Questions arose as to which Maori owned what and who could effect a sale. The problem is not only that the Government's answers were wrong, but that the Government presumed to decide the questions at all, for it is the right of peoples to determine (for) themselves such matters as their own membership, leadership, and land entitlements.

Remarkably, it was presumed that the Government could determine matters of Maori custom and policy better than Maori and that it should have the exclusive right to rule on what Maori custom meant.

– Waitangi Tribunal 1996:5

To assess events in contemporary context the Tribunal must consider custom and tradition in western, lineal terms, but this does not and should not be seen to invalidate modern custom, or require that custom should change to fit historical modes. It was custom that people lived by the laws and structure that suited them at the time, and modern preferences and ideologies adjusted to new needs are as much a part of custom as that which existed before.

– Durie 1994:1–2

The Native School thus was intended as a structured interface between Māori culture and European culture – a site where the two cultures would be brought into an organised collision, as it were – with one culture being confronted by the other in a systematic way. Pākehā teachers appointed to these schools were expected to engage with Māori in specific ways designed to systematically undermine their culture and replace it with that of the Pākehā. While the overall goal of the state might be seen as the reinforcing of Pākehā dominance in the structural relations of Māori and Pākehā, the process itself involved Māori–Pākehā relations at a personal level. As agents of the state, the teachers were expected to carry out their professional tasks in ways that would assist the fulfilment of the state's structural goals. However, the dynamics of personal as well as professional relations and the ways in which power operated within them could allow for numerous factors to intervene in and influence this process.

– **Simon & Smith 2001:3**

2
Ngā Āhuatanga o te Tikanga Māori
The Nature of Tikanga Māori

A number of issues relating to the suppression of tikanga Māori and the likely reasons for hiding it away were discussed in chapter 1. Then followed discussion relating to its emergence into the world of light. While these events were all part of the general movement identified as the cultural renaissance of Māoritanga through the decades leading up to the close of the twentieth century there were some key events which helped tikanga Māori in particular. Now tikanga Māori has found new favour, new legitimacy and new importance in the life of the nation.

In this chapter a number of questions are discussed, beginning with the most obvious ones: What is tikanga Māori? How are we to understand it? What underpins it? I turn now to definitions of tikanga Māori.

Definition of tikanga

As chapter 1 has noted tikanga Māori is defined in legislation as Māori customary values and practices. But this is hardly sufficient. It will be helpful, therefore, to develop a definition by beginning with meanings given by the dictionary.

Williams' *Dictionary of the Maori Language* (1971:416–17) provides a range of meanings for tikanga. For example, tikanga can refer to a 'rule, plan' or 'method', and, more generally, to 'custom' and 'habit'. Indeed, for many people tikanga Māori means 'the Māori way' or done 'according to Māori custom'. Another set of meanings refers to reason, motive or purpose. And there is the obvious meaning of correctness, or tika, as the very name suggests.

This book takes the position that tikanga is the set of beliefs associated with practices and procedures to be followed in conducting the affairs of a group or an individual. These procedures are established by precedents through time, are held to be ritually correct, are validated by usually more than one generation and are always subject to what a group or an individual is able to do.

Tikanga differ in scale. Some are large, involve many participants and are very public. The tangihanga is an example of an intricate and public cultural event. It is a complex of several tikanga which are interrelated and underpinned by a body of mātauranga Māori and a set of beliefs. The number of people involved in it can vary from between a modest 100 to 10,000. Other tikanga, as we shall see, are small in scale and are less public. Some may be carried out by individuals in isolation from the public, and at other times participation is limited to the immediate family. There are thus great differences in the social, cultural and economic requirements of particular tikanga.

Tikanga are tools of thought and understanding. They are packages of ideas which help to organise behaviour and provide some predictability in how certain activities are carried out. They provide templates and frameworks to guide our actions and help steer us through some huge gatherings of people and some tense moments in our ceremonial life. They help us to differentiate between right and wrong in everything we do and in all of the activities that we engage in. There is a right and proper way to conduct one's self.

Āhuatanga Māori and tikanga Māori

Tikanga Māori is included in the definition of a wānanga in the Education Act of 1989. Clearly this term refers to the tikanga that we are discussing. But what is āhuatanga Māori which is also mentioned in the Act? The dictionary definition of āhuatanga refers to form and character and probably refers to knowledge and practices which have the character and form of being Māori. Thus, according to the Act, knowledge that has the form and character of being Māori is to be presented and handled according to procedures that flow from tikanga Māori. The Act translates āhuatanga Māori as 'Māori tradition' and tikanga Māori as 'Māori custom'. The Act is not really clear about either tikanga Māori or āhuatanga Māori.

The linking of āhuatanga Māori with tikanga Māori was done by officials of the Ministry of Education who drafted the Bill that became the Education Amendment Act 1989. One can conjecture that the reason for it was to emphasise an aspect of tikanga Maori that focuses upon the integrity and validity of knowledge. This aspect is signalled by the base word tika which means, in a broader sense, that the knowledge and tikanga Maori taught at wānanga should be genuine and right and not made up. The term āhuatanga Maori substitutes for pono (true to the principles of the culture) and tūturu, which means 'genuine'. These latter terms are discussed more fully later.

The knowledge base of tikanga

Tikanga comes out of the accumulated knowledge of generations of Māori and is part of the intellectual property of Māori. The knowledge base of tikanga is a segment of mātauranga Māori. This base consists of ideas, interpretations and modifications added by generations of Māori. Often the modifications are so small as not to be noticed, but in the end they add to the pool of knowledge about a particular tikanga. Concepts such as tapu (the state of being set apart), mana (prestige), noa (neutrality), manaakitanga (hospitality), take (cause), utu (reciprocation), ea (satisfaction), and many others all play a part in explaining our customary practices. These concepts are also referred to as values, and are discussed as such in chapter 3.

A culture that sets aside its pool of tikanga is depriving itself of a valuable segment of knowledge and is limiting its cultural options. This leads to rejection of many or most of the peoples' ceremonies. Generally speaking cultures that do this

1. are minority cultures that are culturally and intellectually oppressed by a dominant and powerful group; or
2. have members who have been converted to a new religion and they are being asked to, or believe they should, repudiate their cultural heritage; or
3. are members of the minority culture who think that the way to win acceptance in the majority culture is to turn against their own; or
4. are people who are just confused because of the mixed signals they receive.

Fortunately, it is always possible to revisit the pool of tikanga and dip into it; and that is what we have done and are continuing to do. Tikanga is an essential part of our heritage and should be embraced, talked about, practised and evaluated.

Aspects of tikanga
Ideas and beliefs

There are several aspects to tikanga. First is the set of ideas and beliefs about a particular tikanga, and this information is carried in the minds of individuals. This aspect might be described as the ideas and knowledge that individuals build up during their lifetimes by seeing, being told, instructed and scolded, and by research and reading. Older individuals generally have a greater familiarity with and knowledge about tikanga because they have participated in tikanga, have observed interpretations of the tikanga at home and other tribal areas. The kaumātua and kuia, the elders, are often the guardians of tikanga. They are expected to know. Tikanga should not be new to them, but for many reasons this is not necessarily the case. Experience is definitely helpful in knowing what to do.

The practice of tikanga

The second aspect is the operation and performance of the idea of tikanga by a group or individual. For instance, the set of beliefs and practices have to be carried out by a hapū (sub-tribe) when they announce that they will open a new meeting house and carry out the ceremony or complex of tikanga called te tā i te kawa o te whare (lifting the tapu of a house). How well the group performs the tikanga depends to a great extent on factors over which the group has varying degrees of control (such as experience, knowledge and availability of expertise), and access to resources (for example, a fully functioning marae, a well-equipped dining room, and piupiu for the welcoming team). Even the weather can play a major role. There are circumstances on the ground that can make it difficult for any one group to do everything properly and to a standard that the visitors would agree that the requirements of, for example, opening a new meeting house, were met adequately. Then, even as the tikanga is being practised, circumstances can arise that require adjustments to be made.

The social validation of tikanga

Obviously the cultural strength and confidence of the hapū is critical in carrying out public tikanga because of the third aspect: the witnessing of the whole operation by dignitaries and visitors from other hapū and other iwi. The witnessing of the event is necessary to validate socially the individual performance of the tikanga. People, including members of the performing hapū, need to be convinced that the tikanga was carried out properly and completely.

Because large-scale tikanga require social validation the host group will go to great lengths to carry out all requirements of the custom. They need to ensure that the ritual dimension of the tikanga is carried out competently and faultlessly, that the house is finished properly in all respects, that the people are afforded proper hospitality. The hosts will make every effort to ensure that the hākari (ritual feast) cannot be criticised on the grounds of inadequacy. The food placed on the tables will be of a standard that qualifies the meal to be called a hākari.

Public and private tikanga

Some tikanga are very public and involve up to hundreds of people, and some are more private. As stated above, tikanga Māori applies to groups and to individuals. Some ceremonies are meant for groups and those vary in scale according to what is planned. A public ceremony can involve a small whānau group or a household group, or it can involve hundreds or even thousands of people. The tikanga sets out the rules of engagement so that everyone knows what is expected of them. Most of the more spectacular ceremonies are public events.

Some tikanga provide guidelines of behaviour for individuals and for family groups. The practices are more personal in many cases, such as the practice of separating the household wash into clothing and bedding on the one hand and cloths associated with food on the other. Dealing with the whenua (placenta) and the pito (umbilical cord) are other examples.

But a family unit can also carry out what could be more public events, such as christening a child by the local river. When it does so, the family acts as though it is being observed and wants to practise the tikanga correctly. The family is bound by the set of beliefs and practices outlined in the definition. Yet there are no witnesses to the events they engage in other than themselves.

The ritual aspect

The reason for a great deal of concern about tikanga is related to the ritual aspect of tikanga. There is a belief that if the rituals are not performed properly some misfortune will be visited upon the group. Thus there is a strong incentive to get it right. The belief that individuals who trample on tikanga or mangle how they are put into practice will cause misfortune to the group is still very strong among several iwi. Some misfortune is expected to be visited upon the culprits as punishment for offending the ancestors and the Gods of the Māori world. There were several examples of 'things' happening to certain people during Te Māori, and the explanation given at the time by several kaumātua was 'ritual punishment'. There would be a nodding of heads in agreement. Carol O'Biso highlighted some 'happenings' in her book *First Light* (1989), but the group of kaumātua who participated in the opening ceremonies – at New York (10 September 1984), Saint Louis (22 February 1985), San Francisco (10 July 1985), and Chicago (6 March 1986) – have their own stories to tell, and theirs have to do with people who were believed to have broken some aspect of tikanga Maori.

The aspect of manaakitanga

It is necessary for the host group to balance several concerns and at the same time be mindful of the high value placed upon manaakitanga. Months of preparation are needed in order that the hosts satisfy themselves that their responsibility of providing manaakitanga is met. Criticism of an event so public as the lifting of the tapu of a house (or consecrating it, as some would say) can hurt and be remembered for years afterwards. The stigma adheres and it may focus totally on the inadequacy of manaakitanga rather than on the main event.

Obligations

Dawn-opening ceremonies are very popular and hundreds of visitors can be expected. Tribal groups from around the country will be invited. Some will come because they remember an obligation from the past. Some will come because of whakapapa (genealogical) affiliations. They come with their gifts of money or of food, or of both. Others come out of interest. Others again make a point of appearing because they have a house to open later. Reciprocal obligations are very important in public events of this sort. The hosts expect that they will receive financial help to defray expenses and usually this is what happens. However, the hosts are expected to keep an accurate account of gifts of money received as these are not usually 'free' gifts. Rather they represent either old obligations met or new obligations established. Someone should remember what the new obligations are and make a return at some time in the future.

Assessing tikanga

The host group listens carefully to the speeches delivered during the day and from them gains an idea from the visiting groups of how the event has been judged. Sometimes visiting speakers can be very critical of what was done and may condemn some of the procedures. On the other hand the speakers may be very impressed and heap praise upon their hosts for the manner in which the tikanga was carried out. Speeches are accompanied with gifts of money, and the size of the gift often gives an indication of support or otherwise. The normative aspect of tikanga is important and will be commented on by the speakers if there are breaches. However, the quality of assessment is mediated by the level of knowledge of the visiting speakers. This factor affects them also and some might not want to comment because they do not have the necessary knowledge.

The pragmatic aspect

There is a pragmatic aspect to some tikanga. In some instances the mātauranga base of a tikanga is founded upon accumulated knowledge which stems from observations of cause and effect. For example, there is a prohibition against menstruating women diving in the sea for sea-food. This prohibition, still standing today but not necessarily followed, can be explained in two ways. Firstly blood is tapu and therefore a menstruating woman is tapu at that time. The status of being tapu and the act of gathering food to eat and the function of water to decrease the level of tapu do not go together. There is a tension in combining these events. However, the more pragmatic explanation is the danger of shark attacks in the sea. Sharks react to the smell of blood. In the same pragmatic way, women who are menstruating are advised not to go and catch a horse at that time. The horse reacts to the smell of blood and may not want to be caught.

Tikanga of this sort are often dismissed as 'old wives' tales' or as 'superstition'. In reality one has to be careful: the problem may be with the attitude of the person rather than the tikanga. The author learnt some sharp lessons about this while doing fieldwork on the island of Santa Ana in the Solomon Islands. There, if one is so stupid as to ignore the tikanga provided by the local people, the consequences could be serious. For example, one was advised to shower and change clothes after walking in the bush. Failure to observe the custom may result in a nasty rash. Some trees give off pollen dust which, if left on the skin, will cause a rash all over the body. It really does not pay to ignore tikanga or dismiss it out of hand without first thinking about it. Accumulated knowledge is important and one should find out what this is before dismissing some potentially very sound advice.

Concept and practice

It is important to note that what we see happening when tikanga is put into practice is not necessarily the ideal manifestation of that tikanga. It is true that precedents have been set and what we witness may well be a perfect example of an interpretation of the concept, but we have no way of knowing this. Other examples have to be seen to identify the essential features, and with this information judgements can be made about the concept. Nor is it possible to be informed about the associated mātauranga by simply observing the ceremony. Tikanga is not that simple. Research is required to get to its knowledge foundations.

To clarify the relationships among the three elements discussed here – namely background knowledge, the concept and the practice – some explanation is necessary. Background knowledge includes the religious ideas and beliefs of the people as well as their general world view. It would include the history of the people and knowledge about their environment. Concepts relating to tikanga come out of that background. For example, in the case of the tangihanga ceremony there are several key concepts associated with it. The concept of death and ideas about it are obviously of key importance. But linked to this are a range of other ideas, principles and values which surround it. What is actually performed at the marae is the tangihanga ceremony as we know it today. A simple diagram summarises the relationship.

It is also true that without the practice and performance aspects of tikanga we would not know about the ideas, concepts and background knowledge that underpin them. One can work backwards from the practice to the idea and the reasons for it. We are fortunate in having access to ethnographic accounts of many tikanga and we are able to study the literature in order to understand and gain some knowledge about them. Masters of karakia such as Henare Tuwhangai and Ruka Broughton were able to explain what they were doing and why. But they are no longer with us. One way of understanding is to study the texts of the karakia: see for example the work of Michael Shirres (1986). The karakia usually follow a set order and there are many similarities among the different iwi. By translating the karakia some understanding can be obtained. Another way is to speak to practising tohunga (skilled spiritual leaders) and get them to explain. However, some tohunga are not very good at explaining what they do and do not really want to be cross-examined. The other way is to attend many of the ceremonies and talk to various people about them.

Breaches of tikanga

Occasionally one learns more about tikanga when a breach occurs and a disagreement degenerates into shouting and abuse. The breach identifies what the tikanga might or should be, and all concerned receive a sharp lesson. It is not a good experience to be at the centre of such a breach, or even to be a witness, but if one were unaware of the appropriate tikanga before the breach, there is no doubt one learns very quickly what to avoid. Thus another role of the visiting public is to point out breaches of tikanga so that everyone learns from them. The hosts may choose to ignore the information and advice because they can rely on another tikanga which holds that tangata whenua (people of the land) are in charge of events that occur on their marae and home ground.

The monitors of tikanga

At most marae there used to be a person who might be described as the 'monitor of tikanga' – some regarded them as 'the monster of tikanga'. This person scolded, admonished and lectured those who breached tikanga. Children especially were targets of their sharp tongues. Just as often though the monitors acted as the tikanga guides to settle any unease and to let people know the rules of the marae. They were particularly helpful to visitors, but rather rough on the locals. This role is not being taken up today at several marae so that people have to rely on their own knowledge.

There is no doubt that an individual who wants to participate in the Māori world needs to know not only the language but also the culture and its tikanga. Without knowledge about tikanga, an individual is uncertain of what is expected, moves with great uncertainty within the culture and becomes very reliant on others for guidance. Peace of mind is greatly assisted by having a fair degree of knowledge about tikanga. Now that there are fewer monitors of tikanga to turn to everyone must rely on their own knowledge.

Linkages with greater Polynesia

Some of the concepts might be described as 'traditional', as being linked to the past and handed down from the ancestors, generation by generation, to the descendants of today. Indeed, on linguistic evidence some concepts such as 'rāhui' and 'tapu' are centuries old and are shared with other cultures in the Pacific. It is important to reflect upon the fact that some tikanga link us to many other cultures in the Pacific and that a part of our Māori knowledge base is pan-Pacific. The ideas of many people long departed from this world remain with us today. Through time, isolation and adaptation, however, the meanings of some of the ancient tikanga have changed or have been extended in new directions. Some customs were developed in Aotearoa – the whole complex of the tangihanga is probably the best example of local development and elaboration. The tangihanga has great antiquity and although the ceremony has been changed it is one of the most enduring and culturally significant tikanga of our world. It is certainly complex and commits a large number of people to participate in it.

Names for new tikanga

In some instances old terms are combined in a new way in order to make a distinction from the traditional usage. An example is 'muru–raupatu', a term that refers to Government- and Pākehā-initiated confiscation of Māori land from its Māori owners. Māori-to-Māori actions which occurred without any Pākehā involvement, especially the involvement of Government officials, are covered by the term 'raupatu', that is, taken by the blade of a patu, by force.

A few terms like 'kōhanga reo' are definitely modern, but they sound traditional. Old terms are being combined in novel ways to cover activities which appear new, yet sound very familiar; which are linked into older aspects of the language system, yet refer to contemporary activities. The terms create links with the past and this, in part, accounts for their general acceptance by the people. Insights from the past are utilised to solve problems of the present. And by giving the activities a significant Māori name the people are able to own them, participate in them with some enthusiasm, and take charge of them.

Links with the past

Tikanga Māori are not frozen in time although some people think that they ought to be. There are some who believe the Treaty of Waitangi is frozen in time, to the period in 1840 when it was signed, and we should have only what was supposedly known then, namely land, trees and fish. There are purists who believe that a concept referred to in the Treaty, such as rangatiratanga, should be understood in terms of its 1840 mean- ing. There are some citizens who go so far as to say that tikanga Māori should remain in the pre-Treaty era and stay there. To them tikanga Māori has no relevance in the lives of contemporary Māori and that body of knowledge belongs to the not-so-noble past of the Māori. Individuals who think this way really have no understanding of what tikanga are and the role tikanga have in our ceremonials and in our daily lives. It is true, however, that tikanga are linked to the past and that is one of the reasons why they are valued so highly by the people. They do link us to the ancestors, to their knowledge base and to their wisdom. What we have today is a rich heritage that requires nurturing, awakening sometimes, adapting to our world and developing further for the next generations.

Conclusions

By now it is clear that tikanga at one level is conceptual and represents a set of ideas, beliefs and practices. At another level it has to do with practice. Tikanga may be translated as custom (which applies especially to the practice of tikanga) or it might be referred to as a customary concept (which focuses on the set of ideas). There are also several aspects of tikanga which help us understand the nature and complexity of our customs. As well as the conceptual and performance aspects already mentioned, there is the ritual component, the witnessing of large-scale events, the value of manaakitanga, the knowledge and experience aspect of the group who are poised to carry out a tikanga, the assessment and judgement aspect, the obligations of participants, and the pragmatic knowledge that underpins some tikanga. In an analysis of tikanga all of these aspects need to be considered, and there are probably others.

As a people we set aside many of our tikanga, but today we are rediscovering and reviving much that was lost. In effect both Te Māori and the 1990 waka taua project of 1990 offered opportunities to learn and recover parts of our culture and relearn associated tikanga. This sort of learning is exciting, is personally enriching, and is spiritually satisfying. It has the power to enrich and transform lives, and to change attitudes. It is a blessing on the mind, as Eruera Stirling said (Salmond, 1980:247), and it empowers the individual. Knowledge enables a person to participate in one's own culture, to move within it in confidence, to meet other people who are following the same path and to enjoy being a Māori. It is a fundamental right of every person of Māori descent to enjoy his or her birthright, and to feel good about it. Tikanga is part of the birthright.

Tikanga Māori is no longer bound geographically, culturally or ethnically. Wherever Māori go we take our tikanga with us. Thus during the overseas tour of Te Māori our customs were displayed as well as our taonga. The dawn ceremony caught the imagination of museum people and now part of our tikanga is being practised by others. It is also true that many non-Māori are becoming involved more and more in our tikanga, and in some cases, as in the area of tapu, they are often drawn into our customs by circumstances outside their control. Some may see this as an inevitable result of partnership and as evidence of greater understanding among us. They may argue that the best way to nurture our customs is to have them widely supported and embraced. Others may argue from the opposite camp and say we need to control our tikanga and maintain them properly. What is actually happening on the ground, however, is the increasing acceptability and popularity of tikanga Māori in the wider community, and evidence of this is the appearance of the term in more recent enactments of the New Zealand Parliament.

Tikanga has emerged as a new area of study, as a field of great opportunities for research, as a body of knowledge that needs to be taught in our schools. It is a set of protocols and a basket of knowledge that our leaders and educators need to know in order to be more effective in what they do. It is knowledge that our people need to understand, discuss, debate and pass on to others. There is every indication that tikanga Māori will become more important in the years to come rather than the reverse. It has come out of hiding and is now in the bright light of day.

Perspectives

a. The question of whether Maori behavioural norms constituted 'law' is an issue of definition. "Were there rules that were viable as governors of conduct?" is usually asked. This comes from analogies with rules-based western law (as distinct, for example, from Christian law). The question might more aptly be whether there were values to which the community generally subscribed. Whether those values were regularly upheld is not the point but whether they had regular influence. Maori operated not by finite rules alone, or even mainly, but as in Christian law, by reference to principles, goals, and values that were not necessarily achievable. They were largely idealised standards attributed to famous ancestors...

b. Whanaungatanga, mana, manaakitanga, aroha, mana tupuna, wairua and utu, may be described as conceptual regulators of tikanga, or as providing fundamental principles or values of Maori law.

Tikanga derived from 'tika', or that which is right or just. 'Tikanga' may be seen as Maori principles for determining justices.

– Durie 1994:3–5

As we have indicated earlier, the 1930s were to see a change in focus in the Native Schools, with the assimilation policy seemingly replaced with a policy of cultural adaptation. This policy allowed for the inclusion of some aspects of Māori culture – mainly arts, crafts and music – into the Native Schools curriculum. D. G. Ball, the inspector responsible for this change, later claimed that Māori language was permitted in Native Schools at this time. However, apart from that included in waiata and kapa haka, there is little evidence of te reo Māori being used in the schools then. Moreover, the oral testimonies show that children were still being punished in schools for speaking Māori during that period.

    – Simon & Smith 2001:168

TU TANGATA: You said earlier on that you have now chosen the Maori way. What does that entail for you?

'Well I see that some of the old ways, nga tikanga Maori need to be revived. At the moment karakia is seen as a relish adding onto something else. I'd like it to be recognised as an official part of Maori religion.'

Ruka says now it's seen as just a performance, very nice and really only ok for the stage, that sort of thing. It's not seen in its appropriate setting.

Ruka believes there are enough young people to transmit the knowledge to. He sees these young people going through much the same wananga he went through, that is going to certain people, learning over a period of years, so that they are properly prepared.

'I have already started baptising because of requests from people. It isn't a thing I rush into, the people and I have a long talk about it. Wairua Maori, it's total commitment.'

    – Broughton 1985:7

3
Ngā Pūtake o te Tikanga
Underlying Principles and Values

This chapter considers the principles and values that underlie tikanga. In putting into practice a large-scale tikanga such as a welcome ceremony to very important guests there are many variables to take into account. Some of these have been discussed in the previous chapter.

Some variables are values (which are themselves subject to variables of various kinds), and some are common variables such as the weather conditions at the time the ceremony is due to commence or while it is happening, the number of people available (and especially knowledge-able people), the seasonal availability of food, and the state of the budget. Principles and values are important words that are discussed in this chapter.

Principles of tika and pono

When evaluating the practical aspects of tikanga, two words are important. I have already briefly discussed the first of these in relation to ethics: the base word tika, which means 'right' or 'correct'. The concept of tika, or being correct, is a base principle that applies to all tikanga. So the practice of a particular tikanga needs to be correct and right. But in making a judgement about correctness there is another key term that should be considered. This is the concept of pono, which means 'true' or 'genuine', that is, true in terms of the principles of Māoritanga. The concept of pono is understood in other parts of Polynesia, in Tahiti and Hawai'i for instance (Tregear 1891:851), but has tended to be neglected here in Aotearoa. The substitute term is tūturu, which is defined in

Williams (1971:460) as 'fixed' or 'permanent' or 'enduring'. Thus in a traditional sense the term tūturu emphasised the aspect of a fixed and never-changing practice, but today its meaning is different. The meaning of the word is similar to that of pono.

In understanding the nature of tikanga it is advisable to emphasise the concept of pono because it is an old idea and because its meaning is free of other connotations. By focusing on pono a judgement may thus be made on whether the practice of a particular tikanga is true to the principles of Māoritanga or is an example of something borrowed from somewhere else. The notion of pono is important today as more and more innovations are being introduced into tikanga. What a spectator observes when witnessing a ceremony advertised as genuine Maori culture might not in fact pass the test of pono. Thus the notion of pono becomes another basic principle of tikanga Maori. In order to qualify as tikanga Maori a ceremony, for example, needs to be correct and true to the principles and values of Maori culture.

The link between tika and pono on the one hand and values on the other is that values have to do with 'principles or standards of behaviour' (*Oxford Compact Dictionary* 2000:1278). Durie (1994:3–4) makes the following points:

> The question might more aptly be whether there were values to which the community generally subscribed. Whether those values were regularly upheld is not the point but whether they had regular influence. Māori operated not by finite rules alone, or even mainly, but as in Christian law, by reference to principles, goals, and values that were not necessarily achievable. They were largely idealised standards attributed to famous ancestors.

This means that a judgement about the application of a particular tikanga in terms of tika or pono is based on whether the principles or standards of behaviour or practice have been observed adequately. The principles, however, encompass all the values which will be described in this chapter and they include assessments about cultural integrity (tika and pono). A judgement is thus made by assessing a range of variables and is not a simple straightforward matter.

Take–utu–ea

If an action is considered to be incorrect this gives ground for alleging a breach of tikanga. The breach becomes the take, which requires a resolution of some sort. A breach, however, involves parties who are aligned with the wrongdoer and with the wronged group. Both parties have to agree that there is a take before a resolution can be contemplated.

Once a take is agreed upon there is often an appropriate utu (recompense), or some equivalent gesture may be given to the wronged party. The reason for doing so is to reach a resolution satisfying all parties so that the matter is resolved. This is the desired outcome, the state of ea.

The threesome concept of take–utu–ea comprises an analytical template for examining behavioural issues, but each term on its own is a principle of tikanga Māori. Each can be applied to a variety of situations and each is subject to many variables such as the mana of the persons involved in an event, the severity of the breach and the economic situation of the wrongdoers.

Values

Williams (2000) argues that tikanga Māori deals not so much with rules and regulations but with values which are subject to various cultural tests of appropriateness, correctness and adequacy. The groundwork for this point of view was prepared several years earlier by Durie (1994). There are differences of opinion about the range of values that underpin tikanga Māori and there is also debate about which values are more important. There may also be some discussion about the place of values in tikanga Māori. Some argue that a value such as manaakitanga is an ideal that few people can attain and sustain. Values could therefore be regarded as unreal. Yet it is true to say that people do try to reach towards the values and practise them to the degree that they can manage. This is the point made earlier by Durie. It is also true that the practical application of tikanga Māori is judged, evaluated and understood in terms of the values described here. Manaakitanga is best understood as a basic principle of behaviour that applies to most ceremonies and should be a guiding principle for everyone. As noted earlier, values have to do with principles or standards of behaviour. So there is an expected standard of manaakitanga that is considered to be appropriate.

Peace agreements (discussed in chapter 10) are the most spectacular manifestations of a state of ea, but traditionally they were difficult to negotiate. That resolutions should reach a state of ea is an ideal that is in the minds of the people. It is important to be able to say 'Kua ea,' that is, the matter is settled and is no longer an issue. Settling an issue is guided by both precedents and by judgements against modern factors. The end result is to reach the state of ea.

Value, values and principles

It could be confusing to use the word 'values' to mean principles and the word 'value' which means 'the regard something is held to deserve; importance or worth' (*Oxford Compact Dictionary* 2000:1277–78). Obviously one is not the plural of the other. Instead we are dealing with two separate words with very different meanings. Manaakitanga is one of the values that underpin tikanga Māori. It refers to an expected standard of behaviour, an ideal that one should aspire to reach. When we say that manaakitanga is 'highly valued' or that there is 'high value' placed upon manaakitanga we are using the base singular word 'value' which means holding something to be important. What values are important, and have been important, to Māori?

Whanaungatanga

One component of the values associated with tikanga is whanaungatanga. Whanaungatanga embraces whakapapa and focuses upon relationships. Individuals expect to be supported by their relatives near and distant, but the collective group also expects the support and help of its individuals. This is a fundamental principle.

There are obligations in terms of whanaungatanga. At a tangihanga relatives are expected to support the whole ceremony. Many tikanga prescribe ways of restoring a balance in relationships because it is recognised that relationships are fragile and need to be nurtured. An associated principle is that of kanohi kitea, a face seen, indicating that kin members need to be seen and the bonds of whanaungatanga kept strong.

The whanaungatanga principle reached beyond actual whakapapa relationships and included relationships to non-kin persons who became like kin through shared experiences and to the ancestral house at the marae, because it is usually named after an ancestor. Although a high value is placed upon whanaungatanga and its obligations the ideal is difficult to achieve.

Manaakitanga and whanaungatanga

All tikanga are underpinned by the high value placed upon manaaki-tanga – nurturing relationships, looking after people, and being very careful about how others are treated. Thus in the tikanga of muru (the ritual redistribution of property discussed in chapter 9), for the groups of people who come to take away the heirlooms, goods, products of the land, sea and forest, the animals and, in fact, anything moveable, the value of manaakitanga still holds: that is, the principle or standard of behaviour must remain in place. These people are given a meal and are allowed to leave in peace. The practice of muru is carefully managed because the values placed on whanaungatanga and manaakitanga must be maintained.

The Law Commission (2001) preferred to call upon the general term aroha to cover this value. Aroha is an essential part of manaakitanga and is an expected dimension of whanaungatanga. It cannot be stressed enough that manaakitanga is always important no matter what the circumstances might be. Some might be motivated by anger or by greed to act against the expected principles of behaviour. In the end, however, a judgement is made about their failure to observe the expected requirements of tikanga. These principles are important in human relationships.

Mana

Personal and group relationships are always mediated and guided by the high value placed upon mana. Mana has to do with the place of the indi-vidual in the social group. Some individuals are regarded as having a high level of mana and others have varying levels. The word as defined by Williams (1957:172) has a range of meanings: 'authority, control', 'influ-ence, prestige, power', 'psychic force', 'effectual, binding, authoritative'.

People with mana tend to be persons in leadership roles in the com-munity. They are well placed in terms of whakapapa and come from chiefly lines or from important families. People of mana draw their prestige and power from their ancestors (mana tipuna). This power is socially founded upon the kinship group, the parents, the whānau, hapū and iwi. There is also a personal increment based on the proven works, skills and/or contributions to the group made over time by an individual that provide human authority (mana tangata). The element of psychic power relates also to whakapapa and connections with the Gods of the Māori world (mana Atua). Few leaders today claim a divine right to be a speaker on the paepae or taumata (the speakers' bench). Yet the most effective speakers are those that have mana and the confidence associated with it.

Mana is in turn mediated by the value placed on the tuakana/taina standing of a person. Tuakana – older siblings, male or female – have a higher position socially than taina, younger siblings. In effect interpersonal relationships are not on a level playing field. They are much more complicated to manage because of other variables. Having skill and experience are advantages in maintaining balance in interpersonal and inter-group relationships. As a general rule mana must be respected and public events should enhance the mana of participants. Actions that diminish mana result in trouble.

Tapu

The concept of tapu is an important element in all tikanga. The source of tapu goes to the heart of Māori religious thought and even though a majority of Māori are members of some Christian church or sect the notion of tapu holds. It is not really a matter of choosing one religion over another. Rather it has to do with integrating different philosophies and making an attempt at reconciling apparent contradictions. Tapu is everywhere in our world. It is present in people, in places, in buildings, in things, words, and in all tikanga. Tapu is inseparable from mana, from our identity as Māori and from our cultural practices.

As Māori we respect the tapu of places and buildings such as the ancestral meeting house. We also respect the tapu of persons including our own. These are ideals and values we believe in. But it has to be admitted that many of us no longer know about these values and often do not know what to do. Notwithstanding this trend, tapu remains an important part of our actions and of our beliefs. When told that we should not step over a sleeping person the reason has to do with the tapu of the person. One should not pass anything over the head of another, the head being the most tapu part of a person. A building is opened at dawn because it is tapu until the moment the builders, carvers and decorators are released from the tapu of creative work and the building is cleared ready for public use. The whole of the tangihanga ceremony cannot be explained unless the notion of tapu is clearly understood.

Utu

While the notion of utu is linked to the analytical framework of the take–utu–ea model already mentioned, there is also a value placed upon utu as compensation, or revenge, or reciprocity. Many commentators have noted the concept of utu, for example in warfare (Vayda 1960:45) and in economic transactions (Firth 1959:412–13). It is sometimes referred to as the principle of reciprocity (Firth) or as the principle of equivalence, and Metge (2001) regards its main purpose as maintaining relationships. As pointed out in this chapter utu is a response to a take and that once the take is admitted the aim is to reach a state of ea, which might be translated as restoring balance and thereby maintaining whanaungatanga.

There are many pathways and responses by which utu is put into practice. Many of the pathways are culturally validated and are regarded as appropriate to the event that triggered a response. Choosing the wrong pathway could be found to be inappropriate.

Noa and ea

The notion of ea to indicate the successful closing of a sequence and the restoration of relationships or the securing of peaceful interrelation-ships is a value that underpins most tikanga. In war, the notion of ea refers specifically to either achieving revenge, which is a limited and one-sided aim, or towards securing peace between both parties, which is more difficult to achieve. In the case of muru, relationships have been upset and a new set of relationships is validated at great cost to one party. The new element in the relationship enters the group at great expense to the receiving hapū and probably needs to foster good future relation-ships. In the context of infringements upon tapu, the response selected reduces the level of tapu to a state of noa, thereby restoring the balance and so reaching the deserved state of ea.

Noa is often paired with tapu indicating that often noa refers to restoring a balance. A high level of tapu is regarded as dangerous. Here the role of tikanga and of tohunga is to reduce the level of dangerous tapu until it is noa or safe. It is not useful to think of noa as being the opposite of tapu or as the absence of tapu. This is plainly not the case. For example a person can be very tapu if one is very ill or there is bleeding and shedding of blood. Once these tapu-increasing symptoms have passed the person returns to a safe state, but still has personal tapu. The state of noa indicates that a balance has been reached, a crisis is over, health is restored and life is normal again. This means relationships are restored. This state coincides with a state of ea and noa. This state might last for several weeks until upset by some unexpected event.

The cycle begins again from a cause, 'take', to a response, 'utu' and finally reaching a state of balance again, 'ea' and 'noa'.

Underlying principles and values are pervasive in any study of tikanga Māori. It follows therefore that these principles and values will arise time and again in the descriptions of the range of tikanga Māori covered in this book.

Perspectives

To look on *tapu* only as 'being with potentiality for power' is to leave out the most important element of *tapu*, the faith element, the link with the spiritual powers. In the understanding of *tapu* presented here, every part of creation has its *tapu*, because every part of creation has its link with one or others of the spiritual powers, and alternately with *Io, Io Matua Kore*, 'the parentless one', *Io Taketake*, 'the source of all'.

It is important to note that this is one view of *tapu*, a view based on some of the Maori writings of the 1840's and 1850's. Each tribe has its own understandings of *tapu* as is evidenced in the Maori manuscripts, what one Maori writer referred to as *tapu*, another referred to as *mana*. Today too, where some tribes speak of *tapu*, others speak of *mana*. Different words are used for the same reality and the use of the different words itself gives us a better understanding of that reality.

– Shirres 1997:33

Again a major factor in having *mana* as a people is the ability to express *mana* through the exercise of hospitality.

So, in the 1850's when Tamehana Te Waharoa approached different chiefs around the country asking them to accept the title of King of Aotearoa, they refused, one after the other. In refusing they referred to the land over which they had no control and to its food resources. The reason they gave for refusing the title was that they did not have the resources to *manaaki*, to look after the people in a way fitting for a King. They felt that their tribal resources would not be equal to the strain of keeping up the position of King.

   – **Shirres 1997:55**

I therefore make a distinction between intrinsic *tapu* and extensions of *tapu*. The intrinsic *tapu* are those things which are *tapu* in themselves. These are the primary *tapu*. The extensions of *tapu* are the restrictions. These are referred to as *tapu* not because of their own intrinsic *tapu* but because of their relationship to some primary *tapu* as a restriction imposed to protect it in some way. They are thus an extension of the primary *tapu*.

   – **Shirres 1997:34**

Ruka says partly the programming of the missionaries and partly Maori misunderstanding resulted in Maori faith-healers and prophets being too ready to brand some tikanga Maori as kehua or evil spirits.

'Our people became frightened of themselves, frightened of their culture, frightened of their tikanga, frightened of their spirituality and they pushed them aside, even their reo.

'I think an example is my kids talking to their grandmother. My belief is to talk Maori to my kids. But their kuia talks Pakeha to them, and tells them to forget their past, 'your future is in the Pakeha world', and that's sad, that was the thinking that permeated that generation.'

Ruka believes this thinking must be undone, not with the older generation but with the coming generation, to win back something.

He says this is what a lot of Maori people are doing, by their search through other religions for their taha Maori. He says Ohakune is a good example, where there is a strong nucleus of Maori young people staunch in their Katorika roots and their taha Maori.

   – **Broughton 1985:7**

4
Te Tapu o te Tangata
The Tapu of the Person

In the world of today it has become important to know who we are, where we come from and what we are born with. There is a felt need to know our roots and to belong to some place that we call home. But as well as being concerned about identity and our place in society there is also the question of birthright. Do we have a birthright or has it been denied, suspended, removed, or is it in doubt that we ever had such a thing? The title of this chapter indicates we are assuming that a person is far more than a mere biological self. There are other aspects of the self and one of these has to do with the spiritual self, the tapu of the person, the sanctity, the special attributes that we are born with and that contribute to defining our place in time, locality and society. The discussion is limited in scope to looking at the notion of birthright, named here as kaihau-waiū, that is, the attributes gained through the mother's milk. It is a working assumption here that a person is born into the world with a birthright that might be very limited or quite extensive. In the Māori case the birthright includes a spiritual aspect and this will be described as we explore the various dimensions of being a Māori person. Others may have similar ideas and give them different names.

In exploring the concept of birthright a number of interesting questions can be asked. The following are examples:

1. What is the birthright of a Māori child?
2. Are there benefits to being Māori?
3. What is the heritage of a Māori child?
4. What are the obligations of the parents?

5. Does tapu apply to both men and women?

6. Is it possible to improve one's social position or is an individual forever locked into a position defined by one's whakapapa?

7. Is mana concerned with being creative and imaginative?

These are interesting questions that have become important today because of the obvious benefits of belonging to an iwi which has just received some compensation money from the nation or has high hopes for the future. Part of the settlement process involves identifying and registering members on hapū lists. Thus iwi are concerned about the rules of eligibility and are setting in place criteria for determining membership, such as whakapapa links, interests in land blocks and association with marae. On the other hand there are individuals who are dusting their whakapapa books and searching for ways of linking in to tribal resources. There are others who are looking for evidence of some Māori blood in their descent lines. A link to a Māori princess or to a chief is a cherished desire.

The abuse of the sanctity of a person

These questions are also very important from an entirely different point of view. In the 1980s and 1990s a disturbing amount of evidence was brought to light concerned with the abuse of the sanctity of the individual: neglect of children, family violence, sexual abuse of children, assault of women, and murder of women. There were appalling cases of violence towards children by adults who exhibited no awareness or acknowledgment of or respect for the individual and their place in Māori society. Nor is it any better in the treatment of women. Was it always like this? Or has there been further erosion of Māori values and cultural norms? Or are there other reasons? How does concern for the well-being of the individual member of the hapū compare with the warlike nature of society at large? While acknowledging the tenuous nature of life in traditional society it is quite plain that within the hapū and the whānau there were rules of behaviour to adhere to, and if these rules were trampled upon there were dire consequences. However, acts of bad behaviour are today no longer controlled by tikanga Māori alone. These are now almost totally matters for the law of the land.

Can one be an individual in Māori society?

Another question is whether it is possible to be an individual in a whānau or hapū when the interests of the group are seen to be supreme. This question can be asked in a different way: if you rejoin your hapū do you lose some or all of your individuality? Firth (1959:135–41) addressed this issue in 1927 when he wrote *Economics of the New Zealand Maori* (first published in 1929). He argued that though the individual person appeared to exist only as a part of a group, the facts did not support this position. He cited writers such as Wilson, Best, and Cowan (Firth 1959:138), and many others over-emphasising the influence of Māori communism. Firth (1959:135) challenges statements such as the following from Best: 'In Maori society the individual could scarcely be termed a social unit, he was lost in the *whanau* or family group.' In fact, there is overwhelming evidence to the contrary, for example in 'rivalry between persons in work, the insistence on utu or an equivalence for gifts and services, quarrels over land and property rights of a personal kind, theft of valuables, gluttonous consumption of food, idleness and the like indicate a definite sphere of action determined primarily by individual interests' (Firth 1959:138). There is no need to push the point any further. It was possible in 1927 to be a Māori individual. If anything, Māori have been increasingly affected by the western ethic of the individual so that we are possibly more individualistic now than in 1927.

Rangatiratanga

The concept of rangatiratanga has been discussed extensively in relation to the Treaty of Waitangi. See for example contributions by Orange 1987, Walker 1996 and Mead 1997. The word appears in article 2 of the Māori text. In these discussions rangatiratanga is associated with political issues such as sovereignty, chieftainship, leadership, self-determination, self-management and the like. When the term was applied to an individual, as in the writings of Te Rangikaheke (Grove 1985:11–12), the issue is about qualities of leadership and chieftainship over a social group, a hapū or iwi. According to Te Rangikaheke the legacy left to a child born of te moenga rangatira (the chiefly marriage bed) would include the essential abilities to lead and conduct meetings of the tribe, know all about agriculture, be brave in battle, be very familiar with military strategies, know the arts, build up the resources of the tribe and be hospitable to visitors.

Te moenga rangatira: the chiefly marriage bed

This is not a discussion about individuals in general or about what any individual Māori might be born with. Te Rangikaheke (Grove 1985: 11–12), however, did discuss a fundamental concept that underpins certain beliefs about the nature of individual talents and characteristics. He was very clear that the source of these characteristics was te moenga rangatira, the chiefly marriage bed. He quoted the following proverb to emphasize the point: 'E kore e hekeheke, he kākano rangatira' (It will never be lost, the seed of chiefly persons) (Grove 1985:12).

Te Rangikaheke meant that a person derived all of their personal characteristics, or pūmanawa as he called them, from the womb of the mother. He called it the belly. From this statement one can postulate that he saw the kākano (seed) as coming from both parents. While the chief might contribute his genes, it was the mother who nurtured the seed and eventually gave birth to a new life that Te Rangikaheke credited to te moenga rangatira. A child born of noble parentage would be referred to as a descendant of a well-known ancestor and as the child of parents of some social standing in the tribal group. Such a child would receive a generous entitlement of assets such as garments and ornaments, and later, interests in land; would be well brought up and well educated, and would by right of birth receive a richer portion of attributes than other children.

The principle of te moenga rangatira is easy to understand. Children born of te moenga rangatira or te takapau wharanui (the great sleeping mat) receive more of everything according to their position of birth in the chiefly lineages. Those unfortunate enough to be far removed from the main chiefly whakapapa lines receive less. While every Māori person is born with a whakapapa which is part of the birthright, there is no common starting point and no level playing field. Every person is different and every one has a unique position in the social system. Te moenga rangatira is an important ranking device which still has relevance and validity in today's society.

Te tapu o te tangata: the sanctity of the person

Once issues of chieftainship and leadership are set aside it is not really appropriate to speak of the rangatiratanga of the individual except in a metaphorical sense. Respect for the individual is better stated as te tapu o te tangata, the sanctity of the person. The reasons for emphasising the tapu aspect of the person will become clear when various attributes are described and discussed. Tapu is a powerful concept when applied to the individual person.

It needs to be said that Te Rangikaheke did not believe that pūmanawa could be passed on to people of low class, such as tūtūā (slaves). In his time tūtūā did not qualify to be treated as human beings. By becoming slaves these people lost their birthright and thus their right to be treated the same as other members of the hapū. But the class divisions of traditional times, namely the chiefly class and the commoners, the ware (low born) or tūtūā (Buck 1987:337), no longer exist and are not recognised. No Māori today will admit to being a commoner or tūtūā. The social divisions of the past have flattened out and there is one class called Māori. Thus Te Rangi-kaheke's notion of te moenga rangatira applies to everyone regardless of social position. However, the differences are accommodated by varying the levels of tapu and mana that individuals receive. This means that fine distinctions are now made within the context of the single class. In other words judgments are still made about rangatira status and proximity to the chiefly line. Also there are discriminating factors, such as order of birth, which separate individuals.

What I shall attempt to do is to present a coherent model of the attributes and characteristics of an individual born of Māori parents, or having one Māori parent. The individual is subject to various social factors, among which is the issue of enculturation so the children know who they are, understand the culture they are born into and know how to behave as adults. The nurturing and sheltering role of the parents is crucial in this process so that the children grow into their culture rather than become alienated from it as happens today in far too many cases.

The concept of kaihau-waiū: birthright

At this point it is useful to think in terms of a birthright which includes everything that a child can expect by being born a Māori. Components of the birthright can be described as attributes that refer to 'any property, quality or characteristic that can be ascribed to a person' (*The Living Webster* 1973:65). The component identified as an attribute will be passed on to the individual as part of the birthright. There is no word in Williams' *Dictionary* for birthright and so I have coined the word kaihau-waiū, meaning property or attribute gained through the mother's milk, that is, through birth.

Te Rangikaheke applied the term pūmanawa in the sense of natural talents to some of the attributes of a person. A more inclusive term for attributes, characteristics and talents is the word āhua, so one can talk about te āhua o te tangata. Āhua refers to form, character and make-up. Thus te āhua o te tangata addresses the notion of the form, character and make-up of the person.

The dynamic aspects of the kaihau-waiū

One's birthright is affected in a number of ways and may be limited or increased according to certain principles and variables. Once having received the kaihau-waiū there are responsibilities upon the parents, the close relatives and the individual person to maintain it and cherish it. Much of the birthright can be lost, or diminished, or damaged by others. At the moment of birth, however, there are discriminating principles which alter the starting point of people. These are listed below:

1. The principle of te moenga rangatira means that those born from a chiefly line inherit more than others.

2. The mātāmua (first born) principle, or the principle of primo-geniture, that is of the priority given to being born first. Order of birth is important in terms of the whakapapa line and privileges which are associated with this principle.

3. The tuakana/taina principle which grants more status to the elder sibling (tuakana) than to the younger (taina). There are extensions of the tuakana principle to other relationships.

4. The principle of utu—ea (compensation—state of balance), which determines whether the birthright remains in a steady state, is increased or substantially reduced.

5. The principle of toa, or personal achievement and service, which enables an individual to make up for lost ground or increase the birthright.

6. The whakatika principle, which enables one to appeal to the Gods through karakia to correct a wrong. This may be effected through a tohunga or minister of a church who will take steps to correct a ritual error. The whakatika principle acknowledges that an individual can make an unwise decision or otherwise do something that damages one's personal mana.

7. The principle of ahi-kā (burning fire), of keeping one's claims warm by being seen (the principle of kanohi kitea, a face seen) and by maintaining contact with the extended family and the hapū.

8. The principle of spiritual nurturing, which comes from observance of proper ceremonies, use of karakia and appeals for divine support.

In addition to maintaining a balance of all these factors there is the added danger of a nanakia, an untrustworthy, hail-fellow-well-met wheeler-dealer in the family who through various means will attempt to disinherit their relatives or harm them. Thus the birthright needs to be protected, discussed, monitored, and maintained in balance so that once the child becomes adult there is something of value to hand over. More importantly the individual is prepared, willing and able to make decisions for one's self because the birthright is a share in the heritage of the Māori nation. When this moment arrives the individual should be keen to receive their share in the inheritance and not reject it, as often happened in the past.

The attributes

Attributes may be grouped into two categories. First is a set of attributes which identify the person and anchor the individual within a social unit that is identified with a known locality. The second group includes attributes that are fundamental to the very nature of human life and are linked to beliefs about the cosmos and the place of human beings within the belief system.

Attributes of identity

Ira tangata, ira atua

Ira tangata refers in general to what results from the moenga tangata, the marriage bed of humans. A new life is created and the new life is human. The word ira means 'life principle' or more specifically 'gene' (Taura Whiri i te Reo Māori 1996:164), while tangata means human. Ira tangata thus refers specifically to a human life that has inherited a collection of genes from the parents. The genes are more than biological elements, however. There is a godlike and spiritual quality to all of them because as human beings, ira tangata descend from ira Atua, the Gods. The first woman was created by the Gods and the seed of human life was planted by Tāne, son of Rangi and Papa, the primeval parents of the Māori cosmos.

Much of a person's prospects in life depend upon the parents and the legacy they pass on: genes, social standing, economic position, education and the like. When adulthood arrives individuals play an important role in shaping their lives and their future. The individual has to act in a social, political, economic and spiritual environment. Education and training prepare the individual for life in this complex cultural environment. But the individual is also a person with a personality known to other persons.

Whakapapa

Whakapapa is a fundamental attribute and gift of birth. It is the social component of the ira, the genes. A child is born into a kinship system which is already in place and has been for many generations. Every individual is a beneficiary of two whakapapa lines, the mother's and the father's. Sometimes a child can claim the whakapapa of only one parent. This single whakapapa line is sufficient to define a place within the hapū of that one parent. Whakapapa provides our identity within a tribal structure and later in life gives an individual the right to say, 'I am Māori.'

One's whakapapa is affected by a number of the principles outlined earlier. The order of birth is important: the mātāmua is accorded more mana than others. It is also affected by the tuakana/taina principle which is also the order of birth. The older sibling has priority over the younger and this principle works its way down to the last born, known as the pōtiki. This person is often treated the same as a mātāmua. Whakapapa is also affected by the ahi-kā principle: one has to be located in the right place and be seen often in order to enjoy the full benefits of whakapapa.

Correct whakapapa is the key to eligibility to interests in tribal lands, to education grants, to attend certain tribal ceremonies, and to be accepted as tangata whenua at the local marae. With it come some responsibilities to play a part in the life of the hapū and iwi. Whakapapa is also the key to membership in the hapū of the parents, to one hapū or to several. Whakapapa legitimises participation in hapū affairs and opens doors to the assets of the iwi. It provides a right to be buried in the local urupā (cemetery), a right to succeed to land interests of the parents and a right to claim membership in the hapū. One can say with certainty 'I am Ngāti Awa' or 'I am Te Tāwera' or 'I am Tūhoe, Te Whānau-a-Apanui, Whakatōhea, Patuheuheu, Ngāti Manawa or Ngāi Te Rangi.' In short, whakapapa is belonging. Without it an individual is outside looking in.

Tūrangawaewae

Whakapapa is also the key to the next component of one's birthright: the right to be associated with a locality. A bundle of attributes come with the fact of being born of Māori parents or even of one Māori parent. One of these attributes is the right to a place for the feet to stand, that is, tūrangawaewae. It is a place where one belongs by right of birth. Tūrangawaewae represents one spot, one locality on planet earth where an individual can say, 'I belong here. I can stand here without challenge. My ancestors stood here before me. My children will stand tall here.' The place includes interests in the land, with the territory of the hapū and of the iwi. It is a place associated with the ancestors and is full of history.

The tūranga is the primary locality, the place intimately associated with the identity of the hapū and therefore with the identity of the person. Today the marae is the centre of identity. Next to it is the cemetery and the wāhi tapu (sacred spots) of the hapū. The place then extends outwards to include the territory of the iwi – the rivers, lakes, mountains, islands, coastline, forests, swamps, harbours and specific land blocks.

These significant places are remembered in proverbs such as 'Ko Pūtauaki te maunga, ko Rangitāiki te awa, ko Rangitukehu te tangata' (Pūtauaki is the mountain, Rangitāiki is the river and Te Rangitukehu is the chief). Another is: 'Ko Taupo te moana, ko Te Heuheu te tangata, ko Tūwharetoa te iwi' (Taupo is the lake, Te Heuheu is the chief and Tūwharetoa is the tribe).

Pūmanawa

Te Rangikaheke refers to inborn talents that are passed on through the genes and come from the seed of rangatira persons. Williams (1957:309) defines pūmanawa as 'natural talents, intuitive, cleverness'. Talents come with the whakapapa and it is assumed that parents pass on talents to their children through te moenga rangatira. A talent for art, for example, may manifest itself in several generations of a descent line. An example, recorded by Neich (1977:109–110) lists a succession of gifted Ngāti Tarāwhai wood carvers.

A bundle of pūmanawa and characteristics is brought together in the genes that comprise the kākano rangatira mentioned earlier by Te Rangikaheke. A propensity for bad temper and violence is believed to characterise a particular family line. A talent for music, or an ability to recite from memory hundreds of names in a whakapapa table, or a talent for weaving, oratory, singing waiata, or art, passes from one generation to the next. This is why orators sometimes refer to the living descendants of an iwi as the hands and feet of previous generations. Sometimes they detect mannerisms or voice qualities that were the same as those of their relatives who have passed on.

The metaphor of the flax bush (te pā harakeke) may be invoked to represent the ongoing passage of attributes. In a flax bush new life comes out from inside the heart. The sheltering leaves in time fall and die away leaving space for the new leaves. But it is the same flax bush and all leaves maintain more or less the characteristics of the whole pā harakeke. So it is with pūmanawa: the new forms maintain some of the same characteristics that were seen before in their ancestors.

Spiritual attributes

The next group of attributes are those in which the spiritual element is dominant. Every Māori is born with these spiritual attributes, but not every Māori is aware of them.

As mentioned earlier, Te Rangikaheke denied these attributes to persons not born of chiefly stock. In order to benefit from the intervention of the Gods an individual needed to come from te moenga rangatira. However, the whole nature of Māori society has changed and the social distinctions of the past no longer exist. An important consequence is that all Māori now belong to the rangatira class. All are related to the chiefs and have nobility of birth. Thus it follows that every child receives a full basket of attributes; although, as stated earlier, the fruit in the basket will not be of the same quantity. It also follows that every Māori child is born with spiritual attributes and every child has personal tapu.

Tapu

The most important spiritual attribute is one's personal tapu. This attribute is inherited from the Māori parent (or parents) and comes with the genes. Te Rangikaheke's notion of te moenga rangatira provides an ideal model of a person born of the appropriate whakapapa, brought up in ideal conditions, supported through life by parents who themselves possess a high level of tapu and who began life with a maximum increment of personal tapu.

All going well these individuals should be able to protect their interests and build their personal tapu through their own good works which are noticed and approved by the people. Others have a more difficult task of improving their lot, but in today's society there are ways for individuals to do so.

The protection of the self is closely linked to tapu and the attribute of mana, which is allied to tapu. I shall describe mana separately. Here however, it needs to be said that as the mana of an individual grows, the tapu rises at the same time. If the level of one's tapu is at a steady state, the individual is well in both a physical and psychological state. Well-being means that the self is in a state of balance. Personal tapu, which pervades all of the other attributes of the self, is safe, not under threat, or likely to be threatened. All hara (transgressions) have been neutralised and dealt with and there are none imminent. Persons of ill will who may harm an individual in some way are not doing so. In other words the attributes of the self are all in a steady state and the forces of good and evil are in balance. Overall the person can say 'Kei te ora ahau' (I am well).

The source of tapu

The source of tapu is traceable to the primeval parents, Rangi and Papa, and their divine children, the departmental Gods such as Tāne, Tangaroa, Tūmatauenga (God of war) and Tāwhirimātea (God of the elements). Descent lines which trace back to the Gods are believed to have a large increment of tapu. Inevitably that means that tapu is greatest among families closest to the main chiefly descent line. Everyone else has to accept a lesser degree of tapu.

The idea of tapu works best when this personal attribute is recognised, known and accepted by the community at large. To be somebody is to know one's identity, be aware of one's personal tapu and be known to many others in the community. A person who is well known in the community is by and large less likely to be abused, ill-treated or assaulted. Individuals possessing a low level of personal tapu tend to be vulnerable to being picked on, bullied, or abused, and often do not enjoy good health. Quite often the bullying begins at school where the children go to learn.

Tapu is pervasive and touches all other attributes. It is like a personal force field which can be felt and sensed by others. It is the sacred life force which supports the mauri (spark of life), another very important spiritual attribute of the person. It reflects the state of the whole person. In fact life can be viewed as protecting one's personal tapu and in doing so one is looking after one's physical, social, psychological and spiritual well-being.

Damage to tapu

Personal tapu was subject to damage and attack. Direct physical assault could damage one's personal tapu, if the assailant was successful. Events of this sort would help build up one's tapu if the attacker was beaten off. Sorcery, gossip, being publicly humiliated, and personal abuse of any form can all damage one's personal tapu. Poor performance in significant tribal affairs that brought shame to the iwi could have a similar effect. Losing a legal battle on behalf of the iwi is treated the same as losing a war against another iwi. One can do harm by breaking the law and bringing the iwi into disrepute, by making a wrong decision, or by breaking a convention of Māori protocol.

Remedies included appealing to divine intervention through a tohunga or a minister of a church, who would then perform karakia or recite various prayers aimed at neutralising the damage done, putting right any errors of a ritual nature, and generally restoring as much as is possible the personal tapu not only of the person seeking help but also the personal tapu of any others who might have been affected. This is the spiritual part. It will also be necessary to restore balance within the hapū or whānau.

Best (1941, 1:38) noted that the vitality of the race was bound up with the condition of tapu. This condition was supported by the power of the Gods which gave hope to the people. Once the institution of tapu was broken down through the intervention of Pākehā governments and missionaries, the people lost their sense of security and of purpose. Many elders told Best (1941, 1:39) 'that the vitality of their race departed with the loss of tapu, leaving the people in a defenseless and helpless condition'. This is a powerful statement.

Observing the rules of tapu

Efforts to recapture some of the traditional values and revive knowledge about tapu are not easy. Barlow (1991:128–29) observed that 'it is difficult for most people of this generation to become tapu'. It might also be difficult for some to practise the customs of personal tapu. However, there are people who have always been aware of personal tapu and others who observe practices which recognise this attribute in some way. It is possible too that some people observe certain practices without realising that these rules are linked to the notion of personal tapu. Many Māori individuals already observe some or most of the following practices by:

1. separating personal clothing items from cloths used for cooking or for washing dishes

2. not washing the baby or the nappies in the kitchen sink

3. collecting the afterbirth from the hospital and burying the whenua of the child at the appropriate place

4. observing practices related to the birth of new life, such as a special welcome and karakia, bringing the social unit together, considering who names the child and what name from the families' whakapapa to give the child

5. looking after the new person, ensuring that the child is seen by whānau members and is known to them, educating the child and generally preparing them for adulthood

6. not burning the hair, and making sure hair is properly collected from the hairdresser or barber and disposed of properly

7. protecting the child from harm or accident, and knowing that in traditional times neglect was punishable by muru, a form of ritual plunder or compensation

8. menstruating women protecting themselves while in a state of extra tapu and not going into the sea to collect seafood, or to the garden to work, or engage in activities such as horse riding

9. observing the tapu of all the phases of the tangihanga ceremony for example by washing one's hands or sprinkling water over oneself after shaking hands with everyone or after leaving the cemetery

10. not passing food over one's head, and not stepping over the feet and bodies of persons who are lying down

11. observing the tapu of various ceremonies, such as pōhiri and tangihanga, and participating in them

12. not putting one's hat or combs or hairbrushes on the kitchen table, and not sitting on any table or bench where food is prepared or eaten.

The tapu of personal space

There is a sense when the whole person is tapu and should be treated with respect. In traditional society persons of great mana and tapu were avoided because contact with them was dangerous. Their high level of tapu threatened a person of a lower level. In a less dramatic setting every person is surrounded by tapu space, and violation of this space can cause discomfort, affront and damage to one's personal tapu and mana. There are, of course, socially approved occasions when it is permissible to approach a person closely and personal space is not seen to be violated. One such occasion is when visitors are greeted with the hongi and shaking of hands. Friends may embrace each other and others may kiss on the cheeks rather than hongi. Within the family unit there are different rules in regard to personal space.

The tapu of the body

Some parts of the body are more tapu than others. It is not permissible to pass anything over another's head. Patting a stranger on the head is not a friendly act, and passing food over this part of the body is a violation because cooked food negates tapu. For example, a roasted kūmara is often used in reducing the level of tapu of a new meeting house, and many elders keep their whakapapa books away from food and away from the kitchen. The sex organs are also tapu, but not the breasts. In traditional times a man's penis was not particularly tapu, except for the prepuce. This part was as tapu as the sex organs of a woman, which after menstruation began were always tapu. Nowadays the sex organs of both men and women are regarded as tapu. In special ceremonies these parts were used − the men's to ward off evil influences and the women's to remove dangerous tapu from warriors.

The tapu of blood

Blood is also very tapu and must be treated with care. When menstruating, a woman is especially tapu because of the flow of blood. There are restrictions placed on her at this time and dangers to be observed. I have already noted that going to sea puts the women in danger of being attacked by sharks that can smell blood, and trying to catch a horse is not recommended because horses can smell blood. During childbirth a woman is also very tapu. Once the flow of blood is over, the level of tapu drops to a normal state in both cases. Childbirth is more complex and there is more anxiety associated with it. Also more people are involved. The mother, the child and the whenua (placenta) are very tapu and all have to be properly attended to. In attendance might be the midwife, members of the family, the father, and a tohunga to perform karakia.

The tapu of death

A person becomes increasingly tapu as death approaches. Death escalates the level of tapu to maximum levels, affecting everything belonging to that person during their lifetime. Because of the extreme tapu on personal effects such as clothes the family might bundle up all their personal effects and bury them at the time of burial. Or they might burn them, or give them away to Pākehā in the belief that Pākehā are not affected by tapu. Sometimes very private belongings such as whakapapa books are destroyed by the family because they are afraid of them. Yet at the same time heirlooms are kept and given to members of the family for safekeeping. Special karakia are requested to protect living members of the family from harm. Tohunga are often very busy during and after a tangihanga.

Even the house where the deceased lived is affected by the personal tapu of that person. A tohunga or minister of a church is required for a whakawātea ceremony, that is, for clearing away and negating the lingering after-effects of the personal tapu of the deceased. This is followed by the takahi whare (tramping the house) ceremony which has been described by some as 'chasing the ghosts away'. While on the one hand one aspect is to clear away, another important aspect is to reintroduce the family into the world of light and help them get over the trauma of death.

The extensions of tapu

An individual is born with tapu which becomes an essential part of their make-up. The level of personal tapu may fluctuate according to the fortunes of the person. A lifetime of successful living combined with services to the tribe consolidates the tapu and may increase it. At critical times the level of tapu increases, at childbirth, for example, or when a person is very ill. Once a person is over the event, the level of tapu reduces to normal. An increase usually results in prohibitions and restrictions on the normal activities of the person. Very high levels of tapu are dangerous to others. This is especially true when the person dies. Many people are affected by the personal tapu of a dead member of the tribe: the immediate family and the extended family, called te kiri mate (the skin of death), are the most affected. But everyone who attends the tangi is affected to lesser degrees. What this emphasises is that while the person is an individual, at death their importance as a member of the tribe is highlighted and their tūrangawaewae is confirmed in the final act of burial in the local cemetery. Here the person takes their place with the ancestors.

Many of the observances and customs arising from the notion of personal tapu are still practised today. In fact, a surprising number of these customs remain and, as mentioned earlier, many people remain committed to being Māori. However, respect for personal tapu is not as generally accepted as one would wish: there are far too many instances where Māori are damaging the personal tapu of other Māori. Yet respect for others is an ideal we must try to achieve in practice.

Mana

Every individual Māori is born with an increment of mana which, as noted already, is closely related to personal tapu. The child's inheritance of mana depends upon the achievements of the parents, their social position, how they are regarded by others, and what they have done to assist the tribal group. Parents with a high level of mana and tapu will pass onto their children a correspondingly enhanced increment of mana. The opposite is also true: other children can be handicapped in this respect.

While an increment of mana is inherited at birth it is possible to build onto it through one's personal achievements, through good works and an ability to lift the mana of the whole group. For example, being chosen as an All Black could be viewed as lifting the mana of the tribe because everyone will know the selected person is a member. Besides the whole nation supports the All Blacks and so it is good publicity for the iwi. Mana is much more open to extension than any other attribute. It can be described as the creative and dynamic force that motivates the individual to do better than others. The rewards are an increase in mana, and an acknowledgement by others of one's special abilities. Praise, in other words, instead of shame. Success leads to further success, and so the inheritance for the children is substantially improved. It was and is possible to rise above the limitations of whakapapa.

Mana is affected by the principles listed earlier. For example, the mātāmua principle, the tuakana/taina principle and the tūrangawaewae principle all influence how an individual was regarded in relation to others. Mana is always a social quality that requires other people to recognise one's achievements and accord respect.

The mana of a child

Today, adults generally tend not to notice the mana of a child, preferring that children are seen and not heard. It was not like this in traditional society. Neglect of the mana of a child could result in the parents being punished. Allowing the child to be burnt or otherwise damaged were serious offences. Children of great mana were made a fuss of, and special oriori, or lullabies, were composed in their honour and sung by the hapū and the iwi. Children were generally well treated in traditional Māori society and there was great affection accorded to them. Aroha tamariki, as noted by Firth (1959:121), was attested to by numerous early writers, for example, by Graham, Earle, Polack and Baucke. Firth quoted a proverb as evidence: 'He aroha whaereere, he potiki piri poho' (A mother's love, a breast-clinging child). Among the children themselves, differences in mana would be obvious. First-borns, for example, would have more mana than others and elder siblings would have more than younger ones and this would be manifested in greater confidence and in more opportunities to assume leadership roles. First-born males would have more mana than first-born females, although not always. Persons of older generations would be accorded more respect because of their mana as elders. As already mentioned, mana depends for its effectiveness on community recognition. It requires some negotiation skills in order to maximise opportunities.

The dynamics of mana

Mana is underpinned by the rules of precedence that are embedded in the kinship system, and a person has to accept these constraints and strive to rise above them as far as this is permitted by the tribe. Brilliant actions and exceptional talent in sport or music will be noticed and will increase one's mana. On the other hand, thoughtless, crooked and evil actions will also be noticed and will have a negative effect upon the culprit's mana. It will diminish.

In the end it is up to individuals to decide the shape of their lives and what they want to do. They have the choice of following the path of evil or of good. They can develop their own talents and make a name for themselves and their iwi. They can coast along under the shadow of their parents and be a clinging vine. Or they can choose to opt out for a number of years and go to the cities, or go abroad, and return to the iwi later. As others have done, they can opt out for good and return to the iwi in a coffin, if they are lucky. Life is a challenge and will always be. Mana is a challenge too.

Mauri

Mauri is defined in Williams (1957:197) as the 'life principle' or 'thymos of man'. The Greek word 'thymos' adds to the mystery of mauri and does not help us understand. Mauri is the spark of life, the active component that indicates the person is alive. Best (1941, 1:304) stated that 'the Maori viewed the mauri as an activity', and that it was 'an activity inside us'. Tīhei mauri ora is the sneeze of life which signals the new independence of the child, breathing independent of the womb and its supporting life lines. The sneeze also is a manifestation of the mauri existing as an essential and inseparable part of that particular person.

There is a mystical and magical quality to life. The heart beats, the many systems of the human body carry out their specific tasks, the blood flows, and the body is warm and alive. However, once the life principle is extinguished, which is signalled by one last breath, all body systems stop and the body becomes cold. The Māori view is that the mauri has left the body and the person dies. When the body dies the mauri ceases to exist. It vanishes completely.

Mauri at peace

The mauri symbolises a marvellous active sign of life and one can talk about the mauri as something separate from the body. The mauri becomes an attribute of the self, something to nurture, to protect, to think about. The self and the mauri are one. If there is something wrong with the mauri, the person is not well. When the person is physically and socially well, the mauri is in a state of balance, described as mauri tau (the mauri is at peace). When a person receives shocking news, or is surprised, or jolted by an electric current, the mauri is startled, and is described as mauri oho. Traditionally it was thought not good for the mauri to be startled this way as it might leave the body and this is dangerous. When the mauri is startled to this degree it is described as mauri rere, literally flying mauri.

The symbols of mauri

According to Williams (1957:197) the mauri of an individual could be represented by a material symbol which was reinforced spiritually and then hidden away. Best (1982, 2:48) reported that Tuta Nihoniho of Ngāti Porou said that a stone or piece of wood was used to represent the mauri of a person. The stone or piece of wood (presumably carved) became a talisman and a tohunga was called to fortify it with karakia and to call spirits to protect it from witchcraft. This notion of abstracting the mauri and representing it in a talisman was a device to protect the real mauri from harm.

Another custom was for a person going on a dangerous mission, a long journey or undertaking an enterprise that was critical to the iwi to give a taonga to a tohunga and have him perform karakia over it to fortify it. This became an extra mauri which the person carried to give additional protection. Or they wore it as an ornament, a neck pendant for example. The taonga acted as a substitute for the real mauri and was a physical representation of it. The taonga thus acted as a constant reminder to the individuals to look after themselves. This custom is still practised by the Ringatū church and possibly by others. It is an old one as it was noted by Best (1982, 2:48).

The mauri is the life force that is bound to an individual and represents the active force of life which enables the heart to beat, the blood to flow, food to be eaten and digested, energy to be expended, the limbs to move, the mind to think and have some control over body systems, and the personality of the person to be vibrant, expressive and impressive. When the mauri leaves the body the activating force of life comes to a dead stop. Life systems cease work and the mauri disappears. The body later reduces to bones and teeth. Once buried in the cemetery, usually after the third day of the tangihanga, the body to which the mauri belonged also disappears from sight.

Wairua

Every Māori child is born with a wairua, which is usually translated as 'soul' or 'spirit'.

The wairua is implanted in the embryo by the parents and the embryo is nurtured in the mother's womb. It is not until the eyes form in the foetus that the wairua begins its existence and association with that particular life (Best 1941, 1:301). Before this the wairua lies dormant and awaits the appropriate moment when it is activated. It is an interesting notion that the foetus possesses a soul or wairua while it is still developing in the womb and that it is when the eyes have formed that the wairua is activated and becomes a spiritual part of the new life.

When the eyes form is also the time when it is believed the new life develops 'rudimentary powers of thought' (1941, 1:301). This is probably the reason why many Māori mothers talk to their developing, yet-to-be-born babies. They believe the baby can hear what they are saying and becomes bonded to their voices. We have to accept that a child is born with a wairua and this wairua became a part of their existence as a person from the time the foetus developed eyes. And as we shall see, it continues to exist long after the death of the life they were attached to.

Unlike the mauri, which never leaves the human life it is part of, the wairua can detach but never strays too far away. It is believed that during dreams the wairua leaves the body and then returns before the person awakens. Apart from this power to detach when the person is dreaming, the wairua is bound to one specific human being for life.

The characteristics of wairua

According to Best (1941, 1:300) the wairua has the following characteristics:

1. it is part of the whole person and is not located at any particular part of the body
2. it is immortal and exists after the death of the person
3. it has the power to warn the individual of impending danger through visions and dreams
4. it is subject to attack.

A consequence of immortality is that the universe is inhabited by wairua. They roam in space, in forests, on mountains, and are believed to be human souls. They are all around us but we cannot see them. The wairua that live around mountains and forests are known as tūrehu (fairy folk) and those who fly in space are called tiramākā (companies of shy but active souls) (Best 1941, 1:302). Evidently, not too many wairua actually reach or remain at distant Hawaiki.

The wairua of a person was subject to damage through the bad deeds of other people such as abuse, neglect, violence and the wizardry of sorcerers, who used mākutu (sorcery). Though mākutu is less of a worry nowadays, modern life provides its own hazards: robbery, violence by strangers, drugs, domestic violence, rape and being made redundant are examples. Illness and injury can also damage the wairua of a person and weaken it.

Tuku wairua: the release of the wairua

But whatever happens to the individual their wairua remains with them until near death. At this time, and if circumstances permit, a special ceremony known as tuku wairua (releasing the spirit or allowing it to leave) is performed. This is done by a minister of a church or by a tohunga reciting appropriate prayers and incantations to release the wairua from the body while the person is still alive. It is often described as administering the last rites to the living before they die. The timing of this event is judged by the attending doctor or nurses and the tohunga and ministers who, through many years of experience, know when there is no hope of recovery and when the patient has begun the process of dying. The whānau gather around, the karakia are performed, last messages are delivered, and an elder addresses the dying person. After this the whānau take up a vigil and watch and wait for the moment when the mauri departs. This is signalled by the last breath, after which the whole body relaxes.

The journey of the wairua

After the tuku wairua ceremony the wairua is believed to leave the body and begin its vigil of hovering above it for several days. The wairua also begins to undergo a transformation of refinement when it 'shakes off its grosser qualities' and becomes a purified, refined, and invisible spirit (Best 1941, 1:303). It flies through space and while the body is lying in state during the tangihanga ceremony it flies round and round (ka rere āmiomio) in the sky above the marae. It observes what is happening and what people are doing. It is believed that if the ceremony is not properly carried out the spirit will become angry and will not leave the locality or the immediate family and it will do all it can to punish the family. On the other hand, if the ceremonies are done properly the wairua will leave willingly and will not harm the living relatives of the deceased. Many iwi believe that wairua fly to Te Rerenga Wairua in the far north and from there take an underwater journey to Hawaiki, the resting place of peaceful wairua. Ngāti Awa in the Bay of Plenty believe that the wairua of their people go first to Paepae-o-Aotea, near Whakaari or White Island. The wairua say their farewells from there and then fly off to join the myriad wairua that fly above the sacred places of the tribe.

During the tangihanga ceremony orations are made to the dead and orators generally speak in a loud voice. They address the dead lying before them, whose mauri has departed and whose wairua is hovering above the marae. The body cannot hear the message, but it is believed that the wairua does. This is why, generally speaking, an orator will stress the positive contributions of the deceased rather than enumerate all of the bad things done by that person during their lifetime. A dissatisfied wairua can take affront and turn nasty.

Messages to the wairua

During the speeches each orator requests the wairua to depart in peace and one often hears the words 'haere, haere, haere'. Some speakers will direct the wairua to 'haere ki Hawaiki-nui, Hawaiki-roa, Hawaiki-pāmamao', that is, to depart for Big Hawaiki, Long Hawaiki and Distant Hawaiki. It is believed that satisfied and good wairua go ultimately to the final resting place of wairua, Hawaiki and remain there. But it is obvious from the statements of Best that not all wairua go there and if they do they do not necessarily remain there. Or one other possibility is that Hawaiki is actually Aotearoa, Te Waipounamu and Wharekauri – the North and South Islands and the Chathams. The wairua of departed ancestors are an essential part of our environment and our universe. They comprise the spiritual world which most of us cannot see. This interpretation makes sense given some of our beliefs.

For example during the kawe mate or hari mate ceremony, during which the tangihanga is at the marae, some very distant, the wairua is requested to come back and hover over the marae where the people are mourning. But again many of the speakers will request the summoned wairua to depart for Hawaiki. The wairua is summoned also during the hura kōhatu ceremony, unveiling a memorial to the deceased. Again the wairua is summoned to return and hover over the marae only to be sent away again. In other words, the wairua seem to be all around and nearby. We frequently call on wairua to come home for certain important occasions. In addition, some speakers refer to the fact that the spirits of the dead are on the shoulders of the living and that we carry them with us wherever we go.

After the tangihanga ceremony is complete in all aspects and the memorial stone is unveiled a year later, the wairua are free to go wherever they wish. Unlike the mauri they live on for eternity and are often summoned to return to their tūrangawaewae to help the living descendants. Some become very special spiritual ancestors and it is believed that they will assist in the affairs of the living when appealed to by their descendants. Some are believed to become stars which look benevolently down at the people and silently observe them. They are like sheltering satellites out there in the universe. All in all, one's wairua is an important part of the person that enables one to transcend death and live on in a different world.

Hau

Hau is a common word meaning wind. It is a component of another common word, hauora, meaning 'spirit of life, health, vigour', or 'healthy, fresh, well'. Hauoratanga means health and whakahauora means to revive, refresh. Thus the word is associated with well-being and being in a healthy state.

As an attribute of one's birthright hau is a difficult notion to understand. Williams (1957:39) glosses the word as 'vitality of man, vital essence of land, etc.'. It is not the same as mauri.

Best (1982, 2:50–53) provides some enlightenment in his *Maori Religion and Mythology*. He makes the following points:

1. It is a quality that pervades the whole body.

2. It is not located in any particular part of the human body.

3. It embraces the aura of the person.

4. It also includes the notion of personality.

5. Person leaves behind a part of their hau at places where they have sat or walked. The warmth of the body that remains after a person has left a chair is part of their hau.

6. Tohunga skilled in black magic are able to scoop up the aura left behind by a person and use that portion as a means of attacking the whole person.

7. The aura of a footprint is called a manea. The soil touched by the bare foot is capable of being scooped up and used for witchcraft.

8. A portion of hau can be gathered from a lock of hair, a piece of

clothing, spit, or anything else that is close to the person. When used this way the portion is called ohonga.

9. A lock of hair taken from a victim of warfare represents the hair of victory and may be brought back as proof. This lock of hair is called māwe.

10. The aura may be described as āhua and what is taken from a person is called the āhua of the hau: namely the material form of the invisible hau.

Thus the hau is an invisible aura that every individual possesses. The *Living Webster* (1973:66) provides this useful explanation of the word aura: 'a subtle influence or quality emanating from or surrounding a person or object'. Best (1982, 2:51) describes the hau as 'a quality intangible and always invisible, even to gifted seers'. Best might have overstated the case of gifted seers not being able to see an aura of a person. Some modern faith healers and tohunga are able to see wairua in the form of coloured rays coming off the body

The hau appears to be the most vulnerable part of a person in that one does not always have control over places where one has been. However, one can take precautions over items such as hair by observing some customary practices. During pregnancy the mother's hair is not cut. After a haircut, the hair should be gathered up and disposed of in such a way that others will not find it. The practice of leaving one's hair at the barbers or with the hairdresser is an example of neglect in protecting one's personal tapu. The hair should be gathered up and given to the owner to take home. As for spitting, the simple remedy is not to spit in public places. Awareness about the attribute of hau will encourage the person to take better care of themselves and to observe good personal hygiene.

Kaihau-waiū

As we have seen, at birth an individual is granted a package of benefits, attributes and rights which comprise the birthright, the kaihau-waiū.

When a child is born there is a dramatic entry into the world of light, te ao mārama. The child leaves the sheltering womb, and its lifelines to the placenta and blood supply of the mother are severed. A new person is born into the whānau. It is always a marvellous revelation to see the result of human creativity when a new version of ira tangata is produced. As has been noted, the new form is born with an inheritance of genes which are passed on by the parents. Characteristics and talents come with the genes and the person is said to be a reflection of the parents. There is a continuation down the descent line.

An essential part of the inheritance of every child consists of the attributes ascribed by the culture. Whakapapa and tūrangawaewae help define a person in time, place and position. These attributes prescribe the degree, extent and size of the birthright, the kaihau-waiū. They help determine entitlement. But what a person is entitled to is affected by some principles. There are three principles which have an immediate effect upon the size of entitlement. These are te moenga rangatira principle, the mātāmua principle and the tuakana/taina principle. These principles rank a person according to the kinship system, in relation to other close relatives and other people. Entitlements are affected in terms of the next group of attributes.

Whakapapa is a key attribute which validates membership into a whānau, hapū and iwi. From this fact the person gains access into the resources of the hapū and iwi although it may not be until adulthood is reached that one is able to experience the full benefits. Rights to be on the hapū roll, to vote in hapū and iwi affairs, to participate in the affairs of the hapū marae – all flow from the attribute of whakapapa. The importance of whakapapa cannot be over-emphasised as it provides the key to many doors.

The spiritual nature of the person

The child is also heir to several spiritual attributes which are fundamental to the spiritual, psychological, and social well-being of the individual. These attributes include personal tapu, mana, mauri, wairua and hau. They all relate to the importance of life, and to the relation of ira tangata to the cosmos and to the world of the Gods, ira Atua.

These are the attributes that define the spiritual nature of the person and which help make sense of many customs that Māori follow and believe in. If an individual is to understand this part of their birthright, certain processes are necessary. These include proper enculturation into the culture, education in tikanga Māori and te reo Māori, participation in ceremonies, and generally becoming comfortable with the fact of being Māori and the responsibilities that come with that fact. One has to be proud to be Māori in order to enjoy the birthright one inherits through being born one. There is a finality about birth: one cannot emulate Māui and try to reverse that process and reject the package of genes, the identity and the culture one is born into.

It is this particular bundle of attributes that define the importance and sanctity of the person. These attributes place a particular responsibility upon the parents to nurture the child successfully into the stage of adulthood. Later, these responsibilities are assumed by the person who then has to actively protect the birthright and later try to improve upon it. One of the continuing challenges of life is to try and improve the birthright that is to be passed on to the next generation. But it is equally challenging to protect and maintain the legacy one receives. For some individuals this is a difficult task and often the reason for this is because the whānau itself is weak and non-supportive. In the case of children, for example, the adults who are supposed to be supporting, nurturing, and preparing them for adult life are not doing so and may be unable to function as responsible caregivers.

Several principles help to maintain and protect the birthright, given that there is always the possibility of a person making mistakes and damaging what they have. These include the principles of utu–ea, whakatika, ahi-kā and spiritual nurturing. Some of these provide avenues for correcting errors and restoring the balance.

The principle of toa, formerly associated with success in war, may now be generalised to include all personal achievements that help build up one's mana and personal tapu. Mana is the attribute most open to change. It will involve individuals in testing their talents through their lifetime. There are now many avenues open to individuals to establish a reputation and so increase their mana.

Service to the iwi

Service to the iwi is one of the important areas of achievement. For example, being an excellent ringa wera (cook) to provide food for visitors, serving as karanga expert for several years, being an orator and 'sitting on the pae' for all occasions year in and year out, carrying out the functions of a marae committee or serving as a trustee of a block of land are tasks that need to be done. Achievements here are often seen as more important than those earned away from the home base. These are the people who maintain the ahi-kā and keep the culture of the tribe alive. Without them the marae would collapse and the hapū will not be able to uphold the mana of the iwi. Amongst other pathways to achievement are sport, music, drama, art, law, teaching, working for large corporations or for the Government, and being a politician.

The gift of birth

Through the gift of receiving a birthright an individual is linked to the ancestors because the birthright is part of the cultural heritage. Genes are passed down the generations and give form to an individual complete with characteristics that could be unique to that descent line. The birthright has the effect of committing an individual to being Māori and to playing a part in the maintenance and development of Māori culture generally. But there are opportunities aplenty for the individual to develop their particular talents and to make a personal contribution to the tribe and to the nation.

It is possible to deny and reject the birthright or sometimes to store it away for later use, or to suddenly grasp it when an advantage can be perceived. Eventually it is the responsibility of the Māori individual to take hold of the birthright, cherish it, build on to it, explain it to the next generation, and develop it and make of it a gift of the ancestors, a taonga tuku iho. The kaihau-waiū is a significant gift of birth and it is very special to every individual person.

Perspectives

When I got sick, some people blamed my taha Maori, but I expected that, I told them that the Pakeha doctors said this that and the other. When I went to the hospital the doctor said it was strange that I took the chemotherapy very well, never vomited … and I told him I talked to those medicines just like I'm talking to you.

My body is the tangata whenua and those are the manuhiri, and I ask my body, my spirit to receive those things because they are going to look after us.

The doctor laughed at me at first but then he saw the positive side of it.

This is central to the wairua, te korero ki taku tinana, korero ki nga rongoa. I actually talk. 'Haere mai koutou, tomohia taku tinana, hei oranga moku'. It's looked upon by some as mumbo jumbo but if you look at the working of the karakia, it's just plain common sense.

– Broughton 1985:7

5

Wāhi Tapu, Taonga Tapu
The Tapu of Places and Things

Some places and things are special in a cultural, historical and spiritual sense and require a change in behaviour from the observers or participants in a ceremony. The special qualities attached to such places and things (and here I include built things such as canoes and carved houses) impose some restrictions upon how we behave towards them. In some cases the tapu of a place varies in intensity as in the case of a marae. When there is no ceremony on a marae the level of tapu is low and people can be relaxed and are able to move about freely. However when a ceremony begins the level of tapu on the marae increases immediately and restrictions upon human behaviour are imposed. Now there are protocols to observe and a process to follow through to completion.

Some places such as urupā are always tapu but even here some urupā are more tapu than others. The important variable is often the antiquity of the urupā and whose remains are buried there. The level of tapu also varies with built things or created things. A carved house, for example, is very tapu during its construction. The state of tapu indicates that the construction stage and the artistic activities associated with the building are highly regarded. A reason for the high regard is that the reputation and mana of the builders and artists together with that of the owning hapū group is at stake. The carpenters and artists are accountable for the quality of their work to the commissioning group and there is a ritual aspect to it. This high level of tapu remains in place until the ceremony called the kawanga whare (which is described later in this chapter) is performed to clear away the dangers associated with a high level of tapu both from the created structure and from the builders, carvers and artists who created it. After this the house is safe. The level of tapu would rise again during tangihanga ceremonies or pōhiri and reduce again afterwards.

Water and tapu

Wai māori (fresh water) plays an important part in many ceremonies. It possesses the power to neutralise the dangerous aspects of tapu and so render people and things safe. Sometimes water by itself is sufficient to do this as for example when tools used to dig and cover a grave are washed in a river or are hosed down with clean water. The tools can then be put away for the next time of use. People coming out of a tapu place or after being engaged in a tapu ceremony can sprinkle or flick water over themselves to lessen the level of tapu and clear themselves from any perceived harmful effects of tapu.

An interesting question is this: Can water be tapu? The logical answer is, no it cannot. But many people will dispute this answer because they have heard about the tapu water associated with Christian churches. When a person drowns in a river or at sea the area where the drowning occurred becomes tapu as it is immediately affected by the tapu of death. The question now is this: Is it the area, the place, or the locality that is tapu, or is it the water? The answer must surely be that the place is tapu, not the water, because water flows. The water in the river does not become tapu but the place where the drowning occurred does. A rāhui (restriction) is placed on the locality for a specified time and then lifted.

The next question is: Can wai tai (sea water) be used instead of fresh water? Some tohunga do use sea water but generally speaking it is fresh water that is used by most tohunga.

But to come back to the general discussion about water. After a death in the family home a minister of the church or a tohunga would sprinkle water in every room of the house and over things owned by the deceased. Water may be sprinkled over a place where a death occurred but in these cases it is expected that the person doing so has some authority within the group or is empowered by the group to conduct a ceremony which could include some karakia.

Water is used mostly by ministers of Christian churches and not so much by tohunga who practise traditional karakia. They are more likely to use a cooked kūmara or sometimes bread that is baked. The essential feature is that the item is cooked, roasted, baked in an oven or in a hāngi (earth oven). And even then they are mostly likely to use a cooked item during the opening ceremony for a meeting house. Water is available to the general public and is something that we can all use. For some people water has the power to heal and this is another quality that clean, fresh uncontaminated water is imbued with. So all in all water is important.

Wāhi tapu

Relationships between people and places are reflected in different ways. Some places are given names and this is always an indication of special significance. The village was always given a name. Rivers, streams, lakes, and springs of fresh water have names. Mountains are always named and become symbols of identity so that the name of the chief and of the tribe or sub-tribe is associated with a mountain. The enduring quality of a mountain, its prominence in the landscape and its image of strength are qualities that chiefs should ideally possess. Mountains have a measure of tapu and are given great respect.

Burial sites have names as well. For example, Opihi-whanaunga-kore (Opihi of no relatives), a famous burial site opposite the township of Whakatane, is an old site rich in history, and it is the resting place of famous chiefs. Formerly, it was a place where first-stage burials occurred, that is, the corpse was left there to decompose. Then at a later stage the bones were cleaned, wrapped and then a second burial took place at which time the bones were deposited in their final resting place, usually a cave. Opihi-whanaunga-kore meets the criteria that define a wāhi tapu. Its antiquity adds to its significance, and its association with death adds to the tapu nature of the site. According to traditions, the site was so tapu that when burials were carried out no women were allowed to cross the Whakatane River with the men. This is quite different from other urupā in the region where no such restrictions occur. Men, women and children attend burials at most cemeteries. Thus while all burial sites are tapu because of the association with death and kōiwi (bones), they may differ in the level of tapu attributed to them.

Another category of tapu place is the site of a tūāhu (altar) where religious ceremonies were performed. There could be several such sites in the territory of an iwi. Activities associated with the Gods are very tapu and the places, as well as any special constructions on them, were also tapu.

Sites where traditionally bones were scraped as part of the old hahunga ceremony were also tapu. The bone-cleaning ceremony is no longer done and burials are one-stage events, not two stage as used to be the case: a period of interment before the remains were dug up and the bones cleaned, wrapped and deposited in caves or in crevasses along cliff faces. These places are regarded as burial sites and are tapu.

The sites of traditional whare wānanga, learning houses, were also tapu because the learning process itself was regarded as tapu. Students who were learning could not eat or drink until instructions of the day were completed. The teachers or tohunga were also tapu and did their teaching under tapu. The buildings and places of teaching were tapu.

Some named features are significant because an important event occurred there or an important chief or tohunga did something. These places might be rocks or sites near the coast where an important person rested after something happened to them. Some are hillocks or a spot near a tree or some unremarkable feature of the land. That place is given a name and it becomes a place of special significance, a wāhi tapu.

A spring, especially a place where someone important drank, would be regarded as a place of great significance. It would be treated as a wāhi tapu but not necessarily as a place not to be visited by others. Places of great cultural significance are regarded as wāhi tapu with differing levels of tapu. The notion of 'great cultural significance' is attached to a wāhi tapu with some history behind it. Associations with important persons, with religious ceremonies, with death, sickness, burial, learning, birth or baptism ceremonies: all may lead to places being classified as wāhi tapu.

Sites of cultural significance occur across the environment in a variety of places. Rocks in the ocean, lake or river can be wāhi tapu. Parts of a river can be regarded as tapu and restricted in the sense that children would not be allowed to swim there. Usually these are places where someone has drowned or there are dangerous currents. A rock out at sea might be a place where an ancestor rested. Te Tahi o Te Rangi, an ancestor of the Mātaatua people, is remembered as a powerful and famous tohunga. Every site associated with him remains tapu to this day. Another Mātaatua ancestor is Irakewa, father of Toroa, captain of the canoe *Mātaatua* in the latter part of its voyaging. His name was given to a rock at the mouth of the Whakatane River and this was a culturally significant site. It was dynamited years ago, before wāhi tapu were recognized nationally. There are still other sites associated with Irakewa which are tapu: on a mountain, in a lake, out at sea.

Tapu restrictions come into play when humans want to take something out from a part of the environment which is under the mantle of the Gods, such as Tāne and Tangaroa, or when they wish to do something like plant kūmara or set a net to catch fish. Once work commences in the forest, on land, in lakes, in the sea, the rituals that take account of tapu are triggered. A kūmara garden, for example, is held to be tapu from the commencement of work to the harvesting of crops. Removing trees from the forest is covered by rituals to appease the God Tāne. At sea it is Tangaroa.

Activities that are held to be of great importance to the community, as well as the environment in which those activities occur, are under the tapu of the Gods and have been in place since time immemorial. When interacting with the environment, rituals are performed to appease the appropriate God and satisfy tikanga.

In his introduction to the report *Sites of Significance*, the chief executive of Te Puni Kōkiri at the time, Ngatata Love, commented that 'wahi tapu and other sites of historical significance to Maori are taonga over which our rangatiratanga is protected under customary title and under Article II of the Treaty of Waitangi' (Te Puni Kōkiri 1996:4).

'Taonga' may be regarded as something highly valued by Māori, and there is also an implication of something being handed down. The term itself is used in the Māori text of the Treaty of Waitangi, and it has been subjected to legal interpretation before the Waitangi Tribunal. Thus the term 'taonga' is quite complex without having to look at the political implications as well as its cultural significance. The important part of the definition is the following: 'Wahi tapu are sites of historical and cultural significance'.

There are appropriate tikanga to be observed with most wāhi tapu. For example Toi-te-huatahi's pā, Kapu-te-rangi at Whakatane, is a wāhi tapu that is regarded with great respect by the people of Mātaatua. It is a tapu place not only because of the ancestor Toi-te-huatahi but also because of the great antiquity of the site. It is associated with the traditions of the *Mātaatua* waka and waka before it. It is certainly not a place to treat lightly. Some karakia are thought to be appropriate and necessary in order to acknowledge the great importance of the site and to reduce the level of tapu so visitors can feel comfortable and safe.

Today, government departments, the Office of Treaty Settlements, local governments, regional councils and environmental groups are respectful of wāhi tapu and want them identified so they may be protected.

Taonga tapu

There are tikanga which apply to all tapu places, to anything tapu and to the process of decreasing the level and thus the danger of tapu. As discussed in chapter 4, too much tapu is dangerous and gives rise to concern about personal safety. There are mechanisms to deal with such danger. These mechanisms are an integral part of tikanga. A tohunga is required to perform the appropriate karakia addressed to the correct God of the traditional world in order to reduce the danger. Nowadays Christian Māori turn to the ministers of their churches to perform these duties. Sometimes both are required in order to convince the people concerned that the tapu has been lifted.

One area in which high levels of tapu are involved and tikanga is called upon to manage tapu is when large community undertakings occur, such as commissioning and building a wharenui (big house). Restrictions are set in place to manage tapu, and then the restrictions need to be removed so that the community – people of all ages and of both sexes – can use its new asset. The tā i te kawa or kawanga-whare ceremony, conducted at dawn, is an important method of managing the levels of tapu involved.

Te kawanga whare/te tā i te kawa: the dawn ceremony

The modern idea of 'opening' something with a ceremony at dawn comes out of the traditions and customary practices of Māori society. The dawn ceremony is called tā i te kawa, that is, to strike (the carved posts) with a branch of leaves (kawakawa, for example) or with a tokotoko (staff). It is also called the kawanga-whare ceremony.

Williams (1957:110, 354) offers meanings such as 'perform the ceremony of kawa', 'strike with a branch' or simply to 'open a new house'.
'Tā' is to strike and 'kawa' is the ceremony to open a house. Today kawa
is usually regarded as marae protocol, a set of procedures that follow in
some order. Indeed, that is the sense of its use in the term 'he tā i te
kawa'. The ceremony involves a series of activities such as the tohunga
striking or touching some of the artwork, especially key pieces, or the
walls of the structure. There is a procedure to follow. In another sense
the opening of the house is but the end of a series of karakia, which
begin with the ceremonies for cutting down the trees to be used for the
carvings. Some elders refer to the ceremony as 'te hiki i te tapu', literally,
the lifting of the tapu. Williams (1957:110) identifies the term 'kawanga'
as a word that could be used for the ceremony, that is, it could be
described as the kawanga ceremony. Cowan (1930:129) refers to it as
the rite of the kawanga-whare. Other terms suggested by him were
'tainga-kawa' and 'whai-kawa'. The most straightforward term to
describe the traditional ceremony is 'kawanga-whare'. It is not an
entirely appropriate term to describe the dawn ceremony of today
because it may not be a whare that is being opened and if it is, it does
not follow that it is a carved house.

The kawanga-whare ceremony was used traditionally to open (in the
sense of freeing something from restrictions and making it safe for social
use) a whare whakairo (carved meeting house), or commonly a wharenui
that had just been completed and was ready to hand over to the hapū
for its use. Such a structure was placed under tapu from the moment
construction began until it was opened. The tapu signalled to all that the
work was important, that the artists and builders were under an obligation to do their best, that there were ritual risks as well as social and
economic risks involved, that the community was investing everything it
owned in the project. Finally, the tapu indicated that the mana of the
hapū, its status and reputation, rested on a good result.

While under restriction the public was not permitted access to the
house. Only the builders, artists and owners of the house were allowed
in the house and in the shed where the carvings were being done.
Females of all ages were restricted. Even the women weavers who did
the tukutuku (lattice work) and the whāriki (floor mats) were not
permitted to enter the house.

Traditionally the carvers were not allowed to smoke while they worked on the carvings. Smoking was categorised as food in the Māori translation kaipaipa (literally: to consume or eat pipe or tobacco). Food is kai, and as all kai was (and still is) prohibited in a tapu environment, smoking was not allowed. Over time that rule has changed and now artists working on a carved house and engaged in whakairo (carving), kōwhaiwhai (painting patterns) and tukutuku may smoke as they work.

Creative work associated with socially and economically important constructions such as a decorated war canoe, a carved house or a storehouse was regarded as very special and highly valued. As a consequence such activity was placed under tapu. Artists were held ritually responsible for their work and poor workmanship and errors in process and execution were targeted for attention on the day of the dawn ceremony. Artists could be condemned to death by public criticism of their work. It was not until the public ceremony was over that the artists were free from the tapu of art and from the consequences of any errors they may have made. Thus an accountability factor was built into creative work and the opening ceremony was an event of some trepidation. But it was also a ceremony of release for the artists.

Traditionally tohunga tā moko (tattoo experts), tohunga whakairo (expert woodcarvers) and in effect all artists worked to a greater or lesser extent under tapu restrictions. These restrictions are discussed in greater detail in chapter 15. Here, however, it needs to be noted that in the case of constructing a carved house or a war canoe, the place, the structure and the workers were all under tapu. Thus in te tā i te kawa o te whare (lifting the tapu of the house) the ceremony is focused on the workers and especially the artists as well as the decorated buildings.

From the very beginning of construction a tapu is placed on the project and the tapu is not lifted until the task is finished and ready for public use. In fact, before work even begins on the building there is a ritual involving the placement and covering of the mauri of the house in the ground. Appropriate karakia are performed and there are speeches and a hākari to complete the tikanga. This ceremony is more private than the kawanga-whare ceremony and is confined to those who need to know.

Once the kawanga-whare ceremony is completed and, in a popular sense, the tapu of the building has been lifted, people may believe the meeting house is no longer tapu. This is not the case. All that has happened is that the tapu of creative work, of construction, and the tapu of the artists, carvers and carpenters has been reduced to safe levels. The marae and the buildings retain a level of tapu at all times.

The author is aware of one case when the tikanga practised to lift the tapu from a house were performed three times in order to satisfy the people. Even then they were not all entirely convinced. Tapu associations with a building or place linger in the minds.

The tohunga

Tohunga who know the karakia tūturu (genuine traditional prayers) and are thoroughly familiar with the kawanga–whare ceremony play an important role in the performance of the ceremony, in explaining what is to happen and in actually conducting the whole ceremony. The leading tohunga may invite others to assist him, but traditionally this was not the case. However, structures have become more complex. For example the whole of a new marae complex might need to be included in the dawn ceremony, and this is an enormous area to cover. Or it might be focused only on the dining room (nowadays often a huge building), or upon the meeting house, or the kōhanga-reo dwelling.

The word 'tohunga' is defined in Williams (1957:431) as a 'skilled person' or as a 'wizard' or 'priest'. Implied in the term is the double notion of highly skilled and priestly knowledge. Traditionally one could not decide to be a tohunga without the knowledge and approval of a mentor and ideally, of the hapū. A period of schooling was necessary and a ceremony had to be performed upon the novice before one dared to practise. The novice might also have to wait until his mentor died before being free to practise as a tohunga in the wider Māori world. A series of karakia had to be mastered, the purpose of each understood, and the protocols learnt by teaching and by observation. A body of mātauranga Māori also had to be absorbed by the novice. This included the philosophy behind the ceremony, knowledge of cosmology, navigation, astronomy, medicine, history, genealogies, the environment, and the nature of the relationship of people to the Gods.

A trained tohunga was a very learned man, an educated person, a healer, a teacher, a person who worked to improve the lot of people by communicating with the Gods and by providing spiritual guidance and by attempting to hold back the hand of fate so there is hope in life. On a very practical level the tohunga was required to be able to recite appropriate karakia with confidence and authority.

Some tohunga, such as Sir James Henare and Henare Tuwhangai, began their training in a whare wānanga at a very young age, and continued for many years. The students were able to observe tohunga perform the kawanga-whare ceremonies and they learnt by participating in a variety of ceremonies. Learning was accumulative. The most important practical parts of the training were the ability to recite a series of karakia without fault and to give confidence to the people by knowing what to do.

A mentor, who was usually an experienced, well-respected and older person, trained many tohunga. Te Hau Tutua of Ngāti Awa, Pou Temara of Tūhoe, Ruka Broughton of Ngā Rauru, Matiu Mareikura of Whanganui and Huirangi Waikerepuru of Ngāti Ruanui were trained under the mentor system. Huirangi Waikerepuru and John Tahuparae were mentored under Ruka Broughton, while both Ruka Broughton and Matiu Mareikura were trained under the same mentor. In Pou Temara's case, his mentor was an expert in karakia tūturu Māori and in the karakia of the Ringatū church. He opened several houses, and so Pou Temara was able to observe the expert in different situations and in different places over many years. In the case of Te Hau Tutua it was the ceremony to clear the way for him to become a tohunga that was important. He went through a ritual that had the effect of making it relatively easy for him to learn karakia. But he too had observed many opening ceremonies and was so keen to learn that he travelled far and wide to see how the customs were performed.

The term tohunga is now used in different senses. Ministers of the Ringatū church are called tohunga and they open houses as well, but according to the teachings of Te Kooti, which are based on Christian doctrine. Carvers are called tohunga because they are highly skilled people who traditionally were taught the karakia appropriate to their profession. However, many carvers today do not have that knowledge.

The sequence

It is the tohunga who commences the dawn ceremony by the gate of the marae by asking in a loud voice, 'Ko wai te ingoa o tēnei whare?'

(What is the name of this house?) The chief of the owning hapū answers this. Then a second question is asked: 'Mō wai tēnei whare?' (For whom is this house?) Again the chief has to answer in a loud voice so that it is clear to all participating in the ceremony the reason why the house was built and what group or groups are free to use it. Then the tohunga begins to recite a set series of prayers or chants, the karakia, all the while moving towards the house. The supporting party of men and women, often a hundred or more, follow behind and join in the formulaic ending of each prayer, such as, 'Hui e! Tāiki e!' (Altogether now! It is confirmed!), or 'Tūturu whakamaua kia tina. Tina! Hui e! Tāiki e!' (Reinforce it, make it firm. It is firm! Altogether now! It is confirmed!) Confirmation by the participating public is an important part of the ceremony.

The tohunga is held responsible for conducting the kawanga ceremony correctly and without a break, which is called a whati. This is defined as missing a line, or omitting several lines, or suddenly stopping because of a memory failure. A whati is regarded as a very bad omen. Thus a tohunga must be given a clear pathway, with no obstructions, no sudden noises and absolutely no one crossing the pathway in front of him.

The tohunga approaches the porch of the house. He may decide to continue the recitation of karakia around the outside of the house and then return to the porch. While going around the outside of the house the tohunga may arrange to throw a cooked kūmara onto the roof. This act in itself assists in lifting the tapu, but it is not sufficient on its own. Not all tohunga go around the outside of the house.

Now the tohunga approaches the door of the new house. At this point it might still be dark, so some dim lights might be required to provide some guidance inside the house. Another very important component of the dawn ceremony is activated at the door. The hapū has already selected a puhi, a woman of high rank, or a ruahine, a woman who has a ritual function to perform, to be the first person to walk across the paepae poto, the threshold of the door, ahead of the tohunga. Nowadays, she is often a young woman, but traditionally the role was given to more mature women. The tohunga meets the puhi at the door and she is dressed in ceremonial costume, wearing a cloak over her clothes and bedecked with ornaments, usually the best the hapū can muster.

The tohunga and the ruahine together now lead the supporting group around the inside of the house, proceeding from the tapu side to the right of the door, and ending on the noa side to the left. Meanwhile, another tohunga might have been called upon to assist because it is difficult to recite continuously for at least thirty minutes or even longer without recourse to a book. As mentioned already, the tohunga strikes some of the main carved forms of the house which include prominent ancestor figures such as the poutokomanawa figure at the base of the centre pole, the pare (lintel above the door and the window), the amo (front upright posts on either side of the house), and inside, the poupou (ancestor posts along the wall).

The speeches

The tohunga and his party have completed the most essential part of the kawanga-whare ceremony. Now they wait inside the house for the speeches to begin. These speeches are limited to expressing thanks to the officiating tohunga, paying tribute to the artists and their work and greeting the new ancestral house. Most carved meeting houses are named after an ancestor and this provides an opportunity to remember the deeds of that person. The spectacular speeches of the day occur later.

The hapū might decide to hold a Christian service inside the house as soon as the traditional ceremony is completed. Some say this is to provide double protection and insurance for the people. Others say it is merely to appease the Christians, especially of the more anti-Māori churches. In some cases the Christian service is left for later, during what is called the public part of the ceremony. This part of the opening ceremonies might begin soon after the in-house speeches are completed or might be timed to begin at a later hour.

If this second phase commences soon after the speeches are concluded, then the tangata whenua, who are the local hapū, welcome all iwi to the new structure and then allow lots of time for orators from visiting iwi to deliver their orations on behalf of their hapū or iwi and then lay upon the ground their whakaaro (thought) or koha (gift to be reciprocated) to assist with the project. Some iwi are paying back through the koha system and remembering the assistance they received many years before. Others are establishing an obligation upon the hosts to reciprocate at some time in the future. These obligations were well-understood formerly, but nowadays many of the old customs have been forgotten. This part of the dawn ceremony usually takes some time to complete and the sun is well up in the sky by then.

The hākari

A hākari follows the speeches, and it is usually a feast to remember. The local hapū would have prepared well in advance for the occasion and gathered in a variety of seafood and delicacies. The hākari that follows a kawanga-whare is never a simple matter of providing food: it is a ceremonial feast. The best that the hosts can provide are set out on the tables. Numbers of people to provide for are usually very high: 500, 700, 1,000 or more, which might require several sittings. If the complex ceremony finished early the feast is a spectacular breakfast. If not it might be lunch or a late lunch. It is the feast that completes the cycle of events that are all part of the kawanga-whare ceremony. After the meal, the tapu has been lifted and the building is now free to be used by the public.

Basic elements of the kawanga ceremony

1. The time is at dawn, before the sun rises.

2. In preparation the people most involved agree to fast from the time of their evening meal until the ceremony is completed.

3. There must be at least one competent tohunga to conduct the ceremony. If more than one, there is usually a senior tohunga who assumes a leading role.

4. The tohunga asks for the name of the house to be announced and asks to identify for whom the house was built. It is assumed that the house is not a personal dwelling but a social amenity for a clearly defined group. He begins after these questions have been answered.

5. Once the tohunga commences the karakia the supporting group maintains silence, joining in only at the conclusion of each sequence.

6. People get in behind the tohunga and follow.

7. When several tohunga are involved the route to be followed is divided among them. The officiating tohunga steps ahead of the rest and leads the group and steps back when his section has been done.

8. If it is a meeting house that is being opened a high point of the ceremony occurs when the tohunga approaches the door to the house. The chosen ruahine is waiting there to be asked to cross the threshold.

9. The tohunga may use a carved tokotoko, staff or twig to gently touch the thing to be opened, the walls of a building, the sides of a canoe, the paintings on the wall, sculptural pieces, cloaks or other woven items.

10. The karakia tūturu are complete when the tohunga recites the closing section of the sequence.

11. A Christian church service may follow at this point.

12. Speeches follow and if a house is opened the first lot of speeches are held in the house. This could be the time when a special ceremony is performed over the artists and their tools. The speeches then focus on the works of art and the artists.

13. If it is an exhibition the main speeches of the event commence.

14. For a meeting house or dining room, the main speeches of the day are held outside and this is the time when visiting groups place their koha on the ground and make a contribution to the event.

15. The hākari or feast is held and this concludes the protocols of the kawanga ceremony.

The sequence of events above represents a model of how the various parts of the ceremony are arranged. There may be variations and additions and omissions. By the time it is completed the visitors are eager for the hākari that completes the ceremony.

The carvers

Tikanga relating to the artists and their tools differed from region to region and depended a great deal on the tohunga. The customs of Ngāti Awa as exemplified in the work of the tohunga Tumutara Pio and recorded by Cowan (1930:262–71), who witnessed an event in 1900, were unusual by today's standards. The tools of the three carvers who carved the house called Rauru were placed on the maihi (the front bargeboards) and a special karakia performed over them to free them from tapu. Cowan may not have observed carefully exactly what happened here because the roof angle on Arawa houses is quite steep and it would have been difficult to place the tools on the maihi. The next procedure is also unusual and the carver might have acted for the tohunga who by this time was an old man and unable to climb up the roof. This has some significance when the second opening is discussed. In any event what transpired according to Cowan was that the master carver climbed up the roof of the house and stood momentarily with arms stretched outwards and positioned immediately behind the tekoteko, the carved figure at the apex of the house. It is not clear what was happening here and why the master carver had to stand behind the tekoteko unless it was a symbolic statement of responsibility for the whole structure.

The tohunga used a twig of the rata tree, which is sacred to the tribes of Mātaatua, to touch the main carved pieces, the maihi, the centre poles and the pare. Cowan (1930:263) put it this way: 'Tumutara tapped reverently the wooden images of ancestors and fabulous demons, and ever repeated in quick monotone the prayers of old Aotearoa to void the house of all evil influences, to bind firmly all of its timbers, to hold it firm against all assault of wind and rain, to make it habitable with comfort and joy'.

Cowan also observed the practices followed by the Tūwharetoa tohunga Te Rangitahau (Cowan 1930: 263–71). Te Rangitahau was supported by a group of Tūwharetoa and Te Arawa who fasted the night before. He performed what was clearly a dawn ceremony. By contrast, Tumutara had conducted his part of the ceremony on the same house the afternoon before. It was highly irregular to employ two sets of tohunga of different iwi and waka to open the one house but Rauru was unusual in many ways. It belonged to a Pākehā dealer and not to a hapū. The kawanga-whare ceremonies were performed to authenticate the house as a traditional work before being sold.

The protocols of Te Arawa

In Te Rangitahau's case the twig he used was kawakawa and his party was dressed in western clothes and covered with traditional cloaks. The time was March 1900. The tohunga asked the master carver to light a small sacred fire, called te umu-a-Tāne (the oven of Tāne), in front of the house and on the window side of the outside centre-pole. A kūmara was placed in the sacred fire. While the kūmara was being cooked the master carver had to attend to the fire. Meanwhile the tohunga walked to the side of the house and climbed up a ladder to the roof and he positioned himself behind the tekoteko at the apex of the house. He began his karakia from there. From that position he recited the karakia to clear the tools of the carvers.

When that was completed, he came down from the top of the house. He walked on the outside of the house to the back and then to the front to where the sacred fire was burning. The master carver was instructed to take the cooked kūmara and all of the carvers were to accompany him to the door. The ruahine to cross the threshold (takahi i te paepae poto) was Ruihi of Ngāti Tarāwhai, wife of Tene the master carver. In the previous afternoon's ceremony conducted by Tumutara, the ruahine was Merenia Puoke, sister-in-law of Neke, one of the carvers. Te Rangitahau and Ruihi crossed the threshold together and he did not allow the public to follow his special group, which consisted of himself, the three carvers and the ruahine, the woman of honour.

He did not go around the house immediately, as tohunga do today, but concentrated on key places such as the fireplace and the poutokomanawa. At the latter place he formed little mounds of earth and on each he placed a kawakawa leaf. Karakia were chanted to appease Tūmatauenga and bring the house under the influences of Rongo, the God of peace. Only after this ceremony did the tohunga walk around the inside of the house to touch the carvings. While he was doing this, carvers chewed on the cooked kūmara. The party stayed in the house for twenty minutes and afterwards came out. That part of the ceremony was complete.

Recent ceremonies

What happened in 1900 when carved houses had earthen floors and fireplaces dug into the earth is not now possible with houses that have wooden or concrete floors. Modern houses now have windows, electric lights, heating systems, sprinkler systems, carpets, illuminated signs to show exits, attached toilets, and ramps for the disabled people. Rauru did not have any of these amenities.

At a recent ceremony the carvers and other artists were made to stand inside the porch and then special karakia were performed on them to free them from tapu. This was followed by a speech of appreciation to them and then the main speech-making part of the day began. At another recent kawanga whare at Masterton, 27 September 1997, there was a revival of the custom of the artist climbing up to the roof of the house and sitting immediately behind the tekoteko. From that position the carver recited a series of karakia and at one point stretched out his arms as described by Cowan. As soon as he finished, the tohunga who remained on the ground began his series of karakia. While he was doing so the carver and the puhi walked around the outside of the house. On the way the carver threw pieces of cooked kūmara onto the roof. When the outside circuit was completed, the carver and the puhi met up with the tohunga at the door. This part of the ceremony followed the usual pattern. After the tohunga completed the karakia inside the house, tohunga of the Ringatū church conducted a service. There were no speeches inside the house. Instead seating was set up outside in the cold morning air and the speeches began. Breakfast was provided, but this was not the hākari. There was a programme of speeches and entertainment before the big feast ended the ceremony of kawanga whare.

Every ceremony is a negotiated event with many factors having some bearing on what actually happens. Some of the variables, referred to already, are the availability of tohunga, the knowledge of the carver, the ability of the hapū to carry the day, the mana of the hapū, the nature of the house, the season, the facilities available to the hapū, and the customs of the owning tribe. Ideally when the ritual opening of the house is completed and the tohunga and his party come out of the house, dawn should be clearly in evidence and the sun about to rise or rising. Strictly speaking this ceremony should not be performed after sunrise.

More variations

The double ceremony

It has been the practice up until very recently to make a clear separation between the traditional karakia and the public part of the ceremony. The first part was carried out more or less 'underground' and was confined to Māori. That was the dawn ceremony, and it could well have been instituted in order to hide it from the gaze and knowledge of non-Māori citizens, or to protect it from them. The public opening was scheduled for about 10 a.m. and a prominent Pākehā official – a governor general, minister of the Crown, prime minister, or local mayor – was invited to cut the ribbon and open the house. It was the name of this official that was put on the plaque which commemorated the opening day. The tohunga who performed the karakia at the dawn ceremony was not mentioned, nor was the name of the puhi recorded on the plaque. The colonial influence persists even today.

The practice of a double ceremony was instituted as early as the 1870s. For example, when Mātaatua was opened in Whakatane in 1875 the early morning ceremony was probably held 8 March 1875. It is significant that this event was not reported in the local newspaper but the public event held later was fully described. Sir Donald McLean, the native minister, had to wait aboard a ship before he was invited to join the tribes of Mātaatua at a 'public' ceremony where the minister was permitted to speak. On this occasion the people met the next day as well so the tribes of Mātaatua could speak to the native minister and he could threaten them by saying 'remember the Pakeha can do anything he makes up his mind to'(Mead et al. 1990:42). This was shortly after the confiscations of Māori land by governments of Aotearoa in the 1800s had occurred in the Bay of Plenty. McLean is the man who is remembered as the official who opened Mātaatua. The name of the tohunga is forgotten. Thus the custom of a double opening, whereby a proper traditional one – the kawanga-whare ceremony held at dawn – was followed by a public one is over a hundred years old.

Some iwi still practise the double-opening ceremony in the mistaken belief that this was the genuine custom. Others have made the dawn ceremony the most important event of the day and opened it to anyone wishing to attend. There is no longer a separation between the two and no longer a fear of the tohunga being arrested and an iwi being accused of practising unfriendly pagan ceremonies. Nowadays, there is renewed interest in the genuine and authentic ceremonies and customs. But it is fair to say that the tension that exists today is between Māori who want to follow the 'true' customs and Māori who want to follow Christian practices and say Christian prayers. The issue is argued at every opening.

Te Māori, and other transformations of the kawanga whare

The kawanga-whare ceremony has become popularised as 'a dawn ceremony'. It has been adapted in various ways to accommodate new structures, such as the Sky City Casino in Auckland and overseas posts belonging to the nation, as well as new events, such as art exhibitions. The most profound effect upon the ceremony was undoubtedly its use in New York in 1984 to open and launch the Te Māori exhibition, easily one of the most influential exhibitions ever mounted by Aotearoa. The dawn ceremony caught the imagination of the international art world and it became a necessary part of the exhibition wherever it was taken in the United States and in New Zealand. The ceremony was impressive, highly charged, eerie because it was performed in semi-darkness, emotionally wrenching for some, providing a taste of the real primitive for others.

The ceremony changed the way museums normally handled exhibition openings. It brought people of the owning culture together with their heritage treasures in a dynamic relationship, startling the dispassionate curators and exhibition experts. In Aotearoa the rangatahi (youth) of the various tribes took turns at being guides and therefore took on the unfamiliar role of explaining their own culture to others. Iwi took turns at welcoming visitors to the exhibition. These were the flow-on consequences of the iwi imposing cultural controls upon the manner in which their heritage items were displayed, opened, discussed and explained.

By the conclusion of Te Māori, the dawn ceremony had become accepted as a normal way of opening an exhibition of traditional art, of weaving and carving. An adaptation had been made of a ceremony meant for carved houses. In the case of Te Māori the emphasis was upon the very tapu nature of the taonga, the treasures in the exhibition, but in every case there were also newly prepared exhibition halls to open. Within the collection of taonga were names of ancestor figures and very sacred objects such as burial chests. These valuable heritage items were taken abroad, displayed in a strange country, a strange city, a strange building and cared for by people of another culture.

There was real concern about some of the items in the exhibition, which were held in awe by many if not most Māori: the burial chests, for example, or Uenuku. The elders wanted the exhibition rendered 'safe', in a ritual sense, for the visitors who came to see the artworks. The dawn ceremony was the vehicle to render the exhibition noa, free from a dangerous level of tapu.

Negotiating a ceremony

The idea of employing the dawn ceremony to open Te Māori in New York was debated and discussed over many months by many elders and several tohunga. The decision was not lightly made because there were many consequences that required negotiation, not only with the American officials of the various museums, but also at diplomatic level. One consequence of the decision was that a group of tohunga and supporters needed to go to each new venue and carry out the ceremony. Museum officials in the United States had to accept the idea because there were many consequences for them. The very idea of opening the doors of a huge institution such as the Metropolitan Museum of Art in New York in the early hours of the morning and before the sun rose required a major shift in thinking. The same held true, and perhaps even more so, for the notion of an early breakfast. Months of negotiations were required to finally agree on the details of the adapted dawn ceremony. The Americans accepted the Māori way of opening an exhibition and the rest is history. However, at each venue of Te Māori the people involved had to hold further negotiations in order that both sides understood exactly what was to happen.

Te Māori acted as a catalyst to revive interest in this traditional custom and to motivate tohunga to test their knowledge and their ability to recite karakia tūturu. It also brought the practice out into the glare of international publicity and out of the closet as it were. It became a means of expressing tino rangatiratanga in this domain, that is, ownership and control over our taonga and our cultural practices. Māori art itself, in traditional and modern forms, became popular and acceptable, for after all, Te Māori had been accepted as a manifestation of one of the great art traditions of the world.

In each instance the exhibition was not open to the public until the tapu-lifting ceremony had been performed. Competent tohunga took charge of the rituals and shared in the ceremony. They began the ceremony from outside the building and when they approached the door to the museum it was opened for them. The chanting of the karakia continued across the main entrance of the building, and in New York up the stairs and finally into the exhibition area. The tohunga struck the main exhibits either with a branch of leaves or with a carved staff.

After the tohunga had completed the traditional rituals, a Christian service was held before the speeches began. In each venue there were speeches of welcome from the home side and speeches of reply from the elders' group and some officials representing the New Zealand Government. Then followed a breakfast with more speeches and some performances from the Aotearoa kapa haka groups (culture teams) selected for a particular venue. The whole event was spectacular, and the dawn ceremony thereafter became a part of the museum and Māori art world. Since then, we have used it at home and exported it overseas.

The position today

The modern form of the dawn ceremony is modelled very much on the procedures successfully negotiated and discussed by kuia and koroua (female and male elders), and by tohunga such as Henare Tuwhangai and Pumi Taituha of Tainui, and Ruka Broughton of Ngā Rauru, who were among the most knowledgeable and experienced at that time. There were also Sir James Henare of Ngāti Hine, Pateriki Rei of Ngāti Toa, Irirangi Tiakiawa of Te Arawa, Hohua Tutengaehe of Ngāi Te Rangi, Te Hau Tutua of Ngāti Awa, Pou Temara of Tūhoe, Huirangi Waikere-puru of Ngāti Ruanui and Matiu Mareikura of Whanganui, who all played prominent roles during Te Māori. Many others took part in the ceremonies, but they were not really competent tohunga. There was a real fear in 1984 that the arts of the kawanga-whare ceremony might have been lost and that we were seeing the last of the great tohunga. The question asked was: who is to replace Henare Tuwhangai, Pumi Taituha, Hohua Tutengaehe, and Pateriki Rei, who have all passed on?

The reality today is that capable tohunga who really understand and have control over karakia tūturu are very unevenly distributed across the iwi of Aotearoa. There are many iwi who have no one capable of carrying out the protocol of kawanga whare adequately. However, so great is the value placed upon conducting the protocol that in some cases very incompetent tohunga are putting themselves forward. They go through the motions and recite something but it is not the karakia tūturu that one expects to hear. Some recite a tauparapara (a formulaic recital to begin a speech), others recite a speech and talk as they go, and others recite Christian prayers.

The assimilated ceremony

There are some who carry out the protocol under the mantle of a Christian church and thereby compromise the kawanga–whare ceremony. In this case an attempt is made to embrace the dawn ceremony or to assimilate it within the ideology of a Christian church because some Māori have difficulty in accepting the traditional protocol as a part of our heritage. They think it is pagan and should be changed. It is a move that does not sit well with a lot of youthful Māori who want to see the authentic ceremony and enjoy being a part of it. Nor does it satisfy those adults who are reviving old customs and rediscovering old knowledge.

An example of an assimilated kawanga–whare ceremony was witnessed at the opening of a carved house in Auckland. In the half-light of dawn, the officiating tohunga approached a white-robed priest at the entrance of the marae, knelt before him, was blessed by the priest and then proceeded to carry out the 'requirements' of the traditional protocol. However, the 'tohunga' did not know the appropriate karakia and was not able to persuade other tohunga who attended the ceremony that the kawanga–whare protocol had been performed properly. Inside the house itself, other tohunga intervened and recited the appropriate karakia in order to satisfy themselves that the house was opened in accordance with traditional protocol.

Where are the tohunga?

At the time, Tainui probably provided the most experienced pool of tohunga because under Kingitanga they were often invited to open new carved houses. Henare Tuwhangai was the dean of all tohunga during his lifetime, and he officiated at opening ceremonies in many parts of New Zealand and in several overseas countries. He was sincere in his work and was able to explain what he was doing and why. He personally did not accept any interference from the churches and insisted on carrying out the protocol properly according to the traditions that he knew. Even after losing two very prominent tohunga, such as Henare Tuwhangai and Pumi Taituha, Tainui is still able to conduct the protocols of the kawanga–whare ceremony.

Another iwi who is comparatively strong in this respect is Taranaki. Together with Whanganui or on their own, the iwi of Taranaki are able to carry the protocols through with style and dignity. They lost Ruka

Broughton and Matiu Mareikura, but there are others among them who are capable of performing the traditional ceremony. Huirangi Waikerepuru and John Tahuparae are examples and there are others being trained.

Te Arawa lost Irirangi Tiakiawa and now has Mauriora Kingi. Mātaatua lost Hohua Tutengaehe but have Pou Temara and Te Hau Tutua. The northern tribes lost Sir James Henare and the Rev. Maori Marsden who both trained at a traditional whare wānanga. Ngāti Kahungunu lost John Tangiora and Wi Hamutana. Many tribes have to train others to assume the roles of tohunga tā i te kawa.

What the situation is with Ngāti Porou is unclear. At present they have Amster Reedy and Dr Tamati Reedy who perform karakia tūturu. Ngāi Tahu has Huata Holmes. A careful audit needs to be conducted in order to see where we are and what needs to be done to train more tohunga. It is obvious that training programmes are needed.

The boundaries of appropriateness

The kawanga ceremony is part of the world of tikanga. As Māori culture has had to change in order to adapt to ever-changing circum-stances, the kawanga ceremony has also changed. This is obvious from the accounts described in this chapter. As well as the changes made for Te Māori, the dawn ceremony was also used to open an exhibition of contemporary Māori art in Australia. Soon afterwards the works on display were offered for sale. In this case the ceremony was being used for commercial purposes. Was this appropriate? Some thought the tikanga was used wrongly.

In another very recent case the ceremony was used to open either the building or the artworks or both at the Sky City Casino in Auck-land. What was shown on television appeared like an opening for the casino building. Was this an appropriate application of the kawanga ceremony?

The new building to house the Museum of New Zealand Te Papa Tongarewa, at Wellington, had been in use for some time before the dawn ceremony. Staff had been working in the building for months, hundreds of people were invited to visit the premises, food and drink had already been consumed. A dawn ceremony was performed on 30 November 1997. At a meeting of local elders at Waiwhetū Marae it was resolved that although the museum had broken many of the rules, it was possible to ritually correct the situation. A very late dawn ceremony could be held and there were karakia tūturu that could be added to the normal list. There was some discomfort with the compromise, but many present at the meeting thought something needed to be done to put things right.

The real question to be asked is this: Who has the right to change the kawanga ceremony when used nationally and internationally and how should it be done? Months of deliberation, discussion and negotiation among many Māori leaders preceded the changes made for Te Māori. At every venue there were further negotiations. There were also briefing hui held for every group involved in a ceremony so that everyone knew (or was supposed to know) what was to happen. These were valuable experiences which provided a process for dealing with change. At the local level among iwi it is clear that the host iwi make the decisions and take the praise when all goes well, or accept criticisms during speech making when things do not go well.

The tapu of things

The detailed discussion of the kawanga-whare ceremony focuses on how a huge piece of creative art, a fully decorated meeting house, is regarded and treated in Māori communities. Such a structure is like an art gallery that is filled with works of art by many carvers, weavers and painters. Many weavers worked on the tukutuku panels, several painters worked on the kōwhaiwhai patterns on the ceiling and the carvers, who were also the carpenters, spent months creating carved panels for the house. All of these works of art were treated as one complex creation called a whare whakairo, a decorated house. There was one ceremony to deal with the whole building and all of the artists were treated as a collective body, but their names are not recorded and often they are not remembered. Yet there were always artists who created individual works of art such as ornaments, greenstone hei tiki, beautiful weapons, cloaks, floormats and baskets. Traditional artists observed the rules of tapu in respect of their works. They gave their works names and the name, often that of an ancestor, gave the object a measure of tapu. While many modern artists do not follow the traditional rituals and protocols, some do. However, what has become custom is that a karakia is expected when a created piece of Māori art is handed over to its owner. This is especially so for taonga that are worn, such as personal ornaments, and more so for created objects that are used as gifts in the context of a social gathering. Weapons and cloaks are treated with great respect and especially for those that are works of art in themselves. Water might be sprinkled on the object or there might be a combination of karakia and water to seal the transfer from the artist to the owner and to render the object safe for the owner.

Some created works that are ancient are accorded great respect, and works such as waka tūpāpaku (burial chests) are regarded as very tapu and people are usually very careful about them, preferring not to touch them. For all other created works Māori people want to touch them and make contact with them. This is a feature of Māori behaviour that museum curators cannot easily control. During Te Māori, for example, our people made contact with the taonga especially if the objects came from their tribal region. Or they might lay green leaves on them or at their feet. The worst fear for curators was realised when a Māori admirer came armed with a jar of water!

The museums are filled with old taonga that are highly valued and some, such as cloaks, have become very fragile and are in fact beginning to disintegrate. Some marae have valuable created objects and many families have their own private collections of very valuable things.

Conclusions

In this chapter we have discussed a number of situations that could have warranted separate consideration. We dealt with wāhi tapu, taonga, and the kawanga–whare ceremony and its relationship to constructions and artistically created works.

A basic reason for wanting to use the kawanga ceremony is that there is something very important and special to open and that this special thing is closely associated with Māori culture. The carved meeting house or a carved waka taua obviously meets all requirements. If the building is overseas or is built for non-Māori purposes some Māori art pieces may be added to it in order to conform to cultural requirements. A huge building might have only one substantial piece of Māori art in it to qualify. If the thing to open is not a building it might be a collection of many Māori art pieces traditional or modern, created by Māori artists. At the very least the thing might be one substantial artwork by an artist of some standing.

Another reason for wanting to have a dawn ceremony is that it is spectacular and unique. It draws people to it because they wish to be part of an authentic Māori ceremony. It is special to Aotearoa and because of Te Māori overseas people expect to witness it. However, the authentic nature of the ceremony needs to be nurtured and its integrity protected in the national interest.

That the ceremony has changed over time is obvious and there is little doubt that other changes are likely to occur in the future. At the moment Māori play a leading role in the ceremony. As the ceremony becomes more popular it is quite possible that other ethnic groups will grasp the essential idea and adapt it to their own ends. Thus it is entirely possible that in the future we may find ourselves watching our ceremony being performed by others.

Wāhi tapu has recently become very important as an issue when applying for resource consents or Treaty of Waitangi settlements. There is a growing literature on wāhi tapu and kaitiaki (guardians) as a new tikanga appearing in reports of various government departments or ministries (Gardiner 1993; Fisheries Task Force 1992; New Zealand Conservation Authority 1997; and see especially Love 1996) and in various enactments of government. Examples are the Resource Management Act 1991 and the Ture Whenua Maori Act 1993. Formerly wāhi tapu were the concern of the tribes in occupation. They were the kaitiaki of all places in their areas of occupation. Today some groups want to be identified as the kaitiaki of a wāhi tapu as a way of asserting an occupation or owning claim.

There are restrictions on human behaviour and interactions with things, their human creators, and places. The level of tapu is increased while the activity is being performed and then decreased to normal after completion. There are tikanga to accomplish this. In the case of places called wāhi tapu, the level of tapu remains the same for as long as the community wishes it. Tikanga is used to reinforce the tapu of places rather than to diminish it although some wāhi tapu are more tapu than others.

Perspectives

In New Zealand the 'tapu' is a custom, which almost supplies the place of law amongst other nations. The laying of the tapu literally means to pronounce the individual or article in question to be sacred for a greater or less period of time.

– Angas 1847, 1:330

In the Waikato district, 1844

As usual I explored the remotest corners of the pah (Kaitote) in search of anything new for my pencil, and seeing a square deal box elevated on posts and covered with a roof raised by means of slender sticks, I was curious to know what it contained, it was evidently tapu and on lifting up the lid found that it was filled with old garments, which I afterwards learned were the property of a very elevated person lately deceased, and these garments had been placed within this wahi tapu, under the most rigorous tapu by the tohunga: who would probably have pulled my ears had he discovered me peeping at these sacred relics.

– Angas 1847, 2:35

Wahi tapu in a house

About half a mile from the present native settlement stands the ruined pah of Paripari which contains, in a state of almost perfect preservation, two of the finest carved and painted Maori houses still existing in New Zealand. This pah was erected on a memorable occasion of the Taranaki war, when the Mokau warriors set out on their expedition to the fated district; where the inhabitants of the principal pah were either slaughtered and eaten or taken as slaves, by the conquering party ... Within a small railing, in one corner of the verandah of the largest house, is a wahi tapu, where the head of Te Kawaw (fowl) with his feathers, hani and mat, were deposited. Te Kawaw was a great warrior and very swift of foot, which allowed for him the appellation of 'bird' or 'fowl'. He was killed during one of the engagements of the Taranaki war close to the pah of the besieged, and his people not being able to remove the body, cut off his head, which they deposited within the sacred enclosure at Paripari.

– Angas 1847, 2:87–88

The fine house was rendered tapu through this action and abandoned. This was in 1844 when Angas visited Paripari at Te Kuiti.

Two-stage burial
Friday 17th September 1819
In returning through the potato grounds we met with the chief Racow (Rakau), Duaterra's father in law. I wished to visit the sacred grove, which was near, where he died, but as I understood was tabooed I could not enter without permission of the chief. Mr. Kendall spoke to him and told him what I wanted. He came and pointed out the tree where his daughter, Duaterra's wife, hung herself and showed us the spot where both their bodies were deposited. The sacred spot was enclosed with a fence about three yards square. Here the bodies remained together till the flesh was decayed, when their bones were carefully collected and carried to their respective family sepulchers.
Observer: Rev. Samuel Marsden at Rangihou
— Elder 1932:178

The tapu of the forest and of things
The forest for instance, was believed to be under the guardianship of the god Tane, who protected trees, rats, birds and all woodland products from unauthorized interference. The tapu lay upon them and only after Tane had been placated and the effects of tapu nullified could the Maori venture to convert these things to his own use. Thus to clip or cut a living, standing tree was thought to be an unlucky act; it was an aitua, an evil omen for the person who did it. A tree should be felled properly and with due ceremony; one should not aimlessly hack it about; nor should one even adze a standing tree for future use. Such an act was pokanoa, a wanton piece of interference, and the elder would chide any young person seen behaving in this manner. Causal meddling with valuable property was thus prevented. The examination of a host of other beliefs and institutions shows that the significant natural resources on which the Maori was dependent for food or the raw materials of industry all had some degree of tapu attaching to them.
— Firth 1959:247

The tapu of things

The tapu of material culture accessories again is recognition of their 'social value' – to adopt a term which Radcliffe Brown has employed to such advantage. Objects of importance to the community, such as large canoes, eel weirs and superior houses always had a certain amount of tapu pertaining to them, whereas small fishing canoes and dwellings of ordinary type were void of such quality. The intensification of the tapu in the case of things of greater social importance is clear. In the production of the more valued economic goods supernatural restrictions invested the object and its surroundings. Thus, when a large fishing net was being put together on the beach, the net and all the workers engaged thereon were tapu, as also the shore around for a considerable distance.

  – Firth 1959:248

Individual ownership of land was not recognised in Māori society. The land and resources were used by Māori rather than owned by them. Māori recognised the land as their ūkaipō, which descended from the kāwai tīpuna and was maintained as such by their tīpuna. Spiritual beliefs and effective leadership helped to maintain effective control over the use of land.

Rights and interests of individuals and whānau in the land derived from the hapū. Similarly, the hapū had special use rights of various places and resource areas but it did not own them. Iwi would base their rights to land on *take*. They maintained their *take* by placing physical signs on the land or through demonstrating their knowledge of the different uses of the land. Ahi kā required those who used the land to maintain the ability to control the land through continued use and occupation. The whānau, hapū and iwi were obliged to protect the land and exercise guardianship over it. This not only ensured that the well being of the present generation would be catered for, but that the following generations would benefit as well.

  – Ministry of Justice 2001:49–50

6
Te Marae: The Ceremonial Courtyard

The first point to be made about the concept and idea of marae is that it is a very old idea and it is part of the heritage of Polynesia. Other Polynesian cultures use the same term, but with slightly different emphasis. The second point is that here in Aotearoa the notion and expression of it has changed over time. Formerly the marae was the clear space in front of the wharenui where certain ceremonies were conducted. The site of the marae was usually referred to as the pā. Williams (1971:243) defines the pā as a 'stockade' or 'fortified place'. Notwithstanding his definition, 'pā' was the common term used to describe the place where the marae was located. Nowadays the word 'marae' encompasses the whole complex. This change would have come about in the late 1960s partly as a result of the publication by the Department of Education's School Publications branch of a book called *Washday at the Pa*, by Ans Westra. There were a lot of negative reactions to the book, after which the word pā became very unpopular. Today we use the word marae to describe the complex of land, buildings and facilities as they exist today. That is how the word is used here.

The idea and the concept of marae as we know it in Aotearoa has caught the imagination of people overseas and here at home. Whereas the marae was very clearly a rural phenomenon that dotted the landscape as one drove through the countryside, today that is not the case. There are marae in the towns and the cities, at universities and polytechnics, at secondary schools and primary schools. Several churches have marae. This wide range of sites for marae suggest that the idea is accepted as being a very useful one and that the idea itself can be put into practice in a number of ways. It follows that marae do not look exactly the same:

some are close to the ideal model of a marae while others have departed, often considerably, from the ideal. But they are still called a marae. So it is fair to ask: When is a marae very clearly a marae and when is it not a marae?

A place for the feet to stand

A marae is an institution that is a vital part of Māori culture. It consists of a space that is defined and has a name. It is usually fenced in and is a significant site for carrying out the ceremonies and cultural practices of the owning group. There are buildings on the site, one of which is usually a whare tipuna, or ancestral house, which also has a name. It is usually the name of a well-known ancestor or it might be a name commemorating some important event. The names are very important. The ancestral name is a uniting force as most of the people associated with the marae can trace a genealogical line to the ancestor. So it is their ancestor and their house and their land. Similarly the name of the marae site is also a name of some significance to the local people.

The land provides another bonding link and establishes tūranga-waewae, the place for the feet to stand discussed in relation to attributes of identity in chapter 4. This is a very important cultural bond to the land. Alongside this place for the feet to stand come a bundle of rights, such as the right to participate and the right to use the marae for ceremonial and social purposes. There is also an obligation to assist in the work of the marae. The marae stands as a symbol of the hapū that owns it. Many marae are very old and the antiquity of the buildings adds to the significance of the marae. The place where it stands is a wāhi tapu, rich in memories. It is a place where previous generations carried out tikanga Māori in a manner that might be very similar to what is done now.

Marae can be classified into two main categories: the traditional and the modern. In the more traditional marae, there are other buildings on the land. These include a large wharekai (dining room), a toilet block, shelters for the visitors, sometimes a whare mate where the dead lie in state. Today there could well be other buildings such as a building for the kōhanga reo and classrooms for various training programmes. Some distance away from the marae site is an urupā.

A cemetery is an essential part of a traditional and rural marae. The tangata whenua organise and run the entire set of complex ceremonies that make up the tangihanga, including the burials. At urban marae the burial has to be arranged with the local cemetery authority at a time to suit the authority. This has consequences for the relatives and for the tikanga of the mourning ceremony. An urban marae can appear very much like a traditional marae, or it may have a single building which encompasses all of the functions of a marae.

Responsibilities

Establishing and running a marae complex places responsibilities upon the local people that are quite heavy but come as part of being a credible hapū. As well as the actual establishment and construction of the marae complex, responsibilities extend to the maintenance and improvement of the complex. Fundraising is a major, continuing task and a major difficulty in building a new marae. Government subsidies are available but are contestable, and some branches of government may give funds for special purposes: Te Waka Toi may do so for artwork. As well as financial commitments, there are tikanga to observe in beginning a project, tikanga for getting tōtara trees for the carvings of the meeting house, tikanga while the buildings are being put up, tikanga guiding the creative art work for the complex, and, as we have seen in the previous chapter, tikanga for opening the complex.

Manaakitanga and hospitality

The marae site is the hub of ceremonial and social events that are hosted by the group that owns the complex. In today's world owning groups are not just kin-based but may include churches, schools, universities, clubs or pan-Māori urban groups. Marae based in the home territory of iwi are normally used every week and sometimes every day. For some ceremonials, such as tangihanga, the whole complex becomes a hive of activity. Those who come to mourn bring a koha to assist with the expenses of the ceremony and the local people must feed them all. Often the number of people given a meal at the dining room will be over one thousand and for big occasions there could be several thousand people.

No matter how many guests arrive, the local people must offer them manaakitanga and hospitality. Food is the final act in the ritual encounters on a marae and must be offered. Manaakitanga is an expected part of the tikanga.

During these occasions, and at other kinds of gatherings, the visitors may stay overnight and are accommodated by the hosts. Mattresses, sheets, pillows and pillowslips are provided. The guests are expected to bring their own blankets and provide their own towels. Marae also provide showers and bathrooms where guests can shower and wash. A necessary part of the tikanga of sleeping in the meeting house is that there are no beds offered; only a mattress on the floor. These are laid out side by side and there is no segregation of the sexes. Manaakitanga again demands of the marae that their facilities are adequate and well-presented, that the toilets are clean and that the showers actually work. The hosts are honour bound, in terms of manaakitanga, to take good care of their visitors.

Tikanga in the meeting house

Everyone is thoroughly mixed together in the meeting house, but nonetheless there are tikanga to be observed. Stepping over sleeping bodies is frowned upon as bad behaviour. An absolute tapu rule is that no one steps over any other person's head, as the head is the most tapu part of the person. It is not good form to step over any person who is lying down or sleeping. Dressing and undressing must be done discreetly: experience teaches people how to do this without embarrassment. Again, tikanga must be observed. In this sense it is very clear that tikanga provides guidelines of proper behaviour in order that the conventions of society are not broken. When dealing with large numbers of people – say a hundred sleeping in a sizeable meeting house – there must be rules of acceptable behaviour. For some people, sleeping together in a meeting house is a novelty. Probably the most difficult part is not being together, but putting up with the chorus of snoring from different parts of the house. It takes a while to learn how to sleep through the cicadas of the night.

Within the meeting house there are tikanga to determine where the visitors sit and sleep and where the hosts sit and sleep. Visitors sleep on the tapu side of the house (along the right wall when one enters the door) and the hosts are on the noa side of the house opposite the tapu side. There are tikanga which indicate where the leading chief of the visitors should sleep and this is linked to the order of speakers when speeches are given. The honoured position is at the tapu side of the house, in the corner by the window. When the person sitting there speaks, that signals the end of the speakers on the visitors' side. Speakers on the hosts' side begin their speeches from the opposite corner, namely from the corner nearest the door on the noa side of the house. The direction of the speeches is from the front corner of the noa wall, along the length of the noa wall to the far corner at the back of the house, then along the back wall and around to the tapu wall and ending where the visiting chief is sitting or lying down.

During a church service, however, the direction of activity begins from the same corner but then goes in the opposite direction. It is not clear why this is so, but that is the protocol in the Bay of Plenty region. The hosts are the advocates and the guides of the tikanga that have to be followed in their house and on their marae. They have the final say in any arguments about correct procedure. What these rules of tikanga indicate is that a marae is where tikanga Māori is expected to prevail and be followed. Therefore, one should not be surprised to find that this is the case and there is some learning to do. Most marae will have their own special tikanga that the hosts have built up over the years.

The urupā

Urupā, as we have seen, is the Māori term for a burial ground such as a cemetery. There is usually an urupā associated with a marae and it may be contiguous or some distance away. An urupā usually has a name and is gazetted as a Māori reservation by the Māori Land Court. The urupā has particular tikanga associated with it that govern behaviour. It is a wāhi tapu, a place where there are restrictions because of the dead whose bones lie there. There is no eating or drinking allowed there, or smoking. In some areas men empty out their pockets and leave their tobacco and matches outside of the urupā. A woman who is an expert in the art of ceremonial karanga may call people attending and bringing the deceased into the urupā. In some iwi they may not do this. People follow behind the coffin and then gather around the hole where the burial will take place. But even before this event, the gravediggers have determined where the hole should be and there are tikanga about this. They have dug it ready for the arrival of the deceased. They are on hand to help lower the coffin into the pit. The tools they use are kept in a very special place and are not to be used for other purposes. Their job ends when the hole is filled in and properly finished by creating a mound against which the floral wreaths are placed. Sometimes they take their tools to the river and clean them as well as cleansing them in a ritual way. The behaviour of the diggers is governed by tikanga because what they do brings them into the proximity of dangerous levels of tapu. Their normal state of noa has to be restored so that they can participate in the affairs of the people and of their own families.

There are tikanga to guide the actual burial ceremony. A religious funeral service is held. The final speeches to the dead are made at the graveside and here close relatives are free to speak. Children are often encouraged to participate by filing past the grave and either depositing a flower on the coffin or some of the dirt that would be used to cover the dead. When leaving the urupā all participants are expected to wash their hands with water and sprinkle some over themselves usually three times. The function of the water is to reduce the level of tapu to the safe state of noa. This is an important step in the process of transformation from tapu to noa. From here the people go back to the marae and take part in the ceremonial feast called the hākari, the final act of whakanoa or of reducing the tapu on everyone so a state of noa prevails once more.

The age of some marae

In respect of the ceremonies of mourning, most marae also have an associated cemetery and this enables the group to mourn, to farewell and to bury their dead themselves. Many of the cemeteries or urupā are over a hundred years old and so contain several generations of dead. These generational changes are often reflected in headstones. By studying the headstones one can read the names, find out their ages at death, and note whether the message on the headstone is in Māori as all the early ones were and then pinpoint when the change to English occurred, and when Māori language began to emerge again. There are also different styles of headstones as one will find in England or the

United States of America. The notion of the headstone has been borrowed from the West. Traditionally a carved post was put up with no words and no name. The relatives were supposed to remember, but that does not work any more (if it ever did in former times).

Many of the ancestral meeting houses at marae are over 100 years old and are held in especial awe because of their relative antiquity and also because of their beauty. They are looked after by the host tribe or hapū just like any other meeting house and they are used just as often. There are no special measures taken to preserve them, such as implementing controlled-atmosphere technology. The people look after them by using them and keeping them warm in a social sense. The most well known of these houses include Porourangi at Waiomatatini, belonging to Ngāti Porou; Te Whai-a-te-motu at Ruatahuna, belonging to Tūhoe; Te Tokanga-nui-a-noho at Te Kuiti, belonging to Ngāti Maniapoto; Rongopai at Manutuke, belonging to Rongowhakaata; Tamatekapua at Ohinemutu, belonging to Te Arawa; and Ruataupare at Kōkōhīnau and Mātaatua at Whakatane, belonging to Ngāti Awa. There is also a second group of beautiful carved houses built from the 1930s to the 1950s, during the time of Sir Apirana Ngata.

The voluntary nature of the work

In former times only the tohunga whakairo were compensated for their services. Everybody else gave their time as tūao (volunteers), working for their hapū or iwi. Today the buildings have become larger and more specialised and require paid carpenters, electricians, plumbers, plasterers and painters to do the work. Once completed, however, the people take over and except in very rare cases all work is carried out on a voluntary basis. Most marae are very busy places that cater for the needs of the hundreds of people who visit them. Meals are provided all day long and into the evening. The people of the marae provide this service on a voluntary basis. It is hard work over usually a three-day period and sometimes longer. The marae provide their own butchers to slaughter pigs or cattle. They are volunteers. Marae located near the sea coast send out their own divers to collect kaimoana (seafood). They are important members of the chain of tūao. The cooks, waitresses and dishwashers are volunteers. When visiting parties stay at the marae, either overnight or for several days, the hosts, again acting in a voluntary capacity, look after them. This is expected as the manaakitanga responsibility of the hosts. So there are good hosts known far and wide for their hospitality, and there are others. The gravediggers are also volunteers and their expertise is critical as there is nothing more embarrassing than to have the people go to the cemetery only to find that somebody forgot to dig the hole. An omission of this sort is a serious breach of tikanga and upsets everybody.

Funding the activities at a marae

Tikanga also play a part in the funding arrangements at marae events. Cultural events are often funded through the contributions that visitors bring to the event. There are ways bound by tikanga as to how visitors do this. They can give their money to their speaker to put down as a koha. Or they can give it personally to a relative. Or they bring food instead and present this to the kitchen. Or if it is very special food it can be presented on the marae as a koha instead of money. This is done by the spokesperson for the group. But there is a catch to koha placed on the marae. Sometimes a group bringing and placing their koha on the marae is repaying help received at some earlier time. Some marae committees regard all koha as requiring the tikanga of reciprocity, and this is especially so at tangihanga and at openings of marae buildings. They list all the contributions and publish the list by displaying it at the meeting house for all to see. The whānau concerned need to be aware of the obligations and reciprocate when they are able. The payback requires the same amount given plus a little more.

Government-sponsored meetings are quite common and are most often funded by a grant given by the department or ministry or agency. Some other events are covered financially through a combination of visitor contributions, grants, and contributions from the marae itself. Tangihanga are funded from the contributions of visitors and by the relatives of the deceased and sometimes by special funding schemes that people of the marae subscribe to. The fund then pays a set amount for each tangi and is a big help for the whānau. Either the whānau or the marae committee running the affairs of the marae meets any shortfall. Many tangi are covered quite adequately by the contributions brought by visitors. Sometimes there is enough to put towards the unveiling of the headstones, which also has to be funded. The marae committee is responsible for everything that happens on their marae and the members look after the plant and the assets of the people. They look after the money of the hapū, and this is often an onerous and risky task. The committee plans for the future both of the people and the marae.

Innovations

With growing confidence artists of the Māori world are employing their talents to introduce interesting innovations in the decoration of meeting houses and dining houses. In woodcarving, for example, there is an increasing tendency towards greater realism in figure work and in the faces of ancestors. The range of images has been extended to reflect modern living and there is a greater use of colour in painting wall slabs. Rafter patterns on the ceilings and along the walls also display new ideas and again there is more evidence of realism in the decorative themes now being created by artists. Murals of many sizes have become a feature of many dining houses and meeting houses and they certainly lift the decor of the dining facilities. New meeting houses tend to have more windows along the side walls than was permitted in the traditional houses. Lighting arrangements are more innovative than the old lamps suspended in ungainly fashion from the ceiling of the house. Modern artists have taken up the challenge of decorating marae structures with new ideas instead of forever copying the styles of the past centuries. This is not to deride the work of the old masters. Their work is of their time and remains a marvellous legacy for the generations of today. The tikanga allows for innovation, but the artists have to judge how far they should go in introducing new ideas.

Types of marae

As already indicated, there are two broad classes of marae, the traditional and the modern. There are in fact several ways of classifying marae. One way is to consider rural and urban locations as a way of distinguishing marae. Another way is to look at who controls the marae, whether it is a kin group or a non-kin group.

Traditional marae

Some marae hold true to the rural ideal of a facility that has the main components of a marae: a meeting house as a separate building, a dining room as a separate building, a toilet building separate from all others, and shelters for the local speakers and visitors. The urupā is separate and may be some distance away. The layout of the traditional marae follows some principles of tikanga, namely that of separating various functions and keeping them apart. The toilet had to be away from all other buildings because it carried a high level of tapu, that is, it used to in former times, but not now, as we shall see.

The elaborate dining room of today used to be a simple cooking shed called a kāuta. The cooking shed idea has been elaborated considerably in the modern wharekai and a place to eat has been added to it. Before this, people ate on the ground or at where they camped and there was a time when, in the absence of a covered place to eat, the people ate in the meeting house. The food was set on the floor along the middle line of the house, going from the front to the back, or to the left of the door, on the noa side. The middle line was the meeting place, the neutral area as it were, of where the tapu side of the house met the noa side.

In a strict sense cooked food is an agent for bringing people back into a safe state of noa. Therefore the kāuta was clearly separated from the meeting house because tikanga dictated there should be a separation. The pātaka (food store) was also a feature of traditional marae in the 1800s. Its functions are now incorporated into the modern dining house. In most rural marae in the Bay of Plenty, East Coast and Waikato, all three buildings are clearly separated. Only in relatively new marae has this rule been changed.

However the tapu side of the meeting house and the tapu of a burial ground are compatible and so it was not unusual formerly to bury the dead beside the meeting house. This no longer happens and the discontinuance of the practice was related to health scares when epidemics swept through the Māori world and decimated the population. Health regulations also had a part to play in requiring a separation of the burial site and in fact several changes within the buildings were required by health and safety regulations.

Marae reservations

Marae and urupā sites are usually registered under Te Ture Whenua Maori Act 1993 as reservations. Each has a set of trustees in charge and nowadays for each Māori Reservation there is a charter which the trustees have negotiated with the beneficiaries of the marae. What is required to be written into the charter are the following:

1. The name of the marae
2. A general description of the marae reservation
3. A list of iwi, hapū, or whānau (whichever is relevant) who are the beneficiaries of the marae reservation
4. The process for nominating and selecting marae trustees
5. Principles to which trustees will have regard in relation to the marae
6. The manner in which the trustees are to be accountable to the beneficiaries
7. The process by which conflicts between beneficiaries and trustees are to be resolved
8. The recognition of existing marae committees
9. The appointment by the trustees of one or more committees for the purpose of carrying out the day-to-day administration of the marae
10. The procedure for altering the charter
11. Provision for the keeping and inspection of the charter
12. Subject to the provisions of the Act any regulations made under the Act, such as matters that the beneficiaries may require.

Some marae reservations record that they exist for the common use and benefit of the people of New Zealand. Thus here is an act that governs the regulations of marae as reservations and sets out very clearly the responsibilities of the trustees to the beneficiaries who are part of the iwi, hapū or whānau.

The dining facility at a marae has become larger to keep pace with the growing population of Māoridom. Whereas in the past visitors to a marae numbered twenty or thirty people in a group, now they range from forty to a hundred. Early dining houses might have accommodated a hundred persons at a sitting and if there were more, the ringa wera who ran the dining facilities would have to have a second setting. Nowadays, dining houses can seat 300 people at one sitting, or even 500 at very large wharekai.

The meeting house has also had to grow in size. Some of the modern city ones, as in Wellington and Christchurch, are huge. Early meeting houses were modest in size. For example, Te Hau ki Tūranga in The National Museum of New Zealand Te Papa Tongarewa is about nine metres long. Now meeting houses of fifteen to twenty metres are common and the larger ones go well beyond twenty metres. The size of a meeting house can be stated also in how many people the hosts can prepare sleeping places for: two busloads – say eighty to a hundred people – are common. More than a hundred people is large. There are many old meeting houses that can barely manage two busloads of visitors and have become too small for today.

Modern marae

Modern marae have fewer buildings and they often have one where the parts are all under the one roof. The separations are in fact still present in the sense of being clearly marked and closed off, but the parts are contiguous.

Traditionalists should be worried that this practice has become quite common, especially in the towns and in non-kin based marae. The tikanga have been modified and accommodated in different ways, and there is no doubt that the primary concern now is for the comfort of people, for their safety and convenience, and to make the facilities of the marae more in tune with modern living. One explanation of why the previously separated parts of a marae are brought together and cause no great concern is that the model for continuity was already present in the meeting house. One half of the house is tapu and the other is noa. The line where the two parts touch is neutral, and this explains why it was possible to eat in the meeting house.

So if it was possible to place the tapu and noa sides of a house together under the same roof in a meeting house then it follows that tapu and noa buildings could be brought together as has been done. In this explanation the tikanga is certainly modified but its main principles remain intact.

Modern marae can be divided into at least five categories.

Urban marae under Māori control

There are a group of marae that are run by urban Māori. This urban group may be pan-tribal (as is the case with the Hoani Waititi Marae at Auckland), or it may be a single iwi group consisting of several hapū (such as the Mātaatua Marae in Mangere, Auckland, or Mātaatua Marae in Rotorua). Mātaatua in Auckland is under Ngāti Awa control, and Mātaatua in Rotorua is under Tūhoe control. Each is established outside of the current tribal territory in an urban setting. This fact breaks tradition, as the general rule is that a kin group builds a marae on its own land. The principle of tūrangawaewae is based on land ownership: one must have ownership rights in the land either directly as an owner or indirectly as a descendant of an owner.

In the urban environment the land issue is important. Even though the land needed for the marae has to be purchased, tikanga dictates that the group wanting to establish a marae must negotiate with the tangata whenua of that region and obtain their permission. Once the approval is obtained the group then proceeds to establish their marae and take full ownership and responsibility for it. Pan-tribal groups and multi-hapū iwi usually take full control over their marae.

Educational marae at universities

Some marae have been established at an educational institution and where the ownership and full control of the complex is not in Māori hands. While Māori staff might run the marae, they do not own it. Ownership remains with the institution, and in these cases the tangata–whenua iwi may claim cultural ownership and will certainly attempt to assert their right to sit on the speakers' bench whenever there is an important event.

At the universities of Auckland, Victoria University of Wellington and Massey University in Palmerston North, the marae are beautiful and the carved meeting houses are stunning examples of Māori art. Here there is more of an effort to maintain separation of the buildings. This is clearly the case at the University of Auckland.

Educational marae at schools

Characteristically, school meeting houses are converted classrooms. In many cases they are not shaped like traditional meeting houses and they have a lot of windows. But these converted classrooms serve as meeting houses for school groups, for pupils and for visitors to the school. The school also provides toilet facilities and cooking and eating facilities, thus fulfilling the main requirements of a marae. These marae serve an extra purpose as teaching and learning facilities very much like the laboratories of science subjects. Educational marae serve as the teaching laboratories of Māori studies and Māori language classes.

Church marae

Marae owned by churches are often sited under one roof and most are in the cities. The Presbyterian, Anglican and Catholic churches all have marae. Most are plain and devoid of Māori carvings because there is a tension between the church and its Māori groups over whether Māori art is compatible with church philosophy and teachings or not.

Some church marae avoid the problem by not having any examples of Māori art while others have no fears and are pleased to decorate their marae structure. At these marae there is also a tension over ownership. In some cases a tribal group has adopted a marae as their own, and they manage the whole complex on behalf of the church.

All of the functions of a traditional marae are carried out at these marae and one can say much more so than in the case of an educational marae.

Other marae

There are other marae differing only in the nature of the institutions that run them. Urban Māori authorities are pan-tribal groups organised as corporate entities. They too have marae which accommodate all of the functions of a traditional marae. The marae are made available to the clients and are used as places where visitors are welcomed, meetings are convened and more tapu ceremonies such as tangihanga are held.

City groups run their own marae and Māori who have formed trusts also run their own. A well-known example of the latter in Wellington is at Tapu Te Ranga, where the group specialise in providing for government groups wanting to hold live-in seminars.

The concept of marae in Polynesia

The idea and concept of the marae is not confined to Aotearoa alone. It is a Polynesian idea that takes different forms and functions in various places. In Eastern Polynesia, for example, the religious aspect of the marae takes precedence over its social purpose. On the other hand in Western Polynesia it is a place for social events where people can meet. In the Cook Islands and Aotearoa New Zealand there is a compromise between the deeply religious aspect and the social.

In Aotearoa New Zealand the marae retains a degree of tapu and it is a place where religious ceremonies do take place, and where very solemn ceremonies such as tangihanga are commonplace. But it is also a place where weddings and birthday parties can be held and visitors can be entertained. The Māori version of a marae is that of a multi-purpose facility, which is the home base for Māori culture and a symbol of Māori identity.

Some marae on the East Coast and in Northland have a church as one of buildings of the complex. In this case the religious ceremonies of Christian churches have been incorporated into the practices of the marae, and a building to accommodate these will be put up by the people. The church becomes another part of the complex and another responsibility for the trustees and the people.

The Cook expedition recorded some of the marae they visited in the years 1769 to 1770. They saw some remarkable ones in Tahiti and Raiatea. These were paved with stone slabs and often had associated structures such as pyramids and altars. Burials were noted in some marae and human sacrifice in others. Some of these marae are indicated on maps in the Beaglehole accounts (1962, 1967, 1968).

The Hawai'ians are very interested in the Māori concept of marae and there are several groups working towards establishing a marae-like structure where their culture can take pride of place.

Tongans have a difficulty with our meeting house and our tikanga of having everyone sleep in the one large room. Tongan tikanga dictates that the sexes be separated and that if the Tongans were to adopt our marae concept they would have to build two ancestral houses, one for the men and one for women.

Conclusions

A marae is a place where Māori culture can be celebrated to the fullest extent, where the language can be spoken, where Māori can meet Māori, where intertribal obligations can be met, where the customs can be explored, practised, debated, continued, or amended, and where necessary ceremonies – such as welcoming visitors or farewelling the dead – can be carried out. It is the place where the generations before the present ones held the mana of the iwi or the hapū, maintained the tikanga to the best of their ability and kept the culture alive. It is a named piece of ground, registered as a Māori reservation where tikanga Māori has pride of place. It is a wāhi tapu, a place of great cultural significance, but the level of tapu is relatively low when compared, for example, with a cemetery. It is a place to be kept 'warm' by the owning group, and as one generation passes on another takes their place in looking after the marae.

People of other cultures often see the marae as the institution that saved Māori culture from being assimilated by western civilisation. It was a place of cultural resistance that helped Māori enjoy what others have called de-facto sovereignty. Māori control their marae to a large extent, but not completely. The trustees of the marae are subject to the laws of the land such as Te Ture Whenua Maori Act 1993. Police are able to enter marae when they have good cause to do so and when invited. The tangata whenua often believe that the marae is a refuge that protects them from the evils of the western world. It is a safe haven, culturally speaking, for the language, the culture, the tikanga. It is a place where Māori can recharge their cultural batteries. But it is not a refuge for persons who have broken the law. It is even doubtful whether it can be a refuge for battered women of the hapū or for abused children. The marae committee is not organised to take on these functions and lacks the expertise to do so. What the marae does very effectively is provide a tūrangawaewae, a place for the feet to stand. It confirms one's position in the world, where one can say, 'This is where I belong and over there is where I shall be buried so that I am with my uncles and aunties, my grandparents and parents, my siblings and cousins.'

Perspectives

Aotearoa

In a strict dictionary sense a marae is the enclosed space in front of a house. It is the courtyard, the village common. As an adjective it means 'generous and hospitable'.

– Williams 1957:180

Rarotonga

... a sacred place which serves both religious and social purposes. As a rule marae consisted of an area of land enclosed by four almost straight sides meeting at angles approaching right angles. In the construction of some marae the ground plan was an almost true square and in others roughly rectangular with the long axis extending between the back and front, and in some marae the back was much wider than the front. There was no fixed dimensions and shape some being roughly 80 x 80 feet, others 120 x 120 feet, more or less and again others which had the sides longer that the width, the sides measuring roughly 150 feet, and the front and back measuring approximately 80 feet, more or less.

– Savage 1962:142–43

Savage goes on to suggest that some eighty traditional marae were built in the name of Tangiia-nui and each was dedicated to a special god. In addition a person was selected to be in charge. The marae was given a name and the person in charge was given a name. The name of the marae was the name of a chief. A marae was an indication of the rank and nobility of the chief. Some marae were held in greater reverence than others. Most of the early marae of Rarotonga were destroyed after the introduction of Christianity.

Samoa

The marae is an 'open space in a village, where public meetings are held'.

– Tregear 1891:213

Tonga

Malae might be a green. *Ana fakamalaelae* referred to an open space resembling a malae. It might refer to clearing a space of trees.

– Tregear 1891:213

Mangaia

A marae is a sacred enclosure where religious rites were performed and sacrifices offered.

– Tregear 1891:213

Te Marae o Hine

This is the place of refuge situated at Mohoanui on the Upper Waikato River and was regarded as a very sacred place. The proverb associated with this refuge was:

Ko te marae of Hine e kore e pikitia e te patu. (The courtyard of Hine is not to be violated by the hand of violence.)

Hine was the daughter of Maniapoto. The place of refuge was named after her and it was clear that a war party was not permitted onto the site of the marae nor anyone bent on violence.

– Tregear 1891:213

The marae is a refuge for the culture, but in the case of the Marae o Hine the marae was a refuge for women and children and elderly people, that is, for those unable to fight.

According to Tregear (1891:213) the notion of a place of refuge was present in other parts of Polynesia. In Hawai'i there were sacred sites that once a person reached one of these sites, no matter what their crime, the person was safe from harm. The refugee came under the protection of the god associated with that sacred place.

The same source indicated that the Samoans had villages where persons defeated in battle could seek sanctuary. The people of the village protected those who sought refuge.

Tongarewa

They had marae each of which was associated with a chief. The marae was named after the chief. Priests were on the marae. Very tapu persons ate of turtle on the marae. Chiefs could drink coconuts

on the marae. There were 24 marae on the atoll and there would have been about 80 persons to each marae.
    – Goldman 1970:71

Tahiti

A marae is a sacred place formerly used for worship, where stones were piled up, altars erected, sacrifices offered, prayer made, and sometimes dead deposited.
    – Tregear 1891:213

New marae were built as branches of older marae. Many were decorated with skulls in honour of the war god Oro. Here the marae was the centre of local authority. The Tahitian marae were built of stone. According to Goldman (1970:174–76) very large limestone slabs were trimmed to build small marae in the Leeward Islands. While in the Windwards 'monumentally and architecturally sophisticated marae were built of small stones that were shaped and dressed'.

    Tahitian marae were, Goldman says, the largest in the Society Group. Monuments of various sizes were associated with the marae. The great marae at Papara 'has a 11 step pyramid 50 feet high and an attached court that measured 367 by 267 feet'. Coastal marae had a truncated pyramid. On other marae there was an ahu, a one-step platform which was a common feature of many marae.
    – Goldman 1970:174–76

Cook visited a marae at Point Utuhaihai in Tahiti in 1773. Cook regarded this as a family marae and he noted the chief was buried here.
    – Beaglehole 1969, 2:213

Cook visited the Marae at Matarai and saw a corpse laid out on the altar, called a fatarau. This was a sacrifice to the atua.
    – Beaglehole 1969, 2:233–34

Rai'atea, French Polynesia

Cook records seeing a remarkable marae at Rai'atea. It was paved and adorned with a pyramid of palm nuts stacked five feet high. On the paved floor they saw three human skulls lined out in a row, and an image of stone about 18 inches tall.

Near the marae was an altar under which they counted the skull bones of 26 hogs and 6 dogs. In a footnote Beaglehole noted that this marae was located, at Mahai'atea and it was 'the greatest in Tahiti and indeed in all Polynesia'. It was built 1766–68. The whole enclosure made up the marae, the ahu forming one end of it. The enclosure measured 267 feet by 377 feet. In 1865 the French authorities used the squared basaltic stones to build a bridge but it was soon washed away.

– Beaglehole 1968:111–12

Cook Islands

The Cook Islands marae were very important in traditional narratives. When an early voyager landed, one of the first things he did was to erect a marae to give thanks to his Gods and to establish his claim to the land occupied. The building of a marae was equivalent of a flag when foreign powers took possession. The Rarotongan ancestor Tangiia is credited with having established 40 marae, the names and sites of which were handed down in local traditions. He appointed priestly guardians (purapura) over most of them. As population increased and new chiefly titles were created, additional marae were established. In spite of the large number created they have been so thoroughly demolished that little visual evidence remains to aid in the reconstruction of their original form.

– Buck 1987:479

The marae in a fortified village: Northland

This information is based on an account by Crozet of Marion du Fresne's expedition of 1772 and reported in Salmond 1991.

The space which divides the two rows of houses, and which is more or less roomy, according to the lay of the ground, serves as a sort of parade ground, and extends the whole length of the village.

This whole space between the two rows of houses is only occupied by three public buildings, of which the first and nearest to the village gate is the general magazine of arms.

A little distance off is the food storehouse, and still farther the storehouse for nets, all the implements used in fishing, as well as all the necessary material for making the nets etc. At about the extremity of the village there are large posts set up in the form of gallows, where the provisions are dried before being placed in the stores. In the centre of this parade ground there is a piece of wooden sculpture representing a hideous figure very badly carved ... The house of the chiefs are larger, they are ornamented with pieces of carved wood and the posts in the interior are also carved ...

The whole of the village which we saw during our two months stay in the Bay of Islands appeared to be constructed on the same plan without any well-defined differences.

Salmond added that 'the central parade ground (marae) was raised up with beaten earth and kept meticulously clean'.

– Salmond 1991:416–17

Comment on kawa and the paepae

These are my observations with the marae. There's a word that is being used a lot now – 'kawa' – it's a word that I never heard until recently. There were certain things done at a marae, and they knew exactly what, but they never used to say, 'te kawa o te marae'. I never heard those old people use this word. Now, our world is such a small one; I know now that Tuhoe do differ from us. And in Te Arawa for instance, I find that the marae is very much the men's domain. And these men they sit on a paepae. But here the only time they used to speak of the paepae is when there is anyone lying on the veranda – when there is tupapaku. They refer to that little bit, that front part of the meeting house, as the paepae and when anyone is dead we know that the area is quite special, at that particular time. But now these men they are saying to us, 'Oh this is just for men only, this paepae. I didn't think anything of it when our chairman said he was going to put a seat there, for whaikorero. I was quite happy for that to happen; but he made it a permanent seat, and I just couldn't accept it when we were told that it was for men only, and no women dare sit here. That puts a difference on it altogether. Because what they are saying to us – we are tapu men; we are so special that you women cannot come and sit here. That's never been a part of us. The men, the orators – and they were orators in the true sense of the word, like old Te Kani Te Ua – those men just used to sit around for they knew who they were, and they knew when they were to stand up. They never made themselves special. And when they came up with this paepae for men only I reacted badly, because I do know something of Te Arawa custom, no women! Now, I never ever saw it done to my Grannies, and I don't see why it should be done to me, and why it should be done to my children, because that was never our way.

    – Heni Sutherland, in Binney & Chaplin 1986:26–27

7
Te Pōhiri: Welcome Ceremonies

Relationships between and among people need to be managed and guided by some rules. In Māori society there are procedures for meeting strangers and visitors. These procedures are part of the tikanga called the pōwhiri or pōhiri, commonly translated as the welcome ceremony. The pōhiri ceremony has been generalised to cover all forms of welcome and is not confined only to very important occasions when manuhiri (visitors and guests) from outside of the tribe or country visit the marae. In one sense the pōhiri is a ceremony to welcome visitors and to show hospitality in an appropriate way.

The word manuhiri covers visitors and guests, and there are manuhiri tūārangi, which Williams (1957:447) says refers to visitors from afar or from a great distance. Today a manuhiri tūārangi is a very important visitor to the marae, or the prominent visitor within an ope (the collective term for a group of visitors). This prominent person might be a chief of another iwi, the Māori queen, a minister of the Crown, the prime minister, the governor-general, a highly ranked military man, a popular entertainer, an All Black, or the local member of Parliament. For some pōhiri ceremonies it is important to identify the prominent person within the visiting group who will become the focus of a challenge. It is expected that this person is a male. But if the important visitor is a woman she will appoint a man to do the menial task of picking up the token of the challenge. The protocols do not allow an important woman to do this. Rather she is expected to stand clear in front of the visiting party with her manservant beside her. He will be exposed to risk, but not her.

Important principles

Several important principles, two of which have already been introduced in chapter 3, underpin the tikanga of pōhiri. The first of these is the tapu–noa principle. The pōhiri as an event is held to be very tapu, and hence it is very formal and tense. There is a concern about being correct because there is a ritual element in the ceremony. From being very tapu the ceremony moves towards a state of balance in which human relationships are normalised so that people can meet more informally. This balanced state is called noa. It is a transition from one state to another. Manuhiri are tapu and are treated as such, especially in very formal ceremonies. The actual steps in performing a pōhiri can be viewed as the gradual reduction of tapu culminating in the eating of food which ends the ceremony and brings about a state of noa.

The next principle is the principle of ea, that is, of meeting the requirements of the occasion and taking into account the importance of the visitors, and especially of the prominent manuhiri among them. The nature of the occasion is an important consideration especially if it is linked to a series of obligations. Not all pōhiri are of the same order, and thus the tangata whenua and manuhiri have to make appropriate adjustments once each side has appraised the situation each faces. Both have an important part to play in meeting the principle of ea. The host group is motivated by the obligation to carry out the pōhiri and meet all the tikanga requirements to the best of their ability and appropriate to the occasion. At the conclusion of the ceremony the hosts should be able to say, 'Kua ea,' meaning they have more than adequately met their obligations. Some might say simply 'it is done'. But this is insufficient. The tikanga has been carried out according to the shared knowledge that Māori hold in their heads and according to the best cultural practices associated with that tikanga.

Occasionally the tangata whenua misjudge the importance of the visiting group and feel great shame for failing to meet the principle of ea. This can happen, for example, by not knowing who the visitors are and not recognising the prominent persons among them. Or it might be that too many people of the marae happen to be away meeting some other obligation and so the ones left behind are not able to carry the mana and prestige of their hapū to the degree appropriate for the occasion. On the manuhiri side it is possible that they misjudge the strength of the marae group or they were not able to persuade appropriate persons to join them in order to handle the requirements of the principle of ea. A visiting group could appear very weak culturally speaking and unprepared for the pōhiri ceremony. Most tangata whenua appreciate a good effort being made to engage in the dynamics of the pōhiri ceremony.

Associated with the principle of ea is another principle that focuses on a standard of performance and is an element in the dynamics of the pōhiri ceremony. This can be called the ihi principle. The coming together of manuhiri and tangata whenua involves what Salmond (1975) has aptly called rituals of encounter. Each side is expected to contribute to the ceremony. For the manuhiri the whakaeke (the approach onto the marae) entitles them to do certain things. They may have a tohunga perform a special karakia to clear the way for their group, or they may have a haka team precede them. These activities add to the excitement of the occasion and help raise it to the ihi principle. The tangata-whenua side may perform a wero (which will be described later) or have two haka teams, one female and another male, or they may perform a pōkeka, a form of haka that men and women perform together. The encounter aspect of the pōhiri can become confrontational, but there is a point when both sides know they have satisfied the principle of ea and that it is time to withdraw. While engaged in the ritual encounter both sides have contributed to raising the stakes of excitement to the level of ihi. Both sides can say, 'i puta te ihi'. What they mean is that the performances were brilliant and exhilarating. The participants know when they have reached the standard of ihi because they feel it, sense it, and are exhilarated by the occasion. The encounter is hair raising and full of tension until finally the parties withdraw and relax.

Different contexts for pōhiri

Not all pōhiri ceremonies are expected to be hair-raising ritual encounters. Many are low key and very friendly occasions. The ceremony itself is adaptable and flexible outside of the marae context. There are pōhiri ceremonies inside the meeting house, or in domestic dwellings, business premises or public buildings in the towns and cities. There are pōhiri ceremonies that are an essential part of other tikanga such as the tangihanga or the kawanga whare. There are pōhiri in cemeteries, on ships, in buses, and in courts and jails. And there are very formal pōhiri that are usually located at marae. The ihi principle is expected of all speakers, singers of traditional songs or waiata, performers of karanga and haka and, in fact, of all who have a part to play in the pōhiri ceremony. It refers to a standard of performance and it is usually expected that the tangata whenua sets the tone of the ceremony and the manuhiri group accepts the challenge and makes a contribution in some way. At one pōhiri ceremony some years ago one of the manuhiri group was heard to say to his party, 'Weren't we brilliant!' This was an acknowledgment that they had done their part very well and the level of ihi raised by the local hapū was matched adequately by them.

The principle of manaakitanga

Another very important principle is that of manaakitanga, or hospitality. As already noted, a high value is placed upon manaakitanga. The principle or tikanga of manaakitanga applies to all social occasions when tangata whenua are put into the role of looking after guests. It is true to say that the visitors are regarded as strangers at the beginning of the pōhiri ceremony. But as soon as the rituals of encounter are completed the visitors become guests who must be cared for and looked after while in the territory of the host group. While manaakitanga is closely linked to the provision of food and lodging it is wider in its implications. For example, the principle begins before the manuhiri arrive, that is, in providing for the visitors, in ensuring the grass is cut, the place is clean, there are seats for the visitors and shelter from the weather.

The principles of manaakitanga operates at the speech-making sector of the ceremony when the tangata whenua might decide to decrease the number of speakers on their side in order to give more time for the visitors or in order to shorten the proceedings. However, the tangata whenua have to make a judgement between meeting the principle of ea as well as that of manaakitanga. They would not want to be accused of belittling the mana of the manuhiri by having too few speakers or by being seen to omit some procedures. In most issues of manaakitanga the welfare of the manuhiri is an important consideration, which is sometimes submerged by an over-concentration on the principle of ea that is often described as 'mana grabbing' or 'mana gobbling'.

The mauri of the marae

Another underlying principle is that of maintaining the mana of the pōhiri in the hands of the tangata-whenua group. Instead of using the word 'mana', some would say that they are maintaining the 'mauri' of the marae and of the tangata whenua, which is really the same thing. This principle works very well in the speaking protocol known as tau-utuutu where the tangata whenua match one-for-one the speakers of the visiting side and always have the last speaker. The woman who is the karanga expert also endeavours to have the last karanga in order to meet this principle. Haka teams engaged in a pōhiri ceremony will also try to have the last say. It is not so much a matter of winning but rather one of maintaining the mana and control of the pōhiri ceremony firmly in the hands of the tangata whenua.

Transformation of status from tapu to noa

Some participants in pōhiri have said that the purpose of the ceremony is to transform a manuhiri into a tangata whenua, which is to change the status of a visitor into that of a host and thus a person of the land. They also think that once the ceremony is complete the visitor now has the same privileges as a tangata-whenua person. This is not true. The transformation from a state of tapu to a state of noa does not equate with becoming a tangata whenua. The idea might be useful if used in a meta-phorical sense. In reality, however, the status of tangata whenua is a matter of birthright. There are special rights which come with being a tangata whenua and there are obligations which a visitor would not want to be encumbered with, as they are quite onerous. After the ceremony the visitor remains a manuhiri and tangata whenua are obligated to treat guests in accordance with the principle of manaakitanga. The obliga-tions of the hosts continue.

The practice of pōhiri

The pōhiri, as we can see, is a complex set of interlocking tikanga that requires hosts and visitors to engage in a series of ritual encounters to the end that the tapu of visitors is reduced to a state of noa and all parties are then free to socialise and take part in whatever else follows. In a typical pōhiri the rituals of encounter may be analysed as a sequence of steps in the transformation process. These steps are as follows:

1. *Preparation.* Tangata whenua and manuhiri prepare themselves for what is known as whakaeke, namely entering the marae. The tangata whenua signal when they are ready.

2. *Karanga 1.* The karanga woman of the marae, usually dressed in black, begins the ceremonial call to the visitors to enter the marae.

3. *Whakaeke.* The manuhiri ope enters and they begin the slow walk in close formation towards the wharenui. A karanga expert from within the manuhiri ope responds to the first karanga of the tangata whenua and indicates who they are.

4. *Karanga 2.* The tangata whenua then deliver karanga number two, which is concentrated on the dead and meanwhile the manuhiri ope is approaching the meeting house but are still some distance away.

5. The manuhiri respond to this karanga and also focus on the dead in the words of the karanga.

6. *Karanga 3.* The karanga woman of the tangata whenua then delivers the third, more general karanga which invites the group to approach.

7. *Their response.* The manuhiri group responds to the third karanga and by now have approached to within the limits of tapu space and must now stop some twenty paces away from the meeting house.

8. *The final karanga.* There could be another karanga from the local side in order to meet the principle of holding the mana of the event in the hands of the tangata whenua.

9. *He tangi ki ngā mate (respecting the dead).* The tangata-whenua group all stood up when the whakaeke process began and at this stage manuhiri and tangata whenua are standing, separated by tapu space. This may be a quiet period of remembering the dead or it might be accompanied by open wailing. A judgement has to be made when it can be said, 'Kua ea,' that is, the requirement to honour the dead has been met.

10. The manuhiri ope now moves towards the seats or shelter provided for them and they organise themselves, the speakers and their waiata support group to be relatively close together, but it is important for the speakers of the visiting side to be clearly identified and ideally to

sit apart from everyone else. In the organisation there are tikanga to observe. Within the tribal region of Mātaatua in the Bay of Plenty the tikanga is that if Mātaatua speakers are present among the visitors they must speak first so that they can identify with the host speakers in welcoming the visitors who have appeared for the first time on a particular marae. First-time visitors are called 'waewae tapu', that is, legs that are tapu on that particular marae, never having set foot there before. The prominent visitor, the manuhiri tūārangi among the visitors, is expected to be the last speaker.

If the visitors have a koha to place on the marae it is expected that the last speaker of their tribe or the assembled group will place it ceremoniously on the ground within the tapu space mentioned earlier. On the other hand, if the ope visitors include several distinct groups that have come together for the occasion, their speakers retain a right to place their own koha on the marae. These are some of the issues the manuhiri have to decide. The visitors should also have a good idea whether the kawa of the marae, that is its speaking tikanga, is tau-utuutu (where the tangata-whenua speakers alternate with the manuhiri speakers) or pāeke (the tangata-whenua side speaks first, followed by the manuhiri speakers). However, it is always the tangata whenua that begins the speech making.

11. When the manuhiri group sit down, the tangata-whenua group sit down as well. There may be a brief moment of silence as the tangata whenua gets ready to speak.

12. *Ngā whaikōrero.* The formal orations of welcome begin. There is usually a minimum of two speakers from the tangata whenua side. The first speaker might be a local chief and it is up to him to signal clearly the purpose of the hui, to ensure he covers all of the different groups within the manuhiri and then to indicate what kawa the marae follows. Each whaikōrero (oration) is concluded with a waiata or haka. The last speaker on the host side supports the others and covers any aspect left out by the others. (It is assumed here the tikanga is pāeke.)

13. The whaikōrero of the tangata whenua are responded to by the manuhiri either in accordance with tau-utututu or pāeke. Whichever one it is, every whaikōrero is expected to be accompanied and completed by a waiata or a performance of some kind.

14. If the tikanga followed is tau-utuutu the last speaker is on the tangata-whenua side and this speaker completes the encounter of orations. If the tikanga is pāeke then the last speaker represents the manuhiri and this is the person who places the koha on the marae. To know and understand the protocol is to know when the speeches have finally come to an end.

15. *Whakaratarata/Hohou rongo.* At this point the tangata-whenua speakers stand and form a reception line on the tangata-whenua side. The manuhiri now file past and perform the hongi, or touching of noses, one by one. Formerly the hongi was all that was required. Nowadays the hongi may be followed by a kiss on the cheek and always includes a shaking of hands, the harirū. Some iwi prefer that kissing is omitted. The emphasis should be on the hongi.

16. This may take quite a time if there are two hundred people in the manuhiri group and all want to meet the reception line. It is not really necessary for everyone to hongi. What is necessary is that all of the prominent members of the manuhiri and certainly all the speakers go and meet the tangata whenua reception line. They are sufficient to meet the principle of ea in this regard.

17. *Te hākari.* There is a call from the dining room that the food is set out and ready for the manuhiri. But there are tikanga to follow. The manuhiri tūārangi or prominent visitors of the day and the persons associated with that person are first to be called. If there are not a sufficient number of places set to accommodate everyone, the tangata whenua may be asked to wait for the second sitting.

18. *Poroporoaki.* Some manuhiri follow the tikanga of rising to say their farewell speech before leaving the dining room and going home. This is especially expected of important and distant visitors. Once someone rises to say their farewell speech or poroporoaki and es-pecially to thank their hosts for the food, others may follow. When the visitors have finished someone from the tangata whenua will respond and have the final say. These speeches are also accompanied by waiata, often of a less formal nature.

19. The manuhiri leave and the tangata whenua begin to clean up the kitchen and dining room, put chairs away, and generally leave the marae ready for the next event.

20. Often the pōhiri is only the beginning of the real purpose of the hui. Other activities may follow.

The series of steps outlined here is what can be expected at standard pōhiri held outside at a marae. There could well be tribal variations to the model or extensions from it. In the next section we will deal with variations according to context and occasion.

Variations to the pōhiri

Indoor pōhiri

In a meeting house

1. Seating is set up inside the meeting house and arranged so that the tangata whenua are on the noa side of the house and the manuhiri will be seated on the tapu side. On the manuhiri side seating might be limited only to the speakers' bench. Others may have to sit on mattresses or on the floor.

2. As before the karanga woman begins the ceremony outside of the house and she will indicate clearly that the visitors are to go inside the meeting house.

3. *Whakaeke.* The manuhiri group responds as before and the group walks slowly towards the meeting house. The group may stand in silence before the meeting house for a short period and then enter the porch of the house.

4. Footwear is taken off and placed neatly along the wall of the house, and after this the group enters the house. A space is provided for the manuhiri to stand inside the house facing the tangata-whenua bench of speakers. There is usually also a space that is left clear which separates the manuhiri and the tangata whenua. This is the tapu space mentioned earlier which the visitors are to avoid. Speakers must respect this space and not cross it while giving their orations.

5. Speeches take place as before but there is a big difference in that the speaker has neither the space in which to move nor the open air to carry the voice. Inside the house speeches are more muted. Koha is placed as before but this time on the floor of the house. When about to place the koha the speaker is permitted to cross into the

noa space of the tangata whenua for that purpose only and retreat walking backwards.

From here on the process is the same as for a formal pōhiri.

The Āti Awa format

In some tribal areas the visitors enter the meeting house and immediately go to the reception line and hongi all around the house. After this they sit down and prepare for the speeches. Te Āti Awa follows this custom inside the house only.

In a building

Nowadays most pōhiri occur in a building that is not part of a marae and the procedure is much like that described for the inside of a meeting house.

Whānau pōhiri

Pōhiri ceremonies held in domestic homes are whānau affairs and there is no formal karanga. The visitors come into the sitting room and hongi with the hosts and then sit down. An elder or the father of the house will welcome the visitors in a simple straight speech with or without a waiata. A person with the visitors' group might reply and should if possible, but if not, it does not matter. The elder may have a brief church service as well, especially if it is welcoming home a relative who had been away for some time. A meal, or tea, coffee and cakes, completes the ceremony.

Internal tribal meetings

Many of these meetings begin with a karakia and then a pōhiri. One speaker welcomes everyone and comments on deaths within the tribe and mentions anything else of general interest to those present. Someone might reply or the rest may say, 'Kua ea,' in which case the pōhiri is finished and then the meeting begins.

The wero and pōhiri

The wero is a ritual challenge of the visitors and has its roots in traditional times when it was important to know whether a visitor and his party came in peace or not. There were instances in the past when visitors turned on their hosts and massacred them. The ceremony that exists now is highly ritualised, but it is still dangerous if people act foolishly.

The challenge is a tikanga in its own right. It precedes a pōhiri and is often mistaken as a welcome ceremony. The wero is strictly not a part of the pōhiri; it is a challenge that has to be carried out before the pōhiri proper commences. Once peaceful intentions are expressed the pōhiri proper may begin.

The wero is usually reserved for very special guests or occasions. Visitors of distinction include chiefs of other tribes, persons who have distinguished themselves in some field of endeavour, ministers of the Crown, the prime minister, the governor general, overseas visitors, a particular large group of Māori representing some national body such as kōhanga reo, or the Māori queen and her entourage. An important occasion might be the start of a tribal week-long festival. In any case the wero is a special ceremony that is usually employed sparingly in order to emphasise the importance of the occasion.

Because the wero is spectacular, tourist promoters like to use it to impress foreign visitors. On such occasions the wero is performed indoors in a building. It is meant to be a marae-based outdoor ceremony that is performed in open space with plenty of room for the challenger to show off his skills. It is important to stress the safety aspect of the challenge as it remains a potentially dangerous ceremony.

As in the case of the pōhiri, it is the tangata whenua who begin the ceremony. There is usually a moment when the host group and the visitor group stand quietly in anticipation of the beginning of the ceremony. The hosts focus upon the challenger who is in traditional costume and stands ready to begin. The host group looks anxiously at the visitor group to ensure that they have identified the important guest visitor who will be the focus of the challenge. This is usually a male, but in cases where the important guest is a woman it is expected that she will have a male with her to accept the challenge. Nonetheless, she remains the focus point of the wero ceremony.

The wero in action

1. *Preparation.* On the hosts' side people have lined up in front of their ancestral house, a men's haka group stands in front to support the challenges and a women's group behind them. The men's team is

usually stripped down to ceremonial costume no matter what the weather. The women's group is characteristically dressed in black or they may be also dressed in costume items. The challenger is clearly visible because he stands to the side of the men's group.

2. The manuhiri group approaches the entrance to the marae. The prominent visitor who will be the subject of a challenge is leading. The party stops at the entrance. There is usually an advisor beside the main visitor to help that person carry out his part properly.

3. The tikanga of the wero ceremony begins. There is no karanga. The wero or challenge is the first event. When the wero exponent begins to move towards the manuhiri the ritual challenge has commenced. A very important visitor may arrange for a young man to pick up the challenge staff or green branch on his or her behalf. Sometimes the visiting side might arrange for a young man to watch every move of the challenger and then at an appropriate time give chase. This practice is not advised because the challenger is armed and is capable of delivering a lethal blow if provoked. One should also ponder upon the fact that the men's group is there to support the challenger. It is best to participate in the ritual without provoking the challenger.

4. The challenger stops a few steps away from the important guest and performs some special moves to show his mastery of the taiaha. Then he crouches and very carefully places a twig or a carved staff on the ground in front of the visitor. The challenger gives a clear signal to the visitor when it is time to pick up the symbol of the challenge by pointing his staff towards the symbol. He remains crouched until the token is picked up and the visitor steps back out of range of the sweep of the taiaha.

5. The visitor bends down, picks up the twig or staff and stands up straight. Meanwhile the challenger retreats.

6. The hosts might have arranged for three challengers or for one. If there is more than one, the visiting group moves forward only a few paces because at this point the bulk of the visiting party is outside of the marae and the people cannot really see what is happening. A challenger signals when the party is free to move as a whole towards the ancestral house. If there are three challengers the visitors will see

three challengers positioned on the marae. The first two will retreat with care and will not perform a certain act which signals that the visitors are to follow. Instead each will perform a few sweeps of the taiaha and hand over to the next challenger.

7. The completion of the wero ceremony is signalled when the challenger, after watching the guest pick up the token, performs a few intricate movements of the taiaha facing the visitor. Then he turns his back to the visitors, slaps the side of his upper thigh and then 'draws' the visitors onto the marae. At the same time the pōhiri begins by the ritual karanga ringing out at this time.

8. While the visiting party slowly approaches towards the space before the ancestral house, the host group now begins several welcome performances. The first is often a men's haka. When they have completed their part they retreat to the back and the women's group comes forward and performs their welcome. The women's group usually gives a clear signal of peace and the end of confrontational war dances that the men perform. Each time they draw the visitors closer and closer. This is all part of an enhanced ceremony to honour the guests.

9. The visiting party might also have a haka team and as they approach they hold their team back until the host group has completed their welcome. Meanwhile their men flank the visiting party and act as guardian warriors of the visitors. They might have a tohunga perform karakia known as waerea, to clear any ritual danger away from the pathway of the visitors. This man might perform in front of the visiting group and lead them, or he might perform his part from within the visiting group.

10. This is a high point of the welcome ceremony when there is a great deal of activity taking place on both sides. Once the visiting group has reached the outer limits of the tapu space in front of the ancestral house, their haka team form up in front of the group, and as soon as there is a break in the performances of the host group, their haka team performs their war dance. The hosts may accept this performance and in a sense let it pass. However it is more likely the host group will perform another item in order to take back the mana or control of the ceremony.

11. There may be a competition of performances until one gives up. It is expected, however, that the visitors give in graciously and allow the pōhiri ceremony to continue.

12. Once completed the series of karanga begin and the visitors move up towards the ancestral house.

13. The two parties regroup and move to where they will be seated during the speeches of welcome, and from this point forward the procedure is the same as for a standard pōhiri.

Very clearly the challenge ceremony runs into the pōhiri and may affect the first part of the welcome by introducing the element of challenge into the ritual encounter. The challenge ceremony certainly raises the stakes in the combined event and is a way of honouring the visitors.

During the wero ceremony the important visitor who is to pick up the token of challenge needs to stay clear of the sweep of the taiaha and maintain a safe distance. Occasionally a young challenger comes too close to the visitor and should not be trusted with the safety of the visitors. An experienced challenger will never put the visitor at risk. Sometimes there are mishaps. A challenger may break his taiaha by inadvertently striking the ground. When this happens he will leave the broken piece of his weapon on the ground, or he may abandon both parts and retreat quickly.

The role of the visiting group is not to add to the embarrassment of the home side by laughing or commenting. A mishap of this kind is regarded as a ritual error for which there are consequences that will be visited upon the challenger and his family. As a mark of acknowledgement, the important guest should pick up the broken pieces of the taiaha (if they were left on the marae) and keep them beside his feet all through the speeches. Then when the visitors go to greet and hongi the hosts these pieces are formally handed back to the hosts.

Sometimes the challenger slips on wet grass or, if the ground is soft and muddy, the worst possible disaster is to slip in the mud. This has happened. There is nothing the visitors can do about this sort of mishap except to express sympathy later in the speeches. Perhaps the kindest act is to ignore the embarrassment altogether and not say a word about it. Some tribal leaders take offence at mistakes of this sort and will lay the blame squarely on the challenger who should have been aware of the conditions of the moment and exercised some judgement. The hapū itself can expect some unkind remarks either serious or in jest.

However, most wero ceremonies are performed and carried through very successfully and most challengers are experienced and competent. It is rare for mishaps to occur, but the unexpected can surprise and embarrass.

Conclusion

It is important to stress that the models described here relate to the regions I am most familiar with. There will be variations to the procedures described here either by way of further elaborations or by streamlining the ceremony to suit local conditions. Obviously, variations are a reality already as these ceremonies are performed all over the country and in some foreign places, at marae and at places that are not marae. These ceremonies have in fact become a necessary part of New Zealand culture.

Perspectives

Thursday, 23 September 1819, at Rangihoua, Bay of Islands.
This morning several chiefs arrived from the River Thames. When they landed they all sat down in silence in one group on the beach. Shortly after the fighting men of Rangiheehoo (Rangihoua) came running in a body from the village, quite naked, like so many furies, with their spears fixed in a threatening posture and making the most horrid noise. They advanced towards the chiefs on the beach as if they were going to make an immediate attack. When they came within a few paces they stopped and performed the war dance, distorting their features in the most frightful manner and making at the same time the most horrid yells. When they had gone through all their martial movements they returned to the village, when the head chief Racow, an old man about eighty, came forward and made a speech to the chiefs. The chiefs had never moved from their place during these transactions.
Observer: Rev. Samuel Marsden
 – Elder 1932:179

Rituals of encounter

The ceremonial part of a *hui* begins when guests start arriving at the *marae*. Each party of visitors *(ope* or *tira)* is separately welcomed with a formal ritual which includes calling, chanting, wailing and oratory, and it is this that we may call the ritual of encounter. On the *marae* it may be called the *mihi*, or simply, the 'welcome'. In earlier times when warfare was endemic and strangers were probably enemies, these rituals were used as a finely-balanced mechanism to manage encounters in peace.

– Salmond 1975:115

The rituals of encounter in some form or other are used whenever Maori groups formally assemble, and it would be an ominous sign if they were omitted. Cowan tells of a time when a Government survey team was sent into Tūhoe country to route an unwanted road. They came to the *marae* to parley with the local chiefs. No call of welcome was given, and the chiefs sat around the *marae* in grim and scornful silence. Only when the visitors began to speak, the chiefs sprang up, and, one by one they cursed the Government and all its works.

– Salmond 1975:119

8
Tangihanga: Ceremonies of the Dead

The tangihanga ceremony is a vital part of Māori culture today and demands the attention of hundreds of people. No other ceremony can mobilise Māori people quite as effectively as the tangihanga. They will travel from all over Aotearoa and from as far away as Australia in order to pay their respects to a relative, or workmate, or leader of some renown. Often they wait for hours before finally being called onto the marae when the tikanga of the tangihanga begins.

Travel arrangements are part of the preparations that all participants in the ceremony have to contend with today. Actually, there are many preparations and obligations that fall upon the bereaved family and not so many on distant relatives and friends for whom the main obligation is to find out where the tangihanga is to be held and to get there in order to become a part of the ceremony.

Once at the marae entrance visitors follow a set of protocols and procedures. No matter what the weather or the demands of the work-place, there are obligations to meet. The death of a relative immediately places obligations upon many people. An important obligation is to gather around the bereaved family, lend support and be part of the work force. The obligation is stated as an aphorism and as a value: he kanohi i kitea (a face seen). Nothing can really replace the fact of a relative or visitor actually being seen at the tangi. Consequently most relatives try their very best to go to the ceremony no matter how far away the marae might be.

Degrees of obligation

There are tikanga for various classes of individuals depending on the whakapapa links or degree of relationship to the deceased. The immediate family members are obliged to gather around first, and many of them have in fact been alerted to the looming crisis beforehand. Many of them may already be present at the time of death. Other relatives are expected to get to the marae where the tangihanga ceremony is being held by the first day. Members of the wider whānau and the hapū of the deceased are expected to have paid their respects by the first day. The other two days are regarded as time for others. During the first day the local hapū closes ranks around the deceased and the ceremony becomes a public event. The more important the tangihanga the more the local hapū has to unite, combine resources, maintain their mana and carry the ceremony through to its proper conclusion.

The first gathering of the whānau

When a member of the whānau is critically ill and not likely to survive, the immediate members of the family are called together and they stay at the hospital. Many of the hospitals of Aotearoa have a facility for the whānau to gather and stay close to their dying relative. A minister of the church is usually on hand to conduct services to comfort the family but there is an important tikanga that the minister has to perform at the hospital and before death is pronounced by the doctors. This is called the tikanga of tuku wairua (discussed in chapter 4), which is at the point when death is sure to follow. Most experienced ministers know when this point has been reached. The family gathers at the bed and the minister conducts a service to send the wairua on its journey up into the sky. This is somewhat like performing the last rites. But in this case the purpose is very clear: it is to send the wairua away from the body of the person.

Once the relative breathes their last breath, their status changes immediately to that of being very tapu and of being classified as a tūpāpaku, meaning to stand shallow rather than stand tall. The traditional way of preparing a corpse was in sitting position with the knees trussed and bound to the body. Nowadays a tūpāpaku is laid out in a prone position.

While the whānau is gathered at the hospital they make their preparations and tasks are assigned to different members to carry out. These tasks are done while an undertaker is preparing the body. When the body leaves the hospital the whānau members disperse to do their preparations. The tasks can be summarised as follows:

1. Communications: relatives to be informed, advertisements put in newspapers.

2. Preparations at the marae: the whānau has to decide where the tangihanga is to be held. Tikanga dictates that the deceased should be taken to the hapū marae. Some families choose to have their relative at home first, sometimes for the first night. For very important people it is difficult to do this because hundreds of people begin to mobilise immediately and the hapū needs to be ready. Family members are assigned to prepare the marae. One person is assigned to look after the meeting house and this may mean finding a person who knows what to do.

3. Preparations for the wharekai are urgent and some people must take charge.

4. Butchers are organised.

5. Seafood divers are alerted. They need to obtain permits and get gear ready.

6. Speakers and karanga experts are arranged.

7. A waiata team is mustered.

8. Ringa wera are organised. They will staff the kitchen and dining room and provide meals.

9. Finally, when the body is ready the kiri mate organise the party to take their relative onto the marae.

The second gathering at the marae

The hapū has meanwhile organised themselves at the marae to receive the deceased and the immediate whānau. A special pōhiri is organised and there are preparations on both sides to ensure tikanga is being followed. The tangata-whenua groups have prepared the place for the body and they are ready for the pōhiri ceremony to commence.

Placement of the body

The rule concerning the actual location of the body once it is brought to the marae varies from region to region. In some tribal areas the body is placed on the centre line against the tuarongo or the back wall of the meeting house. This is the custom in parts of the north and west of the North Island. In the eastern areas the custom is to place the body inside the house, against the tapu wall (the right wall when facing the house) and usually up against the third or fourth wall post or poupou from the window. This is the practice when the weather is not good or there is no whare mate. Where there is a whare mate at the marae the body is more likely to be placed there. This is an option. In this case the body is usually placed against the back wall of the whare mate in the central position. Some marae have a permanent whare mate placed beside the meeting house, usually on the tapu side. Yet another option which is used when the weather permits and in the summer time is to place the body on the verandah of the meeting house, and towards the tapu side of the house on the right-hand side when one is outside facing the front of the house. There the body is laid out in state, in a coffin with the lid off so that the people can see the face of the deceased.

The whakaeke: entrance onto the marae

Meanwhile, the kiri-mate group and their supporters have lined up at the gate with the pallbearers in front ready to approach.

1. A karanga signals the beginning and the kiri mate approach carrying the coffin with the feet of the tūpāpaku facing the marae.

2. Unlike other pōhiri, this whakaeke is accompanied with wailing on both sides.

3. The pallbearers take the tūpāpaku to the meeting house and they lead the party of mourners. Their progress is like a slow procession, the whole of which is conducted with the seriousness and dignity of the tangihanga ceremony.

4. The pallbearers are told where to take and place the body. They are advised by senior relatives and by the kuia who is looking after the meeting house. The coffin is placed, the lid is removed and kiri mate take up their places around the deceased. Meanwhile the

support group of speakers, together with the singers of waiata, separate themselves from them and go towards where they will sit.

5. For quite a period of time all parties stand as they pay their respects to the dead. When sufficient time has elapsed someone will say, 'Kua ea,' and all of the participants take up their appointed places. The cooks and waitresses very quickly leave and go to the wharekai.

6. Speeches begin, following the protocol of that tribe.

7. At the conclusion of speeches the parties come together and shake hands, hongi, hug and kiss one another. This is often punctuated by bursts of wailing.

8. There is a meal to follow.

9. The hapū may reorganise very quickly and become a unified and coordinated group to begin receiving the groups of visiting mourners who might have meanwhile collected outside the marae while the pōhiri for the tūpāpaku was taking place.

10. Many other individuals who take up well-understood roles support the kiri-mate group. It is one of the marvels of Māori society that a hapū organises itself, sets up an efficient organisation to manage three or more days of the ceremony, and then settles down to carry out the requirements of tikanga, ideally without a hitch. A well-organised tangihanga lightens the burdens upon the bereaved and makes everything much easier for everyone else.

The rituals of tangihanga

The group organised to manage the tangihanga is a segment of the hapū or the iwi. Each deceased brings together a slightly different constellation of people. However, the people who carry out important cultural roles, such as karanga, whaikōrero, church services, and waiata performances, are basically the same people. They participate in practically all of the tangihanga ceremonies of their marae. If they are not available – and there are occasions when this happens – the tangata whenua have to scramble to find others to fill these important roles. People generally know what is expected of them. If they do not, they face a very steep learning curve and must cope the best they can.

1. The kitchen and dining-room group provide meals for all visitors and they need to have everything under control: ordering food, butchering and preparing meat; arranging for cooks to cook the food, waitresses to wait at the tables, dishwashers to wash up. They are prepared to provide meals for hundreds of visitors who come in waves all day. Every few hours, meals have to be provided. Some marae are well known for their efficiency and the goodwill with which they provide for their guests. At the same time they are preparing for the hākari, the final meal that completes the ceremony.

2. Someone is looking after the flag or flags of the marae, putting them up in the morning and taking them down at sunset.

3. At some marae, the kiri mate eat only twice a day, the first before sunrise and the second after sunset. Members of the kiri mate are under the tapu of death and there are restrictions upon what they can or cannot do. They keep together as a group and sustain one another through the whole ceremony. They need to drink in-between meals otherwise they suffer from dehydration. Their evening meal is often an elaborate meal that is a reward for the heavy burdens upon them. The burden is often referred to as 'he kākahu whakataratara' (a cloak of nettles) or a 'kapua pōuri' (a dark cloud).

4. A member of the kiri mate has been allocated the task of looking after the koha that manuhiri bring. This person records all koha given with the name of the donor group and the amount. The list is printed out and at some marae put up in the meeting house for all to see. There are two functions of 'publishing' the list this way. One is accountability to the hapū. Everybody in the hapū knows who appeared at the tangi and the amount they gave. If there are queries about the list, the kiri mate are required to provide explanations. There is usually a list of anonymous donors because a name was not written on an envelope or their money was lumped in with others. The second reason is that the list represents a set of obligations upon the kiri mate following the principle of reciprocity. The whānau will know who came to 'pay back' and hence cancel an obligation and who is establishing a new obligation. In other cases the whānau keeps the list and its members set about meeting some of their obligations as soon as they are able. Some may not be met until years later.

5. The kiri mate has meanwhile decided the hour and date of the burial service at the marae. Sometimes there are arguments about where the burial should take place. The speakers on the speaker's bench usually inform all visitors of the time, which is often 11 a.m. on the nominated day.

6. The kiri mate have also organised the gravediggers and decided on the exact position in the urupā where their relative is to be buried.

7. Some marae close at sundown the reception of visiting mourners to the marae. There is usually a cultural expert of the marae to advise and direct on these matters. What this means is that the home team, who have carried the ritual burdens all day, call for a rest and they leave their post. The main reason for this protocol is to allow the kiri mate to relax and have their evening meal at a reasonable time. Without such a tikanga the kiri mate might be required to remain at their appointed posts until 9 p.m. at night and this is far too long and onerous. Other marae vary this protocol by closing down the formal pōhiri at a set time, releasing the kiri mate and putting in place a relief team to welcome any latecomers. Relatives are free to come at night, but there may be no formal welcome for them.

8. The whānau have arranged a minister to conduct services every evening and often it is this service which closes the reception of visitors to the marae.

9. Relatives from overseas usually take some days to arrive at the marae and the burial might be delayed to accommodate them. On some occasions the deceased has been sent back from overseas to be buried at their traditional urupā.

10. The kiri mate are offered some relief in the speeches of the visiting groups when they refer to aspects of the work of their relative they were completely unaware of. Sometimes speakers refer to shared activities that go back many years. Sometimes they talk about death itself and at other times the focus might be upon some humorous events. Some visiting groups bring singers to provide some light entertainment later in the proceedings or they may bring a kapa-haka team and sing. They may bring a haka team who will perform a war dance. All of these activities are possible and permitted. A tangihanga ceremony does have its lighter moments.

Te pō whakamutunga: the final night

The events of the day follow the previous day except that this day it is more likely that the visitors come from further afield.

In many tribal areas the final night, called te pō whakamutunga, is a special event which is managed in different ways. It is not simply a matter of the poignancy of a last evening at the traditional marae. In fact, it signals an important stage in the gradual lifting of the heavy mantle of tapu that is upon the kiri mate.

1. The protocol of the pō whakamutunga begins with the church service after the evening meal.

2. Once the service is completed, speeches begin. These focus upon farewelling the deceased. If conducted inside the meeting house, the order of speeches is from the tangata-whenua corner from which the church service was conducted. Speakers follow from the corner along the noa wall of the house to the back wall and then to the tapu side of the house.

3. Waiata might be lighter than those performed during the day, but this depends upon the marae and the tribe.

4. The last speaker comes from the kiri mate who, up until this very moment, have been required to remain silent. Now their speaker breaks the tapu of silence. If the deceased is a father, then it is expected that his eldest adult son will speak. If not, the kiri mate selects one of their men to speak. This speech is the highlight of the evening and it is often a tearful introduction into the world of whaikōrero for the speaker. In some tribal areas the kiri mate do not speak until the day of the funeral.

5. There is a break for a cup of tea.

6. The rest of the evening is given over to light entertainment to take the kiri mate further into their transformation from a highly tapu state to a gradual reduction of it. This is a transitional stage and an important one because of the high level of stress that has been upon the kiri mate.

7. At some marae, the entertainment goes all night and it is all conducted informally. The formal part of the evening ended with the speech of the representative of the kiri mate and, from that point on, light-hearted entertainment reigns.

The final day

The first business of the last day of mourning is the gathering of the whānau early in the morning to witness the closing of the coffin. Up until this moment the face of the deceased has been uncovered and visible to all mourners. When the lid is screwed down the face of the deceased will never be seen again. An important moment in the ceremony has been reached and it is often a sad and poignant one. Mourners arriving on this day will see only the coffin, but they understand the tikanga.

Closing the coffin early in the morning allows the bereaved family time to themselves and affords an opportunity to mourn in a less public context. If they fail to do this before the mourners begin to arrive then the closing of the coffin becomes more formal and more public. On the part of the organisers of the whole ceremony the delay will cause problems later in the day.

1. The bereaved whānau and their supporters gather early in the morning to witness the closing of the coffin.

2. A minister stands by ready to conduct a service of closure.

3. The whānau might take the opportunity to say some words of farewell to their relative.

4. If not, the lid is closed amidst considerable wailing.

5. The kiri mate and the hapū prepare for the last groups of mourners who will begin to arrive soon after sunrise.

6. Some mourners have delayed their visit for now so as to catch the funeral service. Some are accused of coming only to catch the hākari. There are many reasons why mourners might be delayed.

7. The last groups of mourners are welcomed as before.

8. At some marae a bell is rung to signal the beginning of the funeral service. This requires a reorganisation of seating, flowers are moved in front of the house on the ground and the coffin may be moved forward to be in full view.

9. The minister of the selected church or several of them begin the service. There are favourite hymns which are sung at this service. A common one is 'Piko Nei te Matenga' in the Anglican list of hymns and it evokes memories of many who have been farewelled at the marae.

10. At some part of the service the kiri mate put forward a person to give a eulogy in either English or Māori or in both languages. This service allows the deceased to leave the marae, but it is not the final service.

11. At the conclusion of this service pallbearers lift the coffin and they begin an alignment of kiri mate behind them. Children are assigned to carry the floral wreaths to the urupā. Others fall in behind them. The ministers of the church might lead the procession. There are variations as to how the procession is organised. At some marae a band might take the lead.

The procession

1. The procession walks slowly to the urupā and halts on arrival at the gate.

2. Meanwhile, groups of people have gathered at the graveside. The karanga expert now issues a karanga to the group to enter the cemetery and proceed to the grave which has already been prepared by the gravediggers. Some iwi do not follow this tikanga.

3. The pallbearers take the coffin to the hole and place it on beams that have been laid across the hole. Ropes are attached to the coffin and the coffin is lifted, the beams taken away and the coffin is lowered into the bottom of the pit with the head towards where the headstone will be placed.

4. The final part of the burial service now takes place.

5. At the conclusion of the service, final speeches are made by any who care to do so. Songs are sung.

6. The immediate whānau file past the pit and throw some dirt onto the coffin. The children are encouraged to join in and throw a flower into the grave.

7. The gravediggers now complete their job which is to cover the hole and shape the top of the grave.

8. Some floral wreaths are placed on the grave.

9. All participants now leave the urupā and go through the water-cleansing ceremony to remove tapu from them.

10. They go back to the marae. The kiri mate are not yet free of the requirements of the tangihanga ceremony. They are ritually welcomed back to the marae and once this is done everyone waits for the call to attend the hākari.

11. Meanwhile, the women of the marae clear away the mats and cloaks that were used for the lying-in-state of the deceased. Ministers or tohunga perform cleansing ceremonies to lift the tapu of death from the place where the deceased lay.

12. The meeting house is cleared and any items for laundering are gathered up.

13. Then comes the call from the wharekai announcing that the final feast is ready. The kiri mate are the first to be called. Others follow.

14. After the shared meal the place and the people are restored to a state of noa and the people are free to go home, except the kiri mate. Obligations upon them are not quite over.

Te takahi whare: tramping the house

The takahi-whare ceremony is an essential component of the tangihanga complex of tikanga. This is a ceremony to clear away the tapu of death from the dwelling place of the deceased. Personal effects of the deceased are a particular problem. Formerly, these were put into bags or suitcases and buried with the deceased. Very personal items of clothing were either buried or burnt.

Nowadays there is a mix of attitudes about this tikanga. The family may share personal items of clothing like coats, suits, dresses and shoes, but there is a reluctance to use underclothing. The latter are usually destroyed or disposed of in some way. Personal ornaments are shared out among family members.

Highly valued heirloom items, such as whānau tiki, greenstone patu and cloaks, are usually given to a responsible member of the whānau to look after on behalf of the whole whānau. They may be brought out on special occasions.

1. The ceremony itself consists of a church service in which a minister cleanses the house with water and prayers, or the whānau may use a traditional tohunga, or both may be employed.

2. Members of the family follow the minister or tohunga as all of the rooms of the house are ritually cleansed, often by the sprinkling of water.

3. When completed, the minister may call the kiri mate together and have a church service to help settle them back into their house.

4. Speeches follow, mainly for two purposes. Firstly, to welcome the family back into their house and to wish them well, and secondly, to thank the officiating minister or tohunga for their part.

5. Food is shared and sometimes liquor is served to help the whānau relax. The ringa wera of the kitchen would have brought some food to the house for this part of the tangihanga ceremony.

6. At some marae the kiri mate and ringa wera and those who carried ritual roles come together for what might be called a debriefing hui. It is one way the kiri mate can thank all of their helpers.

7. Some whānau turn this tikanga into a big event which might last all night.

8. Others keep it short and so allow the family to settle back into normal life.

Kawe mate: taking the event to other places

There is an obligation upon the kiri mate to take their mate to neighbouring tangihanga. If there is another death in the tribal region they are obliged to go there. If there is a relative lying at a marae miles away they are required to go. The whānau usually know or are told or are invited to take their mate to other marae and dates are negotiated for when this is to happen. There are variations in the protocols of kawe mate.

1. The kiri mate arrive at the gate of the marae.

2. The party is called onto the marae. Often a photo of the deceased is displayed as the party approaches.

3. They are treated to a formal pōhiri and the speakers refer to the death that is being honoured.

4. Sometimes the kiri mate are invited to sit at the verandah of the meeting house and put their photo up against the wall for all to see. Their speakers, however, are treated formally as manuhiri.

5. Once the speeches are over there is the usual coming-together to shake hands, hongi and so on.

6. The visitors share a meal.

7. Then they might be invited to stay overnight and not leave until the next morning. On other occasions the meal completes the ritual exchange.

Te hura kōhatu: unveiling the headstone

Usually one year after the tangihanga ceremony was held the unveiling of the headstone falls due. Sometimes the time lapse may be shorter or longer depending upon whether there are other headstones to do. The unveiling is an event that the kiri mate have prepared for both in terms of finance and in the preparation of food.

Once the hura kōhatu is completed the obligations upon the kiri mate are virtually over. All that remains are reciprocal obligations in relation to koha. But this ceremony also signals another milestone in the whole grieving and mourning complex of tikanga. The widow or widower is freed of obligations to the deceased spouse and may remarry after the unveiling.

The same group that organised and supported the tangihanga gather again to honour the dead in this final ceremony.

1. Visitors assemble at the marae and they are formally welcomed to the marae and to the event.

2. Speeches follow the usual pattern, followed by a church service.

3. Then everybody retires to the urupā.

4. They are formally called to enter the urupā.

5. The people gather around the headstone, which has been covered with a cloak.

6. The minister now conducts a service during which the cloak is ritually removed from the headstone.

7. At some point a member of the kiri mate is invited to read the inscription, which might be in English or in Māori depending upon the language preference of the immediate whānau.

8. The service is completed.

9. Sometimes several have to be unveiled at the same ceremony, in which case each one is done in turn and then there is a final common part of the service to cover them all.

10. Relatives will make a point of placing a hand on the headstone and rubbing it gently. They may say some words to the deceased. Now it is the wairua that receives and hears the message. But to the relatives the explanations do not matter. They speak to their relatives whenever they want to.

11. There is a hākari to complete the ceremony and it is handled very much like the hākari of the main tangihanga ceremony.

12. There may be speeches of farewell (the poroporoaki) after the meal is over especially if there are representatives of other iwi present. This is a common factor in all hākari.

Ideas about death

There is a saying to the effect that people make decisions about their lives and their activities and they do what they want to do, but there comes a moment when Hine-nui-te-pō, the Great Maid of the Night, makes her decision and that spells the end of life. Another saying points to the vulnerability of humans. Māui, that demigod who performed such marvellous feats such as fishing up the North Island and taming the sun, failed to gain immortality for humans. He attempted to reverse the birth process and enter the Great Maid of the Night in order to find the source of life. Instead the Great Maid crushed him and as a result all human beings inevitably die. In one of the journeys the dead are believed to make, one part of the wairua visits the underworld and is attended to by Hine-nui-te-pō. She mothers the souls that travel to the underworld. That is her appointed task. So at a tangihanga one might hear an orator recommend that the spirit of the deceased go to Hine-nui-te-pō. (Haere, haere ki tō tipuna ki a Hine-nui-te-pō. Depart and journey to your ancestor Hine-nui-te-pō.)

Some images in woodcarving mirror attitudes towards death. One image depicts an ancestor figure biting the tail of a lizard. Here the attitude is that life is a contest with death. The role of humans is to tease the tail of the lizard and cheat death wherever possible. Another image depicts the head of the lizard entering the mouth of an ancestor figure. In this case the contest has been won by death.

The lizard is a sign of death and it is regarded as an instrument of death. When a sorcerer wishes someone to die he sends a lizard to enter the body of the victim, and this lizard is the metaphor for the disease that takes over the body of a victim and kills them. There are many carvings of ancestor figures which show a lizard entering the mouth. Some say that this means the ancestor died a natural death and was not killed by a weapon. It is bad luck to have a lizard cross your path while out walking. People were afraid of lizards.

It is recognised in our beliefs that human beings are transient and are not permanent features of the social landscape, as some youth mistakenly believe. The condition of human life is compared with the apparent permanence of the land or of a mountain range. Thus there are many ways of talking about death and of explaining it to relatives of the deceased, who often wonder why it should be their relative who lies in state in the meeting house. There are Christian explanations and there are traditional Māori explanations.

At death the mauri that a person is born with dies and disappears. It is extinguished when the spark of life ceases, breathing stops and the heartbeat throbs no more. But the wairua that is released either prior to or immediately after death leaves the body and journeys upwards towards Ranginui, the Sky Father. It is not clear how far up the wairua travels, but common belief indicates that it hovers immediately above the body it left. All through the tangihanga ceremony the wairua hovers, lingers and watches over the proceedings to make sure that the rituals are being done properly. The belief is that if the ceremony has not been done properly the wairua will not leave but it will hover for a long time, bringing bad luck in its wake.

Another spirit or wairua travels to the underworld, which in Māori belief is more akin to a heaven. It is a beautiful place where there is no evil, no violence and no abuse. It is a world of light and peace. Hine-nui-te-pō is the protecting mother of the souls that took that journey. Those souls remain there. The other wairua that hovers above the body departs once the funeral is conducted and the body is returned to the whenua. There are a number of beliefs about the journeys of the wairua. Some say that the wairua leaves the place where the body is buried and flies to Te Rerenga Wairua at the North Island's northern-most point and there it enters the ocean and travels to distant Hawaiki. That is a common belief. In our tribal area the wairua leaves the marae and flies over Opihi-whanaunga-kore, a very tapu and ancient burial ground at Whakatane, alights on a rock at the mouth of the Whakatane River called Turuturu Roimata, and sheds its final tears, hence the name of the rock. Then it flies to Te Paepae-o-Aotea which is about fifty kilometres out to sea and away from Whakatane, and there some say their farewells and depart for Hawaiki.

Others however, do not make that journey. Instead they hover permanently around the burial grounds, the mountains and culturally significant sights and are never ever far away from their kin. There is the belief that when the karanga women say 'Hoki wairua mai e ngā tīpuna' (Return oh spirits of the ancestors) the spirits are close by and are not at some distant location across the sea. They are the spiritual dimensions of the Māori universe, always present and never too far away. So when they are called they come closer to the event to which they are invited. Some of the priests say they can see the wairua and can talk to them. Some say they feel the presence of their ancestors and are uplifted by it.

However there are others who are troubled by the notion that our wairua are close by. These people cannot come to terms with the belief system. For them, it is all too real and their lives are affected, not positively but negatively. The wairua become ghosts that haunt them and frighten them. However, a majority of Māori live happily with images of their ancestors all around them in a carved meeting house, with the wairua of the ancestors above them, with the bones of their ancestors at the burial ground near by and surrounded by their living relatives. All are part of the reality of being Māori. All elements are parts of the whole and death itself is not a frightening experience. Some say it is but another dimension of life. Even the children who attend tangihanga and participate in the whole ceremony accept that death is something we need to understand. It is manageable because we have tikanga to guide us and help us through a crisis and a reality of life.

There is a time before death when the wairua of the person is more able to commune with the wairua of the ancestors. Some report being visited by their relatives long-since dead. It is almost as though the wairua of their ancestors had come to welcome another soul to the spiritual world. In this transitional period the world takes on a different hue. There is an acceptance of a move towards another world where the wairua, cleansed of all the human frailties of its human body, moves and exists forever. Close relatives may see the wairua of the deceased immediately after the funeral. They say they saw the ghost of their relative. Others believe that only the specially gifted among us can actually see wairua and talk to them. For most of us, that world exists as a concept and as an influence that we are aware of but may not ever see, until perhaps at the transitional stage when death is near.

What endures after death is the flax bush, te pā harakeke, a metaphor for the children who inherit parts of the gene pools of the two parents. A mother lives on in her children who may exhibit some of her characteristics and may even look like her. Similarly the father is reflected in the children. Where there is no pā harakeke the family is referred to as a whare ngaro, a lost house, in which the genes are lost and come to the end of a line that may have had great potential. But that is life.

Perspectives

Funeral Rites

Witchcraft possesses a strong hold over the minds of the people; and even those natives who have embraced Christianity are not altogether free from the dread of its supposed power. Diseases are usually attributed to the influence of witchcraft or sorcery, and not to natural causes.

On the death of a chief, or any individual of rank amongst them, a great lamentation ensues, which is called a *tangi*. The women cut their arms and lacerate their faces and breasts in a dreadful manner, with the sharp and broken shells of the pipi or the mussel, until they become covered with blood. The clothes and property of the chief are generally put into the tomb with him; or they are collected together and placed in a *wahi tapu*, or sacred place, surrounded with railings, where they rot away exposed to the winds and the weather. The body is enclosed in a mausoleum of carved woodwork within the *pa* for several months, and at the expiration of this period, the ceremony of lifting the bones takes place, which is performed by the nearest relation of the deceased. The bones, after being well scraped and cleaned, are then deposited in a *whata*, or elevated box, somewhat resembling a provision store; or they are secreted in a cavern, or some sacred place, known only to the *tohunga*.

– Angas 1847, 1:331

Tombs

The tomb or mausoleum of E Tohi is erected near to the '*Kai tangata*'. It consists of a semi-circular erection of wood, within which the body was placed in an upright position. The roof is square and projects like a verandah all round, sloping towards the back; it is supported by posts at the corners and like the central coffin or box, is richly ornamented with spiral arabesques. The ornamental work on the coffin is entirely red and white, whilst the other portions, together with the double row of paling that surrounds it, are coloured black and red. In front of the projecting roof is suspended a richly embroidered kaitaka mat; and tufts of feathers of the albatross are arranged, at intervals, along the framework. This spot, and the ground for a certain distance surrounding it, are strictly tapu; and it would be more than his life was worth for a slave, or an inferior native, to infringe upon its sanctity.

Place: Mana Island, period 1840s

– Angas 1847, 1:265–66

A monument to three native children stands not far from Thom's house at Te awa iti. It consists of an upright series of flat boards, with a post at each end, on the top of which is a rude representation of a head; and the boards are richly painted with black, red and white, each board displaying a different pattern.

Place: Te Awa iti at Tom Channel, period 1840s

– Angas 1847, 1:275

9
Te Muru
The Concept of Ritual Compensation

Grounds for muru

No longer practised today, muru was a well-known response to certain offences, which were regarded as providing sufficient cause to invoke it. Maning (1912:103) described muru as 'the regular legalised and established system of plundering as a penalty for offences, which in a rough way resembled our law where by a man is obliged to pay "damages".' The offences included the following:

1. Threats to the institution of marriage. Examples in the recorded literature focus on the break-up of marriages and the forging of new relationships. Punishment of the first and main offence validated the second.

2. Accidents of a serious nature that threatened life. Maning (1912:104, 113) points to two examples, the first against a father whose child was severely burnt in a fire. The parent was held to be negligent. The second muru was against a person in charge of a waka when several people 'in his charge' were drowned. Again, the offence was negligence and poor judgment.

3. Damaging a wāhi tapu and trampling on tapu. Maning (1912:103) cited the case of a fire lit to clear ground for a garden that accidentally burnt a neighbouring wāhi tapu. Taylor (1870:166) described in detail what happened to a party of travellers after they defied a rāhui or aukati (a line across which the movement of people is ritually restricted or prohibited). Again the focus of the offence was

disturbing the tapu, whether permanent, as in the case of a wāhi tapu, or temporary, as in the case of a rāhui or aukati.

4. Defeat in war. The leader of a defeated expedition often faced the prospect of women performing a manawa wera, or derisive chant, on his return. But in addition to having to face up to the anger of the women whose husbands died there was the prospect of muru as described by Te Rangi Hiroa (Buck 1987:421).

It seems clear from the evidence of the early printed record that the fullest expression of muru and the most common take was in the response to a marriage break-up. There are two examples to be analysed under this category of take.

Case 1

The first example of muru here is one observed by 'A Taranaki Veteran' and published as 'The Great Muru' (1919). This article should be perused for the detail. The Taranaki veteran was manager of the Opunake Company flax mill and he observed a part of the tikanga and was told about most of it. His company was involved in the tikanga by being asked to hide some of the goods that should have been offered up to the muru.

The time was the summer of 1873. This particular muru was described as 'the greatest muru that had been known on that coast in the memory of the oldest Maori'. The place was the village of Te Namu on the banks of the Otahi Stream in Taranaki.

The take

Te Kahui Te Kararehe, a chief of Opunake, lived at Te Namu with his wife Betty, who was of part-African descent. Aperama lived with his wife Lydia at Parihaka. Both men were chiefs of high rank. Te Kahui wanted to marry Lydia, but the local chiefs would not allow him to do so. To break the impasse, Te Kahui eloped with Lydia. This provided a cause for muru and the villagers of Te Kahui Te Kararehe became liable to be plundered.

Preliminary actions

1. There was great excitement in the village as soon as news of the elopement was announced. The people anticipated that utu would be demanded.

2. Steps were taken to hide some valuable goods, mostly guns, within the flax mill. Perhaps this was an innovation because a neutral third party was present. But food was also hidden because manaakitanga still had to be offered at a certain point in the muru.

3. The villagers prepared themselves for the institution of muru to be applied to them. They were required to put out on the marae their moveable valuable goods that would be taken by visiting groups called taua wahine, war parties targeted at trouble over women. The war party was not assembled to kill anyone, but rather to carry out a ritual plunder of the party held to be responsible. The villagers had to stand back and allow the socially and culturally validated tikanga of muru to proceed.

The muru begins

Day one

1. That very afternoon, after the news of the elopement had been announced, the first party arrived. They were from the nearest village of Matakaha, about a mile away from Te Namu.

2. There is no record of how this group was received at the marae. As they were close neighbours one assumes this party was closely related.

3. They took 'old clothes, blankets, boxes, kits, eel-baskets, cooking utensils and anything moveable that they could carry away'. The observer was not an actual witness to these events, but saw the people with their goods walking past the flax mill.

Day two

4. Taua muru (muru war parties) arrived from Umuroa, Nuku-Te-Apiapi and Waitaha in the morning and took, 'fowl, duck, goose, turkey and pig in the vicinity of or on the lands belonging to the village'. The author noted that the people of Te Namu 'began to look exceedingly gloomy', but he may have found this out later as the local chiefs were in touch with the flax mill throughout.

Day three

5. Taua muru came from Taungatara, Punehu and Ouri, villages from the area between Opunake and Oeo. They took away 'every horse, bullock, cow and calf they could find'.

Day four

6. The taua muru from Parihaka arrived at 11 a.m. This was the main aggrieved party, but most of the goods had already been taken. This time the author and his team of workers from the flax mill gathered at the village and actually observed what happened.

7. The taua made a lot of noise as they approached, but when they arrived there was silence, a long silence.

8. The people of Te Namu had to face the visiting taua on their own. Supporters were not expected to stand with them. This was part of the tikanga. By now the people were under considerable strain. The men were 'rigid and immoveable as statues, but for an occasional quiver of a muscle, showing the intensity of the strain upon them, they might have been images of wood or stone'.

9. The taua now approached. Two naked old women came leaping and dancing onto the marae. They had rolled in black mud and each held a firebrand. The women cut their cheeks and their breasts with their sharp nails and the blood flowed. All the while they danced. Finally they torched all of the houses. When all were burning the old women retired, their work done. The main taua were hiding while the torching was undertaken.

10. Just then one of the local women yelled out that there was a sick person in one of the houses. At this the muru was immediately suspended and both taua and tangata whenua began furiously to take down the walls of the burning house to rescue the patient. But there was no one there. As soon as this was established, the two parties went back to their positions. The taua hid behind some flax and scrub as before.

11. When the burning was complete the taua advanced onto the marae. They were led by their chief, Tamihana, who began his speech when his party of men were in squatting position with their guns between their legs.

12. Tamihana castigated the people of Te Namu for the shame brought upon his people of Parihaka. The speech was fiery and delivered with force. When he finished he squatted down in front of his men.

13. Then the women of Te Namu brought out the food which they had cooked for the taua of Parihaka, and provided hospitality for their visitors. Those who participated in the meal were confined to the visiting taua wahine group.

14. At the conclusion of the feast, members of the Parihaka taua rose and left the marae. And as the author noted: 'Everything had been done in perfect order, and in accordance with the best of their old traditions.'

15. There was now nothing left and the people of Te Namu had been thoroughly plundered except for the hidden items. Many thought the muru was now complete, but it was not yet quite over.

Day five

16. Titokowaru, well-known warrior of Taranaki, had organised a taua from his people at Omuturangi. News came that his taua was on the way.

17. There was nothing left for this taua except the lives of the people and they did not really know how they would cope with Titokowaru.

18. At 11 a.m. word was delivered to Te Namu that the chief Hone Pihama of Oeo 'had intercepted Titikowaru, and bribed him with a present of bullocks to turn back'. Titikowaru accepted, and the muru was now over. We do not know the relationship of Hone Pihama to Te Kahui Te Kararehe.

Day six

19. Te Kahui Te Kararehe and his bride Lydia came back to Te Namu 'all smiles and jubilant at having won his old flame, and Lydia dignified but a little shy at the new honours which had come to her'.

Discussion

Plainly, therefore, the objectives of muru were to compensate the wronged partners, Aperama and his relatives, for the break-up of his marriage and thereby validate the new arrangement that Te Kahui had begun with Lydia. The cost to Te Kahui and his people was very high indeed and provided an example to others about the sanctity of marriage.

This example is not described as the 'great muru' for no reason. It was unusually far-reaching and embracing of a wide community. Unusual, too, was its thorough-going nature over many days.

The next example, case 2, is more confined and controlled and this could be a result of a perception of less mana involved in this instance.

Case 2

This is documented by Te Rangi Hiroa (Buck 1987:371). The incident occurred in the Bay of Plenty region at a valley near Te Teko, probably in the early 1920s. Te Rangi Hiroa participated in the muru so his observations are based on first-hand experience.

The take

The wife and her lover fled the district but her people accepted 'the clouds of trouble' quite cheerfully because Te Rangi Hiroa said that the tribe accepted their status as a 'lofty peak'. That is to say the local tribe accepted that they were people of some mana and of some means.

Preparations

1. The taua wahine assembled at Rotorua and so it is fair to assume that the wronged husband came from that district. Te Rangi Hiroa was invited to join the taua, and he accepted.
2. They travelled from Rotorua to Te Teko.
3. On arrival the men stripped to 'loin cloths', armed themselves with mānuka poles that they took from a village fence and arranged themselves into columns of fours.

The muru begins

1. The taua marched onto the marae in columns of fours.
2. The men lined up and performed a haka with much vigour.
3. Then the taua settled into position and the chiefs began their orations. Fiery speeches were made.
4. The purpose of the speeches was to accuse the local tribe of doing wrong and chastise them for their guilt: rude songs were sung.
5. The village chief admitted they were at fault.
6. The people of the village then began to lay out various articles on the marae and in front of the taua. There was a definite protocol followed.

7. Each person who contributed to the pile of jade ornaments, bolts of print cloth, money in pound notes came forward and announced the nature of the taonga they were contributing.

8. Some gave horses and cattle.

9. The taua wahine group employed two secretaries to write down the names of the donors of cattle and horses so these animals could be collected later.

10. When the local tribe had completed their contributions to the taonga they invited the taua to come forward and hongi.

11. This was followed by a hākari.

12. After the feast the taua distributed the taonga among their members. Te Rangi Hiroa received a jade ornament and five one-pound notes. He did not wish to share in the plunder, but as a participant he had to accept.

13. The taua arranged to collect the animals later and they went home.

Discussion

The second example was carried out in a day, except for the collection of the animals. The offence is similar, except in this case the wife, who came from Te Teko, left her husband from Rotorua and went away with someone else. Te Rangi Hiroa quoted a useful translation of a proverb: The clouds of heaven settle only on the peaks of lofty mountains and the clouds of trouble settle only on the heads of high chiefs (Buck 1987:371).

This is an important principle, which will differentiate the extent of the muru. The higher the status of the principals the greater the cost to the offending whānau, hapū or iwi. In fact, if the offenders were not of chiefly status the muru may not be invoked at all because there would be nothing to distribute.

Economists such as Firth (1959) viewed the muru as a means of redistribution of wealth and it certainly did result in redistribution of treasured ornaments and a sharp reduction in the wealth of the plundered group.

From a sociological point of view the tikanga of muru could be viewed as an incentive for maintaining the institution of marriage. As case 1 clearly shows the muru was a severe sanction that could not be taken lightly. Buck (1987:371) made the point that the victims took comfort from the fact that they were regarded as 'lofty mountain peaks'. There was pride in surviving a muru and starting to build up an economic base all over again.

Accidents and muru

There are no detailed accounts of muru having been carried out as a result of a serious accident. There are two clear examples in the record, but these are described as general cases.

Case 3

Frederick Maning was a justice of the peace and judge of the Native Land Court in 1865. He spent many years in the far north of the North Island. He died in England 25 January 1883 and was brought back to New Zealand and buried at Auckland. Maning (1912:103–110) reports a case where a boy was badly burnt in a fire and the father was held to be responsible. The boy was 'considered to belong to the family of the mother more than to that of the father'. He was a 'promising lump of a boy' and a future warrior, belonging to a rangatira family. It is assumed that the incident occurred in the far north of the North Island.

The take

The negligent behaviour of the father who allowed a child of the whānau to be badly burned.

Preparations

1. The brother of the mother, that is, the uncle of the boy, assembled a taua muru.

2. A messenger was sent to the father to let them know when the taua group planned to arrive. The father queried the messenger about the size of the group.

3. The father set about preparing a great hākari for the day of the muru. 'Pigs are killed and baked whole, potatoes are piled up in great heaps, all is made ready' (Maning 1912:108).

4. On the day, the father mustered his taua. All were armed with a 'spear and a club' and they stood silently to receive the visiting group.

The muru

1. The taua muru arrived.

2. The tangata whenua issued a welcome karanga.

3. The father's taua charged out of the marae in a feigned attack, then formed up and performed a haka which was answered by the taua muru.

4. Then the uncle stood before his group and began his whaikōrero, but first he challenged the father. 'Stand up! Stand up! I will kill you this day!' This was an invitation for the father to stand ready for a duel.

5. The father came forward and a duel with spears began. The father suffered a wound and some blood flowed. The uncle also had a wound. That signalled the end of the duel.

6. The uncle then called out, 'Murua! Murua!' That is, he gave the order to begin collecting goods.

7. The ritual plunder began.

8. Meanwhile the two principals, the father and uncle of the child, sat facing each other and, according to Maning, chatted while the father's possessions were being taken (Maning 1912:109).

9. The hākari followed.

10. The muru was completed and the aggrieved party could say, 'Kua ea.'

Discussion

In some cases Maning suggests that the person held to be responsible for the accident is subject to the spear test. This means that he must stand up to the leader of the aggrieved party. The aggrieved leader has the right to one thrust of the spear aimed at a thigh and nowhere else. The victim has the right to parry the thrust. However sometimes the victim feels so overcome with shame and guilt that he fails to parry the spear thrust. He accepts the wound and the consequences, which sometimes end in death. On other occasions, such as the one being discussed, a duel may be fought until both parties receive a wound. There appears to be some flexibility about what is required.

When the principals are of rangatira category a muru becomes highly public. Whakapapa status is very high and there are goods to be taken. The economic standing of the group held responsible may be taken into consideration when deciding whether to apply the muru or not. Can the group stand up to the severity of a muru?

It is also clear that the muru is a social institution and the cooperation of the group is absolutely essential to its success. The more public the event the higher the number involved on both sides. There are muru which are private and less public and can be settled within a short time and with a very limited range of goods involved. However in these instances the principles of muru still apply. It is the scale of event that is reduced.

Maning (1912:109–110) cited the case of a certain taonga or valued item circulated six times through muru. This was a 'nice coat' obtained from the captain of a trading schooner and 'much coveted'. Through the muru it passed through six different hands and eventually came back to the first owner. Maning commented on the 'private' occasions when muru was applied for 'little accidents'. He wrote (1912:110) 'I have been myself paid the compliment of being robbed for little accidents occurring in my family and have several times also, from a feeling of politeness robbed my Maori friends. Though I can't say I was a great gainer to these benefactions.' He went on to say that he 'resisted the muru' and preferred to pay compensation right away than risk a full-scale public muru.

Wāhi tapu and muru

In traditional times the tikanga associated with tapu places and structures was reinforced through the institutions of muru, and the risk of being subjected to muru in addition to having to deal with religious sanctions was an extra hazard. Thus the tapu of places and structures was integrated into the system of law and order, and woe betide those who deliberately or even accidentally infringed the rules of tapu.

Two examples of muru arising out of trampling on tapu regulations are discussed here.

Case 4

The case is documented by Taylor (1870:166) and is described in the perspectives section p.165. Here the case is analysed as with those associated with threats to marriage.

The take

A tapu had been placed on a river, thus preventing anyone from using waka for any reason. The reason for the rāhui was not provided. A Christian mission group keen to reach the next village became impatient and decided to defy the rāhui.

The muru

1. The group was seen and men of the village launched their waka and gave chase.
2. The boat of the missionaries was seized and dragged ashore.
3. All of the moveable objects in the boat were seized. The plunder included bottles of medicine and pots of preserves.
4. Speeches of wrath and indignation were made.
5. The medicine and the preserves were consumed on the spot.
6. The muru was complete.

Discussion

Taylor suggested that they (the missionary party) 'conquered' the villagers and there is a suggestion the medicine had something to do with it. Insufficient information was provided by Taylor to give a full picture of the content, the circumstance and the consequences. One can only guess that once muru had been carried out the missionary party would have been allowed to proceed on their way because they had paid compensation for the offence.

Case 5

This is described in Maning (1912:110–11) and is an unusual case.

The take

On a journey by foot Maning made camp at a certain spot and lit a fire under a certain tree. The tree caught fire and was burnt. This was a special tree associated with death. The corpse of a certain ancestor had been hung up in the tree to decompose and the bones had been taken away for final burial in a cave. Maning was unaware of the history of the tree.

The muru

There were no preparations and no advance notice given to Frederick Maning who was held responsible and regarded as being negligent. As already mentioned, ignorance of the laws of tapu was no defence.

1. Early in the morning Maning was roused by a person of the aggrieved side shouting, 'Get up! Get up! I will kill you this day. You have roasted my grandfather. Get up! Stand up!'

2. Maning came out of his house 'spear in hand' to face 'my friend the sometime owner of the bag of shot'. Maning had obtained a bag of shot from him in a previous muru. We will refer to him as the grandson because Maning does not reveal his name.

3. The grandson was armed with a bayonet fixed at the end of a pole. He charged at Maning 'with pretended fury' and thrust with the bayonet.

4. Maning successfully parried the thrusts. A duel was carried out.

5. The grandson then explained to Maning what he had done and that he had cooked his grandfather. He demanded compensation and if this were not done the grandson would apply the tikanga of muru and ransack the house.

6. Maning offered 'two whole bags of shot, two blankets, divers fish-hooks and a quantity of tobacco'.

7. The utu was accepted as adequate for accidentally 'roasting his grandfather'.

Discussion

Maning was an interesting observer of tikanga Māori. He lived with tikanga and observed it at close hand and sometimes was involved in it as illustrated by this example. Because of his nature, Maning was quick to see the humorous side of tikanga. In this case Maning focused on the bag of shot. He had gained a half bag of shot from a muru he carried out on his own behalf. But he had personally sold a full bag for full value to the same man. Thus Maning gained half a bag of shot, but now he was about to lose his gain and to the same person. Finally, in respect of tikanga he concluded that he would be better off: 'After a few experiences of this nature, to perceive that I had better avail myself of my privileges as a Pakeha and having nothing further to do with the law of Muru.'

Defeat in war and muru

Te Rangi Hiroa (Buck 1987:421) made the comment that a chief who led a tribe into defeat was subject to muru, but he did not cite an actual example. The discussion is important, however, in illustrating the powerful incentives that existed for success in warfare. Defeat put the leader at great risk because he lost mana and the loss gave opportunities for actions against him such as being beaten by the hands of the widows of those slain in battle. This punishment he had to endure without defence. He had to stand there and accept these expressions of grief. He and his party could have been subjected to derisive chants which highlighted their shame. And where the people felt that the cause was not a good one or that the leader was negligent he could be publicly rebuked by way of a chant and such rebuke would remain for years to come. The final shame could be the application of muru, but we do not have an actual case of this happening.

Conclusions

The tikanga of muru was an important means of social control and one of its consequences was to circulate wealth and move valuable taonga among relatives and among those in a marriage relationship. It is important to note that muru occurred among groups of people who were linked either by whakapapa or by marriage. Offences by persons outside of the circle more often than not resulted in more violent reprisals or in warfare.

It is clear that full-scale muru is a very social occasion which links neighbouring villages together in a collective response. While each village whānau or hapū is free to act in its own interest, in the end all of the villages are social groups and they are drawn together to share in the delivery of punishment. This reinforces the severity of the offence and at the same time reconfirms relationships. The people who delivered the punishment are the same groups that will offer assistance to the whānau who lost all their possessions.

Obviously there is an incentive for neighbouring descent groups to become involved in a collective response. They acquire goods that they did not have before. The transfer of ownership is legitimised by the tikanga of muru. Highly valued items could change hands and whānau who might have coveted a particular treasured heirloom may be able to acquire it through muru. But there is no guarantee of this as the transfers are on a first-come first-serve basis.

In the cultural-contact context it is quite possible that the tikanga of muru was used creatively either to acquire desired European goods or to make things difficult for Pākehā traders or missionaries. Some of the instances described by Maning suggest a stretching of the rules. It is obvious in the examples given that negligence that results either in loss of life or in severe damage to the life of a person – and especially of a child – was regarded as a serious offence. Considering some modern cases of serious neglect and abuse of children that have resulted ultimately in the loss of life, some thought has been given to how such offences would have been regarded in traditional times. The examples provided in the literature lend support to the idea that the punishment would have been either the tikanga of muru or the offenders would have had to forfeit their lives. Offences of that nature were serious and negligence was strongly disapproved and supported by sanctions.

Today the tikanga of muru occurs only in a private domestic sense and is between one household and another. The case of a visitor being bitten by a dog and utu being provided follows the principles of muru, but the scale of the operation has been sharply reduced to manageable levels. Whether the full-scale muru will ever be revived is a matter of some speculation.

Perspectives

The woods in which they hunted the rat were tapu, until the sport was over, and so were the rivers, no canoe could pass by until the rāhui was taken down.

In the early days of the Mission, the tapu was a great annoyance, the members were often unable to communicate with each other, until the dreaded pole was removed, but at last they determined to observe the tapu no longer; their boat was manned and they rowed along in defiance of the sacred prohibition; they had not gone far however before they were pursued, the boat was dragged ashore, and all the articles in it seized amongst which were some bottles of medicine and pots of preserves; these were immediately eaten, and great wrath and indignation expressed; but preserving a firm deport-ment the natives were conquered; the medicine perhaps had its share in obtaining the victory, as they found they could not meddle with Europeans with impunity; they held a meeting, it was then resolved that for the future, as Europeans were a foreign race, and subject to a different religion, the tapu should not apply to them ...

– Taylor 1870:166

Simulated muru

The missionary's servant, a former slave was married to a free girl. This of course conflicted with custom. The girl's mother had told Yate privately that she was well pleased with the match but that she must be angry about it with her mouth lest the tribe should become angry and take away all her possessions and destroy her crops. She accordingly protested against the marriage in public and demanded compensation which, in the form of a blanket, was given to her by Yate. So by simulating dissatisfaction, and by demanding compen-sation from the missionary the mother deprived others of a *take* for a *taua muru* directed against herself as a consenting party.

– Biggs 1960:50–51

Use of taonga

It has been noted already that a marriage might be confirmed simply by making a love affair public. Although this is so the discovery of the affair did not mark the end of proceedings. Such a marriage was irregular, offending the social creed which said that marriage should be aata koorerotia (well discussed) beforehand. Therefore, a take (cause) existed for a taua muru against the offending party or parties, usually the boy and his relatives. The utu (payment) demanded was taonga (valuable property) which was said to avert the consequences which would attend a serious quarrel. The surrendering of valuable property may be regarded both as compensation for the loss to the girl's group of her services and as atonement for the irregularities in the marriage.

   – Biggs 1960:50

10
Te Tatau Pounamu: Peace Agreements

Traditional Māori society was often known more for its propensity to wage war and engage in battles of revenge than for peace agreements. Yet there are many examples of peace agreements that involved diplomacy, negotiations, ratifications and confirmations. A consequence of warfare means ways have to be found to bring hostilities to an end, or to try to prevent the loss of life in the first place. A military settlement was often a case of winning a battle, overcoming another social group, sometimes banishing them from their homelands and extinguishing the rights of the conquered group to their lands and resources. This sort of settlement was not a peace agreement. Often the vanquished group would reassemble and at a later date attempt to recover their lands. A peace agreement was necessary to bring about a state of peace and calm that lasted for some time and accepted the status quo.

To make peace

The process of negotiating a peace agreement was called hohou rongo, to make peace. A state of peace achieved after a battle was called rongo, 'peace' (Williams 1957:346). The word which clarifies the process is hohou and its primary meaning is to bind and lash together. This is the aim of negotiating a peace agreement that holds through time. The objective is to bind the parties together, to lash them together so that each side accepts a responsibility to uphold the agreement. When it does hold, the statement made is this: 'Kua mau te rongo.' Such a peace might be called rongomau, a peace accord that is properly bound and lashed together.

Williams provides two more interesting terms. A peace agreement negotiated and brought about by a woman is 'rongo-ā-whare'. This suggests a peace secured in a house. One negotiated by a male is 'rongo-ā-marae', that is a peace negotiated out on the village plaza, in the open air. But these categories do not in fact make much sense.

A well-established peace is a 'rongo taketake' and one that is enduring is called a 'tatau pounamu', or greenstone door. The difference between rongo taketake and tatau pounamu is probably one of degree, with the latter suggesting an agreement that holds for all time.

To secure a state of peace

In tikanga that focuses on utu the important result desired is adequate compensation and equivalence. In warfare the desired outcome is revenge or the restoration of mana or the elevation of mana. By contrast, the emphasis of the process of hohou rongo is to stop further hostilities, secure a state of peace, confirm it and bind it so that it endures. In very simple terms the aim is to accept the political situation at the time. The sequence of take–utu–ea discussed in chapter 3 has been acted out and closure has been achieved.

Traditionally the process aimed at binding the parties to a peace agreement and it sought ways of accomplishing this and symbolising it. In some instances, highly valued taonga were exchanged between the parties, or special marriages were arranged, or features of the landscape were identified as symbols of peace. Negotiations may have been pitched at a higher level where diplomacy was required and iwi leaders were required to vouch for the settlement and stake their reputations on maintaining an agreement.

In other tikanga, such as muru and the tangihanga, decisions are made by those immediately involved in the events. There is no expectation of validating and ratifying what was done. Once completed, the event that triggered the tikanga has been addressed and appropriate practices have been followed to a successful conclusion. A major difference between that sort of tikanga and suing for peace is that a peace agreement is binding on the whole tribe and not just on a section of it, for example, the hapū that negotiated the agreement. Furthermore a tapu is placed on the event, meaning there are conditions to maintain and rituals to follow.

Negotiating an agreement

There are different levels of peace agreements. Some are achieved in a dramatic manner within a very short time. Others are negotiated over a long period of time, and they require ratification and confirmation by the various divisions within an iwi. Some require a minimum of ceremony while others, by their very nature, require several ceremonies and may need extra measures to be put in place in order to ensure that the two sides are bound together.

Often the parties require that concrete symbols of the peace agreement are identified and become a necessary binding mechanism. For example, a tatau pounamu is a concept or a metaphor for peace. There is no door to be seen and there is no pounamu or greenstone. The concept is a beautiful one, however, emphasizing as it does the qualities of permanence, vivid colour and beauty. Each side to a peace agreement would select a hill to symbolise the greenstone door and to remind each party that they are bound to an agreement. The hill then carries an extra measure of cultural significance as it stands for peace and it is understood that it is a constant reminder of a binding peace. To see is to believe.

This visible symbol standing lonely in the landscape might be seen as reaching towards Ranginui, the Sky Father, and standing firmly on Papa-tū-ā-nuku, the Earth Mother. It is a mediator, a symbol of mediation, negotiation and confirmation.

Arranged marriages

But often this powerful symbol was not considered to be sufficient to really bind the two sides together in a visible and real way. So, in order to make the binding real, political marriages were arranged and so the parties were bound together in a symbolic marriage. Each partner to the marriage would be a person of standing in their iwi.

While the marriage itself was an effective visible way of binding the parties together, it was not until children were born of the marriage that the binding became real, since the children belonged to both sides. They could be relied upon to play their part in acting as symbols of the agreement and as mediators between the two sides. Nicholson (2000) calls them takawaenga – mediators, or the people in-between. Their families became takawaenga, and Nicholson argues that these families continued to bind the sides together by arranging further marriages and by literally acting as mediators. Takawaenga families were known and respected because of the important role they played in inter-iwi relationships. They are the living symbols of peace. They play an active role in continuing to remind the parties to the agreement to maintain peace.

Valued heirlooms

In yet other cases highly valued heirlooms or weapons of great mana were exchanged between the parties and the heirloom became the visible symbol of the peace agreement. This symbol was often of greenstone. Firth (1959:415) referred to this practice as 'the ancient customs of exchanging heirlooms such as greenstone mere between chiefs of rank as a ratification of peace'. An example was the mere called Hine-nui-o-te-paua that was given by the Kawerau people to Ngāti Paoa many generations ago. Firth (1959:415) sets out what happened to this heirloom of peace. It was given by Ngāti Paoa to Ngā Puhi at Maumaina to secure peace, then it was later returned by Ngā Puhi to Ngāti Paoa during the 'time of great feast at Kohimarama'. Then Ngāti Paoa gave it to Governor George Grey 'as a token of their desire to keep peace with the white man'. It was not given lightly to Grey but was wept over by the chiefs of Ngāti Paoa. By the time of the gifting the taonga was thought to have acquired such a high level of mana and tapu that it could bring about peace and influence the parties to concentrate on peace. The mere was regarded as having mana and power in itself.

Rongo-ā-marae: peace agreements negotiated by chiefs

Case 1

Sometimes a peace agreement was arranged on the spot between two important chiefs. The strategy might be for one combatant to suggest to his opponent that he should lay down his weapon and agree that the two should settle for peace without putting their warriors to the test of battle. An example is the peace agreement between Te Maitaranui, a great chief of both Ngāti Awa and Tūhoe, and Pomare, a well-known warrior of Ngā Puhi. Pomare invaded Whakatane and cleared the ground wherever he went. Both Ngāti Awa and Tūhoe fled to Ruatahuna and Maunga-pohatu (Smith 1910:267–69).

Pomare took his army to Ruatahuna and camped at Manawaru. Then Te Maitaranui sent a scouting party to Manawaru with a dual purpose: to find out who were the leaders of the invading force and to gain an indication of the strength of their forces. Once Te Maitaranui received the information needed, he proposed to go himself to meet Pomare with the idea of seeking peace. But according to Smith (1910:270) the other chiefs would not agree so a delegation of four chiefs was sent to meet Pomare and his army. They were first met by Pomare's scouts, who then escorted them to Pomare. On learning that the delegation had been sent by Te Maitaranui, Pomare ordered them to return to their base and ask Te Maitaranui to come and meet him. So Te Maitaranui visited Pomare and put his proposal forward. He is reported to have said to Pomare, 'Tō patu tukua ki raro!' (Your weapon, lay it down!)

Pomare agreed to do this and a formal peace agreement was concluded on the spot and then ratified at a huge feast at Maunga-pohatu. The initiative in this case was with Te Maitaranui, the defender of the territory. As a result Ngā Puhi never ever invaded the territory of Tūhoe again.

Case 2

In a different example, at the battle of Haowhenua on the North Island's Kapiti coast in 1834, the Tūwharetoa chief Te Heuheu II Tukino broke his taiaha across his knee. This was on learning that his younger brother Papaka had been killed. He then declared that he and his people would never again take up arms against Te Āti Awa. Information about the battle is in 'He Tangi mo Papaka Te Naeroa' by Te Heuheu II Tukino (Ngata 1, 1959: 210-15), and in Nicholson (2000).

In order to fully understand the initiative taken by Te Heuheu one needs to know that Tūwharetoa was not the principal combatant in this battle but had been called on to assist. Furthermore, it was an accepted practice for an army to immediately stop fighting when an important chief was killed. It was a mark of respect to the chief and an acknowledgement by the other side that sufficient utu had been obtained on the battlefield through the death of an important chief.

Case 3: a tatau pounamu between Tūhoe and Ngāti Kahungunu

It is clear that there are at least three stages in negotiating a tatau pounamu. The first step is to discuss the possibility of a peace agreement. For example in the tatau pounamu between Ngāti Kahungunu and Tūhoe the first step was taken by some chiefs of Ngāti Kahungunu – Hipara, Puhirua and Ngārangi-mataeo – who requested a meeting with the Tūhoe chiefs Te Ikapoto and Moko-nui-a-rangi (Best 1972:550–57). They met at Pohatu-nui Pā, discussed the issue and decided that the two sides would enter into negotiations for a tatau pounamu. The second step was intended to discuss the idea of a permanent peace agreement and then to see how to implement it. This meeting occurred at a later date and the two principal negotiators were Te Ahura of Tūhoe and Hipara of Ngāti Kahungunu. This meeting was held at Hipara's pā and there he offered his daughter Hine-ki-runga to Tūhoe to symbolise the peace. He also offered a hill, Kahu-tarewa, from his side of Lake Waikaremoana as a marriage partner for the Tūhoe hill named Turi-o-kahu. There was a symbolic marriage of the two hills to represent the tatau pounamu.

The third step was the ratification of the agreement in a series of meetings with different groups. For example Tai-turakina of Tūhoe met Te Rangiaia at Puhi-nui to ratify and celebrate the agreement. Then Te Rangi-aniwaniwa of Tūhoe and Tama-uia of Kahungunu had their meeting, likewise Te Kapu-whakarito of Tūhoe called a meeting at O-rakau-whawhapo. Another was held at Titi-o-kura. These meetings helped to bind the parties to the tatau pounamu.

According to Best, while Hipara's daughter was offered in marriage to Tūhoe this was really a symbolic gesture. She would be remembered as the woman representing the tatau pounamu but she was not actually made to marry a Tūhoe husband. The 'marriage' of the hills was sufficient.

Again it is important to note that the preliminary step was important, and once taken, the tapu was in place and breaking it at that stage was fraught with danger. There are two instances that illustrate the point.

The first case relates to Te Tatau Pounamu o Pukekaikahu in which the principal chiefs were Te Purewa of Tūhoe and Moko-nui-a-rangi of Te Arawa (Best 1972:445–47). This Moko-nui-a-rangi is not to be confused with the Tūhoe chief of the same name. One section of Tūhoe objected to the peace agreement and set out to attack Te Arawa while the latter were on their way back from the negotiations for a peace agreement. In this case the negotiators of Tūhoe sent a scout to Te Arawa to inform them that they were to be attacked. A person chosen to be the messenger is called – rather disparagingly – a pūrahorua, literally 'a man of two testicles'; that is, one who is related by whakapapa to both sides. The result of the intervention was that the Tūhoe objectors were severely beaten and the rest of Tūhoe had no sympathy for them.

The second example refers to the peace negotiations between Ngāti Awa and Tūhoe. In this case the first step was not universally approved by both sides, especially by Tūhoe. But as already mentioned the tapu of the tatau pounamu had already taken hold and there was an obligation to hold the peace. In this example a section of Ngāti Awa decided to challenge the agreement. Again a messenger, named Te Au, was sent to warn Tūhoe. The result was a heavy defeat of Ngāti Awa at Te Kaunga, estimated by Best (1996:363) to have occurred at about 1832. The chief who negotiated the preliminary agreement was Tikitu and it was he who sent Te Au to warn Tūhoe. Te Au was reluctant to go but, in effect, he had been chosen because of his whakapapa and he had to go or risk being killed by his Ngāti Awa side.

The tapu placed upon a tatau pounamu transformed it into a serious event that had penalties attached to it. Probably through many years of experience our tīpuna realized that such agreements were fraught with difficulties and often difficult to obtain the complete support of all parties. Modern-day experience bears out the difficulties of getting unanimous support for a settlement.

Rongo-ā-wahine: peace agreements initiated by women
Case 1: Mereaira, Ngāti Hokopū and Ngāti Awa

In the example described here there are several aspects of it to keep in mind. Firstly, it was through the dramatic action of a chiefly woman that peace was secured. Secondly, the family at the centre of the event was a whānau takawaenga, a mediating family whose marriage brought two sides together, namely Ngāti Awa and Whakatōhea. A child was involved in the event. This child, related by blood and thus by whaka-papa to the two sides, was a unifying influence. (In fact, there were several key marriages between Ngāti Awa and Whakatōhea that should have resulted in a rongo taketake but did not. For example, Wepiha, a chief of Ngāti Awa, also married a woman of Whakatōhea.)

Mereaira was the daughter of the chief Te Keepa Toihau of Ngāti Hokopū and Ngāti Awa. She married Te Kape Tautini, a chief of Whakatōhea. They lived happily at Tauwhare Pā, which was on the Ngāti Awa side of Ohiwa Harbour, and they had a child named Te Pirini Tautini. However Mereaira had noticed her husband had become restless and one day he disappeared from Tauwhare and did not return. This made Mereaira and her father suspicious. The two could not guess what her husband might have done. But one morning a Whakatōhea taua arrived ready to drive Ngāti Awa out of Tauwhare Pā. Ngāti Awa was caught unprepared. A marriage was supposed to bind the two parties together. The pā was virtually empty except for Mereaira and her immediate whānau, who were in a helpless situation.

Meanwhile Whakatōhea had lined up on the beach and performed a haka or two. Then they made some fiery speeches. Right in the middle of the taua was Mereaira's husband, Te Kape Tautini. Te Keepa Toihau, we are told, did not know what to do and was prepared to submit to his fate. But Mereaira took the initiative. From where they stood above the beach they had a clear view of the Whakatōhea war party below them. She called out to Whakatōhea and held her son above her head. She told them that her son was a symbol of peace between the two iwi. She had had enough of the constant warring over Ohiwa. Then she said, 'I will throw my child onto the rocks below and his blood will be on your hands and a symbol of your disgrace for all time!' Before she could throw him down Te Kape left the war party and rushed up to save his son. He and his wife were reunited and peace was established between the two sides.

Case 2: Hine-i-turama, Te Arawa

Hine-i-turama was a chieftainess of Te Arawa and wife of Te Hurinui who was killed by Tūhoe at the battle of Puke-kai-kāhu fought near Lake Rerewhakaitu and Mount Tarawera. Several other high-ranking chiefs of Te Arawa were also killed there – Tionga, Te Waha-kai-kapua and Te Rangi-ka-tukua – as well as many other Te Arawa warriors. Killing had gone on for many years in a never-ending series of guerrilla raids. Hine-i-turama was so incensed and upset by the death of her husband and others that she decided to take some action (Best 1996:445).

Hine-i-turama composed a suitable kaioraora (derogatory song) to vent her feelings against Tūhoe. But she did more than this. She also rallied a group of 400–800 men to accompany her into the heart of Tūhoe, to Ruatahuna, in order to ask for the head of her husband to be returned to her. Her huge party arrived at Taumata-o-Te Riu Pā, at a place called Tahora, and was met by Tūhoe (Best 1996:445). Once there, she herself asked for the head of Te Hurinui to be returned.

Her request was granted and so appropriate steps were taken to present the head of her husband to her. The tikanga adopted by Tūhoe was to wrap the head, which of course had been preserved, in a fine cape and it was escorted by fifty men and presented ceremonially before Hine-i-turama. On arrival before her the Tūhoe group unwrapped the head, stuck it on a short stake and wrapped the cape around it more or less according to how they prepared a corpse in traditional times for the tangihanga ceremony. This act signalled the beginning of the mourning ceremony as the whole party wept for Te Hurinui. Then Te Arawa performed Hine-i-turama's kaioraora and the group gave a stirring performance resulting in Tūhoe uttering an expression that is now a proverb: 'He whatitiri ki te rangi. Ko Te Arawa ki te whenua' (Thunder in the heavens. Te Arawa on earth) (Best 1996:445).

Te Arawa remained for several days as guests of Tūhoe. The action taken by Hine-i-turama became the preliminary to a series of discussions about a peace agreement. The chiefs Te Purewa, of Tūhoe, and Moko-nui-a-rangi, of Te Arawa, negotiated a tatau pounamu. The Tama-kaimoana section of Tūhoe did not support the tatau pounamu and in fact challenged it by attacking Hine-i-turama's party. But the results were disastrous for Tama-kaimoana, and the peace agreement held.

Case 3: Te Karau-uhi-rangi, Ngāi Te Rangi

A Te Arawa war party led by Te Roro-o-te-rangi attacked Ngāi Te Rangi at Maketu. His army was reputed to be a thousand strong (Stafford 1967:123). As the battle raged on, Te Roro and his army could see that they were beginning to gain the upper hand and it looked as though they would win. Therefore many people would be killed or made prisoners. During the thick of battle the attackers heard a woman, Te Kurau-uhi-rangi, singing a farewell song to her children. She is reputed to have said to her husband, 'I am crying over our children. Our male children I do not care so much about as they are men of war.' After her song she climbed up the parapet of the fortified pā and called out to Te Roro-o-te-rangi, 'Will you not spare this pā?'

He replied that he was willing to do so. So she called out again, 'Will your war party listen to you?'

He replied that they would obey him. So the battle ceased. Te Kurau-uhi-rangi came out with presents to seal a peace agreement between the warring group. She brought a greenstone mere called Kaitangata, a gourd ornamented with albatross feathers, and a special kind of cloak. Following this event some key marriages were arranged. According to Stafford (1967:123) Maruhinga-ata, a woman of Tapuika, was given to a man of Ngāi Te Rangi. Ure-taka-roa was given to Tahere of Ngāi Te Rangi and Paruhi-te-rangi of Te Arawa was given as wife to Pare-wai-tai of Ngāi Te Rangi.

Case 4: Te Ao-kapu-rangi, Tapuika and Ngāti Rangiwewehi

In about 1823 Hongi, with an army of 1200, arrived at Rotorua to storm Mokoia. Among the party were several women. One of them was Te Ao-kapu-rangi, an Arawa woman taken to wife by Te Wera Hauraki, one of the leading chiefs of the northern army. She belonged to Tapuika and Ngāti Rangiwewehi (Stafford 1967:177). This woman played a remarkable role in the relationship between Hongi Hika and his people on the one hand and Te Arawa on the other. Even though she had been captured and taken to wife by a Ngā Puhi chief she had managed to win the respect of the warrior chiefs. She made it known that she feared and cared for her people and did not want to see them slaughtered.

The first remarkable event she initiated was to persuade the attackers to spare her Ngāti Rangiwewehi relatives (Stafford 1967:178). Her request was discussed and agreed to. So she and a co-wife set off in a small canoe to Mokoia to ask her Ngāti Rangiwewehi relatives to leave Mokoia in peace. Hikairo, the chief of Ngāti Rangiwewehi, thanked her and said that Ngā Puhi was generous in their offer of safety for them, but his people would remain at Mokoia with the rest of Te Arawa.

Ngā Puhi did not attack Mokoia straight away. They took their time. On the third day they landed a force on the island and the actual battle began.

During the heat of the battle, and when many Te Arawa men had been shot, Te Ao-kapu-rangi appealed again to spare her people. And after much persuasion Hongi agreed to spare only those who were prepared to follow an old tikanga well known by warriors. He agreed to spare any Te Arawa person who walked or crawled between her thighs and was thus rendered noa and no longer able to fight.

But she was able to extend the tikanga. What she did was to run to the house, Tama-te-kapua, climb up on the roof and sit astride the top so that more people could 'pass between her thighs'. Her people responded by filling the house so it was crammed with people. Through her action many people were saved.

Her final act afterwards was to play a leading role in negotiating a peace agreement. She gathered the chiefs of Te Arawa together – Hikairo of Ngāti Rangiwewehi was prominent among them – and a peace agreement was settled at Kaiweka. Then they all went to Mokoia where the majority of Ngā Puhi were and, in front of the house Tama-te-kapua, Pomare and Te Wera spoke in support of the peace agreement. Te Wera was reputed to have said something like this: 'This is a binding peace with thee, O Hikairo! also with your young relative Hihiko and your cousin Te Ao-kapu-rangi which will not be broken by me or Ngapuhi, for ever and ever' (Stafford 1967:182).

Peace agreements with the government
Case 1

The Government set aside a piece of land known as Te Putere near Matata and various tribal groups who had been fighting against the government of the day were sent to this place. Te Kooti sent women to Whakatane to make peace with the settlers. Elements of Ngāti Whare and Warahoe went to Te Putere, and stayed there. This group met Mr Clarke, the native commissioner, and arranged a peace agreement with him. They took a famous greenstone patu named Hau-kapua as the symbol of a tatau pounamu (Best 1996:664).

Case 2

Another event occurred at Ruatoki on 25 September 1870 when a peace agreement was negotiated between Te Whenua-nui and Major Mair. In order to bind the peace Tūhoe offered two greenstone weapons and three cloaks which were handed over to the Government. Major Mair offered in return a watch, a gold pen, a gold ring and a shawl. The watch was called Maunga-a-rongo (Best 1996:665).

Conclusions

It is evident from the literature that the process of hohou rongo, of seeking a peace agreement, was common and it was, in fact, a necessary part of warfare. Tribal groups that had many borders to protect, such as Ngāti Awa and Tūhoe, were frequently involved in warfare and so it is not surprising that both were involved in a number of peace agreements. Political reality led and persuaded chiefs to agree to settle differences and bring about a state of peace in the land so that the people were able to enjoy their culture and concentrate on the food quest without fear of constant attack.

The peace agreements show a different side to the character of our tīpuna. Where diplomacy was required, it was forthcoming. Skill in negotiating was necessary, and once a peace agreement was firmly in place the parties had to honour it and would do so for many years. The word of a chief backed up by the hapū and iwi was his bond. But it was a bond that was properly lashed together and given a ritual cover.

These agreements also illustrate the humanitarian aspect of Māori leadership. It was not all slaughter, and winning at any cost. Some heroic deeds relating to a real concern for the people were evident. We speak of the value 'he aroha ki te tangata' (love for the people). That value was manifested in some of the battles that took place. Most important, however, was the willingness to forgive and show compassion for the people. This great human value often becomes a victim of warfare and is set aside as the warriors give way to the other value of seeking revenge, utu.

Some leaders stand out from their peers as being noble in their thinking, compassionate and able to look beyond the events of the day. They are often compared to the ruthless type of leader who showed no mercy, expected none, and slaughtered hundreds. The leaders who negotiated peace agreements were often warriors themselves, but they were also diplomats and politicians and understood human nature. They were sometimes seen as weak because they showed compassion.

Chieftainesses involved in diplomacy and peace agreements were renowned for their concern for the community and for the people at large. Their actions were clearly seen as arising from a concern for the whānau, for the hapū and the tribe as a whole. They had their own way of persuading leaders of the attacking groups to show compassion. They did this by exhibiting great compassion themselves and being unequivocal about this. They were convincing advocates for their people and probably had a reputation for caring.

The chiefs, on the other hand, were also concerned about their personal mana, because they stood as a symbol for the whole group. Sometimes this concern got in the way of compassion and opportunities for diplomacy were lost. In the end, great mana was attributed to these leaders who exhibited a real compassion for people and where possible avoided wholesale slaughter. There is no doubt there is a beauty in a tatau pounamu, in a peace agreement that is meant to be permanent. Leaders who were prominent in bringing this sort of agreement to a successful conclusion are remembered for their humanitarian spirit. Likewise prominent women who saved many lives in their time are remembered and need to be given more credit for what they accomplished on behalf of the people.

Perspectives

Peace between Te Urewera and Ngāti Kahungunu

The Urewera and their allies now advanced to the attack on Puke-karoro, before reaching there they were met by Te Ra-ka-tau, the father of the late Ihaka Whanga (our ally in the war with Te Kooti, 1869–70) who was distantly related to some of the Urewera, and therefore, although a member of Ngati Kahungunu was quite safe amongst the latter tribe's enemies. He endeavoured to make peace with the others and for that purpose presented the Urewera people with a valuable mere named 'Te Rama-apakura'. His overtures were clearly not acceptable to the whole of the chiefs for after telling Te

Ra-ka-tau not to enter Puke-karoro, they laid siege to the latter pa.

After some time Te Ra-ka-tau again attempted to make peace, and presented the allies with two other mere, named 'Kahawai' and 'Kauae-hurihia'. But the siege went on, until the inhabitants were reduced to great straits ...

The pa eventually fell to the allies and there was a great slaughter ... After this a peace was made and some guns were given to Ngati Kahungunu to bind it. My informant, Tamarau, said the pa fell in the month of August, and we know that the year was 1824.

– Smith 1910:328

This was a singular peace-making. When Te Ahuru of Tuhoe met Hipara of Kahu-ngunu in order to arrange a peace, he had with him his dog, named Te Iwi-mokomoko. It appears that our old friend Mohaka, the tohunga or priest of Te Wai-roa, had again been indulging in visions and prophecies, after the manner of his kind. He had, in a dream, seen a dog, and seems to have considered it as a sign from the gods. He told his people (Ngati-Kahu-ngunu) that if the dream dog be seen in life, then a permanent peace would be assured. When Te Ahuru arrived at the meeting place, Mohaka at once claimed that the dog accompanying the Tuhoean envoy was the one he had seen in his dream. This was an excellent omen. Of a verity peace was assured. Then Mohaka renamed the dog Awhi-nuku. Hipara said, 'I will give my daughter Hine-ki-runga to Tuhoe, in order to firmly cement the peace-making.' Puhi-rua and the tribe agreed. The boundary between the two tribes, Tuhoe and Ngati-Kahu-ngunu, was laid down at Kuha-tarewa and Turi-o-Kahu, two hills near the Wai-kare-taheke River. Then the hill Kuha-tarewa was 'set up' by the Kahungunu tribe as a female, and Turi-o-Kahu as a male. This act was as an equivalent for the word of Hipara, viz., that he would give his daughter in marriage to Tuhoe. The mountain marriage corresponded to the human marriage. It was to end the war. And so peace has endured and endured even unto this time, the time of the white man.

– Best 1972:551

11

Te Takoha: Gift Giving

When a person makes a presentation of a gift to another they may use the words 'he koha tēnā nāku ki a koe' (that is a gift, which I present to you) (Williams 1967:123) or 'tēnei te taonga ki a koe' (this is a highly prized object that is presented to you) (Firth 1959:315). Or they may use other words. But some prized object is being transferred from one group or individual to another group or individual. The transaction is either the beginning of a new exchange relationship with others or it is part of a series begun long ago by a member of the whānau, hapū or iwi.

Firth (1959:423) stated that the transaction of making a gift appeared on the surface to be a spontaneous act based on free will and choice and given in good grace. But he implied that exchanging gifts in the Māori world occurred within a cultural and historical context (although he did not use these words). Instead he focused upon obligations, and he thought that there was a compulsion to give something and there was an obligation upon the recipient to accept the gift 'in good grace'.

The proper way

An important point to make about gift giving is that there is a tradition behind it, there are tikanga involved in the exchange and there are many precedents as models of proper ways of behaving. While much has changed since contact with another culture, some of the more traditional forms of gift giving are still being practised and the same customary practices apply.

Another point is that gift giving is part of an exchange of gifts. A return gift is expected some time in the future. In some cases the return may be made fairly soon after the initial gift transaction. But often the recipient looks for an opportune occasion to make a return presentation and this may be many years later. Sometimes the object given as a gift is returned to the donor having fulfilled its purpose of cementing relationships or honouring a particular important guest. There are many instances of prized objects such as cloaks being returned years later to the family of the donors.

The return gift

The next point is that the return gift cannot be less in value than the initial gift. The guiding principle, according to Firth (1959:423), is 'to give as much as possible in return for anything received'. One may give the same gift back, or one similar to it, or one equivalent to it, but the preferred option is to improve the value. Some have likened this to interest accruing on the value of the object. But the important issue is not to give offence to the partner in the transaction or belittle the thought behind the gift or the gift itself. There are many factors to weigh up and there are long-term relationships to consider. The object returned carries a burden of social, economic and political considerations. The pragmatic outcome desired is that the exchange partner is satisfied and the relationship is enhanced.

The rule of taonga

The object given needs to fit into the category of taonga, that is, it must be highly prized and preferably an heirloom. Greenstone objects, big or small, qualify as taonga because greenstone itself is highly regarded throughout the Māori world. Heirlooms or objects made of parāoa (whalebone) also qualify. Cloaks commonly feature as gifts and have always been highly regarded. Tiki are especially favoured as gifts and this appears to be the case whether they are heirloom items or recently made. The important factor is the quality of workmanship and the symbolic value of the object. Decorated baskets can be regarded as qualifying for gifts and again, quality is the key factor. Whāriki used to be highly valued as gifts but have become rare and are less likely to be included as gifts. It is notable that floor mats feature prominently in the gifts made by members of other Polynesian cultures.

Relationships

An important factor in gift giving is the whakapapa of the partners, that is, their genealogical position which in part governs their social standing. Whakapapa implies mana and so the exchange relationship should enhance mana. Not all relationships are equal and some are quite unequal. But all require care in decision-making. The culmination of expectations and judgments about appropriateness is the gift itself. The taonga chosen enhances the exchange relationship.

According to Firth (1959:297–98) the 'quantity and value of these gifts tended to increase with the rank and hereditary position of the chief of the tribe, his prestige, and the following which he was able to gather around him'. It was expected, however, that a chief would be liberal towards his people and that his resources would be made available at gatherings of the people to honour births, marriages, birthdays and deaths. A general principle is that the exchange of gifts should add some-thing to the mana of the partners and not in any way diminish their mana. Some gift exchanges are pitched at an intertribal level and are essentially ceremonial in nature. Some are made as affirmations of kin-ship ties that originated in earlier times as a result of political alliances symbolised in arranged marriages. The alliances are reaffirmed from time to time either by arranging further marriages or by simply exchanging feasts. Thus, gift giving might serve political, social, and economic ends. Some gifts may focus on friendships and alliances at hapū and whānau level and others might serve interpersonal ends.

Exchange of products

Some intertribal gift exchanges were formerly largely economic in purpose as when coastal dwellers exchanged food supplies with inland tribes. Here, items of food not necessarily available to inland tribes were given to them in exchange for food items that were a specialty in inland areas such as huahua (preserved birds). Seafood was always highly desired by inland-dwelling people and one way of having access was by way of an exchange relationship. Some of these exchanges extended to other desired items such as greenstone, either in raw form or already fashioned into adze blades, tiki and other ornaments. Finely made cloaks were formerly acquired through these relationships and networks.

Tika: good grace

Principles of reciprocity, equivalence and manaakitanga mediated by whakapapa, mana and relationships guided the actions of gift-exchange partners. Haggling over whether a gift is appropriate or not was not a part of traditional gift giving. The donor needed to make a wise judgment as the responsibility for the selection of the gift was placed squarely on the shoulders of the party presenting a gift. Negotiation by haggling was not regarded as 'good grace' or as tika. And as already mentioned the recipients were bound to accept the choice in good grace and keep their complaints, if any, to themselves.

However, Firth (1959:296) recorded an instance where the recipient did not receive the gift in good grace. This involved the Wairarapa chief Te Akitu-o-te-rangi, who asked his neighbours to help fill his store of preserved birds. The people responded by giving their time and one day brought the gourds of preserved birds to the chief. There were ten gourds, all full to the top except the last one. Te Akitu-o-te-rangi asked for the name of the man who brought the tenth calabash that was half full. He ordered this man to be killed and eaten. Apparently, a tikanga had been broken: a half-filled calabash was presented and should not have been. It would have been more acceptable to present nine full calabashes than to include a tenth. The story could be far-fetched and told to emphasise the tikanga of never presenting a gift in a receptacle that is half full or half empty.

The role of tapu

The most important thing about a gift exchange is that, once activated, the exchange comes under the rules of tapu. There is an expectation of good faith among the parties that each will act according to the tikanga of gift giving. This means that a relationship is established and that the relationship needs to be nurtured and protected. Failure to reciprocate in a transaction is regarded as a breach of tapu and of good faith. Utu might be expected in such a case. Firth (1959:337) recorded the case of Te Angiangi who gave land to the Kahungunu chief Te Whatu-i-apiti because he was unable to reciprocate with a hākari. Failure to reciprocate resulted in feelings of guilt, which preyed on the mind, affected relationships and made the guilty one open to ritual forms of punishment.

Gifts of food

Gift giving is usually an essential part of social ceremonies such as birthdays, weddings, anniversaries and events such as pokinga taringa (piercing the ears of a child), a practice currently undergoing a revival, or receiving moko or welcoming important guests. Providing a hākari is not only an expected part of manaakitanga but it is also an occasion for gift giving in the form of food. Huge amounts of food might be set before the guests for them to eat or to take away. Specialist and delicacy items were often presented.

Binding a marriage

Feasts were an expected part of traditional marriage ceremonies such as the following:

1. Pākūwhā: a feast given at the handing over of the bride. Taonga were presented as well.
2. Whare tuatahi: a feast given by the husband's group.
3. Tahua roa: heaps of food were presented to the guests to be consumed on site. (Firth 1959:315–16)

Guests brought their gifts of fine cloaks, ornaments, and weapons and laid them at the feet of the married couple. Today there is usually one main feast for a marriage and gifts are brought and laid upon a special table and displayed for the people to see. Display was an essential part of traditional gift giving.

Hākari taonga: feast for exchanging gifts

In traditional times iwi might be invited to attend a hākari taonga as the main focus of the meeting. This was a special feast at which taonga were displayed and exchanged. There were feast exchanges. Each feast was set in a context of tikanga with chants and songs composed for the occasion. If it was a matter of distributing food an expert orator was assigned to carry out this function with wit and a sure knowledge of whakapapa. If cooked food was being presented the hosts might call upon their young women to deliver the food ceremonially and as they walked towards the guests they sang a special song for each type of food.

A hākari taonga implied that taonga would be exchanged during the day. The tangata whenua would display their taonga such as cloaks, blankets, floor mats and baskets, and the guests would be expected to add to the collection which would then be distributed ceremonially by calling guests to come forward to receive their allocation of gifts.

Te Wherowhero's hākari of 1844 at Remuera is a classic example of a huge feast that lasted a whole week and went through a vast amount of food. For Te Wherowhero the hākari itself was a gift to his guests, a paying back for various favours and a return of what was done for him at some earlier date. Some would say the feast was a display of his great mana and wealth. According to Firth (1959:321–31) the food consisted of dried shark, potatoes, pork, flour, sugar, rice and other delicacies. There were 11,000 baskets of potatoes, 9,000 sharks and 100 pigs consumed at the hākari. Obviously a hākari of this magnitude ended a transaction rather than continued or even began one. A hākari on this level tended to impoverish the contributing tribes.

Te tuku whenua: gifting land

Land was sometimes gifted and would be classified as whenua tuku. Sometimes military allies were rewarded for their services by a gift of land. Maning, former chief judge of the Native Land Court, stated in a letter written by him on 26 November 1877 that 'gifts of land unconditional were sometimes made by one tribe to another in acknowledgement of services as allies of war. Such a gift would, of course, constitute good ground of title' (Smith 1942:43).

On other occasions land might be gifted to hapū who had been dispossessed or banished. In this case, use of the land was gifted, not necessarily the title. The recipients were required to make an annual tribute to the landlords as an acknowledgement of the gift. According to Firth (1959:295–96) if no tribute was offered and there was no protest about this fact, the users considered themselves to be the owners. Acceptance of an annual return gift from the users was based on the right to use the land with the goodwill of the owners. Tributes kept the exchange relationship in place. Over time the practice could have become intolerable.

Land might be gifted as part of the gift exchanges expected in important marriages. For example the prospective husband might be offered a piece of land to encourage him to live with his wife's people. The land would be regarded as belonging to him whether he lived on it or not.

In the case of Te Angiangi land was gifted to his exchange partner as a way of terminating a series of exchanges. As taonga, land was regarded as probably the ultimate gift. One could not do better than receive a gift of land.

Koha at the marae

Williams (1957:123) defines koha as 'respect', 'regard', 'present' and 'gift'. It is a term that has wider implications and connotations than its common contemporary meaning of a gift of money. The notion of koha has today become a very common but often misunderstood term. In traditional times koha was not given in the form of money. Rather individuals made a contribution, say, to a tangihanga. They gave food, or lent taonga for display, or went out to the sea to gather shellfish, or gave their time in support of the bereaved whānau. Visitors who came from specialist food regions might contribute some preserved birds or dried shark, or they might bring crayfish. Families living close to the marae contributed baskets of cooked food. All were giving koha and all were contributing to the occasion in a display of kinship solidarity. Others gave their time and skills to the occasion, sometimes for several days. Each was giving a koha.

Today, koha are mostly given in the form of money and visitors to the marae rarely bring food. Local people, however, are expected to give what they can in the way of food such as meat, kūmara, kamokamo in season, water melons in season, pūhā, watercress and so on. There is the rare gift of a bucket of mutton-birds from a visitor from the South Island. More commonly, distant visitors find it easier and much more convenient to bring money.

The public koha

At a tangihanga however there are tikanga associated with giving a koha and most people who have attended a tangihanga know the tikanga. Usually at the end of the series of whaikōrero given by orators of a specific tribe the koha of money is placed on the ground around about the middle of the space between the two sets of speakers. This occurs usually after a concluding waiata has been performed. The speaker then sits down and a person from the marae side walks over to collect the koha and acknowledge it. In some tribal areas there is a karanga to acknowledge the koha before the collector moves. The koha is collected, a short speech of acknowledgement given and then the collector retreats backwards so as not to turn his back on the visitors until a reasonable distance is covered. Then he turns and walks straight back to his seat.

Often the donor thinks of their koha as a whakaaro that is, it is only a thought. The orator might announce their koha as follows: 'He whakaaro tēnei nā taku hapū' (This is a thought contributed by my hapū).

This form of gift giving is very public and is located within a ceremony. The act is seen and witnessed, but the amount given is not disclosed. At some marae, a receipt is given before the visitors leave and so a record is kept of all donors and the amounts given. As noted previously, at some marae the complete list is put up on the window of the wharenui and in this sense is 'published'. This is done for a variety of reasons. The first is to let the hapū know that the record of koha was properly documented by the whānau and displayed for all to see. Next, hapū members are informed about who contributed and who did not. But most important is the obligation upon the recipients of the koha to reciprocate in the future. Members who study the lists are able to recognise who had paid back their koha and who were initiating an exchange.

The private koha

In some cases, especially at a tangi, the contribution or koha is given privately to a member of the bereaved family. When this happens there is a clear signal that the contribution is a one-way one. No return is expected. Increasingly today most of the koha placed formally on the marae are regarded as one-way. The reason is that the generations of today have forgotten about the importance of koha and the expectation of reciprocity. We no longer hear stories of koroua and kuia who made it their life's work to return the koha given to them by attending tangihanga all over the country and through their presence, whakaaro and aroha effectively paid up all the outstanding ceremonial debts of their people and their iwi.

The modern koha of money still carries with it the obligation to help, to show manaakitanga and aroha for the people. What has decreased is the obligation of reciprocity, of some time in the future returning the gift, of someone or a group within the hapū taking on the responsibility of repaying the thought by undertaking to go to a host of hui for several years at great personal cost. In the modern context of difficulties in finding employment and in not having sufficient money to meet daily needs, this part of the obligation to reciprocate is becoming too difficult to meet. The obligation to help one's kin and friends remain strong, but often the helper is also struggling to make ends meet and can ill afford to assist anyone else. Nonetheless, they are expected to help in some way, however big or small. It is fair to say that it is only during a tangihanga that kin appear to rally in force and come from all parts of the country and sometimes from all parts of the world in order to fulfil social obligations.

He kanohi i kitea: a face seen

The other important aspect of the koha is the presence of the individual and supporting group presenting it. Making the effort to visit and be seen at the marae is appreciated. This adds a meaningful social dimension to the presentation and emphasises the seriousness of the process of gift giving. Sometimes the supporting group is large, say a busload or two, and they make a big impression which adds to the mana of the occasion and hence contributes to the tapu nature of the event. Sometimes it is the manner in which the koha is put down that enhances the occasion. A face seen, he kanohi i kitea, is an important value in itself and this could be a gift. But if that face is backed up by an impressive haka team and a tohunga well versed in traditional karakia it can be seen that they are all part of the gift that is given with due solemnity. They enhance the process.

Conclusions

Although many of the tikanga associated with gift giving have become onerous and it is difficult to meet traditional obligations, there are groups around the country who still practise a range of procedures and strive to meet the obligations set down by custom. There are others who practise parts such as keeping a list of all donors to a tangihanga and putting the list up on a board at the marae for all to see. This is a transparency measure so that all know who gave to the occasion. It is also a monitoring mechanism to ensure that several people of the hapū are aware of an obligation to reciprocate.

At many tangihanga today a member of the whānau keeps a notebook into which all koha received are recorded with amounts and names of the donors when this is possible. Often it is difficult to know the exact donors because visitors pool their contributions.

At important tribal hui gifts might be given and exchanged. While it appears much has been lost, a surprising amount of gift giving is still practised among many iwi and we might, in fact, see more of it in the future rather than less!

Perspectives

Koha

Often the generosity of the guests leaves a credit balance; for example, at one *hui* I attended the bills amounted to $350 and the donations to $445. Any extra money is paid into the *marae* or family account, depending on who is running the hui, or to the bereaved family after a *tangi*. A detailed list of donations is kept so that each can be handsomely repaid when the time comes. If the *hui* runs at a loss the default will be met by those who attend the meeting, or out of the *marae* account.

– Salmond 1975:114

gift. A present given to someone, which may be a major distribution technique in early society. Giving presents has an important economic function in all the North American tribes and Polynesia. It is closely linked with a strong sense of personal dignity and self-appreciation. Gift-giving peoples often have institutionalised boasting and indulge in intentional and conspicuous waste. A gift as a voluntary offering to please or propitiate is often found on ceremonial occasions.

gift, fatal. A gift given to an enemy, who unwittingly takes and uses it as if it came from a friend. Fatal gifts may bring the recipient death or misfortunes.

gift, Indian. A gift for which it is understood that another gift is to be given in return. The term arose from the common American Indian custom of asking a gift for a gift.

gift, morning. A gift given by the husband to his wife on the morning after the wedding takes place.
  – Winick 1970:231

The process of exchange by gifts with an absence of bargaining raises two questions the elimination of which will do much to make clear the central motive of the return gift and what determined its quantity or value? When we proceed to a further analysis of the situation we find that for both of these aspects there was a definite mechanism of regulation. Beneath the surface of spontaneity and liberality worked a set of forces which impelled people to act in the presented way, and ensured that every man received approximately his due.
  – Firth 1959:411

12
Rāhui, Aukati: Ritual Prohibitions

In this chapter two forms of tikanga are described – rāhui and aukati. The tikanga of rāhui has often appeared to include the aukati, but it will be useful to separate them.

Both tikanga focus on prohibiting and preventing people from having free access either to food resources or to land and water. The rāhui may embrace an extensive area, as in the case of the rāhui established on the authority of Muriwai (famous sister of Toroa, captain of the *Mātaatua* waka) when her twin sons drowned near Tauranga: a rāhui that prohibited the taking of seafood was placed on the coast from Nga Kuri a Wharei (Cape Colville) to Tikirau (near Te Kaha). Or the rāhui can be applied to a more confined space: a bend in a river, or a particular part of a coast where a drowning occurred. Similarly, an aukati can also be extensive or very restricted. The aukati is much like the notion of 'drawing a line in the sand' that cannot be crossed, or it might be a sign on a post or tree that blocks access to a pathway. Again, however, the aim of the aukati is to prohibit and limit access of people to where they might want to go and to what they might want to do beyond the line.

Types of rāhui
Basically, the rāhui is a means of prohibiting a specific human activity from occurring or from continuing. It might be directed at a group of people or it might be focused upon a single individual; there might be a visible signal, such as a post, to let people know that a rāhui has been stood up (whakatū – to cause to stand). There may be a special ceremony to introduce it or it may be simply announced or proclaimed. Similarly

its conclusion might be marked by ritually pulling down something – the post, or the leaves or cloth tied around it – or by an appropriate announcement, or by everyone noting that the time of restriction agreed upon at the commencement had expired.

Rāhui may be categorised in various ways. There are those with 'teeth' and those without, as suggested in Best's writings (1924). Firth (1929:259–60) distinguishes between 'severe' and 'mild' rāhui, a distinction which he learnt from Best. Probably the most useful way of beginning to differentiate between various examples of rāhui is by examining the take, and/or the sequences of events when a rāhui was regarded as an appropriate response.

The most common types of rāhui are drowning rāhui and the conservation rāhui. These two are closely interlinked and, in fact, one implies the other. A third type might be referred to as the 'political rāhui' or as the 'punitive rāhui'. But this is more like an aukati, which will be described later.

In the first type, the cause which warrants imposition of the rāhui is that the land or the water, or both, have become affected to a dangerous level by the tapu of death. This in turn affects the food supply. The drowning rāhui might be described as the more common model of rāhui. It is one remembered by the elders and is still practised today. Deaths on land, formerly another cause for the application of the rāhui, are rarely considered today.

The tapu rāhui

The examples given by Best (1904:84) cover a range of take. In one case a rāhui was placed on the land and water of Okahu at Te Whaiti when the children of the chief died. According to Best, this 'was simply a ban placed upon the food products of that district'. The ban was lifted in 1847. Unfortunately, Best did not give the precise cause of death (we can only guess that it was by misadventure) nor how long the rāhui lasted. But he did say that no post was put up and no special ceremony was performed. This was a rāhui by proclamation.

In another example from the same area of the Urewera, Best says that the Whirinaki River was made tapu when the blood of warriors slain at the defence of Okarea Pā stained its usually clear waters. In this case, Best

(1904:84) noted that a special whakanoa ritual was performed in order to return the river to normal use. A human sacrifice, a slave named Taupoki, was killed, cooked at Waikotikoti Pā, Te Whaiti, and eaten by the people. No reason is given as to why the rāhui was terminated in this way.

The intensity of the pollution varies according to the rank of the victims. In the example discussed in chapter 10 when several Arawa chiefs – Tionga, Te Waha-kai-kapua, Te Hurinui and Te Rangi-ka-tukua – were killed at the battle of Puke-kai-kāhu, a large area, which included Lake Rerewhakaitu, was placed under a rāhui for several years. So intense was the tapu that the land and water in the area was completely avoided. On genealogical evidence, the rāhui was probably placed around the 1830s. It was not lifted until 1869 (Stafford 1967:174).

A widely known example is the Tūwharetoa case when the paramount chief Te Heuheu Tukino and his people were buried in a landslide at Mount Kakaramea on the shores of Lake Taupo in May 1846 (Ngata 1959, 1:190–95). As in the previous case, land and water in the immediate vicinity were made out of bounds and no food resources of any sort could be taken. The rāhui lasted for five years. This was the length of time that was thought necessary for the 'radioactive' nature of the tapu of death to dissipate into the atmosphere and become harmless.

As soon as the rāhui was lifted, the first fish caught in Lake Taupo were taken to the high priest Te Takinga, cooked and eaten ritually by him alone (Buller 1895:152). In this case, too, Buller notes that the chief of the land, Te Heuheu Iwikau, exercised his right both to apply the rāhui and to lift it.

The drowning rāhui

A classic example of the rāhui, following a drowning, is provided by James Cowan (1930:70–71). The incident occurred in August 1900. A party of schoolchildren from Omaio were drowned near the mouth of the Motu River while attempting to cross it in a canoe. The Whānau-a-Apanui tribe immediately applied a rāhui upon the land and water near the site of the disaster. The outer regions of the affected area from Te Kaha to Opape were under restriction for one year, while the central area was banned for four years. The restriction was observed and anyone challenging the ban was likely to find himself the target of yet another means of social control, the muru. A neighbouring chief of Maraenui 'trampled on' the rāhui quite unwittingly when he took a drink from the restricted portion of the river. Cowan (1930:71) informs us that a taua muru from a hundred miles away (Gisborne) paid him a visit and the drink cost him an estimated fifty pounds.

The rāhui with 'teeth'

The last examples given above would be regarded by contemporary Māori elders as the most severe form of rāhui. However, it is very doubtful whether this is true. What Best (1904:84) regarded as 'the kind which is endowed with magic or supernatural powers' is certainly not the Christian rāhui of modern times. Rather it is the one which has 'teeth' and is believed capable of 'biting' those who challenge it. A tohunga versed in the karakia requisite to establishing the power of the rāhui is needed to provide the 'teeth'. He must also know the incantations for 'sharpening the teeth' and for reinforcing its biting power (turuki i te kapu rāhui).

Best (1904:85) explains that there is a pou rāhui (a post) to which is attached a maro (apron) consisting of a few fronds, leaves, or a fragment of cloth. In the incantations, the maro is added to a stone which together form the whatu of the rāhui. According to Best, it is the whatu which contains the 'true power' and the 'life destroying, magic power' that is put there in the first place, by the tohunga when he calls upon Tangaroa, God of the sea, to sharpen his teeth and cause the flies to swarm and the maggots to crawl.

These material symbols of the power of the rāhui are concealed some distance away from the rāhui post. A false maro is attached to replace the one over which special karakia had been recited. The charmed tokens, hidden away in this manner, are called kapu, another term for whatu. It is the kapu which inflicts punishment upon anyone challenging its effectiveness. However, it is not guaranteed to act in all circumstances because the kapu is believed to lose power and 'go to sleep'. That power has to be brought to full strength by periodic karakia turuki.

The conservation rāhui

This type of rāhui is usually described as the mild one, the one with no teeth or the one over which the karakia whakaoho (incantations to awaken) are recited. Its purpose is apparently not to destroy but rather to restore the productivity of the land (Best 1904:86). In this case, the kapu together with the mauri of the land are taken periodically to a sacred fire (ahi taitai) and there special invocations are recited 'in order to restore and retain the productiveness, health, welfare etc. of the food products, as also of the land and people'.

In recent times, the rituals that restore to tired and misused earth and water their vitality and essence have been rarely if ever performed.

The conservation rāhui was used to protect the products of the land and water. Best (1904:83) mentions forest products (berries, birds, fish, cultivated crops, fern root, flax) and places where red ochre was obtained. What is interesting is that the list is not confined to food resources alone but includes other products.

An example, described by Best (1904:88), concerns the Ngāti Apa (of Murupara) chief Tukuha, who set up a rāhui post at Te Rautawhiri. The post remained in the same position, but whenever the chief wanted to rāhui the eels of his part of the Rangitaiki River, he would hang 'one of his old garments' on it. That would signal a complete ban on that one resource, eels. In this instance, the name of the place, Te Rautawhiri (the leaves twisted on) indicates that it was used by custom as a place to signal a rāhui. Other stories told about Tukuha (Best 1904) also suggest that one of his particular tasks was controlling the supply of eels.

This seems to have been the case in other localities. For example, Piri Sciascia recalls that their chief at Porangahau always controlled the karengo (seaweed) season. No one could take any until he had obtained the 'first fruits'. Richard Taylor (1870:171–72) mentioned that kiekie (a plant used in tukutuku work) would be put under a rāhui until the fruit was properly ripe. A young man would be sent by the chief to check the fruit until it was deemed ready. At that point, the rāhui post was pulled down and according to Taylor 'the entire population go to "takahi" or "trample the wood".' In this instance, too, the first fruit was presented to the chief.

It seems that in most cases involving a conservation rāhui a post is 'put up'. In the Murupara example a garment was hung on the post.

Firth (1929:2601), however, mentions that in a case involving the conservation of the fish and bird life of the three lakes Tara, Kiwa and Poukawa, the posts were smeared with red ochre and this, apparently, was equivalent to tying an apron on each one. It is interesting in this instance that a challenger came along later and not only pulled out the rāhui posts but also burnt them.

The no-trespass rāhui or aukati

Most of the early ethnographers draw attention to the no–trespass rāhui that was put up in a place where it would be seen on a tree, across a track and so on. This type of rāhui could also be regarded as a conservation rāhui when it was used to protect resources. Best (1904:84) suggests, however, that more often than not, its purpose was to stop people from using a particular pathway. Best regarded this type as a 'minor form of tapu or rāhui', but he was mistaken in his opinion.

Interestingly, it is this sort of rāhui which is widely known in the Pacific and seems to have been used by both Melanesians and Polynesians. It is evidently an ancient cultural trait that might go back to the Lapita people who were the ancestors of the Polynesians.

The no-trespass rāhui is more commonly known as an 'aukati'. The word means to block and prevent one from passing over or through a defined line or it may refer to the 'line which one may not pass' (Williams 1957:22). Examples of the application of the aukati are many, but it is possible that its frequent use became necessary in the culture-contact situation especially during the 1860s when the sale of land to Pākehā buyers became a burning issue.

An aukati was established by a variety of means. A person who is an 'owner' or guardian of a property might declare an aukati without reference to anybody else. In this instance rights of use or of occupation, say over a block of land, are firmly established and not in dispute. A more usual way was for a meeting of the hapū or iwi to be called. The issue was then discussed and a decision agreed upon. Then the aukati would be established by public declaration and by the use of appropriate ritual. The tohunga would add the element of tapu to the aukati.

In all types of rāhui, power relations come into play and leaders put their reputations at risk. However, the political nature of the rāhui is most obvious when neither conservation or the tapu of death is the main reason for its application. Thus, it follows that the no-trespass rāhui or aukati is perhaps the most vulnerable to political use. There are, in fact, several examples of the aukati being used as a weapon to punish or to thwart for political reasons. On occasion, the rāhui may be used as a reaction to hearing something offensive.

For example, Tukaha, the Ngāti Apa chief mentioned earlier, put a rāhui on the eels of the Rangitaiki River because someone passed a disparaging remark about a hapū to which he belonged (Best 1904:88). Another instance of the same sort of reaction was recorded from the Taranaki area by Richard Taylor (1870:168–69). Up the Mokau River lived the chief, Te Kuri, and his community, at Motu Karamu. They were all Roman Catholics. Into their group came a German Protestant missionary, whom the chief's head-wife liked very much: she became his patron and his convert. Later, when the priest called into the village on his regular rounds, he scolded Te Kuri 'for suffering a heretical missionary to be located in his district' and he apparently called the intruder some insulting names. This infuriated the chief's wife who next morning put a rāhui on the river. The priest could not continue his journey because no one would take a canoe out. Eventually he was forced to go back. Although Taylor terms this a rāhui, it seems more like an aukati.

The aukati

The best example of a case involving high politics is the Ngāti Pikiao incident in the Rotorua area (Stafford 1967:368–70). In 1864, in an endeavour to get to Orakau to help the Ngāti Maniapoto leader Rewi Maniapoto in his fight against the Government, a party of volunteers made up of Ngāti Porou, Te Whānau-a-Apanui, Whakatōhea and Ngāti Awa men tried to cross Te Arawa territory at Lake Rotoiti. The chiefs of Ngāti Pikiao, a division of Te Arawa, declared an aukati and established a line which was not to be crossed by the volunteers. To understand the full significance of the action the reader needs to know that at this time Te Arawa was fighting on the government side. This rāhui, therefore, was to aid the Pākehā settlers and the Government. The volunteers tried to breach the line, but Te Arawa, with the backing of the Government, defended it successfully.

Later, when the volunteers tried to go via Maketu, they were blocked again by the aukati which had been extended to the coast and once more a battle followed. This time the hand of the Government was much more evident and the full political implications were not lost on those who participated.

This is a case where the rāhui was used to delay reinforcements to Waikato and so help government forces win the battle. The example is not one which is remembered with any relish or pride, but it is worth noting that Ngāti Pikiao also sent a hundred men to help Rewi Maniapoto. This fact is worth stressing if only to show that the chief might move in one direction while the people go in another.

An interesting example is recorded in a letter by Wiremu Kingi and several other Māori chiefs from Taranaki to Buller, resident magistrate in Wanganui. The chiefs complained about the Government trying to assert its mana over their land at Waikawa: 'Kaore matou e pai kia eke mai te mana o te Kawanatanga ki runga'. They had heard that the Government had put a rāhui on their land which removed from the Māori any right to go onto the land: 'Kua rongo hoki matou ka rahuitia e Kawanatanga kia kore ai he mana a nga Maori ki runga'. No date is given for the letter, but it was probably written in the 1840s. The incident referred to might have occurred on 4 November 1842 as the Williams refer in their diaries to Wiremu Kingi being upset over a rāhui (Porter 1974:226). In this instance what is identified as a rāhui is really an aukati.

As one may expect, the rāhui has been used in land disputes quite often. The Waikawa incident illustrates the use of the trespass or aukati concept in a manner so much akin to the rāhui that the owners saw it as such. It is possible that the resident magistrates and land agents actually modelled some of their land legislation on Māori concepts of control. There is little doubt that the Māori used the rāhui when they thought it was the right thing to do.

For example, Taylor White (1892:275) draws attention to a court case in Hastings on 25 February 1892. In the evidence, it was revealed that two men, Te Rangi-ka-mangungu and Hawea, had possession of a block of land extending from Te Whanga to Puketitiri and Titiokura at Mohaka. Ownership of the block was disputed by Ngāi Te Upokoiri. Rangi-ka-mangungu and Hawea, the occupiers of the block, 'put up rāhui all over it'. At Puketitiri, it was said that the rāhui was Piko, while at

Oinga or Hauhau it was Kauhoarangi, but it was not made clear if these were dead men or living men. White asked, 'How could men be "put up as rāhui?"' This question followed upon his discussion of the fact that at Hauhau, on the Omahu block, the chief Te Hauwaho impaled a woman on a rāhui post. Apparently she gave mana not 'only to the rāhui but also the claim of ownership'. Perhaps a further question could be asked: Was a person belonging to the tribe (or not necessarily of the tribe) sacrificed in order to transform a political rāhui or aukati into a rāhui tapu?

To conclude this section on political uses of the rāhui, it is as well to report again the words of Richard Taylor (1870:172) who said that a chief 'laid a ban upon whatever he felt disposed'. Continuing, he said, 'It was a great power, which could at all times be exercised for his own advantage, and the maintenance of his mana or dignity, which in some respects corresponded with manorial rights; frequently he would make some trifling circumstance the reason for putting a whole community to great inconvenience, rendering a road to the pa, perhaps the most direct and frequented, a grove, fountain or anything else, tapu, by his arbitrary will'. It is plain that the Reverend Richard Taylor did not like customs that affected his freedom of movement.

Kairāmua: eating the day before

When a rāhui is challenged or breached it is expected that there will be utu. An offence against a rāhui is called kairāmua (Best 1904:86) which refers to eating before the right time. The person who commits the offence is also called by the same name. On the authority of a Mātaatua informant, Williams' *Dictionary* (1957:89) says that the punishment for a kairāmua was to be killed, cooked and eaten. I have not so far found any reported case of this actually happening, but the threat was probably an effective deterrent.

In reference to either a conservation or a political rāhui which is applied on the basis of mana alone, Best (1904:87) says that 'witchcraft may be resorted to, in order to punish the offenders'. However, it is part of contemporary folk knowledge that some form of witchcraft is always associated with an aukati and especially with a rāhui. It is believed, for instance, that if you commit a kairāmua, some form of aituā (disaster) will follow. Typically, what is expected to happen is that some members of the offender's family will die and it is not until the third death has occurred that full utu is believed to have been made.

In earlier times, the punishment was apparently some wasting disease (Firth 1959:262) which infected the culprit. In this case, the notion of punishment by aituā still holds. The significant difference is that formerly the culprit alone was the target of utu whereas in more modern times it is the whānau or hapū.

There is little doubt that 'meddling with a rahui', as Firth (1959:262) put it, was dangerous and foolish because if magic failed then the kairāmua was open to reprisals of various sorts. The use of muru has already been referred to. Another instance of utu is recorded by Taylor (see perspectives, chapter 9). Probably the most important deterrent to breaching any rāhui, but especially the aukati, was fear of confrontation and violence. Firth (1972:262) drew attention to the Rangitāne case when that group applied a rāhui on their land in order to prevent another from occupying it. They erected a post called Puahi-te-ao. When the opposing tribe cut down the post, war between the tribes began in earnest.

The Arawa aukati mentioned earlier resulted in confrontation between opposing groups and ultimately men were killed. Defending the aukati was clearly linked to the defence of the integrity of the group. This was so at Lake Rotoiti when Ngāti Pikiao applied the aukati and had to defend it. Later, when the confrontation shifted to the Maketu end of Arawa territory, the result was the same: a battle, this time a huge loss of life, the integrity of the defenders was maintained and the transgressing group retreated. There must be numerous cases, however, of the sequence ending in triumph for the challengers. An infamous case is that of Ngāti Awa who, after declaring their aukati, were overrun by government forces which included men from neighbouring tribes. Their property was taken or destroyed.

In 1929 Firth was clearly of the opinion that it was fear of reprisals and loss of life that restrained people from committing a kairāmua. In his mind the moral aspect − the justice or correctness of the rāhui − was an issue of secondary importance. Today, however, the rāhui is still honoured because it is regarded as a sacred ritual of the traditional past and still useful today. This applies both to the conservation rāhui which is sometimes applied to conserve shellfish, and the rāhui tapu that is triggered by the loss of life through drowning. It is very noticeable, however, that the duration of a drowning rāhui is sharply reduced. This is due in part to the difficulty of persuading the community at large to observe the rāhui. Today seafood is in great demand by all sectors of our population. Efforts at conserving resources are often not appreciated by some of the public. Yet if rāhui are not applied resources may be exhausted and everyone suffers through such depletion.

Conclusions

It would be seen in the review of how the rāhui was used as a means of social and political control in times past that it was a creative tool capable of being applied in a variety of situations for a wide variety of reasons. I grouped the reasons into three main categories – death, conservation and political – and regarded each as a type of rāhui. In the first case, the tapu of death, the rāhui was closely associated with the religious beliefs of the Māori and with the traditional notion that death affects land, water, and people. A rāhui was a device for separating people from contaminated land, water and the products thereof. After an agreed lapse of time (several years formerly and now about three months for drowning) people become free once more to exploit the resources of land and water.

Conservation rāhui seem to have been associated not only with control of resources or the good of the whole community but also with the political use of resources. In the former, common-sense regulation of bird, fish and plant life seems to have been a consideration. It might even have been a technique of survival which enabled a group to act for the good of all members rather than allowing the greedy and the powerful to take all.

Nonetheless, it is evident that the conservation rāhui was sometimes used by the chiefs for political reasons which might have been related to the 'foreign policy' of the tribe or might have been for the personal aggrandisement of the rulers. In every case, however, the object was to separate the resources from the people and allow them to grow unmolested. In Grey's overland journey in 1841, which Firth (1972:260) mentioned, the party arrived at Lake Rotomahana and found it under a conservation rāhui. It was teeming with ducks and it was the breeding season. When the appropriate time came to take down the rāhui, the community hunted as a group.

In the third type of rāhui, or the aukati, the political factions were ritually separated and this separation provided an opportunity for the target group to consider its position and decide whether it was strong enough to challenge the defending group. The political advantage remained with the group that ordered the separation, put up the pou rāhui and stood by ready to defend it. Nonetheless, it needed to assess its strength relative to the other side and to calculate the political benefits that would accrue from such action.

An understanding of the rāhui used in its various forms indicates that the Māori of former times was not the political innocent that we of today might believe. They were able to act in a variety of ways; act imaginatively and boldly on a number of issues. The instrument that they thought with and with which they acted out their decisions and desires was the rāhui.

Perspectives

Challenging a rāhui

On purely economic grounds, also, a rāhui might be instituted to save the resources of a shell bank or a patch of forest from becoming depleted, the chief of the hapu might proclaim a rahui over it in consequence of which no one would be allowed to take supplies from there for a time. He would set up a post – but with no magic spells. This rāhui could be proclaimed by word of mouth. This type of rahui was the privilege of a chief and its observance was a tribute to his rank and status. Sometimes the rahui was an act of reservation of the food supply – not a complete ban. Thus when Wanikai of Te Roto-a-Tara wished to protect the fish and birds of the three lakes of Tara, Kiwa and Pou-Kawa, he did so in the usual manner by setting up a post on the shore of each lake and smearing them with *kokowai* (red ochre). This preserved the food supplies for Wanikau until one Mautahi pulled down and burned the posts.

– Firth 1959:259–60

Conserving food resources

In 1841 the writer of the account of Grey's overland journey remarks on having seen a small lake which the natives said abounded in eels. On a ridge just above the lake, a *rahui* was erected – made of an old musket barrel stuck in the ground – with a bunch of reeds fixed on. Such a *rahui* was treated with extreme respect – natives considering it an act of dishonesty to catch eels, fish, to hunt pigs, or destroy any game which it was erected to preserve. Dishonesty, however, is hardly the correct word; it was an immoral but foolhardy act, since, as he observes, the infringements of a *rahui* was a *casus belli*. It was fear of reprisals and not moral obloquy that restrained a person from disregarding such a sign.

When the same party arrived at Roto-Mahana, they found the lakes swarming with ducks – it being the breeding season. The birds were preserved by a most rigid tapu until the young were fledged. After this, the rāhui was lifted, birds caught and a great feast held.

– Firth 1959:260

Rāhuitia

The unfortunate drowning of a young Maori man earlier this week had been respected by the local Maori community at Plimmerton.

The Maori people have imposed the customary observance of not taking any seafood or fishing in the area between Hongoeka Bay and Wairaka Rock, Pukerua Bay, until the observance of the tapu is lifted after November 30th, 1978.

Maui Pomare, JP
25th October 1978

The concept of rāhui as observed in various Pacific islands
Marquesas

Kahui were temporary restrictions placed on foods by chiefs supported by the religious power of an inspirational priest. Such periods of prohibition preceded or followed the great festivals. Kahui on a smaller scale were placed by chiefs or other proprietors of the land on single plantations, groves, or sometimes on single trees.

Closely related to the kahui were seasonal tapu relating to foods. These differed from the kahui in being permanent prohibitions or restrictions. They were established laws, so to speak, and are to be distinguished from the occasional ordinances (kahui). Such a restriction was that which forbade fishing during the season when the breadfruit was maturing.

– Handy 1923:59–61

Temporary restrictions (kahui)

The *kahui,* or *ahui,* was a restriction or prohibition which owners had the right to put on produce of land in which they had vested interests. A chief, being regarded as owner of the tribal land as a whole, was able to lay such restriction on all the land or on particular crops when it was necessary. This was done before or in preparation for great festivals when much food was consumed, and after such festivals when the food supply had been exhausted. Thus, when necessary, the chief would place the *kahui* on fresh breadfruit, or on taro, or on coconuts, or on pigs, or *on* all of them if need be.

The *kahui* was announced by the chief's administrative tuhuna, and was enforced by them, and also by the fear of the evil consequences that would result from the infringement of a regulation which had received supernatural sanction because of some rite performed at the tribal temple. I was unable to obtain from informants any description of these rites. *Kahui* on smaller bits of property were signified by signs of certain kinds attached to the objects restricted. They were laid by means of the rite called *ko'aho,* which was performed by the *tuhuna ko'aho.* This accomplished the enforcement of the *kahui* by supernatural means. The custom of indicating restriction by means of *kahui* signs still persists in the islands. A coconut *kahui* was observed and photographed in the valley of Hana Upe on Hiva Oa. A pole about six feet long was erected on a deserted house platform.

– Handy 1923

Ceremonial food restrictions
The Society Islands

The laying of a rahui (ceremonial restrictions on localities, produce, or goods) required some sort of consecratory rite by which it was endowed with the power of some god or spell that would automatically inflict punishment on any who disregarded it. The removal of the rahui was accomplished by releasing the subject of restriction from tapu by the ritualistic presentation of a thanks-offering in kind – a pig, if pigs had been restricted, fish, fruits, etc. – and it was celebrated by a feast that betokened the release. Any land owner could place a rāhui upon his own property, or upon any part of it, as a single tree, supporting it by whatever psychic powers he could invoke on his marae or through witchcraft. A sign would be put up, such as a leaf of breadfruit or coconut or a stalk of sugar cane attached upside down to the trunk of a tree, indicating what kind of rahui it was, or as a fishing mimi, a pole with a piece of cloth attached stuck up on the reef. Various types of general rahui affecting his district or island were declared at times by the Arii. Such were the rahui maa restricting the use of land fruits, rahui ia, on fish in general, or on certain species at particular seasons, rahui roto i'a on fish traps and ponds, and rahui peho on the inner valleys, prohibiting the eating of pigs and fei. In addition to these there were the general rahui termed rahui o te ara roa, restrictions of the long road, which might last six months or even a year, declared in preparation for great festivals connected with birth, marriage, and death of Arii. These prohibited the consumption of all the best foods and the use of any new cloth, mats, canoes, etc., all of which were reserved for the great festival. The rahui of the Arii were inaugurated by means of a sacrificial rite on his marae, and were announced throughout his domain by messengers. When it came time for their removal, this was likewise announced in advance, and upon the prescribed day the people presented generous portions of their produce and the products of their craft to the Arii who made a division of the accumulated gifts, assigning a share for the gods, another for the priests, and others to the various groups and persons attached to his service, and then turning back a large portion to the people who scrambled for it, believing that in these returned shares of the offerings resided good luck.

– Handy 1930:49–50

13
Whakahuihui Tangata: Social Groupings

The literature on the social organisation of Māori is extensive and there are countless accounts of whānau, hapū and iwi. The aim here is not to review the literature but to look at the tikanga Māori aspects of the various groups that make up the Māori population today.

There was a time when it was feared that as a result of the culture contact situation we as a people encountered, we might fall by the wayside. But that is clearly not the case and now we number over half a million. But in growing and multiplying the traditional system has not kept pace with the changing situation. This is not a fault of the traditional social system but rather is due to various government measures which removed from Māori the ability to control and govern ourselves. The traditional system of whānau, hapū and iwi was frozen in the early 1900s.

Population decline would have caused some strains on the system, but by far the most obvious strains have been caused by the increase of population and the lack of an acceptable mechanism to recognise new groupings.

Urbanisation has been a large factor in scattering tribal populations so although the population is growing this fact is not reflected in the rural homelands where ancestral marae are situated. So on the one hand there is a shortage of personnel at the rural homelands and on the other there is a proliferation of small clusters of tribal members in various parts of Aotearoa and overseas, especially in Australia.

The rebuilding of Humpty Dumpty

It was Professor Bruce Biggs who first used the traditional nursery rhyme figure of Humpty Dumpty to indicate what had happened to Māori society, its systems and its knowledge base. He enshrined the metaphor in a 1989 article entitled 'Humpty Dumpty and the Treaty of Waitangi'. The situation is this. The bits of Humpty Dumpty, a metaphor for Māori culture, are scattered over New Zealand and in Australia, the United States and Great Britain. Only very rarely is Humpty Dumpty able to be rebuilt. This occurs at tangihanga when members of a whānau, or hapū, or iwi make an effort to return to the homelands. The other occasion is when a whānau reunion is organised and the whānau, now greatly expanded because of being frozen in time, gather together. In cases such as these – while it is a wonderful experience to meet everyone – the strains on the social system are easy to see. The dynamic aspects of the system have been knocked out and they need to be reinstituted and reformed.

New whānau need to be recognised, new hapū and new iwi. New terms such as whāmere (a transliterated word for family, the basic household unit) need to be accommodated. In other words there is a need for processes for growing out of one group and into another even though some authorities such as Steven Webster (1998:127–52) doubt that this is a natural progression.

A new Humpty Dumpty is required to take into account the scattered nature of tribal groups and the fact that most are reconstituting themselves in urban centres, the people themselves are finding ways of organising themselves and of accommodating to what may be called euphemistically the realities of the modern world.

Dynamic factors

In traditional times the system was subject to constant change. Warfare resulted in some groups being virtually wiped out, others forced to amalgamate with another hapū or iwi and others forced to forge alliances for survival. Epidemics also affected the system by reducing the capacity of the hapū or iwi to defend itself. But because epidemics are now under control, the food quest is no longer the issue it used to be, and warfare is a thing of the past, every descent group expands and none disappear.

During the New Zealand Wars and the period of confiscations many hapū were destroyed or dislocated or depopulated and are only now coming back again. The only real challenge to the system now appears in the form of assimilation: through defections to the great New Zealand society or through education out of Māori culture, through shifts in the marketplace and the quest for jobs. In the process the collectivity can become fragmented and the tribal estate deserted. On the other hand, there are social and economic forces at work which encourage Māori to regroup and reconstitute themselves. These combined forces sometimes conspire to enhance the traditional system and at other times they encourage some groups to compete with one another, which leads to conflict.

The creative and dynamic aspects of the social system need to be activated in order to allow large groups to segment if they so wish. In this case the number of hapū in an iwi would grow. More marae would be established and more meeting houses built. Groups of hapū in turn may want to become an iwi. The number of iwi could increase.

The legislative pathway

Unfortunately, when the Government in 1990 passed the Runanga Iwi Act an opportunity was presented for aspiring groups to appeal to an Act of Parliament to recognise them as iwi. When the Government changed, the Act was repealed. Recently, some pressure for change and for an agreed process to be put in place has come from urban groups, some of which want to be regarded as iwi. A powerful incentive has been to qualify for a share of the assets of Te Ohu Kaimoana The Treaty of Waitangi Fisheries Commission. The question is, what is the process to become recognised as iwi? Were the criteria set out in the Bill a true reflection of the traditional system? Was the legislative path the correct way to go or is it a matter for iwi to decide?

Should recognition be given by Parliament, or should there be a representative council of elders, of koroua and kuia, to draw up the criteria, establish protocols of compliance, have these discussed, amended and finally approved by Māori? How should such a process be resourced? Obviously there are many issues that can be raised and chief among them is the issue of rangatiratanga, of self-determination and our ability to make binding decisions that affect our own affairs.

Unidentified members

An issue for discussion is the fact that the 1996 Census identified 112,566 persons who either did not know their iwi or chose to identify ethnically rather than tribally. This number was down from the 1991 Census when 113,193 were in this category (Statistics New Zealand 1998:19). The number is rather large and poses the problem of why so many should not know their iwi or do not want to identify as a member of an iwi, or who object to having to choose one over several possible iwi affiliations. There are many explanations to account for this, including the general view that these figures are one of the consequences of assimilation policies. These policies contributed to a long period of successive undermining of the traditional system, and of chronic neglect and underfunding of iwi. Thus the iwi themselves lacked the resources to find their people who meanwhile have become scattered and difficult to find. However, as the Ngāi Tahu case shows when an effort is made at a critical time and resources are available thousands of beneficiaries are discovered. The key component was resources that enabled the iwi to mount an effective advertising campaign to find their people.

The whānau unit

The Māori world is full of social groups that call themselves a whānau. Some are household units and some are large extended families numbering up to several thousand members. This is the basic building block of the whole social system. The word whānau is defined by Williams (1971:487) as meaning 'be born', 'be in childbed', 'offspring, family group', 'family', but modern, and 'a familiar term of address'. Whanaunga is a relative and whakawhānau means to give birth, or, as the dictionary puts it, 'come to the birth'. A key characteristic of the group called a whānau is that members are born into it and that the members are all relatives (although there are looser uses of the term, as we shall see in chapter 19). The term used to label this group contains within it the defining characteristic that distinguishes a whānau from some other group of people. The whānau principle, which is described by anthropologists as the kinship principle and by Māori as the whakapapa principle, underpins the whole social system, that is, one must be born into the fundamental building block of the system in order to be a member as of right. The act of whakawhānau (giving birth) produces a newborn child, a whenua (placenta) and eventually a pito (umbilical cord). The whenua and the pito are buried or placed within the land of the whānau and that establishes a spiritual link between the land and the child. Once born the child inherits a number of rights – the birthright that I have discussed in chapter 4.

Firth's analysis

According to Firth (1959:111) the traditional whānau functioned as the unit for ordinary social and economic affairs. The whānau occupied either one dwelling house or several contiguous houses within a village. Under their head man, the group was able to undertake several important economic tasks such as working a kūmara plot, building an eel weir, building a waka, fishing, rat trapping or bird hunting. Each whānau was fairly self-sufficient and as a rule managed its own affairs without interference, except in such cases as came within the sphere of village or tribal policy.

The size of whānau

Firth regarded this unit as being 'of the utmost importance' because it had cohesion and very close relationships. It consisted of three generations, such as grandchildren, their parents and the siblings of the parents, and the grandparents. Numbers varied from a small extended family to up to ninety persons. A minimal whānau would consist of the children of one set of parents, the uncles and aunts of the children and some grandparents. But if each uncle and aunt married, had children and remained as part of the whānau, the working force would increase dramatically. It is possible therefore for the whānau to have several nuclear families within it.

The whānau nui tonu

There are many whānau present today whose membership is greater than a thousand. Some are over two thousand and still growing. For many of these groups the difficulty is in maintaining the collectivity as a group that is held together by strong kinship bonds but recognising that the group is scattered and divided by geography and by interests. When gathered together as for a tangi or a reunion the whānau has clearly outgrown that category. It is like a super whānau which comes together only very occasionally and may be described as consisting of dispersed elements located most often at urban centres. When they do come together the whānau nui tonu does appear like a super whānau. After the special occasion it disperses and virtually disappears. The reason a super whānau does not divide into smaller units is because the members are not in one place but are scattered over the country. In other words, it is already broken up and what they want to do is to link back to their roots.

As the whānau continues to grow and generational depth increases, a time comes when the whānau has become so large in number that it will either have to divide into several whānau or be regarded as a hapū. By that time it will be acting like a hapū and will be recognised by other hapū as being no longer a whānau.

Towards hapū status

The promotion to hapū is signalled by the establishment of a marae or by the intention to do so. The first hurdle is in gaining agreement from neighbouring groups about the land on which the marae is to be built. There are many examples of social groups splitting and going off to establish their own identity and their own marae. The next test is the ability of the group to resource the project and actually complete it. The difficulty is partly the result of fragmentation as in many cases today there are more members of the whānau living outside the tribal estate than in it. Whānau members have regrouped in different places, especially in large cities, and return only occasionally. Because of this factor the whānau at home is unable to assert itself because it does not have the population base present every day to justify a case to become a hapū. Nor can it guarantee a sufficient degree of commitment to build, pay for, and manage a marae on its own. Sometimes the fragmentation becomes a positive factor when a group is able to raise money through its employed members working in big cities.

The hapū unit

The primary thing to say about a hapū is that it consists generally of more than one whānau and the units within it are bound as before by strong kinship ties and by the whakapapa principle. A hapū is defined in the dictionary (Williams 1957:36) as follows: 'pregnant'; 'conceived in the womb'; and a 'section of a large tribe, clan, secondary tribe'. The term itself emphasises the importance of being born into the group. The metaphor used by our ancestors was that of a pregnancy, of the belly swollen by pregnancy, and of the members being born of the same womb. The metaphor also conveys the idea of growth, indicating that a hapū is capable of containing many whānau.

The whanaungatanga and whakapapa principles

Hapū number several hundred people who are all whanaunga except for marriage partners brought in from other hapū, other iwi, and cross-cultural marriages. The larger hapū may number over two thousand. Within my own iwi there are twenty traditional hapū and two urban hapū with numbers varying from a hundred to a thousand-plus registered members in each. The urban hapū of Ngāti Awa are still kinship-based as every member has to be able to whakapapa to a hapū of Ngāti Awa. The difference here is that the whanaunga link is not as close as in the home-based hapū. Moreover, the hapū is a constant that brings together a slice of the iwi and provides the urban members of Ngāti Awa a connection to the rūnanga and a place in the organisation of the iwi. There are revived hapū, urban hapū, traditional hapū and hapū that are both hapū and iwi. All are members of Ngāti Awa. A group can be a hapū in one context or an iwi in another. That is to say, a well-established hapū of an iwi would be welcomed as Ngāti Awa, the iwi, because on that occasion that hapū is the face of Ngāti Awa. There are several very large hapū that could legitimately claim to be iwi. They choose to work within the larger iwi category because they have been traditionally recognised as a part of the iwi. The iwi is, in effect, an alliance of groups that play the role of hapū at times and become iwi at other times. In other words, there is a degree of flexibility in how the terms whānau, hapū and iwi are used.

The importance of marae

Every well-established hapū has at least one marae which it has managed for a very long time. For well-established hapū the period is over a hundred years. There are varying periods of time for others. For an urban hapū the marae is much more recent. The meeting house at the marae is a point of focus for all members. Because it is characteristically named after an ancestor and because hundreds of members of the group from several generations long since gone played their part in maintaining the mana of the hapū there is also a mystical quality to the meeting house, elements of ihi (essential force), wehi (fearsomeness), and wana (sublimity). In other words the whare tipuna has awe (strength, power and influence), it is imbued with the mana of those gone by, and it is tapu, highly respected, and symbolic of the group and all that it stands for. That was the place where important decisions were made. Big hapū may have more than one marae. A hapū without a marae is not recognised by others as being real. Tikanga demands that a hapū must have a marae, or some building that substitutes for a marae, such as a culture centre.

The naming of hapū

As already emphasised, membership into the hapū is by an act of birth and this can be either through one parent or through both. Where both parents belong to the same hapū, the children have a very strong link to the group and are not divided in their loyalties. There are principal ancestors of the hapū to whom all members are able to trace a link. Ideally, however, members are able to whakapapa back to the common ancestor of the hapū. Thus, if the named ancestor is Pukeko then everyone should be able to link to him. However, there are cases where the name of the hapū is not that of an ancestor. There are many hapū named after an event, for example Patuwai (killed at sea) or Hokopū (buy guns). In such a case, it may not be possible to identify one recognised ancestor for all members. Instead there is a group of ancestors whose names are listed in blocks of land belonging to the hapū.

Hapū as political units

The hapū is the basic political unit (Schwimmer 1966:34) within Māori society. Traditionally it occupied an area of land, and controlled a number of resources, such as mahinga kai (seafood gardens and other regular sources of food), specific fishing grounds, wetlands, and forest lands. The leader of the hapū was the chief, its rangatira or ariki (high chief). The primary function of the leader was to ensure that the group survived and that its land base and resources were protected and defended. The hapū was responsible for its own defence and could enter into alliances to protect its integrity, its resources and its people. It could count on the assistance of neighbouring hapū if attacked by an outside force.

It was responsible for building cultural resources such as a marae, a carved meeting house, a carved pātaka, and canoes for trade and warfare. Some fishing expeditions could be undertaken by calling on the labour force of the hapū. A large and well-organised hapū was a very effective economic, social and political force.

However it would be incorrect to assert that the hapū was like an independent nation and that it stood alone against all odds. This is not true. Hapū did not stand alone and could not survive on their own. Each depended on alliances and always on kin-related groups such as other hapū of the iwi. A badly behaved hapū could find itself subject to attack from the rest of the iwi or banished altogether and forced to give up its land. A hapū was definitely a part of a larger whole.

Decision making

In hapū discussions the kaumātua or rangatira of the whānau gathered together and shared in the decision making. The task of the hapū chief was to listen to the opinions of the kaumātua and others, consider the essential points and then, at the very end of discussion, summarise and make a collective decision. The word of the chief then became the policy for all to follow.

Reviving extinct hapū

The historical record describes many instances of hapū that no longer exist. Many in the Bay of Plenty region faded out, disappeared, dispersed, or joined other hapū. Some hapū live on in the minds of the descendants who remember. Some had quite disappeared from the collective memory until rediscovered by researchers. For example Smith (1910:241) identified the following as hapū of Ngāti Awa: Ngāti Wharepaia, Ngāti Ikapuku, Ngāti Maumoana, Ngāti Paraheka, Ngāti Whetenui, Ngāti Hokopū and Te Pahipoto. By the year 1980 only two hapū of that list were still active, namely Ngāti Hokopū and Te Pahipoto. There is a possibility of reviving some of them, as happened to Ngāti Maumoana and Ngāti Wharepaia, but this depends entirely on whether there are a sufficient number of descendants to reconstitute a hapū, and whether other hapū agree to their revival. There is a period of testing for revived hapū and it is possible to fail to live up to expectations.

Urban hapū

There is also the possibility of forming urban hapū where the members and their families of the various branches of an iwi can form themselves into a hapū, build and run a marae, have a marae committee, hold tangihanga ceremonies, and attempt to meet the needs of their people. Here the building blocks of the urban hapū are smaller whānau groups belonging to many hapū of the tribe. They cluster together, take a name such as Ngāti Awa-ki-Tāmaki and begin to behave like a hapū. Ngāti Awa-ki-Tāmaki chose the ancestor name of Awanuiārangi for their wharenui thus ensuring that every member of the hapū is able to relate to that ancestor. For this group the act of building a marae, paying for it and managing it every day for several years is proof of their ability to be a hapū. The day the marae was opened was an important moment of recognition and validation by the rest of Ngāti Awa and of other tribes who gathered on that occasion. The marae is a huge investment and commitment by the group and the dawn ceremony to open the meeting house was a public test of validation. When the other hapū of the iwi gathered in support, a real milestone had been achieved.

The fundamental criterion of membership

It is worth mentioning that locality by itself or even long association with a hapū, including years of toil at the local marae, do not qualify a person to membership of a hapū. Even the fact of being the mother of many of the hapū children or the grandparent of an even larger number of persons is not sufficient. The whakapapa principle and the simple fact of being born into the group is the most important and fundamental criterion of membership. I have attended meetings where these issues were discussed and argued with great passion. The children especially argue for the inclusion of their rāwaho (outsider) parents and while some hapū are willing to be inclusive in some circumstances they draw the line at land meetings, at giving shares in hapū land, and especially in election of officers for participation in iwi business.

However Schwimmer (1966:36) noted that even though the hapū acted as an 'autonomous' body and enjoyed a large measure of control over everyday affairs, it could not stand alone in both a military and a social sense. The hapū was part of a larger social and political entity called an iwi.

The iwi unit

In his March 1998 submission to the High Court case in which urban Māori authorities were challenging the definition of iwi, Cleve Barlow surveyed the various editions of Williams dictionary and noted a change in the meanings given for the word iwi. In earlier editions it meant 'bone' or 'tribe'. In the 1917 edition it continued to mean 'bone', but the word 'tribe' was changed to 'nation' and 'people'. More recent versions of the dictionary, such as Williams (1957:80), set out the range of meanings for iwi as follows: 'bone', 'stone of a fruit', 'strength', 'nation', 'people'. Through time the association with bone has not changed. And this is important because the metaphor for the social unit above birth (whānau) and pregnancy (hapū) is bone. Relatives are often described as 'bones' and, in this sense, the members of an iwi are 'bones' which emphasises again the importance of shared whakapapa.

That the basic meaning of the word is 'bone' is borne out in Tregear's *Comparative Dictionary* (1891:109) where in Samoa, Tahiti, Futuna, Marquesas and Mangareva the word for bone is 'ivi', in Moriori it is 'imi', and in Hawaii it is 'iwi'. Tregear's other gloss for iwi is 'tribe'.

The metaphor of bones

An important component of the metaphor of bones is that it provides strength. Iwikore (literally no bones), means feeble and without strength. Bones make a body strong and give form to it. Thus bones in the sense of whakapapa and in giving strength to anything is important in understanding the concept of iwi. The important aspect of the word iwi is its function as a metaphor for whanaungatanga and the strength that arises from that fact.

The quality of whakapapa

The iwi is logically larger than a hapū, far more numerous, richer in resources and occupies a far larger area of land. Characteristically the iwi embraces many hapū whose members acknowledge descent from a common ancestor. For example, Best (1972:214–15) in his classic work on Tūhoe listed fifty-eight hapū as being part of the one iwi. The meaning of the word emphasises that the kinship principle remains a significant criterion of belonging. Persons nominated to fulfil ceremonial roles tend to be those individuals who have clear rights of membership. The more important the hui the more this principle applies. And that is not the end of it; the quality of one's whakapapa is also considered. For example one might be a taina (belong to a younger and more junior line) or tuakana (belong to an older and more senior line). Or one may come directly down the aho ariki, a chiefly line. There are advantages to being tuakana. As before, membership can be through either parent. But there is a preference for descent from a senior male line. A chiefly line would be even better. Being born into the iwi and establishing an identity, whakapapa, and a birthright is an essential compliance requirement.

The rohe or estate of iwi

The iwi is the social group that claims an estate or rohe and defends it against all threats of attack from others. At the time of the signing of the Treaty of Waitangi the land was occupied by a number of iwi and their hapū and though much of the land has been lost the idea of a rohe or takiwā (the territory, district or space occupied by an iwi) and te hau kāinga (home) remains strong. Each iwi has an idea of the boundaries of their rohe and forthrightly claims a certain area as their base. Neighbouring iwi, however, rarely ever agree to such assertions and when they draw their map a lot of overlapping of interests will become apparent.

Negotiation of alliances

The iwi is a political entity that maintains an alliance of hapū which can be difficult to hold in place as each hapū also engaged in arranging alliances of its own. In most cases, the allied hapū could be relied upon to band together to defend the tribal estate or to attack another iwi. Skirmishes with bordering iwi could be prolonged affairs which tested the military strength of each side and tested also the internal alliances of the constituent hapū. It was not unusual for the iwi to have factions of hapū sometimes cooperating and sometimes opposing one another.

In cases where a hapū tested the political will of the leaders too far, the iwi could turn against the offender and either destroy it altogether or banish it from the estate for a period of time. At a later time the hapū may be invited back and allocated land, and not necessarily the same land that it had before.

Examples of alliances

There are many instances of iwi engaged in negotiating external alliances either to pay back for assistance given earlier or to create new alliances for specific purposes. For example:

1. Tupaea of Ngāi Te Rangi and Te Waharoa of Ngāti Hauā were joint commanders of an army of 1,000 warriors that attacked and defeated Te Haramiti's army of Ngā Puhi invaders at Tuhua (Mayor Island) (Stafford 1967:198–99).

2. In 1833 Ngāti Rangiwewehi, a hapū of Te Arawa, allied with Ngāi Te Rangi to attack other hapū of Te Arawa that had formed an alliance with Ngā Puhi. The Te Arawa–Ngā Puhi alliance was defeated (Stafford 1967:212).

3. In the late 1820s the Ngāti Awa and Tūhoe chief Te Maitaranui brokered an amazing alliance of many tribes by personally visiting the chiefs. The result of his negotiations was an army consisting of forces from Ngāti Maru of Hauraki, Ngā Puhi of the Bay of Islands, and Te Arawa, Whakatōhea, Ngāti Awa and Tūhoe of the coastal and inland Bay of Plenty that combined to wage war against Ngāti Kahungunu (Best 1972:537–39).

The essence of good leadership was to ensure that if an attack was to be made against an external force the chances of winning were fairly positive. To achieve such a result other iwi were invited to contribute fighting men. Some external alliances were far reaching, and the battlefield could be many days away. Thus the northern tribes ranged all over the North Island and distance appeared to be of little consequence. Ngāti Awa of the Bay of Plenty arranged alliances with Ngāti Maru, with Waikato tribes, with Ngāti Kahungunu, and with Ngāti Raukawa. There were inter-waka alliances. For example, the iwi of Te Arawa would unite against Tūhoe who would have called on other Mātaatua tribes to assist. In a well-documented case already mentioned, we see how Te Maitaranui, chief of Tūhoe and Ngāti Awa, assembled a military alliance to wage war against Ngāti Kahungunu. Best (1972:537) describes how this was done:

> Te Mai-taranui first went to his own people of the Ngati Awa tribe, in order to get them to assist in the east Coast raid. He went up the coast to Tauranga, where Te Waru of Ngai-Te Rangi agreed to take part in the expedition. From there Te Mai' went on to Hauraki, where he visited Tu-te-rangi-anini at Kauaeranga, with the result that Ngati-Tama-te-ra and Ngati-Maru joined the coalition against the Rising Sun.
>
> From Hauraki Te Mai' went north to the Bay of Islands and met Po-mare of Nga-puhi at Taiamai.

The coalition also included Whakatōhea and Te Arawa (Best 1972:538). The stature and mana of the chief brokering an alliance played an important part in its success.

The independence of iwi

In the case of the tribes of Mātaatua, each iwi acted as autonomous and competing entities within the waka confederation. Some of the fiercest battles in the region were within the rohe of Mātaatua and were fought over resources and land. In these battles the names of chiefs killed were remembered and their iwi affiliation recited. The iwi unit was very much a self-contained entity that took care of its affairs with as much diplomacy as was necessary and with the threat of resorting to warfare when diplomacy failed. The iwi acted like an independent nation that was jealous of its mana and was prepared to fight its neighbours to maintain their political standing. There is no question that at this level of operation the hapū was a part of the collective and that the hapū was not an autonomous unit that could do as it pleased.

How many iwi are there?

The 1840 frozen list of iwi

Ngata (1940:158–59) published a list of iwi that were in existence in 1840. There were forty-three tribes in his list. Te Aupōuri, Te Rarawa, Ngā Puhi, Te Uri-o-Hau and Ngāti Whātua are the tribes of the North.

In the Auckland region is Ngāti Tahi. The Hauraki tribes are Ngāti Pāoa, Ngāti Maru, Ngāti Tamaterā, and Ngāti Whanaunga. The Tainui tribes are divided into two main groups: Waikato and Maniapoto. In the Waiariki district Te Arawa and Tūwharetoa are indicated and for Mātaatua the iwi are Ngāi Te Rangi, Ngāti Awa, Whakatōhea, Te Whānau-a-Apanui and Te Urewera (Tūhoe). For Taranaki the iwi are Ngāti Tama, Taranaki, Ngāti Awa, Ngāti Ruanui and for Whanganui they are Ngā Rauru and Ngāti Hau. In the Manawatu region are Ngāti Raukawa, Ngāti Apa, Muaūpoko, and Rangitāne. In the Wellington region there are Ngāti Toa and Ngāti Awa. On the eastern coast are Ngāti Porou, Rongowhakaata, Te Aitanga-a-Māhaki, and Ngāti Kahungunu. These are the North Island iwi in 1840, thirty-five in number. In the South Island the iwi are Ngāti Tama, Ngāti Rarua, Ngāti Koata, Ngāti Kuia, Te Āti Awa and Ngāti Toa in the northern section of the island and in the rest of the island are Ngāi Tahu as the dominant iwi together with Poutini, and Ngāti Mamoe.

The Edward Stanford list

Firth (1959:114) published a map attributed to Edward Stanford, of 55 Charing Cross, London, which was entitled 'Disposition of Maori Tribes about the End of the Eighteenth Century'. The map listed the tribes and gave a location on the map. Ngata (1940:156) confirmed that with one or two modifications the list could be accepted as correct. Metge (1967:121) comments that: 'Once lists and maps were made they came to be accepted as definitive and "right", and the fluidity of the traditional system was frozen.' She, too, drew attention to the fact that hapū continue to grow bigger and bigger without segmenting or changing in category.

The Joan Metge list

Up until recently there were forty-two to forty-four recognised iwi. The Edward Stanford map listed a similar number. Metge (1967:121–24) provided a 1961 list which has been a standard list until revised for Te Māori in 1984. The list for Te Māori was related very much to the groups that needed to be consulted about allowing their taonga to be included in the exhibition and taken offshore. In the 1984 list there were fifty iwi.

The 1996 Statistics New Zealand list

A more recent list is that used by Statistics New Zealand Te Tari Tatau in 1996 for census purposes, in their 1996 publication *Population Census: Iwi Affiliation*. There are approximately ninety iwi identified with several falling far below the population numbers required of the traditionally recognised iwi. The Census list records the name people want to be identified with and the iwi name chosen does not necessarily accord with an actual organisation on the ground.

Population figures for large iwi

1996 population figures for the largest iwi indicate how large some have become. For example, Ngā Puhi have 95,451 members; Ngāti Porou 54,219; Ngāti Kahungunu 45,261; Ngāi Tahu 29,133; Tūwharetoa 28,998: Tūhoe 25,917; Maniapoto 23,733 and Waikato 23,808. Why the largest iwi have not divided into several related iwi as happened in the case of Te Arawa and Tūwharetoa provides evidence of the importance of being a strong iwi. But what it also shows is that the constituent tribes that make up Ngā Puhi have turned it into a super tribe, Ngā Puhi-nui-tonu or Ngā Puhi Whānui.

Population dynamics

As numbers for some iwi have changed since the previous census – for example Ngāi Tahu was 29,133 in 1996 as against 20,304 in 1991 – there is evidence of some mobility and changing affiliations. Thus some iwi are becoming even larger while others are either reducing or remaining small. The group of individuals with multiple iwi affiliations provides a pool of members who are capable of being drawn away from one primary affiliation to another. Impending settlements with the Crown could affect affiliations, and so could the movement towards positive identification as Māori.

The growth of urban groups

Since World War Two, which lasted from 1939 to 1945, Māori have been migrating to the cities in search of work. Some fifty years later, the Māori population has become largely urban. Many groups have organised themselves either as taura here (bound ropes), that is as iwi groups that are still linked to the home tribe, or as urban hapū, or as urban representatives of their iwi, or as urban authorities. There are two urban authorities in Auckland, Manukau Urban Māori Authority (MUMA) and Te Whānau o Waipareira Trust. Both are powerful entities of a corporate nature and are definitely pan-Māori and cater to the training needs of hundreds of Māori. They provide services to client groups and over the years have been seen to be anti-iwi in some of the statements made by their spokespeople. It is therefore ironic that they should now want to be regarded as iwi or to be more exact, they want the definition of iwi to be so broad as to include them.

Ngāti Pōneke

Ngāti Pōneke in Wellington would be one of the first pan-Māori groups to declare themselves an iwi, simply by calling themselves Ngāti Pōneke. The group is essentially a kapa haka or performing-arts group. It is associated with a marae in Wellington, at Pipitea, and the kapa-haka team is still a force to reckon with in the competitions. The tangata whenua of the marae is Te Āti Awa and no one pretends that Ngāti Pōneke is equal in status to Te Āti Awa. Ngāti Pōneke is an honorific term. The tikanga is that the tangata whenua of a region are always recognised by urban groups.

Hoani Waititi marae

The Hoani Waititi Marae in Auckland was established as a memorial to a very popular educationist and it has a community supporting it. This community acts as an urban authority as well as a tribe that runs a kōhanga reo, a kura kaupapa Māori, tuatahi and tuarua (primary and secondary), and is developing a tertiary institution. It also has a kapa-haka team that has featured in national competitions. It has a marae which functions like any other marae in the country and by now would have hosted tens of thousands of people. The community of this marae is not recognised as an iwi and is not referred to as one. There is no honorific term such as Ngāti Pōneke to identify them.

Taura here

Over recent decades the concept of a taura here, representing an urban or dislocated segment of an iwi, has become widely accepted. An important element of the term 'taura here' is that it expresses the urban group's ties to the base group at the homeland. The taura-here grouping differs from urban authorities such as Waipareira in that membership is still based on whakapapa to the iwi to which the group is related.

The taura-here group is similar to an urban hapū – that is, a group made up of members of several hapū who band together as a single unit so that they are able to interact with the tribal centre. There are taura-here groups in many cities and all of them recognise their links to the iwi. They do not attempt to break away and form a new iwi. An urban hapū differs only in that it is regarded as a hapū, or may be regarded as a hapū, when it seeks a place on the board of the iwi authority.

Characteristics of iwi

During the years 1989 and 1990 the late Wishy Jaram, an officer of the Department of Māori Affairs, was seconded to the office in Wellington to prepare some background data for the Runanga Iwi Bill. He interviewed a number of people about what they considered were the essential characteristics of iwi. Some of his findings were included in the first draft of the Bill dated 28 August 1990. Section 5 of the Bill recognised the importance of iwi as 'an enduring, traditional, and significant form of social, political, and economic organisation for Maori'.

Some of the characteristics of iwi in section 4 of the first draft of the Runanga Iwi Act were amended by the Māori Affairs Select Committee. The original essential characteristics are listed below:

1. Descent from (commonly acknowledged) tupuna.

2. Collective possession of a demonstrable cultural and historical identity, based on a shared body of traditional lore. (This was struck out.)

3. A developed political organisation with widely shared aspirations. (Struck out.)

4. A structure of hapū. (Struck out and replaced with the single word hapū.)

5. A network of functioning marae. (Struck out and replaced with the single word marae.)

6. Belonging historically to a (clearly delineated rohe) takiwā.

7. Continuous existence traditionally and widely acknowledged by other iwi. (Reworded but essential point maintained.)

This is an important list of characteristics against which groups wanting to be recognised as iwi can be judged. It is also a useful summary.

Compliance requirements under the Runanga Iwi Bill

A group was required to hold a hui to gain a mandate to apply for registration. A charter had to be prepared and the takiwā or rohe identified and described. It was proposed that the rūnanga of the iwi exercise its authority within this takiwā. The charter had to include, among other things, the name of the iwi, the description of the rohe, the principles by which the rūnanga would be guided in the conduct of its affairs, the manner in which the rūnanga was to be accountable to iwi, issues of equity, method of election of officers, and to describe relationships with taura here or manuhiri groups within the rohe of the iwi. To be accepted as an iwi by the Government, the applicant had to meet most if not all of the essential characteristics of iwi.

Conclusions

The limited list of iwi

For a long time in our history no one appeared to have worried too much about how many iwi there were. For over a century the number accepted as iwi appears to have varied between forty-two and forty-four. This unusual circumstance resulted from various factors. First was the factor of depopulation which would have made it difficult for some whānau, hapū and iwi to exist and function effectively. Government confiscation of land and military actions against some iwi would have contributed to the break-up and scattering of some whānau and hapū. Now the number of iwi has more than doubled.

The move to the cities

During the Second World War a policy of shifting workers from rural areas to the factories in the cities began another depopulation movement, this time from the rural tribal estates to urban centres. The manpower policy opened the way for migration into the cities so that now the population is largely urban. At the same time, the Māori population began to expand – at first relatively slowly before the Second World War, and then after that more dramatically. So while the population has expanded it has also relocated to the cities. Some Māori have migrated further afield to other countries such as Australia. The general effect of these movements have been to reduce numbers at the tribal estates, except for those iwi who live near a big city or town and except those iwi experiencing a return to home base of several of their whānau.

The growing importance of iwi

Despite the addition of new groupings called whāmere or taura here, the traditional system of whānau, hapū and iwi will live on well into the future mainly because it continues to make sense to some of the people. As rallying points for action and for calling the people together the whānau, hapū and iwi have no peers. People respond to the call of their whānau, which remains the most supportive and important group in the life of any Māori. The hapū is also a powerful symbol of identity and its call to action is also difficult to ignore. This group comes together frequently in meeting the ceremonial requirements of whānau, such as tangihanga. For some Māori the iwi is becoming an increasingly important political entity. As the 1996 Census figures show, some Māori prefer to identify by iwi rather than by hapū.

A new category for pan-tribal groups such as urban authorities

For Māori people everywhere the social-organisation model that they know belongs to them and to no one else is the 'whānau, hapū, iwi, waka' model. Thus one understands why urban Māori want to use the traditional categories in order to give themselves a place under the sun. The category taura here is adequate for single-iwi groups living in the cities, but for multi-iwi groups such as the urban Māori authorities a different category needs to be found. Nobody has found one and the main difficulties are the issues of whakapapa.

Urban authorities reach across waka boundaries and ethnic boundaries. They are not waka akin to *Tainui*, *Te Arawa* and *Mātaatua* in which all iwi are seen to be related and tied together in an enduring waka alliance. Urban Māori authorities are unique institutions created to meet certain purposes and focus predominantly on the needs of urban Māori. They have a place in the social-organisation systems of today.

Iwi identity

In issues of Treaty settlements and in allocations of fisheries assets the iwi has become the most important political and economic unit in the whole system. Its importance was clearly signalled in the Runanga Iwi Bill of 1990. And it is this new importance that is encouraging some groups to assert an identification as an iwi with a bit more vigour than previously. For some groups this is but one incentive, albeit a powerful one. There are other incentives, such as wanting to revive an iwi that was lost and scattered and embraced in another iwi. Members want to break away and take on what they may consider to be their proper identity. Iwi identity is obviously important.

The sentiment expressed in the Runanga Iwi 1990 Bill remains an important statement on the importance of iwi: 'The iwi is hereby acknowledged as an enduring, traditional, and significant form of social, political, and economic organisation for Maori.'

The need for an authority and a process

Another statement that confirms the significance of iwi is that the number has risen from the long-standing forty-two or forty-three threshold to ninety or more today. That is, there are forty-seven groups claiming to be iwi who weren't included in earlier lists, but there is no process and no authority to test the validity of their claims. Clearly a process is needed and criteria set out against which applicants are judged. There also needs to be a Māori authority to act as the responsible body to weigh up a case, hear the evidence for and against and then make a decision.

Finally, it needs to be said that the terms used today – whānau, hapū and iwi –are not firmly attached to one kind of kinship grouping. These terms are used creatively and a term such as whānau could apply to all three groups as in the case of Te Whānau-a-Apanui. In their case a whānau can be a whānau or a hapū or an iwi.

In many other cases a hapū is a hapū in some contexts and an iwi in others. Sometimes the hapū represents the iwi and on such occasions will be addressed as the iwi or even as the waka confederation. The nuclear family will be called a whānau, even though it is but one element of the larger grouping. A group of people who rally to support an individual in trouble or in seeking a job will be called a whānau. The point is that these terms are used creatively and that other terms might be brought into the vocabulary, such as whāmere for the nuclear group.

All of these factors do not mean that the traditional concepts and values have disappeared. They remain and come to the fore in huge Māori gatherings. In these contexts the whakapapa principle endures, traditional notions of rangatira, tuakana and taina remain meaningful, traditional values such as manaakitanga and aroha ki te tangata are still important, and hapū and iwi are still judged on their ability to display unity of purpose, strength in tikanga Māori and adherence to traditional practices on the marae.

Perspectives

The essay on Porangahau [Ballara 1995] used concepts of hapu 'community', 'cluster' and 'core' to conceptualise processes of change among several hapu in a specific historical context. It is also increasingly clear from her [Ballara's] analysis that not iwi but hapu or their equivalents were the controllers of marine as well as land resources at the crucial time of the Treaty of Waitangi. It is significant that the overwhelming evidence of the role of hapu has been ignored by the Crown and the Fisheries Commission in their determination to institutionalise holders of the Maori share of fisheries property rights.

— **Webster 1998:148**

Whakapapa is central to Māori society. Whakapapa defines both the individual and kin groups, and governs relationships between them. Whakapapa confirms an individual membership within the kin groups that constitute Māori society and provides the means for learning about the history of their tīpuna. Māori recognised four kin groups: whānau, hapū, iwi and waka. In general terms the iwi was the sum total of its hapū, the hapū an aggregation of whānau, and the whānau an association of close relatives.

— **Ministry of Justice 2001:27**

14
Te Āhua o te Tangata
The Behaviour of People

All cultures have ideas about good behaviour and rules about behaviour that is not acceptable. There are usually clear rules to deal with breaches of good conduct. On the other hand, it is not always clear how a particular society rewards those whose behaviour is above reproach. In our case, the concepts of noa and ea suggest that good behaviour is a matter of balancing the competing requirements of religion and society. Thus one had to ensure that there are no transgressions in the spiritual domain and that one's relationships with the Gods were in a state of balance and harmony. That was no easy task. However, one also had to ensure that one's relationships within the whānau, the hapū and the iwi were also in balance and harmony. And this was certainly no easy matter. At some time or other one was likely to upset the balance either through one's own actions or through the actions of one's relatives. It is clear from previous chapters that punishments were often aimed at the whānau or hapū and not necessarily only at the individual responsible.

Social controls

According to Best (1941, 1:356–57), in traditional Māori society there were systems of control in place.

> The forces that controlled the social system were the institution of tapu, public opinion, the influence of respected chiefs, and, to some extent, the custom of muru ... Now the institution of tapu and magic, as also the mana of superior chiefs, were most effective corrective forces, and all possessed the same vivifying power. The

hidden power that lay behind these institutions, that made them effective, was the power of the gods ... People did not transgress the laws of tapu, simply because they firmly believed that the punishment of the gods would be swift and certain.

Best was describing the traditional system of controls. Today most of these systems have been set aside and the remains are but a pale shadow of the past. Among some tribes some tikanga still hold, but by and large it is Pākehā law that controls behaviour throughout the country. However, the controls of Pākehā law appear to be much more distant and difficult to see and feel. Often it is not until a major crisis occurs that the system is seen and felt. This system also relies heavily on public opinion as we have seen in some notable cases, which dramatise the position of some Māori families in crisis. For example, there were some highly publicised cases of extreme forms of child abuse that involved Māori families (see perspectives, pp. 250–51). Several of the victims died as a result. In the year 2000 alone there were several bad cases, each well publicised by the media.

Earlier there was the 1992 case of the murder of Lou Erueti Tawhai in circumstances that were absolutely bizarre. Tawhai – aged seventy-nine at the time – was murdered, castrated, gutted, beheaded and burnt by his wife Ngahuia Tawhai, aged fifty-two, assisted by Wallace Waru Iopata on 15 August 1992 (Farmer 2001). Earlier in the same year – and widely reported in the days following 25 June 1992 – Raymond Wahia Ratima murdered seven members of his family plus an unborn child. There is growing evidence of dysfunction in some Māori families in which children are no longer safe and parents are out of control and do not know what they are doing. Pākehā law is not sufficient to deal with the human debris left in the wake of recent changes in economic and political policies, continuing policies of assimilation and a host of other reasons, such as drug taking and alcoholism. Associate Minister of Health and Māori Affairs Tariana Turia, in a speech delivered at the University of Waikato to the New Zealand Psychological Society on 29 August 2001, has raised the idea of a psychological state which she called post-colonial traumatic stress syndrome as accounting for some of the difficulties that some Māori families face today, namely the lack of means, of resources, of identity, of control over their lives. Some are overburdened by the problems around them, are ill-equipped to deal with them and cannot find a way forward. Sometimes the problem is caused by competing ideologies. For example, the great value placed on the rights of the individual often hinders collective action and collective control within a whānau or hapū. Sometimes the reason might be poor education that could have been caused by lack of opportunity, or by poor family background, or by simply by not having the mental capacity to accept education and so develop to full potential. There are many reasons.

The role of the whānau

When cases of very bad behaviour come before the public, questions are asked about the role of the whānau and the hapū in controlling their members. Why are they not able to exercise some influence on their members? Where is the spirit of aroha and manaakitanga that we value? What are the leaders of the Māori world doing? Māori leaders and the whānau are often blamed for the social problems that loom before us from time to time. But let us be fair about this. Obviously, past policies of governments – such as the many land acts and the Tohunga Suppression Act 1907 – in dismantling the traditional leadership and social systems and in suppressing tikanga Māori must carry some of the blame. Also, more recent policies of starving tribal authorities of funds and thus making it difficult for them to be proactive is another factor. General issues such as unemployment and drug taking are also factors. On the Māori side there is a lack of authority and resources to do anything but talk. There is also a lack of expertise to deal with the complex social problems of today. Then there is the factor of fragmentation of whānau and hapū so that the members are scattered all over the place. If the whānau or the hapū once were able to exercise some influence it is now very difficult to do so because their members are mostly living away from the home base. Families are isolated and reduced to the basic nuclear unit. In addition, tikanga Māori has been suppressed for so long that most Māori are unfamiliar with this important body of knowledge and do not know what to do.

There is a danger in focusing too much on negative statistics. The fact is, many Māori families are not in trouble and have never seen themselves as being in trouble. They may feel the stresses of modern-day living but they cope and they have various strategies for doing so. Some do it by abandoning their Māori heritage. Some do it by cross-marriages. Others do it by balancing the demands of the greater society with their hapū obligations. Yet others do it by recovering what they have lost and by taking their place as active members of their hapū and whānau. The good thing is that they survive. They make a contribution to the life of society at large and to their whānau and hapū. Some have discovered that they can actually accomplish both outcomes without having to give up their culture.

These difficulties cannot be allowed to overshadow our aspirations, our visions for the future and our development as a people. We must pull ourselves together and begin to help ourselves. In fact, many whānau are doing so. The proposition they adopt is that there is great value and meaning in cultural reconnection and the recovery of mātauranga Māori and tikanga. Their approach has been to look at their history, traditions, traditional waiata and tikanga and begin from that base to face the future. This thesis was first tried in the 1930s by Sir Apirana Ngata when he launched his whare whakairo programme. While Ngata (1940:321) did not use the language of cultural reconnection it is in fact what he was preaching and practising in the 1930s and 40s:

> The realization that so large a part of the Maori people had lost, or was about to lose, its expert artists was the chief reason behind the representations made to the Government of the day which resulted in the establishment of the School of Maori Arts and Crafts at Rotorua. Fundamentally the motive here was the same as that lying behind other phases of *Maoritanga*. The setting up of the school at Rotorua in 1927 represented one of the most important measures taken towards the rehabilitation of the Maori.

It is fundamentally the same idea that the Department of Corrections is using to underpin its cultural programmes for Māori prisoners. Mr Charlie Tawhiao, manager of Treaty relationships within the Department of Corrections supports this when he is reported by journalist Margot Butcher (2003:42) as saying:

> Every part of your whakapapa matters and asks you to think about those values that made you. I've seen guys shift. In thinking about

cultural responsibilities [Māori or Pākehā], who they are becomes inconsistent with who they were.

Butcher goes on to say about Charlie Tawhiao: 'Call him a Pollyanna if you must, but Tawhiao's found healthy cultural identity a very powerful force for change.'

Culture remains the foundation of one's identity and modern technology cannot replace it. Once cultural confidence is established, individuals are better prepared to deal with their own futures. Thus there is an important role for tikanga and culture.

Alternative justice systems

Alternative justice systems have been talked about for many years. This makes it possible to have a marae-based justice system to handle minor offences and would have the benefit of encouraging whānau to act collectively in giving support where appropriate, and in having a say where the authority of the whānau and the hapū needs to be affirmed.

Past governments have been reluctant to introduce an alternative justice system for Māori arguing that there should be one law for all. But this is not the issue. What Māori want to do is to have a culturally relevant way of handling a host of minor offences and of having a hand in reducing the incarceration rate of Māori in our country. We are over-represented in rates of apprehension, prosecution and conviction in the nation's justice system. In 2000, over fifty percent of males and about eighty percent of females in prison were Māori (Department of Corrections 2000). When our overall population is about thirteen percent of the total for the country, these incarceration rates are appalling. The idea is not actually new. It has been tried out before under the Social and Economic Advancement Act 1967. Those who remember those times say the idea was effective and did work.

Another possibility is to have courses on tikanga Māori readily available for youth so that they are familiar with this part of their heritage. This information might be very helpful in providing some guidelines on how to behave and what to do in various situations. Education and more education will not go amiss, and to know is to be empowered. Māramatanga (enlightenment) is to be preferred any day to pōuritanga (darkness).

Over the years there has been a softening of attitude in the Department of Corrections and Māori are being brought into the arena of rehabilitative justice more and more. For example, there are tikanga Māori programmes offered to Māori inmates in some prisons. There are also Māori focus units and whānau liaison positions, which indicates that Corrections acknowledges the power of culture in transforming the lives of Māori inmates.

Marae justice is another avenue which is frequently advanced by Māori proponents as the most appropriate cultural way of dealing with trouble. But there seems to be some reluctance on the part of government to incorporate it into our justice system. It is an alternative way of dealing with Māori who have broken the law and it allows one to be judged by one's cultural peers. In addition the victims of crime become part of the resolution. All discussions and deliberations are grounded in tikanga Māori and so the difficulties of cross-cultural misunderstanding should not be a factor.

When the cultural factor is accepted as normal, the issues of offending can be faced squarely and honestly. Māori might actually be more severe on their own than the national justice system. But a tikanga-based justice system is also likely to find culturally appropriate ways of exacting utu for the crime. In the end we are not talking about severe criminal cases, such as murder, which are probably better dealt with through the national system. We are looking at the principle of community involvement in the justice system and, in the Māori case, giving back to the whānau and hapū some of the authority they possessed before, so that they can deal with unacceptable behaviour. We cannot do any worse than the present system and, in fact, we might be a lot more successful.

The fragments of Māori culture

In chapter 13 I referred in broad terms to Bruce Biggs' metaphor that equates Māori culture to Humpty Dumpty. The policy of mainstreaming Māori activities became very noticeable at the time when the Department of Māori Affairs, that took a global view of the indigenous population of Aotearoa, was disestablished in 1989. The department itself was another Humpty Dumpty that fell off the wall and its parts, most of its functions and its money were distributed to other departments and managed by them. Whereas before there was one point of contact for Māori people now there were many and most of them were not used to dealing with Māori. There were no particular acts that put their policy in place. Rather, it was laid down as policy decisions by various cabinets. The present National opposition (2003) is overtly mainstream in its pronouncements under the guise of one standard of citizenship for all. If Māori are to control their people more effectively they must also be able to control their destinies to a greater degree than is possible today, and have the wherewithal to do so. These larger issues are outside the scope of this book. The focus here is on tikanga Māori and the role it might have in helping to restore balance and harmony in the lives of our people. Some urgency is required in addressing the issues of dysfunction in Māori society. Cultural options need to be considered seriously, and tikanga Māori is an important cultural component. There are obviously other options and all might need to be brought to bear on the problem in order to bring about effective change.

The misuse of tikanga

Behaviour seems to be governed by a kind of fatalism. One behaves in a certain manner because that was how one's parents behaved and that can be used as an excuse and a justification for that behaviour, whether it be good or bad. We are inclined to agree with this line of thinking if the talent is for something positive, like a talent for singing. However, fatalism is too convenient as an explanation for negative behaviour as it allows a ready-made excuse and denies free will. On the other hand, science might lend support to the excuse by saying that a person's behaviour is determined largely by their inheritance of genes. In Māori terms the pūmanawa for crime was handed down to the individual, but the behaviour that resulted from it was still condemned by Māori society and various forms of utu applied. Thus that excuse could not have been used in traditional times.

It is known that some individuals turn to tikanga Māori in order to explain and justify their behaviour. Tikanga Māori has been used in some custody cases as a way of strengthening the application of a family member. Most adoptions, for example, were within the whānau and the hapū. Thus that is the tikanga.

Also, tikanga Māori has been used by some abusive husbands to justify violence against their wives. They have argued that men are tapu and women are not tapu and therefore they are allowed to beat them. Unfortunately for them, tikanga Māori does not support such an argument. In fact, all Māori are tapu regardless of gender, but some are more tapu than others. There are times when a woman is more tapu than a man and does this justify her beating up the children and her husband? It is a stupid argument.

There was also the case (*Police v Cooper* 1999) of a woman who argued that the police could not take blood from her to test her level of alcohol, because according to tikanga Māori her blood is tapu. She was absolutely right on the issue of tapu, but found wanting on other aspects of tikanga. But I understand this defence was ruled inadequate: 'where there was a conflict between cultural values and legal principles, the court was required to give priority to legal principles'. What these examples show is that some of us are quick to appeal to tikanga Māori when we are in trouble and are not so keen on it when we are trouble-free.

Whanonga

The word whanonga means behaviour. Obviously there are many kinds of behaviour ranging from good to evil. There is a saying to that effect: 'Mā te kino ka kitea te pai' (Through evil one is able to see what is good). This indicates that good behaviour is often defined by its opposites. One learns how to maintain balance in one's life by avoiding behaviour that is known to trigger reprisals or rebukes. Most people want to get on with their lives and avoid any activity or action that might get them offside with their whānau. As Best has indicated, public opinion is a powerful force.

Personal traits

There are many words that describe different behaviours and personal traits. Some are viewed as positive and others as negative. There are tikanga that relate to various disapproved actions.

The word 'puku' means stomach. It appears frequently as a prefix in adjectives to describe a variety of behaviours.

He tangata pukuaroha: a sympathetic person.

He tangata pukukai: a greedy person.

He tangata pukukata: a person given to much laughter.

He tangata pukumahara: a person who is cautious.

He tangata pukumahi: a hardworking, industrious person.

He tangata pukunui: a person with a large stomach and therefore held to be greedy.

He tangata pukungangare: a quarrelsome, obstructive and aggressive person.

He tangata pukuriri: an angry person.

He tangata pukutākaro: a playful person.

In Māori thinking, the stomach of a person has much to do with their behaviour. A person is described as having a stomach for angry behaviour or for being industrious and it implies that the person has a propensity to act that way all the time. In these cases the trait can be seen in some sort of action. Persons who are no good at anything and are of no account at all are described as being hauwarea. Such persons are regarded as being morose, weak, cowardly, non-focused and lacking in direction.

Everybody is assumed to inherit pūmanawa. Some pūmanawa are positive and are useful and good for the individual who possesses them as well as benefiting the community. Other pūmanawa are negative and bad both for the person and for the community. The inherited pūmanawa play a part in how a person behaves. Some of that behaviour reflects whānau traits that were observed either in the parents' or grandparents' generations or in the behaviour of other close relatives. Other behaviour might be seen to be a characteristic of the individual and the criticism might be that he or she is nothing like their parents.

Positive traits

Most often we read the nature of a person by studying their face and eyes and then look to their actual behaviour to confirm or modify our judgement. There are many terms for people who are seen as being positive. I have used the term 'tangata' to mean person and not 'male'. The proper word for male is tāne.

The positive people are described in the following ways:

1. He tangata māhaki is a person who is self-possessed, calm, quiet, mild mannered and humble.

2. He tangata pūkenga is a person who is skilled, very knowledgeable, and can be considered a learned person.

3. He tangata pūmahara is a thoughtful and wise person.

4. He tangata manaaki, atawhai is a caring person who is helpful to others and considers the welfare of others besides themselves.

5. He tangata aroha ki te tangata is a person who is concerned about people and wants to help wherever possible. The marae might be a focus of their life, and they are always helping those in need, always present at tangihanga and other collective events.

Negative traits

Some people, by their very demeanour, make other people uneasy. There is something about them that raises caution. On the other hand there are some who exhibit charm but mean harm and some who make a practice of inveigling themselves into a group and then taking advantage of them, for example, absconding with a committee's funds.

The negative and troublesome people are the following:

1. He tangata kōhuru is a murderer, a person who kills by stealth, is treacherous and dangerous. In former times this kind of action was frequently the cause of war. Depending on circumstances the offenders may have forfeited their own lives, or their hapū as a whole was held responsible. Today, the person is sent to prison.

2. He tangata whānako, tangata tāhae is a person who steals. The traditional punishment was either a savage beating or capital punishment or subjection to mākutu (witchcraft).

3. He tangata patu wahine, kōhuru tamariki: There are some extremely angry people who vent their anger on women and children and often with horrific results. They are bad-tempered, quick to anger, and once they began to hurt people, they do not know when or how to stop. The traditional punishment was either muru or, if a life was taken, the life of the culprit. These are now punishable under the law of the land.

4. He tangata pūremu is a person who commits adultery. As seen in chapter 9 the punishment for adultery and running off with someone

else's wife was muru. The punishment was very public and involved all of the kin of the one accused of wrong-doing. As a group they suffered the consequences of an action of one of their members. This action was breaking up a marriage and undoing a relationship that the whānau and hapū had recognised as being socially sanctioned. The consequences upon the children would also be a factor, because a change in the relationship of the parents would result in new arrangements being negotiated for the children. Thus the consequences of a break-up are quite far reaching and affect many people.

Persons were advised to marry within their own circle of relatives in order to minimise the loss of land and property through the use of muru. Here the key word was tuahine, meaning sister or cousin. The marriage rule was directed at cousins and not at sisters in the western sense.

5. He tangata ngau whiore is a person who commits incest. Once identified the matter is either brought to the attention of the police or it may be discussed at the marae. In the case of the Ringatū church the matter is discussed by the congregation and decisions are made on how to deal with the case. It is not clear how cases of incest were dealt with in traditional society and even in how they were defined. What we can do is point to the story of Tāne cohabiting with his daughter and the consequences of this action as a starting point. Today, incest is defined by New Zealand law, and breaches of this law are taken to court to be dealt with.

6. He tangata whakamomori is a person who takes his or her own life and commits suicide. This kind of action was recognised as the ultimate weapon an individual had if they disagreed with the decisions of their elders. There are many stories of young women committing suicide because they disagreed with the choice of a husband made on their behalf. It was a clear signal to the elders that they had gone too far in insisting on a course of action that the young woman had not agreed to. There is no record of any punishment being meted out for being the cause of whakamomori. Today, suicide among youth has become a national problem.

7. He tangata mauāhara is a person who nurses grievances, harbours ill-feeling towards others and refuse to let bygones be bygones. This

person feels intensely any hurt that was aimed at them and will not forgive those who caused the hurt. He or she is consumed by resentment, broods and plots to find ways of paying back. Such people are usually known for this kind of behaviour and they tend to be difficult in their relationships with others.

8. He tangata wairangi is a person who is suffering from mental illness. Historically the whānau tried their best to care for their relative and not let them harm themselves or others. Another word that is sometimes used to describe people suffering from mental illness is 'pōrangi'. But this word is less specific and is more of a general word to describe an action that might be said to be mad. Such action is not necessarily that of a mentally ill person, but it is unusual. Most whānau are not equipped to deal effectively with mental illness. Tolerating it is not really sufficient.

9. He tangata kai-tarukino: Tarukino is a general word for drugs. It was coined to describe the bad weed known as marijuana. Drug abuse is a huge problem among Māori communities everywhere and some strange behaviours, such as extreme cases of child abuse, have been noted of people who are heavily involved in tarukino. In fact, tarukino has become a factor in contributing to the dysfunction of many Māori families. The repercussions are being felt at the primary school level. In some rural areas marijuana has become the only viable crop for raising money in a context of high unemployment, no industries and no rural development prospects.

10. He tangata keka: In Mātaatua territory a keka is a person who loses self-control when stressed. They do not just get angry like other persons, but rather quickly get into a rage from which they later recover. Williams' *Dictionary* gives the additional meanings of 'mentally deranged' and 'beside oneself with grief'. The main sense of the word, however, is to lose control of oneself at critical moments. At other times a keka person can be quite calm and sensible. The keka phenomenon has become a problem on highways where some drivers lose control of themselves and become enraged. This is called road rage or he keka huarahi.

11. He tangata whano-kē is a person who acts in a strange way, is erratic and different from anybody else.

12. He tangata matapiko is a mean person who does want to share what they have with anyone else.

13. He tangata kino is a general term for any person who is considered by the community to be consistently badly behaved.

14. He tangata māngere is a lazy person, who was generally spoken of in disparaging terms. Women were advised not to marry such a person. Great value was placed on a man having ringaringa raupā (calloused hands), a sign of a worker.

Models from the traditions
Domestic violence

Traditional thinking about behavioural issues can be found in the origin stories, thus linking actions and resolutions to the realm of the Gods. For example, wife beating is an essential part of the story of Mataora and Niwareka as told by Te Matorohanga and recorded by Te Whatohoro and Aporo Te Kumeroa in Smith (1913, 1:67–76).

The events of the story can be summarised as follows:

1. Mataora married Niwareka who was of the underworld but was a visitor to the upper world. She was the daughter of Ue-tonga, a high chief of Rarohenga.

2. One day Mataora became jealous of his older brother Tautoru who seemed to pay too much attention to his Niwareka. Mataora beat Niwareka.

3. Niwareka immediately ran off and returned to her people.

4. Mataora regretted what he had done and grieved for Niwareka. After a time of reflection he set off to find her.

5. Mataora eventually came to Pou-tere-rangi and met Te Kuwatawata, keeper of the entrance to Rarohenga. Mataora was allowed to pass through the door.

6. He arrived at the home of Ue-tonga, father of Niwareka, and came upon him applying moko (tattoo) which was different from the moko Mataora had on his face. The moko of Rarohenga was permanent and was carved into the skin. There was a discussion between Mataora and Ue-tonga, the result of which Mataora received the permanent moko of Rarohenga. His moko became a model for tā moko Māori.

7. At this point the people Mataora had met in the underworld did not know who he was. He was identified later by Niwareka.

8. Once identified he was taken to the house of Ue-tonga and he stayed with them for some time.

9. Mataora discovered new things while he was there, such as a new form of moko, the arts of weaving and tāniko. He learnt that the world of Rarohenga was peace loving and creative, where people were respectful of one another. It was a world of light where night was not known.

10. Eventually Mataora wished to return to Te Aotūroa, to his world. An interesting discussion occurred.

11. First, Mataora suggested that he and Niwareka should make the decision about returning by themselves. Niwareka disagreed and said the matter should be left with her and her kin group to decide.

12. Niwareka consulted her parents and brothers. Ue-tonga told Mataora to go home by himself as he did not like the practice of wife beating in Aotūroa.

13. Mataora was shamed into silence and he suffered shame.

14. Niwareka's brother Tauwehe encouraged Mataora to remain with them because eventually all the people above would die through warfare and crime and come to Rarohenga. The advice to Mataora was to make a clean break between his violent world and Niwareka's.

15. Mataora then made a promise before the family that he would adopt the ways of Rarohenga as the model of behaviour for his world.

16. Ue-tonga then reminded Mataora about the nature of his world where crime and darkness were known. In contrast there was no crime and no darkness in Rarohenga. Mataora was told to never again practise the bad deeds of his world, such as wife beating.

17. So when Mataora returned to Te Aotūroa with Niwareka he was a transformed and retrained person. His appearance was different because he returned with a beautiful moko on his face and wearing a beautiful cloak called Te Rangi-haupapa which means The Sky of Peace. He had gained new knowledge and new insights, and his mind was focused on creativity and non-violence.

The story leaves no doubt that wife beating was regarded as unacceptable behaviour. It is interesting that the party, guilty of violence towards his wife, went to Rarohenga to the spirit world. In a sense both husband and wife approached death and could have died if Ue-tonga and his family decided that there was no hope for them. Instead, convinced that Mataora had left behind the bad ways of his world and had genuinely adopted the values of Rarohenga, he and his wife were sent back to Te Aotūroa. A change of attitude was required.

It is also instructive that Mataora was not allowed to make the decision to return to his place. Nor was it a matter only for the couple to consider. Rather the decision rested with Niwareka and her immediate family.

Murder

It is evident in the many waiata celebrating the death of chiefs that to die in battle was considered to be an ideal end. But to die through a murderous act was not a noble way to die and the repercussions of such an act would be far reaching. An example is the murder of the Tūhoe and Ngāti Awa chief Te Maitaranui by Tuakiaki of Te Reinga. A waiata tangi (lament) was composed for him by Pikihuia (Waiata 117 in Ngata 2:68–71). A description of the murder is given in Best (1972:542–46).

The immediate consequence was that Tūhoe and Ngāti Awa, with help from Whakatōhea and Ngāti Maru, attacked Raki-roa Pā and killed Tuakiaki and others. As Tuakiaki was of Ngāti Kahungunu the army turned to attacking Ngāti Kahungunu in battles known as Rotokaha and Hauturu. According to Best, Pomare of Ngā Puhi came to assist in avenging the murder of Te Maitaranui.

The seeking of utu did not end here. Later a Ngāti Kahungunu ope was invited to Ruatahuna by Te Purewa Kotete (Best 1972:549) to share in a feast. They came and were slaughtered. Clearly, murder was regarded as a serious offence and the utu demanded was not confined to the accused and his hapū but extended to the whole tribe. This was common practice and a recognition that a person was part of a group.

Incest

The God Tāne created the first woman, Hine-ahu-one, and together they had several daughters, the first born being Hine-titama (Smith 1913, 1:139). Tāne married Hine-titama, his daughter, and so caused the first case of incest in the world. Hine-titama was not aware at first, but later was shocked to hear that her husband was also her father. Great was her pain when she discovered this.

Early the next morning she cast a spell over her children and their father Tāne and she fled, eventually arriving at Pou-tere-rangi, the gateway to Rarohenga. She was questioned by Te Kuwatawata, the guardian of the entrance, as to whether she understood what she was leaving behind. Tāne caught up with her and was weeping for her. She told him to return to their family and care for them. She was severing the link to Te Aotūroa for ever, and her task was now to care for the dead. She then passed through the gateway of Pou-tere-rangi and went to Rarohenga. Here her name was changed to Hine-nui-te-pō.

The model here is a difficult one in some respects. First, the emphasis is on the victim of incest and her transformation from the world of life to the world of death. Tāne is portrayed as weeping for Hine-titama and no more. For Tāne there is neither transformation nor utu. That incest is not condoned is, however, very clear in the story.

The important point is that incest caused a transformation for Hine-titama, a movement from the world above to the world below, from the dawn and the world of light to the night, and darkness. Incest is a kind of death.

The issue of homosexuality

Attitudes vary in regard to the issue of homosexual men and lesbian women in Maori society. But there are two different issues here. One is about a person of one sex having a predisposition to be the other. The second is about pairing and the modern issue of wanting to have same-sex marriages validated by the state. Women acting like men and men acting like women were recognised and incorporated into the community. There were terms for them, such as tangata whaka-wahine, whaka-tāne. Tangata whaka-wahine were men who preferred to associate with women and take up feminine occupations such as weaving. They were easily accommodated in Māori society. Likewise tangata whaka-tāne – women who acted like men and preferred to take up masculine occupations such as becoming a warrior and engaging in heavy labouring tasks – were accepted without stigma. They played their roles openly and with the support of their communities.

As indicated earlier, same-sex pairing in a marriage-like relationship was a different matter. Such relationships were not recognised as marriages. Rather, people in such relationships were regarded as close friends who worked together, travelled together and probably lived in the same village. Such friendships were tolerated by the community as they are today.

Conclusions

In traditional times there was a close link between the people and their culture and all that the term implies. People tended to live in communities of relatives and they were members of several supporting groups such as the whānau and the hapū. There was a religious system and a kin group of Atua (Gods) that were descendants of Ranginui and Papa-tū-ā-nuku, the primal parents. Tapu was an important part of the religious system and it was like an invisible policeman that was always around. Once the system of tapu controls was understood, people could live their lives in relative harmony with their Gods.

People also tended in those days to live together in clusters, some quite large and some quite small. Individuals had to contend with the members of their group and learn to live in harmony. The collective opinion of the group was a very useful social force in seeing that children were well treated, and members of the whānau were encouraged to be good citizens. There were always relatives around to help in various ways: to bring food, to share in the catch of the day, to help look after the sick, to share information, and to ask for help when help was needed. The local tohunga was handy and the elders were close by when advice was needed. Today the support systems are no longer in place, except perhaps in a few isolated cases. For many families living in the cities there is no one close by to turn to. The whānau is scattered. The elders are back home at the tribal base. And then there are the varied offerings of city life – the pubs, the nightclubs, the sports clubs, and mixing with people who are in the drug scene. In some cases the support systems have broken down even at the tribal base. Today Māori society is subject to every temptation that is known in the western world.

Tikanga could be very helpful in providing some support and guidelines for people who have lost their way in life. The pathway towards balanced living points to being situated comfortably within a culture and knowing who, what, where and why we exist. Disconnection causes many problems and the way back to the pathway appears to be based on reconnection with the wāhi ngaro, or the missing part of one's life. The focus today is on cultural reconnection for Māori and this could be a solution for other ethnic groups as well. Cultural identity, learning te reo Māori, becoming familiar with the history of the hapū and the iwi and restoring cultural pride and confidence are all ingredients of a balanced life. Tikanga Māori provides guidelines for behaviour and as such comprises an important part of cultural identity.

Perspectives

City children

But, you see, other people went in. That's how I see these kids that have gone into the city who became misfits, who are utterly dislocated. There was no connection for them. They belong to nowhere. A lot of our young people have got into gangs in the city and they do ask, 'Who am I? What am I doing here: I am just a 'black' Maori, lost, and it's these damn Pakehas who did this!' There are a lot of people who back them up – verbally – just to suit themselves – just too many of them! My own personal view – I support kōhanga reo a hundred per cent plus.

For the reason – for me – this upsurge, this feeling, with parents wanting to go back, wanting to learn, and for their children to learn Maori and things Maori – it's not just the language, it is the language and things Maori – it will give them confidence in themselves. They will never, ever question, 'Am I a Maori?' or, 'What kind of a Maori am I?' So these children of ours will not be disadvantaged, as I was when I went to school. Disadvantaged in this way, well, there was no paper, no pencils; I had to learn hard! But these kids of ours, we are of one mind in the kōhanga reo, that is, to give to these little ones every opportunity to learn the language and to know themselves. Also, because it is bilingual what we are doing, at Manutuke, we are preparing our kids for when they move from the kōhanga into the school. By that time, we should have given them all those things they need as a Maori child.

– Heni Sunderland, in Binney & Chaplin 1986:125

Incest

I was a community officer for twenty-one years. This is why I do say it was that kind of background that I had which was a lot of my own strength, that I was able to draw from. Quite a number of families, family situations, truly, I had no answer for! Because they were in such a muddle! I never, ever imagined people could let themselves and their families get into that kind of mix. Oh, I have actually got down on my knees with them. Now, in a Maori situation I could do this; if I was working with a Pakeha family I don't know if it would have worked. We had to get these strengths. We had to ask for some guidance. With a Maori, as long as you have got your facts, and you are sure, they'll tell you the rest. They just say to you, 'Yes', and they will tell you all about it.

There were some situations – some I can't – incest was one of the things I found very hard. The first case I had was fairly close to home, too. It was an adopted child brought up from tiny as their own. I had to take myself quite apart: if you are very sure this is happening, then, what are we going to do about it? The mother and I decided we would take the girl back to its natural mother. I thought it was all finished with when this gentleman comes into the office, asking me what right did I have to take this girl? Well, that was enough for me! Ah, I let him have it! He is one of the very few men I have actually cursed in Maori.

– Heni Sunderland, in Binney & Chaplin 1986:124–25

Tapu

People did not transgress the laws of *tapu* simply because they firmly believed that the punishment of the Gods would be swift and certain.

– Best 1941, 1:359–60

Punishment for ill-treatment of a child

The case is summarised as follows.

Place: Ruatahuna   Tribe: Tūhoe

Child badly ill-treated; father held to be responsible. Taua muru advanced onto marae. Local people assembled to receive them. Taua muru led by a woman armed with a stick. She walked up to the father and 'belaboured him with that stick'. The party then demanded 'payment' for the assault. The fine was produced and piled on the plaza. This all taken by the visitors.

Goods – five guns, two rolls of print, some new garments, greenstone ornaments, one horse, and five shillings in silver, the monetary wealth of the family group.

– Best 1941, 1:359–60

Quarrels

As a rule a native community lived in harmony in the hamlet, but quarrels might cause a noisy and boisterous scene when some cause of dissension arose. Idlers were almost unknown, for all engaged in the industrial activities of the community.

– Best 1941, 1:17

Mākutu

The pseudo-science of *makutu* was often called upon when a thief was ripe for punishment. Of such punishment there were several grades. The injured person might desire that the thief be utterly destroyed, or perhaps visited with some less severe form of punishment. A magic rite called *ahi matiti*, or *whakamatiti* caused the thief to become mentally deranged, and also constricted and weakened his fingers in such a manner that he would find it very difficult to steal again. There were a number of spells that were believed to have similar effects. When the thief was unknown the *tohunga* could ascertain his identity by performing a certain rite, when the *wairua* or image of the thief would appear before him.

– Best 1941, 1:336

Child abuse

Maori children are about five times more likely to be abused than Pakeha children, according to figures issued by the Department of Child, Youth and Family Services.

The figures show that in the 1998–1999 year 2405 children said to be Maori were assessed by the service as abused, compared with 2467 New Zealand European children. Though the abuse figures are similar for the groups, about five times more New Zealanders identify as being Pakeha than Maori.

Maori Affairs Minister Parekura Horomia said though most Maori parents did a good job, professionals and whanau needed to work together to tackle the problem. Children's Commissioner Roger McClay said the statistics – which included neglect, sexual, physical and emotional abuse, self-harm and suicide – were clearly unacceptable. 'It's not about Maori bashing, it's about child bashing,' he said. Figures included in Mr McClay's investigation into the death of 4-year-old James Whakaruru last year showed Maori children were nearly four times as likely to be admitted to hospital for injuries through deliberately inflicted harm. Mr McClay said Maori women aged 15 to 24 were seven times more likely than non-Maori women to be admitted to hospital after an assault.

– *Dominion*, 1 August 2000

Culture no excuse

I wish to set the record straight regarding my views surrounding the recent case involving a Samoan couple sent to prison for child abuse.

Two of your correspondents have made some rather unfortunate statements about my position. I have long campaigned against child abuse and especially child abuse in my own community. My position has always been that culture is no excuse for abuse, and that very public view hasn't changed.

Your story reporting my comments on the 'ifoga' protocol failed to reflect my criticism of the couple for their absolutely unacceptable behaviour. My comments on getting the courts to better understand the ifoga process were made with the view that if they did, then the courts would have been in a far stronger position to judge and even punish offenders for the misuse of the ifoga protocol as a form of defence.

The comments were never meant to support any use of violence against children, nor any attempt to use culture to blunt the exercise of the law in this abusive situation. The Samoan Council doesn't support abusive and violent behaviour and neither does Samoan culture.

Chairman, Samoan Advisory Council
– *Evening Post* 2 August 2000

15
Ngā Mahi Auaha
Creativity and Performance

Few would doubt that in their time our ancestors developed the arts to a very sophisticated and unique expression of the creative genius of the people. Woodcarving was especially rich and was elaborated in storehouses, meeting houses, canoes and countless tools, weapons and everyday appliances. The weaving arts gave us beautiful cloaks of tāniko and of multicoloured feathers. There were floor mats and baskets. There were intricate works in bone and ivory, greenstone, obsidian and various other stones. Painted designs adorned war canoes, memorials, paddles and meeting houses.

In the area of performing arts they developed the war dance, poi dances, traditional waiata and action songs. We are still performing the same dances but the styles have changed and the tunes have become very modern. The performing arts today are very much alive, actively pursued and performed all around the country. Traditional chants are still performed today and now some groups are composing new ones and so adding to the repertoire of traditional-type waiata.

The art legacy passed down from the ancestors to the generations of today is a gift of great magnificence, a thing of beauty to many, a gift that touches our very souls. We are enriched and we can stand tall in the international arena of art. We have something of which we can be immensely proud.

Often the question is asked: How was it that our ancestors were able to create such beautiful art forms and produce such fine and measured work? There are many answers to the questions. An obvious one is that the artists worked with their people and for their people in a cultural context. They all shared. There were shared beliefs and shared values. Creative work was highly respected and protected. The artists were learned people who were well versed in the background knowledge pertaining to their art forms and they knew the rituals. Perhaps the most powerful reason why our ancestors produced great art was that such work was placed under the tapu of creative work.

This statement poses an immediate question as to what the tapu of creative work means. The question may be asked in a different way. Creative work is exciting and usually very enjoyable. Why then should it be placed under tapu and restrictions built around such activity? There are several aspects to the answer.

Pūmanawa: creative talent

In the modern world credit for a particular talent is usually given to the individual fortunate enough to have it. The rewards to that person could be considerable in terms of personal wealth and standing. Some become world champions or international celebrities.

In traditional Māori belief a talent for creativity comes to the individual through the parents and down through one's ancestry. In a creative activity, for example woodcarving, a study conducted by Roger Neich (2001) found that the talent for whakairo or woodcarving in a particular tribal group was a characteristic of a single whakapapa line. It was in the family, as it were. Each generation produced one or more individuals with the same talent. All of them were great carvers and their names are remembered. One of them, Kaka Niao of Te Teko, died in July 2001. There was no question that he was a gifted carver and the meeting houses that he carved remain as testimony to his genius.

In this particular case no one can argue that the pūmanawa was unique to the individual. A more correct statement is that the pūmanawa was unique to the whānau or family and that it is expected that this talent will manifest itself in one or more of the descendants from time to time. As chapter 4 has discussed, Te Rangikaheke of Ngāti Rangiwewehi was quite clear in his mind that pūmanawa came from a moenga rangatira, a chiefly marriage bed. The assumption was that there was a pool of talents in the people who belonged to the chiefly families. We might not agree with the other part of his argument, however, which was that in families that did not have access to a pool of talents one should not expect the emergence of a genius or a great artist. His main point was that one was more likely to emerge from a chiefly marriage bed. That is, whakapapa determines the distribution of talents.

In this sense a talent for creativity is not an individual's good fortune but rather it is the good fortune of a kin group, of the tribal group, of the community. It follows, therefore, that the results of such a talent should enhance the group, and the individual and the kin group should share the rewards. Our best-known carvers worked with the people and for them and spent years working in poverty. Few of them ever became wealthy after a lifetime of service to the people.

Some artists might have done better than others – for example, the tohunga-tā-moko probably did better than the weavers and the wood-carvers. By and large most of them made great contributions to the cultural enhancement of the tribe or of the local hapū. Some worked across tribal boundaries and were looked after and rewarded by other tribes.

Divine origins of the arts

Woodcarving

According to traditional beliefs the source of woodcarving traces back either to a mythical otherworldly ancestor or to a God. Some tribes credit a mythical ancestor called Rua with the more realistic three-dimensional ancestor figures. Others credit Tangaroa. One version was recorded by the Ngāti Porou and Ngāti Hauiti ancestor Mokena Romio about 1890 (Mead 1984:64–65). The story is very detailed and credits Ruatepupuke with committing a breach of protocol in respect of Tangaroa, God of the sea. The utu demanded by Tangaroa was to take Ruatepupuke's son named Manuruhi down into his realm. There he transformed Manuruhi into a bird and hung him up on the gable of his carved house as decoration. He took away his human form, but not his personality and ability to speak.

Eventually the father searched for his son and found him in the realm of Tangaroa. Ruatepupuke discovered a fully carved house on the ocean floor. The ancestor figures moved and spoke, but they could not leave the slab onto which they were fixed. Manuruhi was able to speak to his father and together they hatched a plan. Ruatepupuke set fire to Tangaroa's house but he took the tekoteko of the house and a poupou and brought them back to earth. The point of the story told against the background of hara–utu–ea (cause–means of resolution–settlement) is that the highest forms of decorative art came from Tangaroa.

Ruatepupuke, who is the central figure of the origin tradition, is a descendant of Tangaroa. He is a grandson of Tangaroa and is essentially part of the divine family (Mead 1984:67). The divine origin of most of the arts explains why they are tapu and very special. According to Tūhoe sources (Hamilton 1901:372) Takataka-putea and Marere-o-tonga were the originators and inventors of dancing, flute playing and various games. Other tribes credit Raukata-uri and Raukata-mea with these arts. The haka is credited to the Summer Maid, Raumati and hence the dance was called Te Haka a Raumati (Raumati's Dance) (Hamilton 1901:376). As we have seen in chapter 14, tattooing originated in the underworld of spirits and it was Mataora who went in search of his wife Niwareka and met up with her family. Ue-tonga, her father, taught the art of tā-moko to Mataora and gave him a beautiful cloak to bring back to earth. It is said that Niwareka was the first woman to have her forehead and cheeks tattooed (Best 1941, 2:547), albeit with simple crosses and not the elaborate patterns that became a hallmark of Māori tā-moko.

The tikanga of weaving

Hine-te-iwaiwa is regarded 'as the patroness and the originator of the art of weaving' (Best 1941, 2:514). Best (1941, 2:511–14) describes the whare pora (house of weaving). This house was not actually a building, but rather it was the collective of weavers old and young who worked within the principles of the house, who protected its traditions and made sure that novices were properly inducted into the tikanga. There was a knowledge base belonging to the house – a mātauranga of weaving – there were procedures for novices to follow, and there was tapu.

The tikanga of weaving is described in Best (1941, 2:511–14) and in Mead (1969:169–70). Erenora Puketapu Hetet (1989:3) refers to some aspects of tapu. The initiation of weavers begins almost at birth when a baby girl is dedicated to weaving. A special karakia is recited over the child to dedicate her to the art form of weaving and this was done during the tohi (baptism) ceremony.

Taylor (1870:186) provides an example of a special karakia for baby girls. The key lines are:

> Hahau kai mau, tangaengae;
> Haere ki te wahie mau, tangaengae
> Whatu kakahu mau, tangaengae.

> Seek food for yourself, make this bind
> Go for firewood for yourself, make this bind
> Weave garments for yourself, make this bind.

> (My translation)

As the girl grew up her aunts and grandmothers observed her to see whether she was keen on weaving. She would be encouraged to watch her mother or her aunts or the elders, the kuia of her family. She would participate in all aspects of weaving and would thus learn quite naturally, almost as a matter of course.

Later in life a girl may have been tested to see whether she was really keen to learn. There may have been some discouragement to ensure there was a strong interest.

1. Once the aunts were convinced of a genuine interest a young woman would then be matched with a recognised expert in weaving that may be her own mother or someone else. At this point she 'enters' the whare pora.

2. A tohunga performs special karakia, which begin the novice's serious training in the various branches of weaving and in the techniques one has to learn. The novice sits before two weaving pegs called pou kurukuru. The right peg is tapu. She attaches wefts across the two pegs. The main weft is called the aho tapu, the sacred thread. Before she actually begins any serious weaving the novice is required to bite the top of the sacred peg as soon as the appropriate karakia is completed.

3. She then weaves the sacred thread. She does not actually do much weaving because the main purpose of the ceremony is ritual confirmation. There may be another karakia to bind the knowledge of weaving.

4. Te hurihanga takapau (turning the floor mat). The weaver was given a leaf of pūhā to chew on. There may be a karakia to clear the tapu so the novice can mingle once again with her family.

5. Once the rituals are completed it is assumed that the weaver is under tapu, notwithstanding the karakia to reduce the level during the hurihanga takapau ceremony. As a dedicated weaver she will always have the status of a tapu weaver. From now on she will not make any human errors in weaving; the errors will be ritual in nature and may portend coming unpleasant events. The weaver becomes a beneficiary of divine strength and support but at the same time she also becomes a 'vehicle' for messages from the Gods.

6. From now on the weaver follows some simple ritual rules (Mead 1969:171).

    a. Fine garments are woven during daylight hours.

    b. When the sun sets the sacred weaving peg is taken down; the work is rolled up and then covered.

    c. It is permissible to work on capes and kilts at night.

    d. Weaving is done under cover. That is, it is not open for public observation.

    e. When strangers arrive work stops and the work is covered.

    f. Weavers should not smoke while weaving. This rule applied formerly to all artists because tobacco was classified as a food. Tapu and cooked food do not go together.

7. Gathering material: Weavers are subject to similar rules that all other artists using natural materials have to observe. Thus for weavers there are special rules for the care of harakeke (flax) plants, for cutting harakeke, preparing the strips needed for some baskets and mats, and for clearing the green material away from a leaf in order to reveal the white fibres needed for quality cloaks.

8. Tikanga with dyeing: There are two aspects to dyeing the fibres of harakeke, the technical processes and the ritual requirements. Here the emphasis is on tikanga or the ritual aspect.

    a. Weavers engaged in dyeing fibres according to traditional methods must avoid sex the night before.

b. Widows and spinsters were often called upon to undertake this task.

c. The placing of the fibres in mud should be done in daylight hours.

d. If a southerly wind is blowing the task must be postponed.

e. Great care is required to ensure success. Failure results in poor colours and loss of mana for the weaver.

f. There is a great deal of anxiety about the process and in understanding the chemical process involved. Weavers have to master the process in order to ensure consistency in the results. Today the whole process is focused on technical mastery and, while the traditions are respected, the rituals are not as important as they used to be.

Other sources of tapu

Enough has been said about the divine origins of the arts and the fact that creative activity was credited to the Gods and god-like figures. Talented human artists developed the divine models, added their own creative genius and produced truly impressive art. The development and elaboration of the arts is credited to the artists, but not the origin of the art form.

The next source of tapu comes from the materials that artists work with. Anything from the forest belonged to the God Tāne. Shells and shark teeth are from the world of Tangaroa. Greenstone is from the earth and credited to Poutini, guardian of greenstone (Best 1941, 1:163–64). Poutini is associated with water and with Tangaroa. Whales are from the realm of Tangaroa.

In fact, wherever artists and craftsmen and women turned in the natural world they dealt with the Gods of the Māori world. Even when the 'material' to be worked on was the human body, as in tā-moko, the tohunga-tā-moko deals with the God Tūmatauenga.

In summary then the following points can be made:

1. The source of the arts leads to the Gods, to the children of Rangi and Papa and to members of divine families.

2. The source of a person's pūmanawa is a gift handed down the family line and is something to be respected and treasured. The talent is tapu.

3. The materials used in creative activities all carry an element of tapu.

4. Artists traditionally worked under tapu and especially (but not only) while doing creative work. There were activities that were prohibited to them while they were at work.

Tikanga and other art activities

I have chosen to use weaving as an example of the tikanga requirements of that art domain. There are similar sorts of requirements for every art form and there is a list of dos and don'ts for each, some quite extensive and others less so. For example, tohunga tārai waka (expert canoe builders) begin at the forest where the trees stand. There they have to perform certain rituals before they fell a tōtara tree and there are many other tikanga they need to follow thereafter. One very important decision that a canoe builder has to make is to determine the natural floating position of a log without having to actually put the log into water. If the expert does not know how to determine this it is best for that person to carry out some practical tests by cutting lengths of logs of varying sizes and immersing these in water. The log will automatically float in one way. The floating position is then compared with the shape and pattern of the tree rings. Eventually one is able to read the tree ring pattern to determine which part of the log will form the keel of the waka and which will be the top part of it. Often there is a relationship between the tikanga and the judgement that a canoe builder has to make in order to build a good waka.

The best way to learn the tikanga of any one art form is to work alongside an experienced worker. This is essential for canoe builders and for woodcarvers who aspire to be a tohunga whakairo who is able to manage all aspects of constructing and decorating a whare whakairo. It is equally important for an artist wanting to be a tohunga tā moko. While many of our best contemporary tohunga tā moko have been largely self taught this practice is unnecessary when there are so many experts in the field today. People who teach themselves do not necessarily get the tikanga right. They may master the technical aspects of the art form and fail to achieve the same level of mastery over the tikanga. It is preferable to have full control over both aspects.

Our ancestors were able to produce some outstanding works of art that hold their own among the best works in the world. They were not lacking in creative talent, nor in sheer technical skill. Perhaps the extra dimension that assisted them was the discipline of tikanga Māori which allied them very closely to their communities and more importantly to the values of their communities. Observing the rules of tapu demands a high level of commitment and dedication to the heritage.

I am aware that many weavers have chosen to work within the tikanga of tapu. This is a personal choice that each weaver has to make. Likewise it is a choice that all artists who work within the art heritage of our people have to make. This applies to tukutuku weavers, tāniko weavers, kōwhaiwhai designers, greenstone artists, bone carvers, wood-carvers who produce waka huia, tokotoko (walking sticks), weapons and ornaments of many types. Artists who feel uncomfortable or inadequate with the tikanga Māori aspects of their work could choose to work outside of the rules of tapu. That is their choice.

Accountability

The other important reason why artists tended to produce works of great skill is that they were accountable to the people and to the community. The level of expected accountability was higher for complex works such as carved houses, decorated pātaka and waka taua. Accountability was locked into the system of tapu. The focus was on errors both in the performing arts as well as in the visual arts. If a glaring error was made in a decorated meeting house for example, the mistake was regarded as a ritual error. In other words, the mistake is not a lapse of memory, a falter in a performance, or a failure to execute a pattern properly or with proper care. That is a human error. Rather the belief was that the Gods spoke through the artist and the error is the first sign of utu or punishment for something done previously by the artist. Once the error is pointed out publicly, and usually at the ceremony that presents the work of art to the people, the second and more deadly phase of utu is expected to take effect. Depending on the seriousness of the error the life of the artist or performer is at stake. No one attacks the artist physically. But the tapu that surrounds the work attacks like an unseen arrow and the person wastes away and dies.

If it is not the life of the artist that is expected as utu, the other possibility is that the family of the artist is subject to a series of misfortunes. It is then believed that the family did something wrong ritually and misfortune is the punishment. Their only recourse is to seek the help of a good tohunga who will recite the appropriate karakia to make amends for the error or to cast it aside. After turning to Christianity many Māori artists, weavers and performers decided that the accountability to the Gods was too onerous and frightening and so decided to give up the tapu of all forms of work, including creative work.

Modern artists, weavers and performers are only just turning attention to taking up some elements of the tapu of creative work but leaving other elements alone. It is a process of rediscovery for many Māori artists, a time for experimentation, for testing, for adopting what seems to be good, sensible practice and rejecting aspects such as accountability to the Gods. Some find inspiration in following tradition and linking back to the roots of the art form and to the artists of generations gone by. Some artists actively reject the tapu of creative work but like the idea of the tikanga of a dawn ceremony to open an art exhibition. Others are more cautious because there is a lingering fear that the power of the Gods has not been extinguished entirely.

Fields of creativity

In traditional times the fields in which artists could exercise their creative talents covered a wide number of activities. We know about tā moko as one of these important fields. Artists could and did make names for themselves by excelling in tā moko and becoming household figures. Tukutuku was another activity that required a high level of skill and offered artists opportunities to be creative. Sir Apirana Ngata had a reputation for demanding high standards of skill in tukutuku weavers. If a panel did not meet the required standard he would use a sharp knife to cut up the work of the weavers. They would have to start again.

Tohunga whakairo would also demand high standards and would reject a piece of work that in their opinion was sub-standard. In woodcarving, artists were given many challenges to show off their skill and creative genius. Kōwhaiwhai is a fascinating field of activity for artists with creative talent. While some artists are content to copy old patterns others create entirely new patterns which enhance the overall beauty of some carved meeting houses as in Te Tumu Herenga Waka at Victoria University of Wellington and Tane-nui-a-rangi at the University of Auckland. Less obvious were the areas of artefacts, tools and ornaments. Artists working whalebone, greenstone and other kinds of bones and stones were able to apply their creative talents and produce some beautiful works of art. This was also the case with woodcarvers who worked with wood to produce canoes, canoe paddles, balers and decorated features for canoes.

In fact, it is difficult to limit the opportunities for creative people to apply and exercise their creative talents. Creative talent was expected to be used to enhance the quality of life, to transform the environment and to apply the stamp of culture upon it. In today's world the opportunities are just as varied. Pūmanawa such as creative talent is expected to be used to put the stamp of Māori culture upon the landscape. Some artists accept the challenge to become global in the fields they choose to work in and the media they want to manipulate.

Opening art exhibitions

Regardless of whether artists work within tikanga Māori or outside of it the idea of a tikanga Māori opening for an exhibition is popular. A large exhibition might even have a special dawn ceremony. More thought actually needs to be given to the nature of an art exhibition. Where does it fit in the scheme of traditional rituals? The model followed by artists is that set by the Te Māori exhibition in New York in 1984, discussed in chapter 5. In this model two things were happening. The first was clearing the site of the exhibition and the second could be described as 'settling our ancestors', preparing them for what was to come and also helping to remove from the works they created any effects that might be harmful to visitors. Because Te Māori was loaded with extremely valuable art creations made long ago and because the works presented our culture and our people to the international world there were heightened concerns about tikanga Māori and about getting it right.

Modern art exhibitions are arranged for entirely different purposes. Now artists are exhibiting their works for the buying public. These works are different from those exhibited in Te Māori and logically the form of the ritual opening ought to be different. An exhibition of modern works by a group of Māori artists does not equate to a new fully carved meeting house that will stand against the four winds for decades to come. Yet the form of ritual being used to open a modern art exhibition is virtually the same as that used for a new building on a marae. The question is this: Is there another tikanga that might be more appropriate for art exhibitions?

The answer is, yes there is one. A suitable tikanga to invoke is the aukati or rāhui. This would mean that the exhibition is not open to the public until the aukati is lifted. Meanwhile the organisers are free to make their preparations regardless of whether they follow the rules of tapu or not. In an aukati a sign is placed on the door as a symbol of an aukati. This sign has to be taken down ritually and by agreement of all parties. The doors are then opened and the tohunga is then able to perform karakia that would clear away all ritual obstacles so that the exhibition is now free of restrictions and the public is free to inspect and reflect on what they see. The ceremony is easier for the tohunga, its purpose is clearer, and in the end everyone is happy.

I have actually witnessed an opening that followed the tikanga of the aukati and it was employed by the Hawai'ian community at the opening of a commemorative exhibition to Sir Peter Buck at the Bishop Museum in 1985. This was witnessed by a huge delegation of Māori from the East Coast. The occasion is remembered by those who participated in it as a momentous meeting of tikanga Māori and tikanga Hawai'ian. All went well and the hākari and manaakitanga that followed is memorable. Thus it was the Hawai'ians who pointed out to us that this ancient tikanga which we share among all Polynesians and most of Melanesia can be used to good effect to open an art exhibition.

Conclusions

In all branches of art there are tikanga to observe. In tā moko, for example, because blood is spilled in the process there are some strict observances to follow. There is also the idea that groups of people prepare themselves for the tohunga tā moko. The itinerant specialist does not visit a village to do one person. Rather, there is a group of men and a group of women. One of each group is selected to represent the whole group. The chosen one has great mana because of whakapapa and becomes the symbolic head of the group. The rest are regarded as 'feathers for his/her feet', that is, they are their supporters.

In woodcarving there are tikanga which are specific to this art form, much of which is described in various books (such as Hamilton 1901; Archey 1977; Mead et al. 1984; Mead 1995) and need not be summarised here. The point to reiterate is that as a highly valued activity art is surrounded and immersed in tikanga. Through time and as a result of culture contact the tikanga has diminished and changed. Whereas before smoking on the job was against the rules of tapu, nowadays carvers may smoke as they carve both traditional and contemporary compositions in wood. Even the kind of wood they use has changed. Some carvers believe that observing the rules of tapu is far too onerous in today's world. Some prefer to set aside the tapu of carving although they still want their work to be included in the ceremony of 'te tā i te kawa o te whare', lifting the tapu of the house. Others, however, want to observe what they consider to be appropriate today, arguing that it is the observance of tapu which accords to the work the seriousness that is required. Weavers face similar concerns and they too have to decide what is appropriate for them. Generally, they lean towards observance of some tapu rules and want to give mana to their work.

There are many artists today who know little or nothing about tikanga and have much learning to do. The observance of the tikanga of creative work actually enhances the activity, gives significance to the work and elevates the activity as something special and highly valued.

Perspectives

The first cross thread woven by the learner is viewed as the *tapu* thread, and the right hand peg of the crude frame is said to have also been *tapu*. Prior to the commencement of the weaving the learner, sitting before the frame or pegs, took a hank of dressed fibre in her hand and sat inactive as the expert recited a charm the object of which was to force the knowledge of the art of weaving into the mind of the learner, and render it permanent. As the expert finished his recitation the scholar leaned forward and bit the upper part of the right hand *turuturu*, or rod, just closing her teeth on it. She then proceeded to weave the first cross thread. She would then weave a few more cross threads under the eye of the expert when her weaving would be discontinued for the day. That first piece of work was styled a *kawhatuwhatu*; it was never finished or continued, but was viewed as a pattern piece, a kind of sampler.

Another ceremony was performed in order to remove the *tapu* of the proceedings from the actors. In this performance the scholar was given a small portion of a herb called *puwha* to eat, and the ceremony itself was sometimes termed *moremore puwha*.

– Best 1941, 2:513

Te whare pora

The whare pora, whare parapara, and whare takutaku, the name differing in different districts. There was a certain amount of tapu and ceremony pertaining to the acquirement of the art of weaving. When a young woman desired to learn how to weave fine garments she obtained the assistance of an expert. She had to weave a small piece of fabric under close supervision, and the task was accompanied by certain ceremonial, including the repetition of charms by the directing expert.

– Best 1941, 2:511

Modern tohunga – tā moko

A descendant of traditional tattoo artists, Inia's first works were in pen on the faces and bodies of actors in such movies as *Once Were Warriors* and *What Becomes of the Broken Hearted*. Friends asked him to design for them, but he often felt frustrated with tattoo artists' efforts to interpret his designs properly. He headed to Europe and America to learn all he could about tattooing.

'I received a lot of assistance,' he says. 'Although [it's] a very secretive world, where trade secrets are kept pretty tight, people realised I wasn't going to be peeing on their lamp post at all. I was actually reviving something that was my family's anyway.'

Inia uses a tattoo machine for much of his work, but he insists on using traditional tools for facial moko. 'When people come to me to get their traditional tattoo, I give it to them exactly the way it was done,' he says.

Just as the integrity of Moko Inc is important to him, Inia also expects people to wear his work with integrity, 'It demands a full-time, seven days a week, 52 weeks a year commitment to wear it, so the least I can do is commit my life to supplying it. There's a thing that starts and stops when you tattoo, which is the design, but there's another part of it that carries on right through life and that's the 'who did that?' I want that 'who did that' to carry as much mana as the rest of it.'

   – Swan, 2001:36

Broadening the concept of creativity

Everyone is potentially creative. An over-emphasis on rationality alone, technocratic reasoning, restrictive organizational or community struc-tures and an over-reliance on traditional approaches can restrict or destroy this potential. This is why it is important that the prestige attached to the arts should not lead to the neglect of countless, modest imaginative undertakings that inject a vital substance into the social fabric. All the people need to communicate their experiences, their hopes and fears, as they have always done, and many local initiative help them to do so without having to ask whether what they are doing is 'creative' or even 'art'. Suffice that it aims at its chosen public in a fresh and stimulating way.

Precisely because the creative approach cannot be taught or commanded, it has to be nurtured wherever it appears. In spite of its universal potential in a favourable environment, the spark of artistic creativity is in fact so rare that it needs careful fanning wherever it flickers, in the hope of generating a fire. Creativity clearly thrives in a fostering environment. But it is also unpredictable and undefin-able. During the past two decades the social and economic conditions of artistic work have been radically transformed.

   – Pérez de Cuéller 1996:79

The tapu of artwork

The people here were exceedingly troublesome about the *tapu*, and E Pera was as bad as any of them: they were angry because my portfolio was placed under the cooking shed to preserve it from the rain, for E Pera had told them that it contained the head of Te Heuheu, and as it is sacrilege for him to enter a place appropriated to food, it is equally sacrilege for his portrait to be placed under similar circumstances.

– Angas 1847, 2:133

16
Te Tuakiri, Te Whenua: Identity and Land

All over the world land is an important issue that groups of people are prepared to fight over, just as our ancestors did long ago. There are international examples of note: Palestine, Kosovo, Bosnia, Kashmir, East Timor, Ireland. When competing claimants fight over land their behaviours tend to change dramatically. Land evokes strong emotions among the people who live upon it. These powerful emotions are often linked to cultural mechanisms of bonding and may be positive and controlled. But fanned by zealots these positive attitudes to land can lead to ethnic cleansing and the slaughter and mutilation of hundreds and thousands of victims as in some parts of Africa and in Kosovo. For most people the traditional notion of a homeland is an important basis of national identity. We want a place that we can call home.

Whenua

The Māori word for land is whenua. But the word whenua means more than land: it also means 'placenta', 'ground', 'country' and 'state'. Williams (1957: 494) adds the further meaning of 'altogether' or 'entirely'. Thus whenua carries a wide range of meanings. Whenua, as placenta, sustains life and the connection between the foetus and the placenta is through the umbilical cord. This fact of life is a metaphor for whenua, as land, and is the basis for the high value placed on land.

As we shall discuss further in the next chapter, when a child is born the placenta is buried in the ground, hence the whenua returns to the whenua, which is similar to the biblical idea of 'dust to dust'. The dried-up remnant of the umbilical cord is hidden in a cliff or in a tree or also buried in the ground. The word whānau is the name of the basic social unit of Māori society, the extended family. Thus the birth unit is a close knit relatively small group into which new members are received. Thus there are associations between whenua as placenta, whenua as ground and whenua as land. There is a mix of birth, placenta, umbilical cords, land and social unit. Today, however, many whānau are dislocated from their traditional land bases and now have to base themselves in other districts.

Tangata whenua: people of the land

The ideology of the culture ties the pieces together and there are cultural practices which focus upon the pieces, such as dealing with the placenta and the umbilical cord. The result is that new members of the group are tied to the land. The people so bonded are called tangata whenua. Internationalise the term tangata whenua and it becomes the indigenous people.

Cultural practices and beliefs lay the foundation for the high value that most Māori give to whenua, as land.

Iwi and bones

As we have seen in chapter 13, the social unit that is larger than the whānau is the hapū, which consists of several whānau or birth units that are bound together through common ancestors. The iwi is the next plank of the system. It consists of several hapū. The word 'iwi' may refer to bones, to one's relatives. What is left of members of the iwi are their bones which are usually buried in caves or in the ground. This cultural practice also creates binding relationships with the land.

Thus pregnancy, birth, the placenta, the umbilical cord and bones (hapū, whenua, pito, iwi) become enmeshed in the concept of whenua, as land.

Burial sites

One of the great fears of losing land is loss of burial sites and their desecration by settlers bent on eliminating the rights of former occupants. The links to the land become evidence of rights of occupation and rights of use. Burial sites are very important in this sense. Burial sites are the resting places of the ancestors, of the elders of the group and close relatives who have passed on. The urupā is as important as the marae in defining who we are.

The whare whakairo

Ancestors are important anchor points in the social system. Not only are they the key points in genealogies but they also give special significance to decorated meeting houses (whare whakairo) which enclose a gallery of ancestor figures. One can claim a direct link to the ancestral meeting house. The ancestral house and the descendents of that ancestor are indivisible. These houses, often named after an ancestor, also provide evidence of land occupation over many years. In addition, a grid of place names is placed over the landscape and these names also link to particular ancestors and so reinforce the emotional connection to the land. The marae on which the ancestral house stands also has a name which might be an ancestral name or some other name of great significance to the people of the marae.

A combination of many elements assist members of a culture to come to terms with the land they live on. Many of these elements are institutionalised and become normal practice. Cultural practices or tikanga associated with birth and death emphasise links to the land and include burial of the placenta, concealment of the dried-up remains of the umbilical cord and burial of the remains of the dead in caves or in the ground. There is also a high value given to the grid of place names, the network of wāhi tapu (the sacred sites discussed in chapter 5), and special features such as mountains, lakes, rivers, islands and coastal sites.

The world of spirits

In addition there are songs and dances which feature significant landmarks and these become a part of the symbolic world of members of the culture. Then there are the spirits of the ancestors: spirits which hover over significant sacred sites, spirits which are called upon to be present at important ceremonial occasions, spirits of the mountains, malevolent spirits and protective spirits in rivers and lakes, guardian spirits in the ocean, new spirits on their way to joining others, and many spirits unseen but ever present in the space between heaven and earth.

Land as the foundation of the social system

The land and the environment in which people live became the foundation of their view of the world, the centre of their universe and the basis of their identity as citizens or as members of a social unit. Traditionally the bonding to the land was necessary as a means of strengthening the resolve of the warriors to fight for their land whenever it was coveted by others. Land had to be defended and protected against all comers. Therefore, a warrior force was necessary.

Land was also necessary as a means of maintaining social solidarity. Land was the foundation of the social system, the base, the means of giving reality to the system in the forms of residences, villages, gardens, special resource regions and so on. Continuity of the group depended very much on a home base called te wā kāinga where people could live like an extended family and actually see it on the ground as a working reality.

Concept of tūrangawaewae

Undoubtedly land provides a place for one to stand. This is inherent in the concept of tūrangawaewae, a place for the feet to stand; where one's rights are not challenged, where one feels secure and at home. The concept of tūrangawaewae will always be important not only for Māori, but most modern citizens. The global society notwithstanding and despite the stunning technology of the modern world, land will always be an important part of how we define ourselves as people. We all need a place for our feet to stand, a place to call our own.

Māori people have been consistent in placing a high value on ancestral land. In more recent times there have been protests and occupations since the 1970s beginning with Bastion Point, which became the benchmark for future protests. This was a protest by Ngāti Whātua of Orakei about their land and involved a 506-day-long occupation of the site by their people and by sympathisers from other tribes. It took on the elements of a pan-iwi protest and appeared to have no satisfactory resolution. The people were pushed off the land by a massive police action on 25 May 1978, but that did not stop other protests over land. There have been many others.

The relationship to the land

The net effect of various cultural bonding mechanisms and traditional tikanga practices was to develop a relationship with the land. This relationship is about bonding to the land and having a place upon which one's feet can be placed with confidence. The relationship is not about owning the land and being master of it, to dispose of as the owner sees fit. The land has been handed down the whakapapa line from generation to generation and the descendant fortunate enough to inherit the land does not really 'own' it. That person did not buy it. The land cannot be regarded as a personal asset to be traded.

Durie (1987:78) puts the position very clearly in the following statement: 'In the beginning land was not something that could be owned or traded. Maoris did not seek to own or possess anything, but to belong. One belonged to a family, that belonged to a hapu, that belonged to a tribe. One did not own land. One belonged to the land.'

The traditional land tenure system was overturned by various acts of Parliament and through the Native Land Court. Now there is little land left in Māori ownership. Bonding to the land has changed since the introduction of shareholdings in land blocks. A result is that larger shareholders have greater voting power than others. Thus relationships among the 'owners' have become divisive. Now the descendants of the ancestors regard themselves as 'owners' because the Māori Land Court says they are owners, and they often call 'meetings of owners'. This concept of owning a commodity has become general. We rarely hear of Māori saying they are bonded to the land. Rather they are asserting ownership rights.

Identity is translated as 'tuakiri' in *Te Matatiki* (Taura Whiri i te Reo Māori 1996:63), and Williams (1957:445) provides a gloss of 'person, personality'. Tua means to be on the farther side of something, and kiri is skin. Tuakiri probably refers to the elements away from the body that help define the identity and personality of a person. That far side is probably the land, the mountains, rivers, lakes, the ocean front, the islands and the sea, all of which ground a personality to a place.

But this way of looking at identity does not sit well with the notion of owning and trading the land. Working it for the collective good lies within tikanga Māori, but selling land to help buy a car and so dispossessing others from belonging to the land is not consistent with tikanga. Thus there are problems in respect of Māori land and there are changes in respect of the relationship to the land. While we speak in glowing terms about the values we hold about our land, others are quietly trading away the foundations of our identity.

Land in treaty settlements

As can be expected land is a very important part of any settlement with the Crown in remedy of Crown breaches of the Treaty of Waitangi. The first major settlement of modern times was the Waikato–Tainui settlement of 22 May 1995. An important principle of negotiation and settlement was the Waikato dictum 'i riro whenua atu, me hoki whenua mai' (as land was taken, land should be returned). The Crown actually agreed 'to return as much land as is possible that the Crown has in its possession…' (Office of Treaty Settlements 1995:6). The quantity returned was 15,553 hectares (29,803 acres). Waikato lost 500,000 hectares (1.2 million acres) by raupatu or confiscation (Ward 1999:54).

For the Ngāi Tahu settlement of 1998, the redress package included 'some high-country pastoral properties in Crown title; some forest lands and license fees from those lands, the right of first refusal over some urban Crown lands (including airports); the title to certain previous sites; and the title to certain reserves' (Ward 1999:57). The Crown and Ngāi Tahu negotiators together agreed to some innovative legal mechanisms for recognising Ngāi Tahu historical and cultural associations in certain lakes, streams and wetlands. One example is the recognition of nohoanga sites which are like camping sites for people who are gathering food, or fishing out at sea, or gathering shellfish close to the shore. The iwi is given the right of use under certain conditions for a prescribed number of days in a year. These are the forms of statutory acknowledgments and deeds of recognition that have now become a standard part of Treaty settlements.

Shares in land blocks

When the land-tenure system of Māori was changed and Māori land was reclassified, surveyed and divided up into blocks of varying sizes, lists of owners were drawn up for the blocks that remained Māori land and shares were allocated to the 'owners'. There are some people with large holdings of shares and others with very small holdings, and very small fractions of a share. Yet the share – no matter how small or big – represents a link to the land and is the basis of an individual's tūranga-waewae in respect of that block of land. Through that share a person belongs and can attend meetings of 'owners', share in decision making and receive a dividend. As 'owners' die the shares become divided among their descendants and so the shares become increasingly fragmented and the dividend so small that it is hardly worth writing out a cheque for it. But that tiny bit of land is the basis of tūrangawaewae. The only way to stop further fragmentation is for a whānau group to apply to the Māori Land Court to establish a whānau trust. The whānau trust alters the basis of tūrangawaewae to whakapapa only, that is to establish a kinship link to the ancestor under whose name the whānau trust is to be formed. A share is no longer necessary.

An interesting by-product of multiple ownership and having hundreds of owners in a block is that the land becomes almost impossible to sell. In that sense it is good to have hundreds of people who belong to a block of land. The descendants have something to belong to and the land cannot be easily sold.

Customary land

It is a truism to say that there was a time when Māori owned all land in Aotearoa under the customary land tenure system. The land belonged to a collective group and its members used it, lived upon it, named various parts of it and established relationships with it. There was no concept of ownership and clear title as in the western case.

The collective group, whānau or hapū occupied the land and defended it from all others. Their fires of occupation, ahikāroa, lasted until such time as the fires were either forcefully extinguished or the land was gifted to some other group. Most of this land is lost and there is very little remaining as customary land that has not been through the Māori Land Court system or converted into Crown grants.

Recently Ngāti Awa was able to claim Te Paepae-o-Aotea, a group of rocky islets about fifty kilometres out to sea from Whakatane, as customary land on behalf of the iwi of Mātaatua. Te Rūnanga o Ngāti Awa was appointed as trustee over this customary land. Later Ngāti Awa claimed customary title to several rocks just out from the mouth of the Whakatane River. Several were included in the claim granted by the Māori Land Court, which has exclusive jurisdiction to investigate Māori customary land.

Categories of Māori land

Māori land is now classified in different ways and administered by a variety of trusts under the Ture Whenua Maori Act 1993. The purpose of the Act is to recognise that land is a taonga tuku iho of special significance to Māori, to promote the retention of the land in the hands of the owners and to assist the Māori people in achieving the implementation of these principles.

Tikanga Māori is defined in the Act to mean 'Maori customary values and practices' (section 3, Te Ture Whenua Maori Act 1993). The Act recognises Māori land as 'taonga tuku iho' that is, as a precious heritage which should be retained and maintained in Māori hands. Tikanga Māori is the main basis of claims for customary or aboriginal title to land and tikanga Māori might be taken into consideration in the deliberations of the Māori Land Court. But tikanga in respect of land is very much in the hands of the Māori Land Court and much has changed from traditional times. For example, land is no longer given as wedding presents and whānau and hapū are no longer forced off the land they occupy. The dynamics of the traditional land tenure system do not function today. We petition the Māori Land Court now and we use the authority of Te Ture Whenua Maori Act 1993.

Māori freehold land

This is land registered in the Māori Land Court as Māori freehold land. The land is held by a group of owners or by individual owners or by Māori incorporations. According to the Law Commission (2001:62–63) there are currently 25,887 Māori freehold titles. 12,441 are not yet surveyed and 14,852 are not registered under the Land Transfer Act. There are 119,000 owners.

1. Altogether, Māori freehold land totals 1,515,071 hectares, or about six percent of the landmass of Aotearoa.
2. The blocks average fifty-eight hectares and the largest blocks average 522 hectares.
3. Ahu whenua trusts administer 49.56% of Māori freehold land.
4. The average number of owners for a block is sixty-two per title, but the larger blocks average 425 owners each.

General land

This is land that is not protected under the Ture Whenua Maori Act 1993 and is registered under the Land Transfer Act 1952. It may be ancestral land which has passed through the Māori Land Court and is classified as general land but is still held by the descendants of the original owners, or it is land purchased by individuals and held by them. These owners can apply to the Māori Land Court to have their general land reclassified as freehold.

Māori reservations

This is a category of Māori freehold land which is classified as a Māori reservation under the Te Ture Whenua Maori Act 1993, part xviii. The Act states that on the recommendation of the Māori Land Court the chief executive can:

> Set apart any Freehold Land or General Land as a Maori Reservation for the purposes of a village site, marae, meeting place, recreation ground, sports ground, bathing place, church site, building site, burial ground, landing place, fishing ground, spring, well, catchment area or other source of water supply, timber reserve, or place of cultural, historical or scenic reserve, or for any other specified purpose.

Māori incorporations

Under section 247 of Te Ture Whenua Maori Act 1993 'the court may, if it considers it in the interests of the owners to do so, make an order incorporating as a Maori Incorporation the owners of any one or more areas of Maori Freehold Land, of which at least 1 area is owned for a legal estate in fee simple by 2 or more owners.'

Shares are allocated and the owners have the authority 'to carry on or undertake any business or activity, do any act or enter into any transactions ... .[with] full rights, powers and privileges' to do so.

Trusts

A variety of trusts were created under Te Ture Whenua Maori Act 1993 and each is set up for a specific purpose.

1. Pūtea trust

The Court may order one to be formed. 'The land, money, and other assets of a pūtea trust constituted under this section shall be held for Maori community purposes, or such as the court may specify...' (s212 (6)).

2. Whānau trust

'The land, money and other assets of a whanau trust shall be applied, for the purposes of promoting health, social, cultural, and economic welfare, education and vocational training, and general advancement in the life of descendants of any tipuna [whether living or dead] ...' (see 214 (3)).

3. Ahu whenua trust

The beneficiaries are the beneficial owners of a block or blocks of land which constitute an ahu whenua trust. 'The land, money and other assets of a whenua topu trust shall be held for Maori community purposes, or for such Maori community purposes as the court may specify...' (see 216 (5)).

4. Kai tiaki trust

A kai tiaki trust is 'constituted where the court is satisfied that the constitution of the trust would best protect and promote the interests of the person under disability'. The land, money and other assets of a kai tiaki trust shall be held in trust for the person under disability (see 217 (8)).

Traditional categories

How land was classified in traditional times is of great interest and elements of the land-tenure system are contested and argued before the Waitangi Tribunal when tribal claims are heard. The issue might be the meaning of the term raupatu (confiscation) or when and how land rights were extinguished in traditional times. What does it mean to have land gifted to a group and when might the gift be transformed into a right of use? Much has changed over the years but the traditional classifications and understandings remain a source of ongoing research in claims brought before the Waitangi Tribunal.

1. Whenua papatipu/papatupu

Williams (1959:261) defines papatipu as 'hard ground' or 'solid mass' and adds the modern gloss of 'Maori land not having a European title'. In other words, whenua papatipu is customary land held under customary title.

2. Whenua taunaha

There are instances in history of well-known Māori explorers and chiefs of high standing naming places as though they discovered them. Stories associated with the settlement of a waka crew often provide a lot of names given to certain landmarks. The new settlers acted as though there were no names given to the landscape and imposed on it their own grid of names. To name is to claim and to claim is to occupy and use. Newly named lands become new land for an occupying group. But naming has to be supported either by tangata-whenua consent, by the use of military force, by arranging political marriages, or by a combination of different tikanga.

Ihenga, the noted explorer of Te Arawa, provides a good example. He named and claimed many places for Te Arawa. These include Te Motu-tapu-a-Tinirau, Te Pera-o-Tangaroa, Te Kauae, Ngongotaha, Weriweri, Te Awahou, Puhirua, Kopu, Tupa-karia-a-Ihenga, Tanewhiti, Ohau, Tua-roto-rua, Te Niho-o-te-kuri and Kahui-kawau. According to Stafford (1967:33–36) Ihenga displaced the original occupiers of the land.

3. Ahikāroa

The Native Land Court system elevated the concept of ahikāroa to that of the supreme right to own a block of land. Claimants had to prove to a judge that their fires of occupation burned continuously for a long period of time and that at no time were their fires ever extinguished.

Evidence included cultivating gardens on the land, establishing a kāinga or village, building canoes, growing peach trees, attending to pigs or cows, building and looking after an eel weir and so on. Several far-fetched claims were put before the courts. The notion of ahikāroa is not consistent with the idea of seasonal occupation when groups moved from one place to another to harvest a food source at the right season. The more permanent village sites came at a later stage at the time of the introduction of Christianity, the Ngā Puhi raids, and the introduction of the musket into the technology of warfare. Major regroupings occurred and large villages were established. Notwithstanding the doubts of others, the concept of ahi-kā-roa remains an ideal of occupation.

4. Whenua raupatu

This is land conquered from another group of occupants. The basis of a claim before the Native Land Court was to argue a take raupatu, that is, to claim by conquest through the blade of a patu. That means of taking land overrode all other tikanga and introduced a new political order into the region.

It was not necessary for the conquering group to establish fires on all parts of the new land. The new group could exert their mana over a large area of land from one part of the estate. Challenges to their mana could occur later and successful challenges would lead eventually to the break-up of the estate.

5. Whenua tuku

This is land that has been gifted to the occupants. The basis of their claim is said to be he take tuku, a claim by way of gift. Such land could be gifted as part of an exchange of gifts in a marriage. It may be land given to an ally as payment for military services. Or it may be land given to a hapū in order to resettle them in the tribal rohe. A conquered group may be given land to work for the landlord, but in time the owners might agree to gift the land to them.

6. Whenua muru

This land is to be differentiated from land taken by the blade of a patu. Whenua muru is land sacrificed by a group in order to compensate others for a wrong done to them. The sacrifice might include a waka, a very valuable weapon, cloaks and land.

7. Take ōhākī

Sinclair (1981:91) included as a distinctive category land that was allocated to an individual as part of an ōhākī, a last testament of a dying chief. An estate may be broken up this way and allocated to the sons of a chief as a way of avoiding discontent and squabbles amongst them later.

The relevance of tikanga Māori

The customary system of land tenure was upheld as law in 1847, but Chief Justice Prendergast undermined the ruling (Williams 2000:5). Only recently has the Privy Council confirmed that there is 'a body of law called native custom' in New Zealand and that it could develop and evolve over time (Williams 2000:5).

Tikanga Māori is being applied in land issues under Te Ture Whenua Maori Act 1993, but it has become increasingly difficult to separate tikanga Māori from western land laws.

Williams (2000:6) sets out examples where tikanga Māori applies in law:

1. land issues in Treaty of Waitangi claims

2. identifying the traditional group for consultation purposes

3. allocation of settlement resources

4. succession to land interests

5. environmental issues

6. child welfare

7. administration of Māori land

8. establishing Treaty claims and mandates.

He argues that the principles of tikanga Māori – which he calls values – underpin the thinking today. He also provides guidelines as to how tikanga Māori might apply in particular cases.

The full impact of tikanga Māori in rules and regulations in respect of Māori land is yet to be realised. The relevance and application of tikanga Māori is still evolving and it would be interesting to see how it develops. It is true to say, however, that many Māori still hold dear to the heart the traditional values relating to their land.

Perspectives

Values in proverbs

He kura tangata e kore e rokohanga; he kura whenua ka rokohanga.
The treasured possessions of men are intangible. The treasures of the land are tangible.

> – Brougham and Reed 1987:57

Te toto o te tangata he kai, te oranga o te tangata he whenua.
Food supplies the blood of human beings, but the welfare of humans is based on land [my translation].

> – Brougham and Reed 1987:56

Māu te wahine mākau te whenua, kia ai koe i te tore tangata, kia ai hoki au i te tore whenua.
You have the woman and I will have the land so that you may copulate with the woman and I will copulate with the land [my translation].

> – Brougham and Reed 1987:56

Tukua mai he kapunga oneone ki ahau, hai tangi.
Send me a handful of soil that I may weep over it.

> – Brougham and Reed 1987:56

The relationship of Māori with the land

The importance of the land and the environment was reflected through whakapapa, ancestral place names and tribal histories. The regard with which Māori had with the kāwai tīpuna. The children of Ranginui and Paptūanuku were the parents of all resources: the patrons of all things tapu. As the descendants of Ranginui and Papatūanuku and the kāwai tīpuna, Māori maintained a continuing relationship with the land, environment, people, kāwai tīpuna, tīpuna and spirits. The way they conducted their lives and the respect they have for their environment and each other stemmed from whakapapa. The system of community co-operation in cultivation and sharing the natural resources inhibited any trend towards individualism and individual ownership of land.

The land is a source of identity for Māori. Being direct descendants of Papatūanuku, Māori see themselves as not only 'of the land', but 'as the land'. The living generations act as the guardians of the land, like their tīpuna had before them. Their uri benefit from that guardianship, because the land holds the link to their parents, grandparents and tīpuna, and the land is the link to future generations. Hence, the land was shared between the dead, the living and the unborn.

– Ministry of Justice 2001:44

The 1840 rule

In contested cases, especially those founded on take raupatu (conquest), the Court applied its so-called '1840 Rule', first set out authoritatively by Fenton in the Compensation Court in the *Oakura* case in 1866. In this case Ngati Tama and Ngati Mutunga were refused compensation for their confiscated lands in Taranaki on the basis that they abandoned these lands prior to 1840 and had not kept their 'fires burning' (the principle of ahi-ka-roa) in the intervening period. Fenton stated:

'We do not think it can reasonably be maintained that the British Government came to this Colony to improve Maori titles or to reinstate persons in possessions from which they had been expelled before 1840 or which they had voluntarily abandoned previously to that time. Having found it absolutely necessary to fix some point of time at which the titles as far as this Court is concerned must be regarded as settled, we have decided that that point of time must be the establishment of the British Government in 1840, and all persons who are proved to have been the actual owners or possessors of that land at that time must be regarded as the owners or possessors of those lands now.'

Oakura was a Compensation Court, not a Land Court, case; nevertheless, said Fenton, 'while the rule cannot be so strictly applied in the Native Land Court, where the questions to be tried are rights between the Maoris *inter se*', nevertheless even in the Land Court 'the rule is adhered to except in rare instances'. As applied in the Land Court, Sinclair sees the rule as having the following aspects:

(1) No use of force could confer rights to land after 1840.

(2) No later assertion of rights could be upheld that did not have the consent of the owners at 1840. This flowed from (1).

(3) Lack of occupation did not destroy a claim which was valid at 1840.

(4) The owners at 1840 could voluntarily dispose of their rights or admit other persons to ownership.

Fenton did not state exactly when in 1840 the clock began running, as it were: there are of course a number of possibilities. One consequence of the rule in the Waikato was that the Court refused to entertain claims that land had been placed under the mana of the Maori King, and insisted instead that title could be determined only by reference to customary use and practice as at 1840.

– Boast et al. 1999:78–79

The functioning of the court

(a) Investigations of title

The Court's main task in its first decades was to inquire into Maori ownership of blocks placed before it and issue titles based on Maori custom. This kind of case was styled an 'investigation of title'; by 1900 most of the remaining Maori-owned land in the country had been investigated and titles issued. Purportedly applying Maori customary law, the Court evolved a number of standardised 'take', or roots of title, including take raupatu (conquest), take tupuna (descent) and take tuku (gift). A sample of the Court's minute books ˙ gives the overwhelming impression that in practice most claims were based on a combination of ancestral descent and settlement, proved by whakapapa (genealogies) and proof of recent cultivations. The Court generally saw its main task of identifying the dominant hapu, proved by descent from an accepted ancestor 'set up' as the basis of the claim and supported by evidence of residence, cultivation, and the management of resources. After the enactment of the Native Lands Act 1873, the Court's standard approach was to make a brief judgment identifying the successful claimant group or groups, but leaving the process of identifying names to the successful claimants, who handed into the Court lists of names to be entered into the Court records.

Sometimes a supplementary hearing would be necessary to deal with objections to the list.

The Court rapidly developed a standardised and routine approach to its work, which quickly became apparent to Maori claimant groups who naturally tailored their claims accordingly. A group of specialist practitioners, sometimes lawyers and sometimes not (the latter were known as 'Native agents' or 'Native conductors' and were often Maori or part-Maori) developed to service Maori applicants and objectors and this no doubt helped with the process of formalisation and simplification of traditional land tenure and history characteristic of the Court process as a whole.

    – Boast et al. 1999:78–79

Definition of custom

Local customs are still regarded as a source of law in England. The requirements for recognition are set out in *Halsbury* (1998, 12(1):par. 606:160):

To be valid, a custom must have four essential attributes:

1. it must be immemorial;
2. it must be reasonable;
3. it must be certain in its terms, and in respect of both of the locality where it is alleged to obtain and of the persons it is alleged to affect;
4. it must be continued without interruption since its immemorial origin.

    Halsbury goes on to say: 'These characteristics serve a practical purpose as rules of evidence when the existence of a custom is to be established or refuted'

    – Halsbury 1998, 12(1):par. 601:160

Halsbury adds the following on the meaning and scope of custom:

A custom is a particular rule which has either actually or presumptively existed from time immemorial in a particular locality and obtained the force of law in that locality, although contrary to, or not consistent with, the general law of the realm.

    – Halsbury 1998, 12(1): par. 601:155

17
Te Whakawhānau: New Life

Before the coming of the settlers from Great Britain and Europe children were born in accordance with tikanga Māori. There was a knowledge base to the tikanga and there were accepted practices that were held to be correct. After Christianity was adopted by the local Māori population and after the people were colonised and shown the civilised and advanced ways of handling many things, including childbirth, the old customs and practices were set aside. Babies were born in hospitals, and we were told what to do not only in preparation for childbirth but for the birth itself and after-care of the newborn child. By the end of the 1900s and with few exceptions we had effectively lost our tikanga in respect of childbirth.

By the 1980s some of our mothers had begun asking questions about our birth customs. Some were alarmed at hospital practices in respect to the placenta. The general understanding was that they were thrown out and burnt. Some mothers wanted to know why they could not have their immediate whānau in attendance at the birth. In the 1950s and 1960s it was unheard of for the whānau to be in attendance. Even the father of the newborn child was not welcome. In those days we believed in the Plunket way and in the absolute authority of the doctor and hospital. Afterwards there was the district nurse, the saviour of all mothers of newborns, including Māori women. She was an institution.

All this has changed now. Whānau are able to attend births, the father of the child has a place in the process and there are home births and a variety of ideas about how best to deliver a newborn. Accompanying this liberalisation of ideas about childbirth we, as a people, have begun to reawaken our customs and try and put them into practice. However in this world of change there are many factors to be considered. Māori are scattered over the country and the world. Many of us are in mixed marriages so that there is no guarantee of understanding on the part of the spouse. Some families are removed from their whānau support and must fend for themselves. Today there are new challenges for Māoridom and, ironically, it is also a time to look back and reflect.

The whenua

One aspect of tikanga Māori is concerned with the placenta. Its common name is whenua; another name is ewe. The whenua is the medium between the mother and child, succouring a new life. After birth the whenua, as land, succours the whānau. The two whenua are similar. Both are real. Whenua as placenta allows a foetus to become a baby, a small human being with all the potential to become a strong and healthy adult. Whenua, as land, sees that person develop and grow, make their contribution to society and then be 'born' into the spirit world.

It makes sense that the whenua as placenta should be returned to whenua as land and deposited within the bosom of the Earth Mother, Papa-tū-ā-nuku. Many mothers today are recovering the whenua of their babies from the hospitals and taking them back to their ancestral tribal lands for burial or are burying them in the cities where they live. Some mothers either make their own special baskets to receive the placenta or they ask a close relative or friend to make one for them. This is taken to the midwife. Later the basket containing the placenta is given either to a grandparent of the child or to the father to take home. It is then expected that the father or the grandfather will take it back to the tribal lands for burial.

The burial itself requires a ceremony as the whenua is tapu; it is a part of the newborn. While it does not share the personality of the child it is still nonetheless a part of them. Where it is buried could have a sign which says 'Te Ewe o —' ('The Placenta of —').

The act of burial is a mechanism of binding the child to the homelands and to the particular named block. Recently I was told that some Māori mothers who give birth to a child overseas are sending the whenua home for burial. The New Zealand Customs Service has special protocols for dealing with returned placenta. Usually the mother comes home as well and ensures that the burial takes place. This practice provides good evidence that modern Māori mothers are aware of tikanga in respect of the placenta and they are carrying out the tikanga to the best of their ability.

The pito

The umbilical cord is another important part of a child and is the vital link between the child and the placenta. There are names for the various portions of the umbilical cord. The shortest part nearest the baby's body is the pito. The word means end bit. The part nearest the placenta is called the rauru and the portion between is called iho. A general word for the umbilical cord is tāngaengae, a word that appears in the traditional karakia and has ritual connotations.

The cord is cut at birth and what is left is the pito. After about eight days it dries and drops off. This bit, the pito, is collected and placed into its own receptacle and it too is taken back to the tribal homelands for burial or placement in a hollow tree or in a crevasse in a cliff face or somewhere else. The pito and the whenua are often placed at different locations. The dried pito is very small while the whenua is large by comparison. The tikanga in respect of the pito is also being revived and adapted to modern conditions and circumstances.

Revival of the tohi ceremony

Some families have revived the custom of taking the child to a stream and there carrying out the tohi ceremony. This is a baptism ceremony, and its traditional practice is discussed below. What is done today is very different from the traditional ceremony. But the idea is being revived and some of the karakia are included. Families who have done this find that the ceremony brings the whānau together and helps to establish a place for the child within it. It emphasises the importance of the child to the whānau and the equally important role of the mother.

The karakia of new life

A perusal of the literature reveals several texts of karakia that were recited in former times. If called upon, some of the tohunga of today are able to recite some appropriate karakia to welcome a new life into this world and to give strength to the mother and ensure her well-being. Some tohunga are able to perform appropriate karakia to baptise the child. The traditional karakia related to new life are being revived and put to use again.

Traditional knowledge base

Human beings belong to the realm of Tūmatauenga and so it is common to see the name of the God in many of the karakia pertaining to new life. The primal parents of all humans were Ranginui, the Sky Father and Papa-tū-ā-nuku, the Earth Mother. Male babies were dedicated to Tūmatauenga and females to Hine-te-iwaiwa.

Another name that appears is that of Hine-titama. As chapter 14 has noted, the God Tāne created the first woman, Hine-ahu-one, took her as a wife and produced a daughter called the Dawn Maid, Hine-titama. Tāne then became the husband of his daughter, reciting special incantations to make her conceive. The child was Hine-rau-wharangi. As already mentioned the union of Tāne and Hine-titama is cited as the first case of incest in our world. There are other events that were considered to be a consequence of this incest and that clearly indicated disapproval.

In respect of childbirth, however, Hine-titama and her daughter Hine-rau-wharangi are remembered and respected as a mother and daughter model. The mother followed the tikanga laid down by Tāne and the result was a beautiful daughter. They were the first, according to some traditions, to undergo the tohi ceremony (Best 1929:20). In some ceremonies the divine mother and child are honoured and their names are remembered.

Conception

Hine-te-iwaiwa is patron of new life and she presides over the whole process of conception, formation of the foetus and the ultimate birth of the infant. She is Goddess of the Moon. With her are the Moon Maidens – Hine-kotea, Hine-korito, Hine-makehu and Hine-korako – all of whom have something to do with childbirth (Best 1929: 20).

In cases where pregnancy was difficult a couple could enlist the help of a tohunga to perform the ceremony known as whakatō tamariki (planting the seed of a child). The tohunga's first act was to clear from the woman any influences upon the mind that might interfere with conception. The karakia were aimed at casting aside 'any wrong acts, indiscretions (hara)' and 'any offences against the laws of tapu' (Best 1929:6). This part of the ceremony was known as whakahoro, the purpose of which was to absolve and purify.

The next part of the ceremony was directed at awakening the woman's power to conceive and providing her with divine support. At the end of the karakia the tohunga placed a leaf at a spot just below the breasts called te morenga o te poho (the lower end of the breast bone). In some cases there were special trees, stones or places which helped to awaken the woman's own power to conceive. Incantations were recited as before, but she was asked to embrace a tree or face a certain direction while doing so.

Others followed a practice of adopting a child or two and often the act of fostering awakened the power to conceive. There were other cases of non-success in conceiving and others where children were born but none grew to adulthood. These families were known as whare ngaro (lost houses), that is in terms of whakapapa and of continuing a family line.

The developing new life

According to Best (1929:7) the belief was that the seed of life was provided by the male and the female was the nurturing bed and often called te whare tangata (the house of human life). New life was nurtured by the woman and it developed within the womb. The birth passage was called te ara tauwhāiti a Tāne. We now know that both parents contribute to the seed of life.

In the karakia recited over Hine-titama by Tāne appear these lines:

> Ka tupu, ka toro, ka whakaiho tangata
> Toro te akaaka, toro te iho nui, toro te iho roa
> Ka whakaupoko, ka whakaringaringa
> Ka whakawaewae, ka whakatinana mai koe.

It grows, it extends, a human form emerges
The limbs extend, and the big heart, the long heart
develops
Then the head develops, the hands
The legs and your body is formed. (Best 1929:8)

In another section of the book Best quotes the following: 'E ki ana nga kaumatua ko nga whatu tonu te timatanga o te ahau, no muri nga wahi katoa' (The elders say that the form begins with the eyes and other parts follow). So in some karakia the following line appears: 'Ka whakawhetu tama i a ia' (The child develops eyes).

What is important is the belief that the wairua of the child is activated when the eyes form. The development of thinking begins soon afterwards and is signalled in the words: 'Ka riro mai a Rua-i-te-pukenga' (Then is obtained the knowledge).

Once the wairua of the child is activated and thinking begins, the foetus is already a tangata, a new human being but it has to develop further in the shelter of the womb.

Childbirth

Women of rank were treated differently from other women. In the latter's case there was little ceremony. The immediate family unit looked after themselves and did what was necessary to care for and assist the mother during and after childbirth. For a woman of rank a whare kōhanga (nest house) was built. In traditional times the house would be kept warm and if necessary a fireplace was built and a smokeless fire lit as a heater. The expectant mother and her tapuhi (midwives) moved into it and stayed there until after the birth. It was like going to the hospital in the modern sense.

As the time of birth approached the level of tapu in the whare kōhanga and on all who worked there gradually increased. When the actual time arrived the level of tapu was at its highest and the behaviour of all partic-ipants became critically important. Restrictions came into play. People not closely related to the new life kept away. Children were kept aside, loiterers banished and the curious chased out. The process of whakawhānau needed concentration, alertness, knowledge and experience because there was always an element of danger in childbirth. Something could happen that would put the life of the child or mother, or both, in danger.

The last six nights or days of confinement were critical and the belief was related to the Earth Mother and how she gave birth to her many sons. They were born on the sixth day of labour.

Three classes of birth

In the expression 'hokai rauru nui, rauru whiwhia, rauru maruaitu' (Best 1929: 11) are identified the three classes of birth recognised traditionally.

1. Rauru nui (large umbilical cord) was a complication-free birth that produced a normal healthy child.

2. Rauru whiria (tangled umbilical cord) was a prolonged and difficult birth and there were several expected reasons. The first could be that the child had become entangled in the umbilical cord. The child might be born either with a leg out first or an arm. The child might be stunted or not well. Karakia were addressed to the child as well as to the mother for both to work together to bring the child out into the taiao, the natural world, and te ao mārama, the world of light. There was a good chance to save both the mother and the child, but an experienced tapuhi needed to be on hand.

3. Rauru maruaitu (umbilical cord of disaster): In this case the baby might be stillborn or there are great complications in the process with the result that the mother is expected to die. The word aitu signals disaster.

Thus there is always great concern at a birth and tremendous relief and happiness for a rauru nui where everything goes well. Experience is required to deal with the second and third classes of birth.

The delivery

The tikanga recorded by Best (1929: 12–13) was as follows:

1. The expectant mother kneels with knees apart.

2. The tapuhi squats or kneels in front of her with her knees braced against those of the mother.

3. The tapuhi clasps the mother under the armpits and uses her knees to assist the process of birth.

4. The mother embraces the tapuhi in a similar fashion and holds on to her. In this manner the tapuhi gets an immediate reading of the contractions of the mother and can support and encourage where required.

5. The two now work together to effect the birth.

6. A third person, another tapuhi, is attending to requirements such as providing warm water and providing soft flax fibre for mopping up blood.

7. Eventually the child is born and the tapuhi tend to the new life and mother.

8. The pito is tied next to the skin, cut and smeared with tītoki oil. According to Best (1929:15) the judgment on where to cut the umbilical cord was guided by either measuring the length of the thumb to the first joint (but this was considered to be rather short) or, the preferred measurement, to the length of the kōiti or little finger. Buck (1949:351) says about an inch and a half (37 mm) was the preferred length.

The welcome to the newborn child

Once the child is cleaned up and dressed and the mother is comfortable and relaxed the maioha ceremony can commence. Today this can be done either at the hospital or when the mother and child come home. In former times the ceremony was held when the mother was sufficiently strong to participate. She held the child in her lap. Speeches were addressed to the child and mother, one from the father's side and one from the mother's side. Then followed a recital of a special karakia of welcome which began with the lines:

> Nau-mai e tama/hine, kia mihi atu au
> I hara mai koe i te kunenga mai o te
> tangata i roto i te ahuru mowai.

> Come forth oh son/daughter, so I can greet you
> You have come from where human life
> begins in the sheltering womb.

> (My translation) (Best 1929:16)

The rest of the karakia is in Best (1929) and there are others to choose from.

There was an exchange of gifts, some from the relatives of the father. It was a time of rejoicing and the occasion was a time to celebrate a new life and a new addition to the whānau.

If done at the home the ceremony ends with a hākari. If done in the hospital the whole ceremony is informal and there is no feast.

The traditional tohi ceremony

The moral justification for the tohi ceremony relates to the activities of the divine family. Best (1929) based his information on information provided by the Ngāti Kahungunu informant Te Matorohanga, and thus we can say that the procedures set out in his book are largely Ngāti Kahungunu practice. The model for the ceremony is based on the model which was believed to have been set by the God Tāne for baptising his granddaughter, Hine-rau-wharangi. During the ceremony a great mat, te takapau wharanui, was used and the ceremony began and ended in front of the ancestral house Hui-te-ananui.

Gudgeon (1885) sets out a different introduction to the tohi ceremony but the main baptism ceremony is very similar. The source of his information is not clear. For the Mātaatua region there is a different explanation and justification for the ceremony. It is Tāwhaki, God of lightning, who took hold of the correct vine that enabled him to climb up to the heavens. His goal was to reach the tenth heaven, the abode of the God Tamaiwaho. Tāwhaki gained knowledge and the appropriate karakia for the ceremonies necessary for human life.

Another theme of the story was Tāwhaki's search for his wife Tangotango who had returned to her heavenly home with their daughter Arahuta or Te Arawhita-i-te-rangi. Eventually they reunite and Tāwhaki then carries out the model of the tohi ceremony that Mātaatua would consider to be their tradition (see details in Mead 1996). The details of the ceremony itself are not so very different from the Ngāti Kahungunu version as set out by Te Matorohanga.

Preparing for the tohi

1. At dawn two tohunga chose a suitable site for laying out the takapau wharanui. The people would be led to the spot by the tohunga.

2. The great mat was laid out very close to the edge of a stream. A fine cloak was placed on top of the mat and then another cloak of superior make was placed on top of the first cloak.

3. The mother was conducted by two tapuhi to the cloaks, one tapuhi in front and the other behind the mother.

4. If the mother was not carrying the child the father was expected to do so and he would bring the child to the mat.

5. The elders and relatives followed behind the father and all stood before the cloaks.

6. One tohunga, clad only in an apron, would be standing in the stream ready to perform his part of the ceremony. He was called the tohunga tohiora.

7. The assistant tohunga stood close to the mother but in front of the mat and to her right.

8. The mother and child should be facing the east.

The pito

1. The child's grandfather meanwhile has brought the pito to the ceremony. It has been encased in a raupō (bullrush) covering.

2. If the child is female the grandparent on the mother's side carried the pito.

3. It was handed to the assistant tohunga.

4. At this time the tohunga tohiora standing in the water chanted a karakia that was directed at the pito. An example is in Best (1929:22).

5. The tohunga tohiora then placed his hand in the water and flicked the water onto the mother and father who were standing on the great mat.

6. The pito was then handed to the tohunga tohiora who dipped it into the water and at the same time chanted another karakia.

7. The pito was then passed from the tohunga tohiora to the assistant and eventually to the father of the child.

The tohi

Attention was now directed at the infant. Great care was taken to hold the newborn baby carefully and to protect its head, which was held against the body of the adult. The father now handed the child to the assistant tohunga who began a karakia and at the same time walked over to the tohunga tohiora. By the time he arrived his karakia would have ended and he then passed the child into the hands of the tohunga tohiora, who began his karakia. The child would be dedicated to the Gods and encouraged to pursue appropriate activities under their protection.

When completed, he immersed himself and the child in the water and only up to the child's neck while holding the child in his left hand and then holding the child in his right hand. After this the tohunga tohiora sprinkled water on the baby's head and recited another karakia called the oho rangi (awakening the sky). Thunder was meant to be heard at this point. In the Mātaatua version lightning was expected.

Then the child was handed back to the mother.

The paparoa ceremony

1. At this point the paparoa, which is the spot where the great mat was spread out, was cleared.

2. Mother and father stepped off the paparoa.

3. The great mat was turned back so as to clear the earth.

4. The chief of the group then picked up a sharpened pole and proceeded to dig a hole with it right in the middle of the paparoa. This would be about where the mother stood on the mat.

5. When the hole was deep enough the father placed the pito into it and then the hole was covered over.

6. Six small stones were placed in the hole, each representing the six nights of labour for the child. The stones were tamped into the hole.

7. The two cloaks that were on the paparoa were placed over the father's shoulders.

8. The reason for this was because the baby was handed over to him and he covered the child with the cloaks, which were the best the whānau could produce.

9. The father then led the procession back to the marae.

The pure ceremony

The procession led straight into the next ceremony. The group was welcomed back to the marae by a karanga. But meanwhile the tohunga tohiora has performed appropriate karakia to clear the way for the group. The great mat has been spread out again on the verandah of the house and other cloaks are placed over it. The spot was now called the tahuaroa.

1. The husband and wife approached the window of the house and stopped before the tahuaroa. At this point they would be facing the window.

2. The tohunga then directed them to step upon the tahuaroa. The father of the child remained standing while the mother sat on the mat and not on the cloaks.

3. It is not clear who was holding up the baby at this point. Best (1929:26–27) indicates that the paternal grandfather of the child had the child and he came up to the mother and handed the child to her. She held the child on her lap.

4. The tohunga tohiora recited a series of karakia each one beginning with a welcome to the child: 'Hara mai e tama/hine' (Welcome oh son/daughter).

5. The karakia were aimed at dedicating the child to great deeds, to a world of knowledge, to the protection of the Gods.

6. When the karakia were completed the people moved to the porch of the house to greet the child. At this point several speeches could be addressed to the child.

7. Meanwhile others have been preparing a hākari. The people partake of the hākari.

8. The child was left on the mat while the parents approach the feast. This had been set out on the ground in front of the house.

9. The mother was 'fed' by her tapuhi and the father was 'fed' by his tapuhi. What this actually meant was not explained.

10. According to Best (1926:28) this ceremony was 'performed by the priests in order to render permanent the sacred and spiritual mana; it was not a removal or lifting of tapu'. Best further added that after this pure ceremony all who participated had to undergo a whakanoa ceremony in order to remove the tapu of the ceremony from them.

The practices set out by Best are very detailed and elaborate and it is doubtful that many iwi followed such practices to the letter.

Baptism as recorded by Gudgeon

Gudgeon probably obtained his information from the eastern tribes among whom he worked.

1. Soon after the birth the tohunga made a number of clay balls and prepared a similar number of mounds in the earth.
2. The mounds were named after the main Gods of the Māori world.
3. The clay balls were named after the child's ancestors.
4. The tohunga then took a branch of karamū or ake or hutu and split it in two.
5. One half of the branch was tied around the waist of the child and while he was doing this the assistant tohunga recited a karakia called a tūāpana. The purpose of the karakia was to clear dangerous elements of tapu from the mother and the settlement and also to give strength to the child. A translation of the text is in Gudgeon (1885:120).
6. The tohunga then went into the middle of a brook or stream and dipped the karamū branch into the water. There was a karakia for this.
7. He then used the thoroughly wet karamū branch to sprinkle water on the mother and child. There was a karakia for this part and appeals to Tūmatauenga, Tāne, Tāwhaki and Tama.
8. The tohunga then planted the karamū branch he used in a suitable place and this plant, if it grew, would be associated thereafter with the person baptised in this ceremony.
9. Three hāngi were prepared, one for the tohunga, one for the mother and one for the Gods. Kūmara were cooked in each of them.
10. The kūmara in the hāngi for the Gods was presented to pumice-stone representations of the Gods. These were arranged in a row and the cooked kūmara placed before each of them.
11. The other kūmara were given as intended, one lot to the tohunga and the second lot to the mother.

12. The child was now shown to the people and the ceremony was completed.

13. This was only the beginning, however. There was another ceremony to follow which was not very different from that described by Best, except that it was less elaborate. For example, the child was not immersed in water but merely sprinkled with water. A karamū branch was used. Gudgeon (1885:123) explained that a ceremony for a girl was not very different. Girls were dedicated to Hine-te-iwaiwa. The procedure was the same for all children born of chiefly families.

Teething

Gudgeon (1885:125) indicated that there were special karakia which the mother recited over the child to encourage a tooth to come out. Unfortunately, he provided only a translation of the text, as follows:

> Growing kernel, grow
> Grow, that thou mayest arrive
> To see the moon now full,
> Come, thou kernel,
> Let the tooth of man
> Be given to the rat
> And the rat's tooth
> To the man.

There is no explanation about the exchange of teeth between human and rats.

First haircut

Cutting the hair of a child, or of anyone in fact, was surrounded with tapu. The hair comes from the head, the most tapu part of a person. According to Gudgeon (1885:125) the first haircut of a boy is done by the boy's grandfather or by a tohunga. Gudgeon did not write about the ceremonies for a girl but the absence of such information does not mean that there was an absence of tikanga for girls.

The day before, the tohunga went to a sacred place, a tūāhu, and spent the night there. Early next morning the child went to him and he was greeted with the words:

> Come, my child,
> And I will cut
> Each of the hairs
> To the honour of Tū.

The tohunga then cut the child's hair with a piece of obsidian.

When completed the father handed over to the tohunga a fire stick called a poporokai-whiria which was used to start a fire by the traditional friction method. Once a fire was lit the hair was burnt and a karakia recited. The translation recorded by Gudgeon (1885:125–26) is as follows:

> The honour thou didst seek, my son,
> Has come and gone.
> Thou was sacred
> And art common
> Thou canst return
> Here I am, my son.
> I have risen up,
> I have received,
> I am satisfied.

The tohunga then cooked a piece of fern root in the sacred fire. When cooked he touched the boy's head with the cooked fern root and then he ate it.

From the time the tohunga went to the sacred place everyone in the village had fasted. Once the tohunga ate the fern root the fast was over and the whole village could light their cooking fires, cook their food and have a meal.

Conclusions

Many of the practices of traditional times would be difficult to duplicate today. No tohunga, for example, would want to strip down to an apron and stand in the middle of a stream, no matter how shallow, and in the middle of winter. Nor would we want to immerse a newborn baby only eight or ten days old in a cold stream in winter. Today we would want to bring the water from some special spring or stream to the place where the baptism is to occur, at a marae, a church or at home.

Families today have to decide for themselves what aspects of tikanga they want to revive and are able to carry through. Already many of the tikanga are being revived and adapted to the conditions of today. It is a fair prediction that many more families will be looking at the tikanga associated with new life with a view toward adopting some of them.

They would want to know the mātauranga that supports the tikanga and accumulated experience of practising them. As pointed out here the background information goes back to the divine family of Ranginui and Papa-tū-ā-nuku. The 'customs' are validated by reference to Tāne, to Hine-ahu-one the first woman, to her daughter Hine-titama and to her daughter Hine-rau-wharangi.

For some iwi the origins of the tohi ceremony are attributed to Tāne and his family. But to some sections of Mātaatua the tohi is attributed to Tāwhaki who gained the knowledge from Tamaiwaho. Tāwhaki performed the tohi ceremony over his daughter Arahuta and this was held as the origin of the ceremony for the iwi of Mātaatua. Other iwi might have different interpretations and tribal lore.

Perspectives

The following karakia was used at the baptism of female children:

> Tohia te tama[hine] nei;
> He aha, he hau ora;
> He hau rangatira;
> Kei runga hei te rangi;
> Ka puha te rangi;
> E iri iria koe ki te iri iri;
> Hahau kai mau, tangaengae;
> Haere ki te wahie mau, tangaengae;
> Whatu kakahu mau, tangaengae.

> Name this child;
> What is it, a living breath;
> A Chief's breath;
> From the heaven above;
> The sky has breathed forth;
> Be you baptized with the baptism;
> Seek food for thyself with panting for breath;
> Go for the firewood with panting for breath;
> Weave garments for thyself with panting for breath.
> – Taylor 1870:186

As soon as the babe was born intricate ceremonies began. The navel-string was cut by a priest, he repeating a charm (tangaengae) in which were enumerated to a boy-infant the many manly virtues, such as courage, energy, etc., he ought to possess, and to a girl-child the qualities expected of her, such as industry, skill in weaving etc. The new-born babe and its mother were both sacred at this time and not to be touched by outsiders till they had been made 'common' (noa). It was particularly to be dreaded if anyone engaged in the planting or harvesting of sweet-potatoes (kumara) should touch or be touched by a woman before her purification.

   – Tregear 1926:42–43

Afterwards came the baptism (tohunga), or rather 'dedication' and naming of the child. A name was sometimes decided on before birth, the father saying 'If it is a boy his name shall be so and so; if a girl, so and so,' but at other times it was left to be settled during the ceremony.

— Tregear 1926:46

It was also a ritual when the babies were born, how to massage the babies; different massage for baby girls, different massage for baby boys. You wouldn't believe it, but according to my grannies I was born with crooked feet, club feet, and I was the ugliest baby born! Granny Tiakiwhare said my head was long and my nose, and she showed me what she did, she said, 'You are so soft, straight off! She straightened my legs, my feet, there and then. Then she put my chin in her hand, and put her (other) hand behind her head and she demonstrated how she pushed, twisted, and shaped my nose, pushed my mouth back. She fashioned me from what I was, from the babe that was.

— Heni Sutherland, in Binney & Chaplin 1986: 113

18
Mātauranga Māori: Knowledge

Learning is a life-long process and even if one chooses not to go to a school, learning occurs. There is, in fact, an ever-changing and expanding pool of knowledge to grasp. There is so much to learn that it is not expected that any one person would ever learn it all. Some of this knowledge is learnt as we go along and participate in the activities of everyday living and join in a cycle of ceremonies that is part of life. We learn by watching television, by reading books, newspapers and magazines or by going to movies, by exploring the internet or simply by attending meetings and listening to various speakers.

Some learning is more structured and formal: there is a curriculum, a body of knowledge and a wide range of subjects in which knowledge is divided and organised. Those of us who have experienced the school system in Aotearoa have become familiar in greater or lesser extent with the subjects offered and the manner in which they were taught at primary schools, intermediate schools and high schools. Some of us have gone on to polytechnics, private training establishments, universities, teacher training colleges and wānanga. As part of our learning we should have been exposed to mātauranga Māori, that is, to Māori knowledge.

Māori knowledge is being revived today and there is a new subject area called mātauranga Māori that is being taught, researched, argued about, and taken very seriously in learning institutions. It is taught at graduate studies level at Te Wānanga o Raukawa and elsewhere. The term 'mātauranga Māori' encompasses all branches of Māori knowledge, past, present and still developing. It is like a super subject because it includes a whole range of subjects that are familiar in our world today, such as philosophy, astronomy, mathematics, language, history, education and so on.

And it will also include subjects we have not yet heard about. Mātauranga Māori has no ending: it will continue to grow for generations to come. Each year its knowledge base is expanded through research, written papers, theses, books, seminars, conferences, debates and discussions.

It would be futile to endeavour to discover the beginning of mātauranga Māori. It comes with the people, with the culture and with the language. Mātauranga Māori is and will be.

As mentioned in chapters 13 and 14, Māori culture can be likened to Humpty Dumpty. When Humpty sat on the wall he or she was a complete being. But when Humpty fell the whole being was shattered and broken into pieces. In the case of Māori culture the pieces have been scattered – some have been destroyed, some hidden and others are just waiting to be reconstructed.

Efforts are now being made to reassemble Humpty Dumpty, but the task has become difficult because meanwhile Humpty is changing and continues to grow and expand despite being shattered and scattered.

One of the major parts being reconstructed is called mātauranga Māori. However, people are not concerned only with recovering the broken pieces. The educators, thinkers and researchers have to put the pieces into new places, embrace new technologies, new information and try to make sense of the changing world at large through mātauranga Māori. Mātauranga Māori is not like an archive of information but rather is like a tool for thinking, organising information, considering the ethics of knowledge, the appropriateness of it all and informing us about our world and our place in it.

Mātauranga Māori is also entwined with the tikanga of learning or the tikanga of knowledge. There are customary ideas, values, and notions of correctness and appropriateness associated with mātauranga Māori. More importantly, there is a tapu aspect to mātauranga Māori. The tapu aspect of mātauranga Māori ties it firmly into the system of beliefs and values of the Māori people.

Traditional ideas about learning

It is clear that formerly higher learning was not available to all and that men were segregated into their school and the women into theirs. Male students were most often dedicated to the God of war and of human affairs, Tūmatauenga. Most often female students were dedicated to the Goddess of the moon, Hine-te-iwaiwa. Students were recommended and often specially chosen by their hapū.

Parents, aunts, uncles and grandparents observed the children as they developed and noted their particular interests. Strong interests in agriculture, fishing, weaving, woodcarving or building canoes were especially noted and the novices would be sometimes encouraged to learn as much as they were able. Or they might be teased and put off to test their interest and commitment.

In most cases there was a ceremony to formally 'enter' a student into a subject area and be dedicated to it. 'Entering' meant coming under the protection of a divine figure and observing some rules so as not to offend the deity. Thus, students of weaving were dedicated to Hine-te-iwaiwa, woodcarving to Ruatepupuke and Tāne, fishing to Tangaroa, seafaring to Tangaroa and Tāwhirimātea. Those learning to be warriors were dedicated to Tūmatauenga and those following agriculture to Rongo and Haumia.

The traditional schools of learning were religious in nature and in all pursuits of learning there were rituals to observe. Learning and the act of teaching were not ordinary or common. The importance of the act of acquiring knowledge was emphasised by surrounding the event with rituals. Religion was not separated from education. Learning was elevated high above the ordinary pursuits of a community.

The house of learning as described by Te Matorohanga (Smith 1913, 1:86) was modelled on a carved meeting house, but with an earthen floor. Apart from the building itself there were few comforts for the students. There was a fireplace to provide heat. Classes began at dawn and finished after midday. There were no breaks for eats or drinks. There were no comfortable chairs to sit on but hard stones set in the ground. Students had to wear special clothing while attending the whare wānanga. After each daily session they had to remove the clothes of learning and wear their ordinary everyday clothing.

Resources for learning included an ahurewa (altar) at the back wall of the house and little pebbles that each student had to swallow at the end of the course. There were no books, no reading and no writing. But each student needed a very good memory in order to 'record' the teachings of the priests of the whare wānanga, retain the information and recite it later without fault. It is not surprising, therefore, that considerable effort was directed at retaining the information taught to students.

Before a course ended the students were required to stand on a special mat near the ahurewa. Under the mat were placed the whatu-kura, or stones of knowledge. The tohunga then grouped the students together and the priests placed their hands on top of the heads of the students and recited a special karakia 'to ensure the permanence of what the pupils had learned' (Smith 1913, 1:90). Here again the importance of retention is obvious.

Because so much reliance was given to good memory the method of teaching was different from what happens today. There was a leading tohunga who was assisted by one or more tohunga. The task of the assistants was to prompt when required and to fill the gaps when there were lapses of memory on the part of the lecturer. Lecturing was very much a group effort, as was learning for the students.

Ceremonies for completing a course were much more complicated and demanding than for the beginning. Rituals were recited to begin the course and to dedicate the students to the serious tasks of learning. When the course began the mantle of tapu was placed over the entire course and the students for the duration of the series of lectures. Each day there was a reinforcement of the tapu at the beginning and a reduction at the conclusion of the course for the day. It is noteworthy that knowledge was expected to enter the stomach and not the mind. A good student was thus a person who had a stomach for learning.

Once the course was completed there was a series of transformation ceremonies that reduced the tapu of learning to a state of noa so a student could rejoin their whānau free of any dangerous elements of tapu. It was necessary to go through the rituals for every course completed. This included going to the sacred latrine and having to bite the paepae tapu (sacred bar), taking off the clothes used in the whare wānanga and returning them to the institution, having a lock of hair and other samples of the student such as spit and sweat collected, being taken to a stream for a complete dunking into the water, changing clothes and then assembling at the porch of the training house for final speeches. Included in all of this was the lighting of a special fire by the priests to signal the removal of the clothes of learning and thereafter the adopting of normal daily wear. Then the students were free to mingle with their families.

Biting the sacred latrine bar embraced a complex of ideas. Te Matorohanga used the words 'ki reira whakahoro ai i nga tapu o Te Kauwae-runga' (Smith 1913, 1:7). A literal translation would be, 'there the tapu of the kauwae-runga session would be removed'. The kauwae runga (upper jaw) refers to 'things celestial' and encompasses the origins of the world and the activities of the divine family of Ranginui and Papa-tū-ā-nuku. A footnote by Smith added that the act helped fix the learning, it demonstrated the determination of the student to adhere to the teaching and declared that the student was willing to undertake whatever was necessary in order to learn.

According to Te Matorohanga (Smith 1913, 1:95) the whare wānanga opened seven times and Smith, the translator, thought that this meant there were seven separate courses or sessions. Ceremonies for the seventh and last course were more elaborate than accorded the other courses.

The place of Io

Te Matorohanga placed Io at the head of the divine family and above Rangi and Papa, the primeval parents. I have great difficulty with the concept of Io and with the very notion that Io was so exalted that the people did not know about him and were not supposed to hear his name. There was no evidence that so important a matter was kept secret or could have been kept secret. There is little or no evidence in the Bay of Plenty area that there was a supreme being organising Ranginui and Papa-tū-ā-nuku. Nor does Io appear in genealogical tables linking to Rangi and Papa.

Te Rangikaheke (Grey 1953) certainly does not mention a supreme God in his explanation of the origins of the world. Te Rangikaheke's opening statement in the chapter 'Nga Tama a Rangi' (The Sons of Rangi) (Grey 1953:1) is as follows: 'Kotahi ano te tupuna o te tangata Maori ko Rangi-nui e tu nei, ko Papa-tua-nuku e takoto nei' (There is but one ancestor of the Maori people, Rangi-nui who stands above and Papa-tua-nuku who lies below). That is a simple and powerful statement and I cannot really envisage a supreme God above the primeval parents. Rather there was Te Kore, The Void, The Nothingness.

Several of the karakia in the lore of the whare wānanga include the name of Io and it could be that in the Ngāti Kahungunu traditions there was a place for a God called Io. It is noticeable that many groups participating in education today dedicate their karakia to Io, the Supreme Being. The point needs to be made that there is doubt about the authenticity of the traditions dealing with Io and that in the case of the Bay of Plenty tribes there is no conformable fit in the whakapapa of the divine family for Io.

For example, it is Tāwhaki who is credited with fetching knowledge from the uppermost heaven and the source of the information was Tamaiwaho. Also there were ten heavens and not twelve, which is the Kahungunu tradition. Thus there are regional differences in our traditions and therefore care needs to be taken in educational institutions that karakia are addressed to the appropriate deity. A national version of our traditions and hence of tikanga does not exist. Regional differences are to be expected and Te Matorohanga noted this in his teaching (Smith 1913, 1: 84).

In examining the workings of the whare wānanga as described here it is not so much the details that we should focus on but rather the principles or the core beliefs that are associated with higher learning. Very often, as in the case of the tohi ceremony, the core beliefs and principles are similar but not the details of the ceremony. The information outlined below is based on the *Lore of the Whare Wananga* (Smith 1913, 1: 85–95).

Characteristics of the traditional whare wānanga

1. The transmission of knowledge was not open to everyone. It was limited to members of a waka confederation or an iwi.

2. Each iwi conducted its teachings and practices according to its tikanga.

3. Students selected by their tribe needed to be alert, intelligent, committed to learning, young and male. The students were tested by their own iwi and if suitable were recommended to attend the whare wānanga.

4. The whare wānanga was a whare tapu, a sacred house. All who participated in teaching and learning were covered by the tapu of the institution and of learning. Knowledge was tapu.

5. The whare wānanga was constructed outside the main village. The whole site with every structure within it was regarded as a marae.

6. Cooking facilities were outside of the whare wānanga site.

7. Women were not permitted on site.

8. The house itself was constructed like a whare whakairo. Details are described by Te Matorohanga (Smith 1913, 1:86).

9. A common practice was to bury the whatu or mauri of the building in the hole where the pou-tuarongo, the rear centrepole, would be placed. Te Matorohanga indicated three whatu were buried in the hole. The whatu consisted of Rakai-ora, a green lizard; Pekerau, a tuatara; and Te Tama a Arawaru, a kārearea or sparrowhawk.

10. At the rear end of the house is the ahurewa. The day before the house was officially opened the priest entered and placed a set of pebbles, called whatu, at the ahurewa. These pebbles were for the students.

11. Other stones, which were to be the seats for the students, were placed four on each side of the ahurewa, and some were placed where the fireplace was located. These stones were set into the ground and could not be moved around.

12. The eight stones at the rear were called Ngā-whatu-mataki and these were used when the teaching was about to close, usually in the month of September.

13. There were three main stones at the front end of the house. These were called 'Te Rongo-taketake o Rongo-marae-roa' (The enduring peace of Rongo, God of peace). The priests taught from these stones.

14. The priest taught from the Kauwhanga or Kauhanga, or open space or centre line, in the house. According to Te Matorohanga there were three priests on the teaching staff. While one was teaching the other two checked and prompted when necessary.

15. Lessons commenced at daylight and ended at midday.

16. When the course came to an end the students were taken through several ceremonies. The first was to stand together on a great mat in front of the ahurewa. The priests placed their hands on the heads of the students and recited the karakia to help them reclaim the knowledge transmitted to them.

17. Then the students were taken to the paepae tapu, the latrine bar which each student had to bite, and the reason for this was to remove the tapu of learning from them.

18. After this they removed the clothes of learning and went to the river for total immersion in the water. This act further reduced the level of tapu from the students.

19. They then put on their own clothes. While attending the whare wānanga the students changed clothing every day. Special clothing was worn while in session. Home clothes were left outside of the whare-wānanga site.

20. Precautions were taken against witchcraft being practised on the students by others who were jealous of them or bore ill will towards them.

21. There was a final meeting of the students with their teachers when speeches were made about their perseverance, praise given to their behaviour and cautions given about the protection of the knowledge they had gained. The beginning of the next session would be announced.

22. The students rejoined their whānau in the activities of the iwi and this would have been like a vacation that is enjoyed by modern students.

23. The clothing worn at the sessions were returned to the whare wānanga and stored at the ahurewa.

24. There were seven sessions of the whare wānanga.

The tikanga of learning today

There are many learning institutions managed by Māori that practise various tikanga in association with their programmes. Wānanga are charged under the Education Act 1989 to run their institutions in accordance with tikanga Māori and āhuatanga Māori. Private training establishments also incorporate some tikanga Māori practices in their work.

Within many mainstream learning institutions are departments or schools of Māori studies which also draw upon tikanga Māori in order to create the appropriate conditions for learning. Several of these institutions, such as the University of Auckland, Victoria University and Massey

University, have marae established on campus and so tikanga Māori is visible and it is accepted as a natural part of the learning environment.

To my knowledge only one institution has been bold enough to revive the notion of the tapu of learning and to attempt to persuade the student body that they should agree to some common understandings as to what this means. This is Te Wānanga o Raukawa at Otaki. The institution, however, has focussed on the 'kawa of learning', that is, on the practices of learning that everyone should accept as binding upon them. The overall aim of the kawa is to lead students towards success and not to impede them. One of the practices is focussed upon good health and there is an agreement to ban smoking on campus. Another agreement looks at encouraging the mind to be alert so that drugs and alcohol are banned from the learning environment.

Many Māori learning institutions either begin each day with a karakia or incorporate karakia whenever appropriate. The karakia can be Christian, traditional Māori or a mixture. Several have kapa-haka groups that are able to enhance the ability of the institution to practise other tikanga, such as traditional waiata, the haka, action songs and poi.

Others practise full-scale pōhiri ceremonies when appropriate and a few have held the tangihanga ceremony at their premises. The tangihanga complex of tikanga is held to be the ultimate in tikanga Māori and if a learning institution is able to carry out such a ceremony the environment has become accepting of tikanga Māori to a high degree. But it does not follow necessarily that the institution believes in or practises elements of the tapu of learning.

The tapu of learning encourages the practice of beginning learning sessions with some karakia. It demands the separation of food and all beverages from the act of formal teaching and learning. Many modern students would find this prohibition to be difficult. In practice, however, what it means is that food and beverages are confined to the intervals. When there are long classes, such as two-hour or four-hour sessions, it is possible to schedule rest periods.

The tapu of learning today also means respecting the rights of one's fellow students for they are following the same values. They respect the sources of knowledge and the repositories of knowledge. The rules of the library are observed so that other students are not prevented from accessing information. The whole group is able individually to advance their learning and eventually complete a course successfully. There is an obligation to work cooperatively in the pursuit of knowledge, but it does not mean copying from one another. If joint projects are scheduled in the course the contributions of each individual are assessed. Lazy students are not tolerated by a group.

Coming to terms with the tapu of learning is a relatively new challenge and not an easy one for modern students. It is much easier to accept parts of the tapu of learning rather than agree to a whole package of prohibitions, even though the aim is to encourage completion of a course with a high level of success. Successful completion of a course of study is today a major focus of teaching institutions. Some would argue, however, that the contestable notion of funding by equivalent full-time students (EFTS) forces institutions to concentrate on the recruitment of students as high priority. If the student roll decreases, funding decreases; if the student roll increases, funding increases. Tertiary institutions are thus forced to compete for students to fill various study programmes. EFTS funding varies according to field of study. Only when the numbers have been secured can the lecturers feel free to give attention to the quality of learning. Often a course cannot begin until a magical viable number is reached.

Attention to the tapu of learning means doing something about the beginning and closure and completion of a course. The first part of the closure ceremony is focussed on retention of the knowledge gained and ensuring that the curriculum was taught and delivered and that the outcomes of the course were reached. Revision exercises are one way of ensuring coverage. Retention of the knowledge is another matter. Traditionally this was accomplished by having the community participate and by insisting that everything was committed to the memory. There was no reliance on books, notes, computers or other devices. The student had to commit the knowledge to the memory and then retain it.

Logically the modern resources available to the student should assist in understanding, acquiring the knowledge, retaining it and then being able to reproduce it when required. But this does not appear to follow.

Graduation

In the modern world graduation is part of an elaborate closure ceremony when students are given a certificate of achievement for having completed a programme of courses that have often taken many years to complete. The question often asked is: 'How does the graduation ceremony of tertiary institutions fit into the tapu of learning? Or is there no fit?' There is probably a better question to address: 'How can we incorporate some of the core ideas of the traditional whare wānanga into the graduation ceremony?'

The first point is this. The graduation ceremony practised by most universities belongs to a different culture and fits well into the traditions of that culture. Thus the tikanga of the graduation ceremony is not Māori but is English or American or European. If we follow it and adopt it we need to acknowledge that point. We may construct our own tikanga from beginning to end or we can adopt the present ceremony and build into it some core ideas that are a part of Māori custom.

Indeed, Māori students are demanding some adaptations or, in some cases, they are taking matters into their own hands. For example, they may wear some items of traditional costume or they may greet the chancellor with a traditional hongi. There may be a karanga from the supporting whānau or even a rousing haka. There are real attempts to indigenise the graduation ceremony of western cultures and the tikanga that is an essential part of it.

Handing out a certificate is new and there is no question of doing away with it. Rather the document itself is being subjected to indigenisation, usually by adding elements of Māori art in order to provide a Māori dimension to it. Another core part of the graduation ceremony is 'capping' the student. This leads to the Māori term 'whakapōtaetanga' for the whole ceremony, that is, placing a hat upon the graduating student. A special cap is passed over the head of the student. After this the graduating student is permitted to wear the graduation hat of their particular institution and to wear the colours of their particular study area. The complete costume consists of gown, the hood and its colours and a hat. The western graduation ceremony is a colourful and very dignified event and it embodies the notion of the clothing of knowledge.

The idea of special clothes is compatible with the tikanga of the traditional whare wānanga. The students had special clothes which students had to wear when in class. At the conclusion of the course students had to hand these special clothes into the institution. In the modern graduation ceremony, however, there is a special costume available to successful graduating student, after the learning is complete. They may wear them at graduation and thereafter at special ceremonies of the institution to which they belong. Most people hire their costumes rather than own them and often the reason for doing so is that the special clothing is used very rarely.

At Victoria University of Wellington a special graduation ceremony is held for graduating Māori students. There is a large measure of indigenisation of the graduation ceremony which is styled a hui whaka-pūmau, that is, a meeting to bind the knowledge gained by the students.

The notion of binding the knowledge so that retention is assisted ritually accords with some of the core ideas of the traditional whare wānanga. At Victoria University the binding or whakapūmau part of the graduation ceremony is very important and is performed by a competent tohunga. Ritually this is a high point of the ceremony and brings it to an end. However, in the western model it is the actual capping that is the high point of the ceremony. Once the graduating student is capped, the degree gained is emphasised at that point and made binding upon the institution to honour the qualification.

The ceremony is often enhanced by including special performances. Musicians and singers may perform pieces from the classical music repertoire. The national anthem is sung and a special graduation song, 'Gaudeamus Igitur', is sung in Latin, lending emphasis to the history of western knowledge. In the indigenised version of the ceremony performances by a kapa-haka team fit easily into the proceedings.

All in all, the modern graduation ceremony practised by many learning institutions incorporates tikanga Māori to a greater or lesser extent. Less so for mainstream institutions and more so for wānanga and for special graduation hui held for Māori students at the main universities of the land.

The other question, of course, pertains to the practice of teaching and learning at the different levels of the schooling system. What is the impact of tikanga Māori in the classroom? What is the learning environment like and what are the specified tikanga-Māori practices that the institution has adopted? There are enormous differences across the country in respect of the incorporation of the principles of 'the tapu of knowledge' or of 'the kawa of learning' into the daily practice of institutions. It is all very well having elaborate ceremonies of entry into a programme and of closure after successful completion. But it is the daily practices of the institutions over the months and weeks of the academic year that make a lasting impression on the lives and fortunes of students.

Clearly Māori providers of education are still working towards developing their own distinctive styles of teaching and learning. Some, like Te Ataarangi, have a clear philosophy of learning. Others, like kura kaupapa Māori and kōhanga reo deliver according to a kaupapa-Māori philosophy. Wānanga reflect tikanga Māori in their practices. But it is fair to say that practices vary, and perhaps that is how it should be.

The tikanga of research

Traditional attitudes to knowledge have a direct bearing on rangahau (research) practices. It is fair to say, however, that up until recently Māori were rarely involved in research activities into our own culture. That was done by others and in those days the others came in and did their research, and we cooperated, made the researchers welcome, allowed them to live among us and then farewelled them.

Those days are gone. Now researchers are required to follow a process and – better still – they are required to pass the requirements of their institution's ethics committee.

Knowledge was tapu, as already noted. Students had to belong to the iwi or the hapū before being admitted. Today there remains a reluctance to share the heritage of the iwi with outsiders, although outsiders from beyond Aotearoa might be trusted more than researchers of our own country.

Researchers now must seek permission from a tribal authority to enter the authority's territory and carry out research among their people. Moreover, the project has to be fully explained, and benefits to the people, if any, need to be outlined. It is expected that copies of papers or reports are sent to the community afterwards. Others might demand that local people are hired if assistants and workers are required to carry out the research project.

Every teaching institution that requires Māori students to seek information from their parents or grandparents for assignments large or small will discover that the students regard the information so gained with some awe. Some want to protect what they learned, some want to restrict access to it and some are reluctant to share it. Others refuse to subject such information to critical analysis. It is tapu, they say.

The tikanga of research in a western sense requires that all information is subject to scrutiny and subject to analysis. This tikanga clashes with the traditional tikanga of the old school of learning. Thus there are sensitivities about research and about the information gained through research. Recipients of the information are obliged to keep apart information given as a family member and in confidence from information that can be included in a report.

The values underpinning tikanga cannot be ignored. They are in the mind and often manifest themselves in the form of difficulties. But remembering them can be helpful. For example, the value of manaakitanga will be helpful in making the right decisions because it encourages the researcher to be respectful towards those who supplied the information and to be respectful towards the information itself.

The mana of people needs to be protected and thus care should be exercised about how information is used. In addition the mana of the researcher is also at risk in the area of rangahau if information is mishandled or if the task is inadequate.

A researcher should always be guided by the principle of tika which is the very basis of the word tikanga. Processes, procedures and consultation need to be correct so that in the end everyone who is connected with the research project is enriched, empowered, enlightened and glad to have been a part of it.

This principle also ensures that the ethics of research are observed and no one is morally offended or outraged by the purpose, methodology or results of a project. What is researched, how it is researched, how the results are presented and used as well as what may follow from such research are all ethical issues.

The values of manaakitanga, whakapapa, mana, tapu, utu and ea are useful to keep in mind. Research in a Māori sense seeks to expand knowledge outwards (te whānuitanga), in depth (te hōhonutanga) and towards light (te māramatanga). These are goals that are demanding and focus upon different directions, for example, laterally in the realm of Tāne and Tūmatauenga, downwards into the depths of the world of Tangaroa and upwards into the world of Ranginui. Thus, it is expected that a researcher will go to considerable lengths to research a topic and thereby gain a worthwhile result which is often described as a 'taonga', that is, as a work of value.

Māori expectations about the results of research are no less onerous than those expected of western scholars. In fact, one can argue that Māori researchers of old were far more accountable to the people. Making mistakes, or missing a line of traditional waiata, or forgetting a name in a whakapapa line, or getting one's facts wrong were all held to be ritual errors punishable by divine means. In addition to the threat of divine intervention there was also the stigma of whakamā (shame), which was socially damaging to the individual.

Examinations

There is a misunderstanding about the nature of examinations in the traditional context of learning. Some Māori students believe that there were no tests and no examinations whatsoever. But that is plainly not the case. A tohunga or teacher-priest was given a special name when he was examining a student. He was called he tūāhu tāpātai or a tohunga patapātai, that is an examining tohunga who conducted the test by oral questioning of each student. The word pātai is not aimed solely at asking questions but also at eliciting information from the student. Thus students were tested to ensure that learning had occurred and that information had been successfully transferred from the lecturer to the student.

Te Matorohanga indicated that when the students of a course met with their lecturers at the end of the programme, evaluations were made of each student's progress. Students who did not reach the standards required were asked to return and repeat the course. Details of how assessments were made are not recorded but the lecturers probably were able to assess the abilities of their students with ease.

Conclusions

A study of the traditional whare wānanga and its practices reveals some interesting points. The most important is that learning was held in high esteem and that the act of transmitting knowledge was taken very seriously. The importance of the art was emphasised by surrounding it with rituals and by placing the whole institution under the tapu of knowledge and thus under the protection of the Gods. Students were made to feel the importance of their learning not only through daily rituals but also by adopting special clothing while learning. Thus there was a clear separation between everyday activities and learning.

The next important idea which comes out of this chapter is the notion of the tapu of knowledge or the tapu of learning and the tikanga associated with it. It is possible to revive some aspects of the tapu of knowledge and to adapt these aspects to the practices of today. Thus, learning in accordance with tikanga Māori could mean adopting protocols that derive from the notion of the tapu of knowledge and ensuring that such protocols are fully discussed and that students are willing to follow them. The objective should always be to enhance the learning of students and to assist them achieve to the best of their abilities.

Perspectives

When a Maori possessed of any prized or hard-earned knowledge wished to pass such on to a son or other relative, together with the mana pertaining to it, then a peculiar ceremony was performed in order to effect the desired transfer. The striking part of the performance was a certain personal contact that was deemed necessary, and which is said to have marked the precise moment at which knowledge passed from a dying parent or other relative to the recipient. Among the Takitimu folk the act is called whakaha and consisted of making contact with the head of the repository of learning or pu Wananga. The recipient placed the mouth to the crown of the head of the dying expert and just closed his teeth on it, at the same time making a short inspiration, a breathing inward. In some districts the act was that known as ngau taringa or ear biting, though no actual biting occurred, but mere contact.

— Best 1982, 2:110

Matauranga Maori is a body of knowledge that seeks to explain phenomena by drawing on concepts handed from one generation of Maori to another. Accordingly, matauranga Maori has no beginning and is without end. It is constantly being enhanced and refined. Each passing generation of Maori make their own contribution to matauranga Maori. The theory, or collection of theories, with associated values and practices, has accumulated mai i te ao Maori / from Maori beginnings and will continue to accumulate providing the whakapapa of matauranga Maori is unbroken.

– Winiata 2001

19
Te Whānuitanga o te Tikanga Māori
Extensions of Tikanga Māori

It has been said already that tikanga Māori accompanies Māori wherever they go and whatever they do. Tikanga Māori is adaptable, flexible, transferable and capable of being applied to entirely new situations. Our ancestors could not have predicted that we would have taken our elders and tikanga to New York and opened a highly successful exhibition of Māori art at the Metropolitan Museum of Modern Art in 1984. This event was a showpiece of tikanga Māori that included a dawn ceremony, traditional karakia, whaikōrero, waiata and performances by a kapa-haka group. Since then, Māori events and custom have been exported to many countries of the world. The New York event launched tikanga Māori into the international scene in a manner we could not have imagined. It did much to make tikanga Māori more acceptable not only to the population at large at Aotearoa but, more importantly, among our own people.

Today there are many new places and new events where tikanga Māori is applied. In previous chapters I wrote about traditional applications of tikanga Māori, of revivals of customs that had been cast aside earlier and of some modern adaptations. The focus here is upon applications to some modern situations not already described.

Tikanga Māori is most visible during performances of Māori performing arts troupes, at openings of art exhibitions, at dawn ceremonies to open important buildings at overseas posts and at home, at conferences, at displays of Māori martial arts and during visits of Māori groups to indigenous groups in other countries. We sometimes see it at openings of Parliament, at special events at Government House, in learning institutions, in hospitals, in various government agencies and in local government buildings. There is very strong evidence that tikanga Māori has become more acceptable nationwide and it appears in new situations.

The job interview, and beginning employment

It has become a custom to accompany a Māori person to a new job and to formally hand that person over to the hiring institution. Tikanga Māori applies to the interview as well. According to tikanga Māori a person is entitled to whānau support and so a 'whānau' appears. In some cases the whānau consists of blood relatives, and in many cases the 'whānau' consists of colleagues and friends who become a support group for their friend. At an interview there will be a speech of welcome, a pōhiri to the candidate, and that is given by a member of the interviewing panel. A member of the whānau-support group replies, usually in Māori. A karakia or prayer follows and then the interview begins. The candidate may answer all the questions put to them by various members of the interviewing panel, but a member of the whānau support group may speak as an advocate for their relative. There may be more speeches at the end of the interview.

If the candidate is successful, another 'ceremony' follows and this is the occasion of the transfer to the new job. This is a more important event than the interview. A day and time is negotiated for the successful applicant to arrive at work and take up the appointment. First, there is a pōhiri and at the conclusion of the speeches, and before the two groups meet and perform the tikanga of hongi, the transfer occurs. The new member of staff is asked to leave the comfort of their support group and cross over to the new group, greet them and then sit with the group that will become colleagues at work.

There may now be a special address in English to the new colleague and after this the new person may be asked to speak, especially if the position is a very important one in the organisation. Otherwise, the speeches may not be necessary. Instead, the two sides come together for the hongi and then have a cup of tea or a meal. The shared meal ends the induction ceremony.

Launching a book

As more Māori writers publish books there is a need to have book launches. The Māori term for this ceremony might be 'he whakarewa pukapuka', launching a book, or 'he tuku pukapuka', letting go of the book and making it available to the public, or 'he whakanoa taonga', that is, removing from the book the tapu associated with the creative act of writing and with everyone who played a part in publishing the book. In the last case the ceremony is similar to the notion of releasing the carvers of a meeting house from the tapu of their great work and from themselves. Once the whole ceremony of opening a meeting house is complete the house becomes free to the public to use it and access to it is no longer restricted. Thus, when a book is launched according to tikanga Māori the tapu is lifted from the work itself and from the author. The writer 'loses' control of the book at this point and the publisher, the distributors and the booksellers take over the task of making the book available to the public.

Many book launches have occurred around the country and in different iwi regions. Here is one way of carrying out a launch at a marae. First the author or authors and their whānau support groups and associated colleagues and friends become the manuhiri or visiting group. This group is formally welcomed to the marae according to a standard pōhiri ceremony, out in front of the ancestral house. The welcome is part one of the ceremony. After this the people are called into the ancestral house where the actual book launch occurs.

There are several ways in which the house can be arranged using either the mattresses or chairs or a combination of both. A better arrangement is to oppose the two main walls of the house. Chairs are more comfortable, especially for older persons. A simple arrangement is to have a few chairs up front on the noa side of the house where the speakers and author(s) will be seated and rows of chairs for the people on the tapu side. There is a master or mistress of ceremonies to manage the ceremony and to introduce the various speakers. The main speaker who is the honoured guest is a person who is able to read the book and give a good analysis of it or a summary of what the book covers. A positive person is required, not an overzealous critic who will upset the author or authors and their support groups. The last speaker will be the author or, if there are several authors, maybe more than one speaker.

The speeches need to be informative and worth listening to. Each is introduced by the master/mistress of ceremonies. Usually there is an invitation which sets out an agenda for the book launch.

The third section of the ceremony is to have a tohunga perform the appropriate karakia to free the authors and the work from the tapu of creative work. Many people prefer to have a tohunga perform traditional karakia over the book. If it is not possible to find one, a minister of a Christian church can be asked to 'bless' the book. Or it is also possible to start with karakia tūturu Māori (traditional karakia) and finish with Christian prayers.

The final part of the book launch ceremony is to have a meal, which might be a set meal or a big feast or a more humble finger-food sort of meal. Wine and beer might be included, if permitted. Some marae do not permit alcoholic drinks. The ceremony is complete once the meal is finished. As pointed out earlier, there are variations to the model described here, which is based on actual happenings.

Awards ceremonies

Awards ceremonies are now relatively common. The national Māori Sports Awards and the Māori Literature Awards are examples of very large events that are covered by television. There are smaller events that are not so public. Tikanga Māori has a place in these events. The main principles are as follows:

1. Every event begins with a pōhiri and perhaps a karakia or opening prayer.

2. The event itself has a tapu aspect to it. The award as well as the person being honoured are under the tapu of the event and this aspect should be respected.

3. Food and drinks are separated from the awards and must come at the end of the event.

4. There may be a closing karakia after the awards are presented and before the meal.

Two models are described as guides.

Model 1: an iwi award

In this case an iwi is honouring one of its own people and a protocol is worked out to suit the occasion. Obviously the nature of the award itself has already been decided. The description that follows is an award that recognises service to the iwi and consists of a printed citation and a taonga such as a tiki.

1. There is a pōhiri to the whānau of the recipient.
2. The purpose of the event is explained by the chair of the organisation.
3. A citation is read out.
4. Then the individual to be honoured comes forward and receives the citation, a certificate of the award and the taonga.
5. At this point a tohunga performs appropriate karakia to ensure that the recipient of the taonga receives it with the blessings and support of the iwi and that the taonga itself is free of any ritual impediments and that it feels good to the wearer.
6. A member of the whānau speaks in acknowledgement of the award.
7. Finally the person given the award speaks.
8. A closing karakia may follow.
9. The people now enjoy a hākari. This ends the award ceremony.

Model 2: national awards

In this case the awards are pan-tribal and is national in scale. It is likely to be a televised event or at least one that is held at some important building such as the National Museum of New Zealand Te Papa Tongarewa at Wellington or some other public building.

1. The event begins with speeches of welcome by an orator and an organiser of the sponsoring organisation.
2. A speaker explains the purpose and the history of the awards.
3. Comperes, especially bilingual ones, manage the ceremony, announce the names of the shortlisted candidates and organise someone to open the envelope which identifies the winner of a particular award, etc.

4. When the winner is announced whānau supporters may sing a song, perform an action song or do a war dance, or do a karanga.

5. If there is a series of awards to be given some entertainment might be provided at certain intervals.

6. The most important award is often left for the last and it becomes the high point of the event.

7. Food and drinks are enjoyed and wine and beer will most likely be included. This concludes the event.

There are many variations of the model. Some mix-up everything so that food and drinks are consumed as the awards are being presented. This does not accord with tikanga Māori.

Award ceremonies are held in different venues ranging from large public buildings to a convention centre, a hall, a marae or a small meeting room. What is right as a venue depends entirely on the size of the event and the nature of the programme and what is offered to participants by way of food and drinks. In events witnessed by the writer Māori culture is in evidence and the Māori language is used freely. Often the tribal affiliations of the winners are announced. It is worth noting that this tikanga of identifying oneself tribally is often over-emphasised. Some individuals give a long list of half a dozen or more tribes and hapū, whereas two would be sufficient, that is, provide the main affiliations and leave the rest out.

The hospital

For many years there was a reluctance among many Māori to go into hospital. Besides being cut off from one's whānau group there was the issue of tikanga Māori. No Māori wants to be put into a bed where the previous occupant died. Some do not want to wear the clothes of the hospital and want to have their own because clothes are affected by the tapu of the person who wears them. Some want to take their own sheets and towels because they do not trust the hospital's laundry system to separate out cloths associated with the human body. Others do not like the food of the hospital.

However everyone agrees that the hospital is the place to be when one is very ill. Visiting hours are now much more flexible than used to be the case and it is a more welcoming place for Māori than a few years ago.

When someone is very ill and life hangs in the balance most hospitals now offer a place where the whānau can stay for several days. The whānau looks after its own food arrangements and bedding, and being on the premises enables the whānau to roster its members so that there is always someone by the bedside of their sick relative. The whānau adopts the value of manaakitanga and will care for distant relatives and friends who come to visit their relative. The whānau vigil may last for several weeks. Each night the whānau will arrange for someone to come and conduct a church service for them. Some hospitals have a roster of chaplains who are available to the whānau.

Once it is clear that the tūroro (patient) is recovering and will not die the whānau support group begins to decrease. Some members have to go back to work and others need to look after the family's home and business if there is one. Some may come and go. In the end only the immediate family is left and eventually they will leave as well. The presence of the whānau close by is seen as the values of manaakitanga, whakapapa and aroha ki te tangata in action and could play a strong role in assisting the patient to hang on to life, that most precious gift that could be lost as a result of a major operation or a major illness. The whānau is an essential part of the recovery process.

If, however, the tūroro is about to transform into a tūpāpaku and the signs are clear, the size of the whānau support group is likely to increase. More and more relatives and friends will gather around to catch a final glimpse of the living person and to lend their support to the whānau. It is a sad moment and one which unites many people as the strong hand of fate, te ringa kaha o aituā, gradually dominates.

This is an entirely different situation from the case of a recovering tūroro. In the latter case the whānau is happy and very hopeful of a full recovery. As the patient recovers the tapu of the illness decreases and so people are much more relaxed and cheerful. However, where the strong hand of fate assumes control the tapu of illness increases and reaches a high point when it becomes the tapu of death. Behaviour becomes subdued, serious and respectful.

A minister of the church or a tohunga might be called in to administer last rites. In the Māori case (discussed in chapter 4) it is called 'te tuku wairua', that is, releasing the wairua of the person so that it leaves the body peacefully and begins its 'journey' of joining the many wairua that have already made a 'journey' to Hawaiki-nui, Hawaiki-roa, Hawaiki-pāmamao. This ceremony is witnessed by the whānau and occurs at the hospital.

After this the whānau prepares itself for the tangihanga ceremony. An undertaker is hired to prepare the body for a journey from the hospital to the morgue and then to the marae. From that point onwards the tikanga of the tangihanga ceremony follows. Meanwhile the hospital prepares for the next whānau support group.

Blessing a home

It has become common for both Māori and Pākehā home owners to request a tohunga or a minister of a church to come and 'bless' the house. There are different understandings of the term 'blessing a house' and the tikanga Māori term of he hiki i te tapu o te whare, lifting the tapu of the house. New-home owners feel more in touch with the new home and more at peace within it if the 'blessing' is carried out.

The ceremony is requested sometimes by families who have occupied the home for some time. The reason given for the request may be that there were disturbing 'happenings' in their house such as apparitions appearing, windows rattling and generally creepy occurrences, to the extent that the family was no longer happy with their lot. For new owners the reasons given are generally to clear away any bad influences in or around the house and to ensure that the family can enjoy their stay in their new home without being frightened or disturbed by unusual noises or dogged by ill fortune.

The tohunga arrives and is welcomed to the house. He may reply and request the family to come outside and follow him or simply to remain outside while he recites the traditional karakia to lift the tapu of the house. He will visit every room of the house except the toilet and the bathroom, which contain water. He may have a branch of green leaves which he uses to strike the walls of each room. A traditional tohunga does not use water to sprinkle over the rooms. A minister of a church may follow very much the same procedure except that the family gathers in the sitting room and the cleansing service begins there. The minister will recite prayers and will sprinkle water in each room to cleanse it of evil influences. At the conclusion the family and the tohunga or minister of a church gather in the kitchen and share a meal which might be just light finger foods and tea or coffee, or it might be a sit-down meal of several courses.

Blessing a factory

In a factory where a substantial part of the workforce is Māori and where accidents frequently occur a tohunga may be asked to visit the factory and lift the tapu from it. Often this is demanded by the workers who feel that there is something wrong with the place, that it might have been built over a burial site, or that there are bad influences in the factory which lead to accidents happening. The procedure adopted by the tohunga is to arrange to visit the factory when there is no one there. Several tohunga may become involved as a team. This occurs especially when tohunga of the Ringatū church are involved. They may use a team approach or they may employ one person. It all depends on the nature of the task. Ringatū tohunga tend to carry out their task early in the morning when it is still dark.

Tohunga not associated with a church may choose their own time and follow their own procedures for clearing the factory floor of influences that are conducive to accidents happening. They will lift the tapu and not really expect a meal because the circumstances are different. On the other hand the owners of the factory may reward them with a gift of money instead.

Te tāpōrena i te roro o te wharenui: the canvas extension to the carved meeting house

As recently as the beginning of the year 2000 a heated debate occurred at one Bay of Plenty marae over the appropriate use of a canvas extension to the porch of a meeting house. At several marae in the Bay of Plenty it is custom to attach a canvas extension to the porch of a meeting house during a tangihanga. This is especially the case where the body of the deceased is placed in the porch and the supporting kiri mate are required to sit there all day from sunrise to sunset. This group needs to be protected from the elements. The canvas is called a tāpōrena (tarpaulin).

In the East Coast region the custom is to drape a huge tāpōrena in the front of the porch to provide cover for the mourning group. Sufficient space is allowed for the visiting groups to actually see the casket and to satisfy themselves that there is a body lying in state before them and that they have come to the right place of mourning.

The Bay of Plenty canvas cover is specially cut to fit the front of a meeting house and it is truly an extension of the house. It is brought out for tangihanga ceremonies and rarely for any other purpose. The debate mentioned occurred when a request was made to put up the tāpōrena in order to protect the officials of a tertiary institution, who were to sit at the porch of the house. The forecast was for a hot summers day and therefore some protection was necessary. The person making the request thought the reasons he advanced in support of the request were reasonable, logical and in the best interests of manaakitanga, that is looking after the health of the visitors. Thus his request was in accordance with the values of tikanga.

However his request sparked a debate on whether the occasion was appropriate after all the extension was attached only for tangihanga. A graduation ceremony is a celebration and therefore did not qualify. The extension was not put in place and the officials were quite red in the face and sunburnt at the end of the day, unaware of the debate that had occurred the day before. However the marae maintained its tikanga in relation to the tāpōrena.

Conclusions

The examples described here emphasise two points. The first is that wherever Māori live and work, tikanga Māori or aspects of it follow them. There is a natural tendency to give meaning to an event by injecting into it some aspects of their own culture and their own customs. A result of doing so is that the participants do not feel as though they are merely observers of someone else's culture. Rather they become active participants. In many instances, such as in some of the examples described here, Māori are actually organising and putting into practice ceremonies that they have seen, liked and then borrowed. There is really no end to the range of non-traditional activities that Māori may adopt and into which tikanga Māori can be injected.

The second point is the growing acceptance of tikanga Māori and the fact that many non-Māori accept it as a matter of course. The tendency is evident in ceremonies organised by non-Māori for non-Māori events. It is now quite common to hear a short speech of welcome in Māori by many office holders and in places where it is not expected. We may hear a greeting in Māori on Air New Zealand jets. Many non-Māori purchase and wear Māori ornaments and some request a ceremony to make the ornament safe for them. Many radio and television announcers really try very hard to pronounce Māori names correctly. As New Zealand citizens seek to identify themselves as uniquely New Zealand we will see an increasing tendency to accept and practise tikanga Māori.

20
Ngā Ahi E Ngiha Mai Nei
The Fires That Flare Up

All around us are issues that have either not yet been addressed, or discussed seriously, or are yet to be verbalised. The Māori world is assailed by these issues that are not just local but tend to be international in scope, issues which are articulated and argued about in New York, London, Paris, Berlin and at other places eventually come here. For a while we may regard these issues as interesting news, but eventually the Māori population has to join the discussions and at this point such matters often become difficult. There is a proverb which provides a useful comment on this dilemma: 'Taku ahi tūtata, taku mata kikoha; taku ahi mamao, taku mata kiporo' (When my fire is close by, the point of the weapon is sharp, but when the fire is distant the point is blunt (Mead & Grove 2001: 355)).

Distant 'fires' have a habit of coming close to home so that we do have to sharpen our wits and deal with them. Issues such as genetic engineering (GE), genetic modification (GM), in-vitro fertilisation (IVF), organ transplants, surrogate motherhood and same-sex marriages are fires that began in other countries. Eventually the same fires are ignited in our country, and so long as we thought that the issues were Pākehā ones and had nothing to do with us we did not have to contend with them. But inevitably we do have to engage in the debates and we do have to attempt to identify a position that we might call a Māori one. In attempting to discover a position, however, we will find that we have to engage with tikanga Māori and its knowledge base, mātauranga Māori.

What I am calling a tikanga Māori position is sometimes referred to by people working in various ethics committees or in the health field as a tikanga Māori framework of assessment. In other words, it provides a method or methods for assessing a situation or event that challenges our thinking and our values. Applying a tikanga Māori framework of assessment should give us a Māori viewpoint, or a Māori position, on whatever the issue might be. The key point here is that the framework provides *a* position and not necessarily *the* position.

The result of applying the framework will differ according to the position of the person making the assessment. The relatives of a person ill in hospital and depending on a new cure for life will rely on their obligation to protect the mauri and therefore the life of their relative. On the other hand, one who is not immediately caught up in the moral dilemma of the family might stress some other aspect of the framework. The latter assessment is more detailed and is free of the immediacy of a life-threatening situation. Others again will question why tikanga Māori should be considered at all and will rely either on a church position or on individual choice. But here we are interested in developing a tikanga Māori framework, and I discuss five tests to apply to new issues. When the fires of ethical controversy flare up close to home they can be tested according to tikanga Māori, and a tikanga Māori perspective developed to guide our actions in controlling the fires.

The role of government bodies

The mainstream population has the benefit of specialised institutions such as ethics committees to assist the people cope with 'brush fire' issues. The Bioethics Council, a newly created body (2003), considers the ethical, spiritual and cultural aspects of new developments in biotechnology and new medicines. There are bodies of this sort in other western countries and so it is possible to gather information from several sources. Government funding is made available to protect the interests of the people and save them from unscrupulous advocates of new cures and new technologies. There are bodies like the Environmental Risk Management Authority (ERMA) which is responsible for assessing and deciding on applications to import, develop, field test or release genetically modified organisms; the independent Biotechnology Advisory Committee that is charged with stimulating dialogue and enhancing public understanding about biotechnology and among other things to advise on developments in human biotechnology; and there is the Bioethics Council that is charged with enhancing New Zealand's understanding of the cultural, ethical and spiritual aspects of biotechnology and ensure that the use of biotechnology has regard for the values held by New Zealanders.

These bodies have responsibilities to the Māori population as well and they do attempt to address Māori concerns about the ethical, spiritual and cultural consequences of these new 'fires'. However, they are some distance away from the iwi and their marae and the people. So it will be useful to place information in the hands of the people and a process of analysis as suggested here will assist families to arrive at a decision that is informed by a more intimate knowledge of tikanga Māori. By the time the reader has read all of the chapters of the book and up to this final chapter it should be possible to work out a tikanga Māori position on whatever the issue might be.

Test 1: the tapu aspect

A starting point is to subject the ethically controversial issue to the tapu test. For example, if the gene of a fish is placed in a tomato, or a human gene into a sheep or a cow, or a part of a pig is placed inside the body of a human being, has tapu been breached? In the first example, fish are under the mantle of Tangaroa, and plants are under Tāne. Is the result to enhance the tomato or to degrade it? Has the tapu of Tangaroa been damaged in the transfer? Probably, one would say, not much.

What about a human gene into a cow or sheep? Or into a pig? This is not an academic question. These transfers are already happening (Bryan & Clare 2001). Māori generally have great difficulty in accepting the use of human genes this way. There is a sense of degrading the tapu of a human being. Then what do we think about the medically successful use of a pig valve surgically attached to a human heart that helps to keep a relative alive? Has that small living part of a pig damaged the tapu of a human being? Is the human being any less human? Plainly the patient is alive and well and must therefore be feeling good. The transfer of part of a pig has not damaged the tapu or mana or mauri of the patient.

In referring again to the use of a fish gene in a tomato plant there remains the issue of the tapu of the individual Gods and their domains. Tangaroa is a powerful God and he cannot be treated with disdain.

Although Tūmatauenga conquered Tangaroa, his people are often claimed in large numbers by Tangaroa or individuals are attacked by the children of Tangaroa. It follows that Tangaroa has to be treated with due regard and that the tapu of his domain is to be greatly respected. This applies to the domains of all of the Gods. While there is a breach of tapu here the degree of the breach is not as great as breaching the tapu of Tūmatauenga. Some may argue that the breach is so slight that it can be ignored for the common good. But this raises another issue. The common good must surely refer to the people, to the consumers, and not to the developers of the technology. So, is the modification a benefit to the common people? And if there is a benefit, who are the beneficiaries? These are tricky questions, the answers to which are by no means clear-cut and could fall either way. The story about Tūmatauenga's defeat of his brothers provides an explanation of why it is right to eat the progeny of other Gods in order to sustain life. The story does not, however, cover the transfer of body parts or genes.

Test 2: the mauri aspect

Every living thing has a mauri and, in fact, we go one step further and say a forest is a living thing, so is a meeting house, and even a rock. But our concern here is with living organisms, with animals, plants and human beings. In considering the case of the tomato plant and the fish gene the question to ask is this: has the mauri of the tomato plant been put at risk? Did the transfer damage the mauri of the tomato plant and its fruit to the end that the tomato is no longer a tomato but is something different? Plainly this is not the case. The tomato still looks like a tomato and the plant behaves like a tomato plant. What is different is the skin, which tends to be thicker than previously, and the taste of the fruit has become more bland, at least in the view of this taster.

The mauri test is essentially a test of the risks to the life of the subjects of, say, gene transfers. When a pig's heart-valve is inserted into a human being does that threaten the mauri of the patient? In this case it does not. In fact, it protects the mauri of the patient. What about the pig? Is the mauri of the pig affected? The answer is, yes. In the final analysis a mauri is sacrificed to save another and this is not an ideal situation. The rationalisation for sacrificing the pig is that we kill it and eat it anyway. But when we eat it we do not call it pig, but rather pork. Eating pork, however, is quite different from using living tissues of a pig to keep us alive. Most of us enjoy pork in various forms, for example as chops, roasts, spare ribs, bones, intestines and even the blood of pigs as black pudding. In fact, there is a close historical relationship between humans with pigs and in some societies, especially in the Pacific region, pigs are important in social and economic exchanges and extremely important as pork in many ceremonies. But many of us have qualms about employing living pig tissues to repair damaged human parts, such as replacing damaged heart valves with pig valves and replacing burn-damaged skin with pig skin. Why is this?

In the case of pork the pig is killed, prepared, cooked and eaten by us. The mauri of the pig is extinguished in the process. When eaten the pork provides sustenance for humans. The act of cooking and consuming the pork renders it noa and therefore safe.

In contrast, living tissue used to repair human parts continues to live. It is not consumed, but provides humans with the ability to improve the state of their mauri. In a sense, the pig tissue has been incorporated into the life-support systems of a human. Pigs contribute to the maintenance of life itself in a different way from the contribution of pork. Part of the mauri of pigs remain in human beings as living tissue. One supposes that if in taking living tissue from the pig the animal is killed and therefore its mauri and its tapu are extinguished. But we doubt that the mauri and tapu of the pig are in fact completely extinguished, and this is a concern. Are there risks to humans in employing the living tissue of animals to repair damaged parts? The natural order of life is that we eat and consume pigs as pork. This order has now been changed and a new net goes fishing and a new order has to be negotiated. But uncertainties remain about using animals in this new way, essentially about using their living tissues that have not been culturally processed and philosophically reconciled with tikanga Māori.

But then there is another problem: the incorporation of human genes into pigs, which makes the pig safer as a source of living parts for transplantation. And when this happens does it mean we can no longer enjoy such pigs as pork? Surely when such a pig is killed in order to use parts of it to improve the quality of life for humans, qualms increase rather than diminish. Part of the mauri and tapu of the pig remains in the living parts and now there is a human component added to them. It could be argued that these are ethical, moral and philosophical issues and not fundamental health issues. But we are guided by our belief systems so the burning issue might be to change the belief and philosophical system, that is, mātauranga Māori and tikanga Māori, in order to accommodate new technologies and new ways of improving the quality of human life and extending life expectancy figures. This takes time, however, and sick people cannot wait.

There are other areas where the mauri test may be applied. For example, genetic modification in the food supply might damage our mauri if we do not know the long-term effects of such changes and if field trials have not been carried out with sufficient rigour.

Cloning, the asexual and artificial reproduction of life, poses problems of risk to the mauri of the cloned form. There are missing elements in the clone which place the mauri at risk. The state of knowledge about reproductive cloning poses some problems of risk to the mauri of the cloned form. Here we are not talking about twins who are conceived and born naturally, but rather about the use of the techniques of biotechnology to create a cloned form. Dolly the cloned sheep is well known in the world of biotechnology (Meek 2003). Dolly was cloned at the Roslin Institute in Scotland, born 5 July 1996, died 14 February 2003 and its stuffed form placed at the Edinburgh Royal Museum on 9 April 2003. Dolly had three mothers, one ewe to provide DNA from an udder cell, the second one to provide the egg into which the DNA was inserted and a third mother acted as the whare hipi, as the nurturing house for the cloned embryo. So Dolly was born and raised into adulthood. She gave birth to six uncloned lambs in her time, but there was a problem with Dolly herself. She is alleged to have aged prematurely and to have suffered from arthritis and a debilitating lung infection which were characteristic signs of age. Ordinary sheep could live up to twelve years. But Dolly died at six years of age.

Thus there is a suspicion that there are problems in the present method of cloning and that the cloned form is not equal in all respects with a sheep produced the orthodox way. Its mauri was fine when Dolly was born except that it was already at risk because its DNA timetable and the trigger points for growth were not quite right.

The biggest fear about cloning is that 'mad scientists' would turn to reproductive cloning to produce human beings of strange alien-like forms. This fear is probably unfounded, but nonetheless people are worried about the ethical and tikanga Māori aspects of cloning.

Euthanasia, the painless killing of a terminally ill patient, aims at terminating the mauri of the patient and therefore is at odds with the value we place on protecting the mauri of human beings especially. In Māori terms it is the unseen hand of misfortune, te ringa kaha o aituā, which takes away the life of a person.

Surrogate motherhood is where a woman bears a child on behalf of another woman. Through advances in biotechnology it is possible for someone else to be the whare whakaira tangata (the house to create a new human being), not the biological mother who might be unable to nurture and carry a child. There may be good reasons why this is necessary. The mother who becomes the surrogate mother is chosen. She may be paid to undertake the task of nurturing the fertilised egg, giving birth to the new life and then handing that new life from her womb to the natural parents.

Surrogacy aims at creating a new mauri in a way that does not follow the accepted norm. Is the mauri of the child put at risk? It is not at all clear what the risks might be, if any, in such cases. Surrogacy aims at producing a new life and thus at creating a new mauri. The concern would be for the life of the new being and for the long-term prospects. Most of the concerns are probably focussed on moral and social issues rather than on risks to the mauri.

Test 3: the take–utu–ea or TUE test

If a breach of tapu and/or mauri is established or is seen to be an issue the next step is to apply the take–utu–ea or TUE test. We deal with each element of the test in turn.

The take traditionally has to be accepted by all parties as a legitimate cause. This means that there has to be recognition that tapu has been or will be breached and the reasons are canvassed and debated. In all of these 'fires' the debates are likely to be contested and since we are now dealing with global rather than local issues, with believers and non-believers, and with Māori and non-Māori it is much more difficult to reach agreement. In fact the cards are stacked against tikanga Māori. One way of dealing with this aspect is for Māori to have their own debates. Since the aim is to arrive at a Māori position it is logical to confine the debate as much as possible to people who know something about mātauranga Māori and tikanga Māori. A real difficulty here is the ideal of achieving mutual acknowledgement of the wrong done.

We suppose now that the take is agreed. The next element is that of utu. What is the form of utu most appropriate to this sort of breach of tapu? Many questions can be asked. For example, who is implicated in the breach? What is the reason for doing this? Is it to harm people, or to benefit them? Before carrying out the deed did they assess the likelihood of damage to the well-being of the people who will use the results of the new modifications or the new technology? These questions need to focus on one particular issue at a time.

The final, desired state is that of ea. Ea, as we have seen, is a state of satisfaction where a sequence has been successfully closed, relationships have been restored, or peaceful interrelationships have been secured.

For example, if it is a new drug does it have some harmful side effects? If the answer is yes, have the people been warned about this? If the answer is no, then the company is liable and compensation needs to be determined so as to reach a state of ea. A cause has been established, the payment of compensation for the breach has been determined by a court or by mutual agreement, and a state of satisfaction has been reached.

Not all cases fit the test. One could say that if it is not possible to establish an agreed-upon take then it is impossible to move to the next stage. For example, workers attempting to establish that their health was affected at the workplace through exposure to toxins usually have great difficulty in persuading all parties to accept the take. Factory owners may be reluctant to agree and may have to be forced to accept culpability though court action. Modern firms are afraid of the financial consequences of agreeing to a cause because either they know the extent of the utu or they have no way of estimating what the utu might be. It is helpful to know what the utu is expected to be, even if it means something like a muru wherein the guilty party loses everything moveable and is forced to make a new start. In today's world the courts determine what is appropriate, and it is not always clear what the outcome might be.

Test 4: the precedent aspect

When confronted with a new 'fire' an obvious response is to look for precedents in the culture. Is there some event in our traditions that might help us understand the issue and help frame a response to it? For example, the current debate on genetic modification is a matter of some concern. What is a response to this matter?

There are stories of ancestors changing form from one being to another or of human forms changing into non-human forms such as rocks and mountains. The means used was magic. In one of the origin stories about the moko Tama transformed himself into a white heron and visited the underworld (Best 1982, 2:237). The demigod Māui was able to change himself into an owl or a hawk, and was able to transform others. For example, he changed his brother-in-law Irawaru into a dog (Best 1982, 2:360). These examples may not be very helpful as precedents and perhaps the most useful idea coming out of these stories is the notion of changing forms and of crossing the domains of the Gods. In another tradition the demigod Tāwhaki was able to give sight to his blind grandmother Whaitiri (Mead 1996:48–57). Some genetic engineering of sorts would have been required to accomplish this feat, but the engineering was done by magical means. In another interesting series of cases a whakapapa model is used to explain the creation of various life forms.

Here is one example:

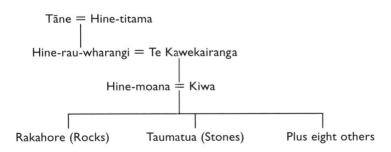

Among the children of Hine-moana were Rakahore and Taumatua and their purpose was to provide for nine kinds of mussels and provide anchor points for seaweed (Best 1982, 2:255–6). Hine-moana created various kinds of shellfish. Demigods marry and have children and they and their children create various natural forms such as rocks and life forms such as shellfish (Best 1982, 2: 255–56).

This is quite a common model of explanation for the creation of life forms. Following this same whakapapa many other life forms were created. The critical ancestor is Hine-moana who had ten children to Kiwa. According to the traditions collected by Best (1982, 2: 257) she and Kiwa created cockles, eels (including blind eels), conger eels, lamprey, mullet, sea urchins, porcupine fish, snapper, gurnard, groper, kingfish, moki, kahawai, terakihi, and the octopus.

Crayfish came from the marriage of Tahu-maeora and Kohurau (ibid.: 257), although in another version it was Kama, a child of Tāwhaki and Hine-murutoka, who created seven kinds of crayfish. These stories are essentially explanations for the manner in which our world is ordered.

Genetic engineering is concerned with the creation of new elements or new characteristics in existing life forms. The sorts of changes scientists are bringing about through the utilising of genes from other life forms could result one day in the creation of new life forms. Genetic engineering in fruit could produce new variations of existing named fruits such as apples. There is now available in shops a new variety of kiwifruit. Thus scientists are like demigods who are able to create new forms of life or transform one life form into another. At the moment scientists are said to modify rather than create, but the technology allows them to create. A tomato might be eventually transformed into a fish, a pig might become more human and a cow eventually produce human milk. Or they may create half forms such as the half human and half taniwha children of taniwha and human parents that storytellers relate to their children.

Thus from a Māori perspective the question is whether there is a whakapapa to which the new event can be linked, or whether there is a tauira, or model, in our traditions.

Test 5: the principles aspect

It is quite possible that the first four tests may not be helpful at all and so one may have to consider the principles test. This test examines the issue at hand against the principles and values of tikanga Māori. Some of the principles and values – utu, ea and tapu – are included in the first four tests. Remaining are the values of whanaungatanga, manaakitanga, mana and noa. These are very important values which embrace other values such as aroha ki te tangata, concern for our people, being a good host and providing hospitality for guests, protecting the mana of people and not doing anything that threatens their mana or, worse still, damages personal mana.

Test 5.1: whanaungatanga

If the person seeking support and assistance is a blood relative one is obliged to be helpful. Relatives are expected to be helpful and to render such assistance as is in their power and means to give. So if one's relative is a scientist at the forefront of genetic engineering there is an obligation upon the relatives to be helpful and to give support as well. It follows that if the victim of industrial misadventure (unprotected exposure to toxins, for example) is a relative, the other kin are obliged to assist and support.

The whanaungatanga principle and value can be extended to include a wider constellation of non-kin colleagues or sympathisers, such as the whole tribe, all of one's workmates, the student body. It might even include a political party whose members see themselves as linked together by a common cause. For example, a political party can agree to a policy of not supporting genetic engineering or nuclear testing, and such a policy would oblige Māori members to support it whether it was supported by tikanga Māori or not.

Test 5.2: manaakitanga

The principle and the values attached to manaakitanga are held to be very important and underpin all tikanga Māori. Manaakitanga focuses on positive human behaviour and encourages people to rise above their personal attitudes and feelings towards others and towards the issues they believe in. Being hospitable and looking after one's visitors is given priority. The aim is to nurture relationships and as far as possible to respect the mana of other people no matter what their standing in society might be. The value is often expressed as 'acting like a rangatira'. Such a person is prepared to hear about the other arguments relating to any particular issue.

The principles of manaakitanga are traditionally to be expected of the chiefs and leaders, that is, the rangatira. It remains a powerful value, and hapū and iwi attempt to live up to it. Not to do so is to bring shame to the whole group. When applied to the notion of genetic engineering, the principle of manaakitanga would be similar to the notion of the common good. Is the modification helpful to human kind, or to people who suffer certain illnesses which are difficult to cure, or to babies or to the poor, the orphans, the widows and the maimed. In applying the manaakitanga test, however, one has to consider that there are other values in the test package. One should not seize on manaakitanga alone as the sole criterion of assessment, but it is clear that ultimately a family group might have no other choice but to appeal to manaakitanga.

Test 5.3: mana

The principle here is that an event should neither damage the mana of a patient, nor a consumer, nor anyone associated with that event. Ideally a new idea should enhance mana, help individuals maintain or even improve their mana, and lift everyone else who participates in the event. This means that the idea itself needs to meet some basic ethical standards and should not be regarded as morally wrong or at the least very doubtful. A controversial innovation could damage the mana of those behind it and of those who take up the idea. Controversial 'fires' evoke strong emotional reactions from sections of the population. In this context the mana of the participants is at risk and can be damaged. For example, doctors who practise abortions are often targeted and denigrated and while they see the service they provide as meeting the principle of manaakitanga their personal mana is put at risk and they themselves are open to personal damage.

Genetic engineering and modifications generate heated debate and supermarkets that sell GM products might find that their clients will boycott their store and go somewhere else. It could be that the scientists who develop these genetically 'enhanced' products are denigrated by the media. As a result, mana is damaged. Many of these innovations that are now possible through new technology or improved processes remain controversial and are yet to be widely supported by the general public. Until that wide support is gained the mana of some people could be damaged.

Test 5.4: noa

Noa has much to do with normality and with reaching a state whereby a new idea is accepted, incorporated into the thinking of people and no longer is a cause for controversy. Pharmaceutical companies probably need to plan a whakanoa campaign, that is a campaign to put people at ease and persuade them that the new drug really is good for the people, that there are no bad side effects and that the price is reasonable. Great attention might need to be paid to how a new product is introduced to the public. It might not be a good idea to focus on persuasion through advertising and acceptance of the new product as something modern thinking citizens ought to accept without full and honest disclosure of relevant information.

With a whakanoa plan the idea is to settle the minds of the people about the new product. For example, people need to know that it will not harm them or their children. In fact, it might enhance them in some way by prolonging life or easing pain. There is a process geared to different peoples and different cultures. In Aotearoa, Māori people may need to be treated differently, and a whakanoa plan is geared to their cultural concerns and it can be said to be similar in purpose to being transparent and accountable to the people.

Test 5.5: tika

There are more general principles, such as public acceptance of a particular tikanga. Most tikanga come down through the generations and are carried out because it is right to do so. The success of tikanga depends very much on public acceptance. But there is a more fundamental principle underlying whether it is right and morally acceptable to adopt a new tikanga that has come from somewhere else but now has to be confronted by us. We too participate in biomedical innovations. We accept body parts belonging to non-kin. We too look for ways to prolong life. So these medical miracle cures have to be considered in terms of tikanga Māori. The basic question to ask is whether the miracle cure is tika, that is, ethically, culturally, spiritually and medically right. After all other considerations have been undertaken, the test of appropriateness and correctness is the final hurdle. The answer should be, yes, it is tika and right for me to participate in the new technology. If there are second thoughts about the decision that could mean it is not passing the critical test about whether it is right.

Whakapapa issues

In the relatively new area of surrogate motherhood an element has been added recently to what is already a matter of ethical concern. It has to do with a sister acting as a surrogate mother for a sibling.

What tikanga Māori issues are raised when a sister carries the fertilised egg of her sister and her sister's husband? Some may say that there is apparently no problem if a sister acts as surrogate mother. The whakapapa link is not a problem. In fact, many would say that this would be an ideal situation. It meets the requirement of whanaungatanga (of obligations to assist family members), of manaakitanga (obligations to assist especially if there are medical reasons as to why the sister should offer help). This would be seen as helping to preserve the tapu and the mauri of the sisters and sharing enhances the whānau, produces a new life and adds a new member to the whānau. The outcomes are considered to be tika, correct.

There was considerable concern, however, when the general public was informed of the case where a sister was assisting her brother and his wife. If a sister-to-sister relationship is accepted as appropriate, why not a sister-to-brother one? Obviously, the notion of incest is raised and some people feel uncomfortable about a sister surrogate mother acting for her brother and his wife. Has tapu been breached in this case, that is, the tapu associated with incest which rejects brother–sister sexual relationships and marriages?

One could say that in the case of the sister acting as surrogate mother the spectre of breaching marriage regulations is still a problem. The husband of the sister and the father of the fertilised egg has no rights of access for any purpose to the whare whakaira tangata of his wife's sister except in Māori tradition if the sisters are both wives of the same man. There would be no breach in the latter case. Some societies permitted a man to have several wives who were not necessarily sisters. Were any of them to act as surrogate mother on behalf of another wife there would be no breach. There is obviously a grey area here where there is no clear-cut general rule. So the element of tapu is not such a big concern in this case. Many cultures would say no to a sister acting as surrogate for her brother, arguing that there should be no relationship whatsoever that is associated with the whare whakaira tangata, the process of creating and nurturing new life and giving birth to that life. The tikanga-Māori position would favour focussing on the issue of te whare whakaira tangata and arguing that this house is tapu and remains a prohibited area to a brother. The utu is the social stigma that is carried by the family. There is some bite in the proverb: 'waiho mā te whakamā e patu' (let shame be the punishment). Or, as in most cases of infringements associated with tapu, there may be an unknown ritual penalty at some unknown time.

Conclusions

Five tests are proposed to assist those who want a tikanga framework to help them develop and justify what may be called a Māori position on current contentious issues. In this chapter an attempt has been made to examine the process of arriving at a tikanga Māori position on many controversial issues which often flare up overseas and then make their way, sometimes very rapidly, to our country. The Māori population cannot ignore these controversial fires. In today's world these global issues eventually come to our marae and we have to confront them. In many cases we do not know how to 'deal' with these issues and how to frame a position. People insist, however, that there must be a tikanga Māori position.

A framework is suggested here for assisting people to arrive at a position in terms of tikanga Māori. This position is not to be confused with a Christian point of view or other views based on other philosophies. We need to be very clear about this and try to focus on tikanga Māori and not some tikanga from some other cultural perspective.

The discussion is firmly based on mātauranga Māori, on our traditions, on our customs and thus, eventually, on the principles of tikanga Māori. Five basic tests are suggested: the tapu test, the mauri test, the take–utu–ea test, the precedent test and finally the principles test. Others may wish to add more principles to the list and that might be helpful. After exploring these tests it should be possible to decide whether it is right to adopt the new technology or the idea of genetic modification, organ transplants or surrogate motherhood. In some cases the issues are so complex that these tests might not help at all. We remember too, that there are old ideas, such as domestic violence, child abuse and abuse of the elderly which we can also subject to the same tests and find some answers.

On the medical front we are beset by diseases such as heart problems, diabetes, gout, cancer, asthma, Aids and mental problems associated with drug taking. There are problems with kidneys and livers, with hearing and sight, with Parkinson's disease and so on. Not only might we need to change our diets and ways of life but we might also need to be more accepting of new ways of improving one's life chances. Many of the decisions that have to be reached are often made by suffering individuals.

The tests identified here could be useful to families confronted by the dilemma of having to decide whether to participate in new technologies, new cures for medical problems, and new ways of doing things. There are steps to take and questions to be asked and answered. The resulting decision would at least be based on a process that would generate much soul searching, many discussions, and result in a greater understanding of tikanga Māori. What remains unclear, however, is whether the decision made puts out the fire. Even if it does, another distant fire, an ahi mamao, will flare up and will soon to become an ahi tūtata, a fire close-up, and the process will be repeated.

Perspectives

Culture change

The emphasis on creativity has led the Navajo to accept, adopt, and adapt many things and practices from other peoples. Many aspects of Navajo culture have been adopted from other cultures and incorporated in Navajo life. This has been done creatively, so that the essence and core of Navajo life and culture have not been disrupted or destroyed but have been enhanced. Many writers and historians have commented on the ability of the Navajo to absorb without being absorbed. This ability is derived from a capacity to make creative syntheses.

  – Witherspoon 1977: 182

But I do wish to argue that apparently major and significant changes can occur on the surface level of a cultural system without alterations to its more fundamental metaphysical assumptions. These surface changes require a process of remodelling through which they are reconciled with the lower level assumptions. Through this process of reconciliation the cultural system returns to an ordered and coherent whole.

  – Witherspoon 1977: 5–6

21
Kua Ea: It Is Done

This book represents a preliminary exploration of tikanga Māori and some reflections upon issues around it and arising from its place in modern Māori society.

It is an introduction to a body of knowledge that had been neglected because tikanga Māori was not in favour earlier and so not in the public mind. Over the last few decades, however, tikanga Māori has been revived, has undergone a transformation and is now discussed openly, taught in the education system and is increasingly entering the public domain. Its time has arrived. Clearly tikanga Māori has its basis in traditional Māori society and because of this fact there are some thinkers who believe that what we do now is the same as our ancestors used to practise. According to them, tikanga Māori endures unchanged and ought to be carried out true to custom. In other words tikanga Māori is grounded in antiquity and its basic core remains constant. While we can accept that the core of tikanga Māori retains its integrity over long periods of time the proposition that tikanga Māori never changes is not supported by the facts of the real world.

As pointed out in this book there is a dynamic aspect to tikanga Māori. Besides the fact that the physical setting for tikanga Māori varies enormously there is the equally compelling fact that the players and the audiences are never the same. On each occasion there is a range of variables that impinge not only on how the tikanga is interpreted but also on its practice. Subtle and sometimes major changes are introduced every time a tikanga is practised. This point is canvassed many times in this book.

Another issue that is explored in various chapters is the question on whether tikanga Māori is only for Māori or whether people of other cultures are free to participate. There is no doubt that Māori rightly consider themselves to be the cultural owners of tikanga Māori. It is our duty to protect its integrity and it remains the duty of Māori generally to be responsible for our tikanga. We are the people who have a responsibility to maintain tikanga, to carry them out properly so as to be correct, to understand the significance of these customs and to value them as expressions of Māori culture.

However, it is part of human nature to borrow customs from other cultures. We ourselves have done a lot of borrowing in our time and continue to do so every year. There is increasing evidence that many government agencies and private institutions are incorporating tikanga Māori into their activities. The pōhiri is a good example. It is commonplace to witness a pōhiri ceremony at all sorts of places in our country. We export it overseas. As described in some chapters the dawn ceremony has become very popular. The idea is appealing and many non-Māori groups want to make use of it. Other cultures are thus being enriched by the influences of tikanga Māori.

Whatever other cultures choose from our pool of tikanga the primary responsibility for reviving, rejuvenating, practising and securing the basket of knowledge remains with Māori. Others pick and choose according to what appeals to them. Māori are committed to the whole package. However, it cannot be denied that some Māori also pick and choose, as is their right in modern society. Yet the collective group has the responsibility to protect our tikanga and to develop our customs and practices to suit the conditions of the present and future.

However, one of the difficulties that face us is that there is no formal process for protecting our tikanga and no structure to keep an eye on what is happening. Every Māori group, or whānau or hapū or iwi, does the best they can. The only effective monitoring mechanism that we have is the individual Māori who speaks up when tikanga is very inappropriately applied. Such individuals continue a tradition. As pointed out, the public have a role not only in supporting tikanga but also in ensuring that tikanga has been carried out correctly and appropriately and preferably with style and verve. Individual monitors emerge and sometimes with great drama.

One of the most enduring and widely practised tikanga is the tangihanga ceremony. This is a remarkable complex tikanga that is carried out with little fuss at marae and sometimes in homes throughout the land. The tangihanga brings together in a coherent way many of the core values of Māori society and many practices that demand use of the Māori language-arts. Oratory is given several days of practise. The karanga is a vital part of the ceremony as is the performance of traditional waiata. There are rituals to carry out and importantly the value of manaakitanga is given full scope as all who participate in this ceremony have to be hosted, given food, and bedding is provided for them should some stay overnight. There is the thought that the tangihanga ceremony is at the very core of Māori culture and that we are fortunate our ancestors insisted on maintaining this tikanga throughout the 1800s and the 1900s. Today the tangihanga remains a powerful and unifying ceremony.

Several tikanga, like the tangihanga, that have endured through time are explored in this book. There are others such as the muru which have gone out of favour and are no longer practised. Then there are new situations where tikanga Māori has been applied quite successfully such that a new protocol is established. Examples are the launching of books written by Māori authors, opening art exhibitions, introducing the tapu of learning into tertiary institutions, opening overseas buildings, setting up facilities for whānau support groups at hospitals and so on. There are many of them.

Then there are old customs that have a new relevance. The revival and widespread popularity of the tā moko is an example. It has become a validating symbol for persons wanting to emphasise their identity as Māori. There is also the tatau pounamu, symbol of a peace agreement. There is a new relevance to how our ancestors negotiated peace agreements and how they made them hold. As more and more Treaty settlements are concluded between the Crown and various iwi groups, peace agreements become increasingly relevant. In the modern context the tikanga associated with peace agreements might need to be revised as it should be between iwi that have old scores to settle.

New grounds have been explored, for example in the chapter on creativity. Here an attempt has been made to describe the tikanga associated with creativity and in various domains of artistic activity. Many Māori are involved in creative activities, and thus presenting a chapter on mahi auaha or creative work is useful to provide some guidelines for artists and creators.

Also new for tikanga Māori is looking at some of the burning issues of our time. An attempt has been made to offer some ideas as to how one may arrive at a tikanga Māori position on an issue such as genetic modification. There are many issues of this sort that fall squarely into the area of ethics. The question whether it is right or wrong to accept the notion of putting human genes into pigs for medical purposes is an example of the sort of issue that we face. Tikanga Māori is about whether an action is right or wrong and whether it is morally appropriate or whether it is absolutely wrong. But in the case of tikanga Māori, judgements are made against a background of Māori values and knowledge. The general public, on the other hand, makes judgements based on other philosophies, other bases of knowledge and other values. Sometimes the contrasting positions might actually be complementary and share some common grounds. These issues are very topical, are often charged with emotions, have dedicated advocates pushing them and often have the effect of splitting communities. Looked at from the point of view of tikanga Māori, these issues remain complex and have the capacity to create interesting discussions among whānau.

Medically driven innovations often require major shifts in thinking and require the establishment of new benchmarks. Some of them require time and a sense of precedent to convince the public that the idea is not harmful to humans and that there are real benefits in these new ways of curing old ailments. Heart operations have explored the frontiers of possibilities beyond the ken of many people and now they have become expected and commonplace.

Sacrificing animals for the common good of humans raises problems for animal activists. They argue that humans have no right to regard themselves as the centre of the universe, and to make all animals subservient to humans, existing to provide for human needs. Māori have problems with the idea of placing human genes into cows, for example, to make cow's milk more compatible for human consumption, or into pigs to provide skin grafts for burn victims. The purpose is good but the means is troublesome and raises moral issues. But while the public at large might take a detached view of these innovations and condemn them, those patients urgently in need of new cures, new solutions and new technology take an entirely different view. If it means saving a life then this conforms with the value we place on the person. He aha te mea nui i tēnei ao? (What is the great value in this world?) Māku e kī atu he tangata, he tangata, he tangata (I will say it is people, it is people, it is people). So eventually it is the high value we place on human life that might win the ethical agreement. Values play a large part in determining a position.

This introduction covers a fair range of tikanga, of situations and issues, but obviously does not pretend to cover everything. However, there is sufficient here to begin the process of understanding, and for some to allay their fears that this is all about hocus-pocus. Every culture has tikanga, and cultures borrow the bits and pieces of customs from other lands that appeal to them. Tikanga is real, it plays a part in the everyday life of Māori. While on the one hand it might weigh heavily as a burden for some individuals, for most others tikanga Māori is empowering, validates being Māori, provides light where there might be darkness, illuminates the highway of life so we know where we are going, and enriches. Lastly, it is a blessing on the mind, a gift from the ancestors, a legacy that we share, and something to nurture and cherish.

Glossary

ahi-kā	burning fire; rights to land by occupation
ahikāroa	fires of occupation; rights to land by occupation
ahi matiti *also* whakamatiti	mākutu – rite that causes a thief to become mentally deranged
ahi taitai	lit. a sacred fire; form of karakia
aho ariki	chiefly line
aho tapu	lit. the sacred thread; main thread in weaving
āhua	aura; attributes, characteristics and talents
āhua o te tangata, te	form, character and make-up of a person
ahurewa	altar in the whare wānanga
aituā	disaster
amo	fixed upright posts on either side of the house
ao mārama, te *also* te aotūroa	world of light
ara tauwhāiti a Tāne, te	the birth passage
ariki	high chief
aroha	love, respect, compassion
aroha ki te tangata, he tangata	a person concerned about people who wants to help wherever possible
aroha tamariki	affection for children
auaha	shape, create, form, fashion
aukati	no-trespass rāhui; a line across which the movement of people is ritually restricted
awe	strength, power, influence
ea	satisfaction
ewe *also* whenua	placenta

hahunga	disinter and clean the bones of the dead
hākari	ritual feast
hākari taonga	feast for exchanging gifts
hāngi	earth oven
hapū	sub-tribe; pregnant
hara	transgression
harakeke	flax
hara–utu–ea	cause–means of resolution–settlement
hari mate also kawe mate	to continue the mourning ceremony at other places
harirū	handshakes in pōhiri reception line
hau	vitality of human life, vital essence of land
hau kāinga, te	home
hauora	health, spirit of life, vigour
hauwarea	morose, weak, cowardly, lacking in direction
hei tiki/tiki	flat figure of greenstone worn about the neck
hiki i te tapu o te whare	lifting the tapu of the house
Hine-ahu-one	Atua – the first woman, created by Tāne; mother of Hine-titama
Hine-nui-te-pō	Atua – the great lady of the night; goddess of death
Hine-titama	Atua – daughter of Tāne and Hine-ahu-one
hōhonutanga, te	the research principle of deepening knowledge
hohou	bind or lash together
hohou rongo also whakaratarata	make peace
hongi	touching of noses
huahua	preserved birds
hui whakapūmau	Māori graduation ceremony – a meeting to bind the knowledge gained by students
hura kōhatu	unveiling a headstone
hurihanga takapau, te	turning the floor mat
ihi	power, authority, essential force
iho	section of the umbilical cord between the pito and the rauru

ira Atua	the Gods
ira tangata	a human life that has inherited a collection of genes from the parents
iwikore	lit. no bones; no energy
kai	food; to eat
kaihau-waiū	birthright; property or attribute gained through the mother's milk
kaimoana	seafood
kaioraora	derogatory song
kaipaipa	to smoke (tobacco)
kairāmua	lit. eating the day before; an offence against a rāhui
kai-tarukino, he tangata	a drug abuser
kaitiaki	guardians
kākahu whakataratara, he	a cloak of nettles (burden borne by the kiri mate)
kākano	seed
kāuta	cooking shed
ka rere āmiomio	flying around in circles
kanohi i kitea, he	a face seen
kapa haka	group performing arts or culture display
kapu *also* whatu	object invested by the tohunga with powers for rendering a rāhui
kapua pōuri, he	a dark cloud (burden borne by the kiri mate)
karakia	incantation
karakia turuki	karakia that recharge the kapu, bringing a rāhui back to full strength
karakia tūturu Māori	traditional karakia
karakia whakaoho	incantation to awaken a conservation rāhui
karamū	shrub, *coprosma robusta* etc.
karengo	seaweed
kauae runga	lit. upper jaw; the domain of things celestial in the whare wānanga
kaumātua	elder or elders
kauwhanga/kauhanga	open space or centre line in the whare wānanga
kawanga whare	ceremony to open a house

kawe mate *also* hari mate	continue the mourning ceremony at other places
keka, he tangata	person who loses self-control when stressed
keka huarahi	road rage
kiekie	plant (*freycinetia banksii*) used in tukutuku work
kino, he tangata	a badly behaved person
kiri mate	lit. skin of death; bereaved family
koha	gift (to be reciprocated), contribution
koroua	male elders
kōhanga reo	lit. language nest; a Māori-language-medium pre-school
kōhuru, he tangata	murderer
kōiti	little finger
kōiwi	bones
kōwhaiwhai	painted patterns
kua ea	the obligation has been met
kuia	female elder or elders
kūmara	sweet potato
kura kaupapa Māori	Māori-language-medium primary and secondary schools
māhaki, he tangata	self-possessed, calm, quiet, mild-mannered, humble person
mahinga kai	seafood gardens and other traditional sources of food
maihi	front bargeboards of a house
maioha	welcome ceremony for a newborn
mākutu	sorcery, witchcraft
mana	prestige
manaaki/atawhai, he tangata	caring person helpful to others
manaakitanga	hospitality
mana Atua	Gods of the Māori world; spiritual authority
mana tangata	human authority
mana tipuna	prestige and power drawn from the ancestors

manawa wera	derisive chant
manea	aura of a footprint
manuhiri	visitors and guests
manuhiri tūārangi	distinguished visitor
māngere, he tangata	a lazy person
māra	garden
marae	ceremonial courtyard; village plaza
māramatanga	enlightenment
māramatanga, te	research principle of expanding knowledge towards light
maro	apron; an apron of fronds, leaves, or a fragment of cloth, attached to a pou rāhui
mātāmua	principle of primogeniture, firstborn
matapiko, he tangata	a mean person
mātauranga Māori	Māori knowledge
mauāhara, he tangata	person who harbours a grudge, nurses resentment
mauri	spark of life, the active component that indicates the person is alive
mauri oho	startled mauri in reaction to a shock
mauri rere	flying mauri, a mauri startled to a great degree
mauri tau	mauri at peace
māwe	lock of hair taken from victim of warfare
moenga rangatira	chiefly marriage bed
moenga tangata	marriage bed of humans
moko	tattoo
morenga o te poho, te	lower end of the breast bone, spot just below a woman's breasts, used in the whakatō tamariki ceremony
muru	ritual redistribution of wealth as compensation/ punishment for an offence
muru–raupatu	Government- and Pākehā-initiated confiscation of Māori land
nanakia	an untrustworthy, hail-fellow-well-met wheeler dealer

noa	balance, neutrality
ngau whiore, he tangata	person who commits incest
ngā-whatu-mataki	stones where students sat in the whare wānanga
ohonga	portion of hau gathered from hair, clothing, saliva etc.
oho rangi	lit. awakening the sky; a karakia recited at the tohi ceremony
ope	collective term for a group of visitors
pā	former name for marae complex
pāeke	pōhiri protocol in which the tangata whenua all speak first, followed by the manuhiri
paepae *also* taumata	speakers' bench
paepae poto	threshold
paepae tapu	sacred bar in the latrine
pā harakeke, te	flax bush; metaphor for generations
pākūwhā	traditional marriage feast given at the handing over of the bride
paparoa	spot where the takapau wharanui was spread out during the tohi
Papa-tū-ā-nuku	Earth Mother
parāoa	whalebone
pare	lintel
pātaka	food store
patu	club, weapon
patu wahine/kōhuru tamariki, he tangata	wife/child abuser
pito	section of the umbilical cord nearest the baby's body
piupiu	a garment
pōhiri/pōwhiri	welcome ceremony
pōkeka	form of haka that men and women perform together
pokinga taringa	piercing the ears of a child
pono	true to the principles of culture
poporokai-whiria	fire stick used in the friction method of fire starting

pōrangi	mad
poroporoaki	leavetaking
pōtiki	lastborn
pou kurukuru	weaving pegs
poupou	ancestor posts along an inside wall
pou rāhui	rāhui post to which is attached a maro and a whatu
pōuritanga	darkness
poutokomanawa	figure at the base of a centre pole in a carved house
pō whakamutunga, te	the final night at a tangihanga
pūhā	*sonchus oleraceus*, sow thistle; boiled as greens and often linked with pork bones
puhi	woman of high rank
pūkenga, he tangata	a skilled, knowledgeable, learned person
pukuaroha	sympathetic
pukukai	greedy
pukukata	given to much laughter
pukumahara	cautiousness
pukumahi	hardworking, industrious
pukunui	greedy
pukungangare	aggressive, obstructive, quarrelsome
pukuriri	angry
pukutākaro	playful
pūmahara, he tangata	a thoughtful and wise person
pūmanawa	personal characteristics, talent
pūrahorua	lit. man of two testicles; a messenger between parties who is related by whakapapa to both sides
pūremu, he tangata	an adulterer
rāhui	ritual prohibition either placed on a place, or part of a river, part of the foreshore or on certain resources
Rakahore	child of the atua Hine-moana and Kiwa; a personification of rocks
rangahau	research
rangatahi	youth

rangatiratanga	political – sovereignty, chieftainship, leadership, self-determination, self-management; individual – qualities of leadership and chieftainship over a social group, a hapū or iwi.
Ranginui	Sky Father
Rarohenga	the underworld
raupatu	taken by the blade of a patu, by force
raupō	bulrush, *typha angustifolia*
rauru	section of the umbilical cord nearest the placenta
rauru maruaitu	lit. umbilical cord of disaster: stillborn baby; severe complications that result in the expected death of the mother
rauru nui	lit. large umbilical cord: birth without complications that produced a normal healthy child
rauru whiria	lit. tangled umbilical cord: prolonged and difficult birth, perhaps with an unwell baby born
rāwaho	outsider
ringa kaha o aituā, te	strong hand of fate
ringaringa raupā	calloused hands; sign of a worker
ringa wera	lit. hot hands; cook
rohe	boundary, territory (of an iwi)
Rongo	Atua – god of peace
rongo-ā-marae	peace negotiated on the marae
rongo-ā-whare	peace agreement brought about by a woman
rongomau	peace accord properly bound and lashed together
rongo taketake	well-established peace, but not to the degree of a tatau pounamu
ruahine	woman who has a ritual to perform
rūnanga	tribal administration headquarters
tahua roa	traditional marriage feast where heaps of food were presented to guests to be consumed on site
tahuaroa	place where the great mat is spread out on the verandah of the house for the pure ceremony
taiao	natural world
taina	junior

tā i te kawa	lifting the tapu; ceremony to manage levels of tapu in a new structure
takahi i te paepae poto	cross the threshold of a house during the kawanga-whare ceremony
takahi whare	lit. tramping the house; part of the protocol for clearing a house of its deceased occupant
takapau wharanui	lit. great sleeping mat; chiefly marriage bed, mat spread out during the tohi ceremony
takawaenga	mediator
take	cause
take ōhākī	land allocated as part of the last testament of a dying chief
take raupatu	claim by conquest through the blade of a patu
take tuku, he	a claim based on rights by way of a gift
take—utu—ea	principle of cause, reciprocation and balance
takiwā	territory, district or space occupied by an iwi
takoha	gift giving
tā moko	tattoo
Tāne	Atua – creator of humanity, God of the forests
tāngaengae	umbilical cord
Tangaroa	Atua – God of the sea
tangata whenua	people of the land
tangihanga/tangi	funeral and burial ceremony
tāniko	woven ornamental border
taonga	a highly prized object
taonga tuku iho	gift of the ancestors, precious heritage
tāpōrena	tarpaulin
tapu	state of being set apart
tapuhi	midwife
tapu o te tangata, te	the sanctity of the person
tatau pounamu	lit. greenstone door; metaphoric reference to a peace agreement that holds for all time
taua	war party, hostile expedition
taua muru	muru war party

taua wahine	war party formed to deal with trouble over women
taumata *also* paepae	speakers' bench
Taumatua	child of the Atua Hine-moana and Kiwa; personification of stones
tauparapara	formulaic recital to begin a speech
taura here	lit. bound ropes; urban iwi groups linked to the home tribe
tau-utuutu	protocol in which tangata whenua speakers alternate with manuhiri speakers
Tāwhirimātea	Atua – God of the elements
te aotūroa *also* te ao mārama	light of day; this world
tekoteko	carved figure at apex of house
Te Kuwatawata	keeper of the entrance to Rarohenga
tīhei mauri ora	the sneeze of life, a formulaic beginning for a speech
tika	appropriate behaviour, good grace
tikanga tuku iho	tikanga passed from generation to generation
tino rangatiratanga	self-determination
tiramākā	companies of shy but active souls, wairua who fly in space
tītoki	tree, *alectryon excelsum*
toa	personal achievement or service, brave
tohi	baptism ceremony
tohunga	priest; skilled spiritual leader; expert
tohunga patapātai	tohunga who conducts an examination by oral questioning
tohunga tā moko	tattoo expert
tohunga tārai waka	expert canoe builder
tohunga tohiora	tohunga who conducts the tohi ceremony
tohunga whakairo	master carver
tokotoko	carved stick, staff
tuahine	sister/cousin
tūāhu	sacred place, altar

tūāhu tāpātai, he	an examining tohunga
tuakana/taina	senior/junior
tuakiri	identity, person, personality
tūao	a volunteer
tūāpana	karakia used to clear dangerous tapu from the mother during the tohi ceremony
tuarongo	back wall of a meeting house
tuku pukapuka, he	letting go of a book and making it available to the public
tukutuku	lattice work
tuku wairua	ceremony to release the wairua
Tūmatauenga	Atua – God of war and human affairs
tūpāpaku	lit. to stand shallow, rather than tall; corpse
tūranga	place or primary locality intimately associated with the identity of the hapū and therefore with the identity of the person
tūrangawaewae	place for the feet to stand, home
tūrehu	fairy folk, wairua that live around mountains and forests
tūroro	a patient
turuki i te kapu rāhui	sharpen the teeth of the rāhui
tūtūā	slaves
tūturu	genuine, permanent , enduring
umu-a-Tāne, te	lit. the oven of Tāne; small sacred fire
urupā	cemetery
utu	reciprocation
utu–ea	compensation–state of balance
waerea	karakia used to clear ritual danger away from visitor's pathway during a wero
waewae tapu	first-time visitor to a marae
wāhi ngaro	the missing part of one's life
wāhi tapu	sacred spots
waiata tangi	lament
wā kāinga	home base

wai māori	fresh water
wairangi, he tangata	a person suffering from mental illness
wairua	soul, spirit
wai tai	sea water
waka taua	war canoe
waka tūpāpaku	burial chest
wana	inspire fear, awe; sublimity
wānanga	Māori tertiary institution
ware	low born
wehi	fearsomeness
wero	ritual challenge to visitors
whaikōrero	oration
whakaaro	thought; a koha or gift
whakaeke	approach onto the marae
whakahauora	cause to be well
whakahoro	casting aside prior offences and wrongs against tapu, part of the whakatō tamariki ceremony
whakairo	carving
whakamā	shame
whakamatiti *also* ahi matiti	mākutu—a magic rite that causes a thief to become mentally deranged
whakamomori, he tangata	a person who commits suicide
whakanoa ritual	tapu-reducing ritual
whakanoa taonga, he	when a book is launched, removing the tapu associated with a book from the book, its writer and publisher
whakapapa	genealogy
whakapōtaetanga	capping a student
whakaratarata	make familiar, friendly
whakarewa pukapuka, he	a book launch
whakatika	correction of error
whakatō tamariki	lit. planting the seed of the child; ceremony to aid fertility

whakatū	cause to stand
whaka-wahine/ whaka-tāne, he tangata	a person who behaves in ways appropriate to the opposite gender; a gay man/lesbian
whakawātea ceremony	ceremony to clear lingering tapu
whakawhānau	give birth, childbirth
whāmere	family
whānako/tāhae, he tangata	a thief
whānau	be born; be in childbed; offspring, family group; family, but modern; familiar term of address
whanaunga	relative
whanaungatanga	relationships
whānau nui tonu	super whānau (in size)
whānau takawaenga	family whose marriage brings two conflicting parties together to secure peace
whano-kē, he tangata	an extreme eccentric
whanonga	behaviour
whānuitanga, te	the research principle of expanding knowledge outwards
wharekai	dining house or room
whare kōhanga	lit. nest house; house for an expectant mother of rank and her midwives
whare mate	lit. house of death; house where the dead lie in state
wharenui	big house
whare ngaro	lit. lost house; family without issue or whose children died before adulthood
whare pora	house of weaving
whare tangata	womb
whare tapu	sacred house for the whare wānanga
whare tipuna	ancestral house
whare tuatahi	traditional marriage feast given by the husband's group
whare wānanga	house of learning
whare whakaira tangata	lit. the house to create a new human being; a woman who acts as a natural or surrogate mother

whare whakairo	carved meeting house
whāriki	floor mats
whati	a break, omission or memory failure in reciting karakia, regarded as a bad omen
whatu	stone invested by the tohunga with powers for rendering a rāhui effective – karakia are said and the whatu is hidden away from the pou rāhui; equivalent to the mauri of a building
whatu-kura	stones of knowledge in the whare wānanga
whenua	earth, placenta
whenua muru	land sacrificed by a group in order to compensate others for a wrong done to them
whenua papatipu/ papatupu	customary land under customary title
whenua taunaha	land named and claimed by discovery
whenua tuku	land that has been gifted to the occupants

Bibliography

A Taranaki Veteran. 1919. 'The Great Muru'. *Journal of the Polynesian Society* 28:97–102.

Angas, George French. 1847. *Savage Life and Scenes in Australia and New Zealand.* London: Smith, Elder and Co.

Archey, Gilbert. 1977. *Whaowhia: Maori Art and its Artists.* Auckland: Collins.

Ballara, Angela. 1995. 'The Formation of an Eighteenth Century Community in Southern Hawke's Bay'. *New Zealand Journal of History* 29:3–18.

Barlow, Cleve. 2001 [1991]. *Tikanga Whakaaro: Key Concepts in Maori Culture.* Auckland: Oxford University Press.

Beaglehole, John C. 1962. *The Endeavour Journal of Joseph Banks 1768–1771.* Vols 1 and 2. Sydney: Angus & Robertson.

——. 1967. *The Journals of Captain James Cook: The Voyage of the Resolution and Discovery, 1776–1780.* Cambridge: Cambridge University Press.

——. 1968. *The Journals of Captain James Cook: The Voyage of the Endeavour 1768–1771.* Cambridge: Cambridge University Press.

Belshaw, Horace. 1940. 'Maori Economic Circumstances.' In Ivan Sutherland, ed. *The Maori People Today: A General Survey.* Christchurch: Whitcombe & Tombs, pp. 182–228.

Best, Elsdon. 1904. 'Notes of the Custom of Rahui'. *Journal of the Polynesian Society* 13:83–88.

——. 1924. *The Maori As He Was.* Wellington: A.R. Shearer Government Printer.

——. 1924. *The Maori.* Vols 1 and 2. Wellington: Harry H. Tombs.

——. 1929. *The Whare Kohanga (the "nest house") and its Lore.* Wellington: Government Printer.

——. 1941. *The Maori.* Vols 1 and 2. Wellington: The Polynesian Society.

——. 1972. *Tuhoe, the Children of the Mist.* 2nd ed. Wellington: Polynesian Society and A.H. & A.W. Reed.

——. 1976 [1924]. *Maori Religion and Mythology.* Part 1. Wellington: Government Printer.

——. 1982. *Maori Religion and Mythology.* Part 2. Wellington: Government Printer.

——. 1996. *Tuhoe, the Children of the Mist.* 4th ed. Auckland: Reed.

Biggs, Bruce. 1960. *Maori Marriages: An Essay in Reconstruction*. Wellington: Polynesian Society.

———. 'Humpty Dumpty and the Treaty of Waitangi'. In I. Hugh Kawharu, ed. *Maori and Pakeha Perspectives of the Treaty of Waitangi*. Auckland: Auckland University Press, pp. 300–311.

Binney, Judith, and Gillian Chaplin. 1996. *Nga Morehu: The Survivors*. Auckland: Auckland University Press and Bridget Williams Books.

Boast, Richard. 1999. 'The Evolution of Maori Land Law, 1862–1992'. In Richard Boast et al. *Maori Land Law*. Wellington: Butterworths, pp. 78–79.

Brougham, A.E. and Alexander W. Reed. 1987 [1963]. *Maori Proverbs*. Auckland: Reed Methuen Publishers.

Broughton, Ruka. 1985. 'Incompatibility between Maoritanga and Christianity'. *Tu Tangata* 27:5–7.

Bryan, Jenny, and John Clare. 2001. *Organ Farm. Pig-to-Human Transplants: Medical Miracle or Genetic Time Bomb?* London: Carlton Books Ltd.

Buck, Peter (Te Rangi Hiroa). 1987 [1925]. *The Coming of the Maori*. Wellington: Maori Purposes Fund Board.

Buller, Walter L. 1895. 'On Some Peculiar Maori Remains'. *Transactions of the New Zealand Institute* 27:151–52.

Butcher, Margot. 2003. 'Treaty Fatigue: What is Maori? Who is Pakeha?' *North and South*. August. 36–47.

Cowan, James. 1930. *Legends of The Maori*. Wellington: Harry H. Tombs.

Dansey, Harry. 1971. *Maori Custom Today*. Auckland: New Zealand Newspapers Ltd.

———. 1981. 'A View of Death.' In Michael King, ed. *Te Ao Hurihuri*. Auckland: Longman Paul, pp. 129–41.

Department of Corrections. 2000. 'Forecast Report'. Wellington: Department of Corrections.

Durie, Eddie. 1986. 'The Maori Understanding of a Gift compared to the Law of Charities'. In *Te Kaupapa Tikanga Rua: Bi-Cultural Development. The Report of the Bi-Cultural Commission of the Anglican Church of the Province of New Zealand*. Auckland: Provincial Secretary of the Church, pp. 44–45.

———. 1987. 'The Law and the Land'. In Jock Phillips, ed. *Te Whenua Te Iwi, The Land and the People*. Wellington: Allen & Unwin and Port Nicholson Press, pp. 78–81.

Durie, Eddie for the Waitangi Tribunal. 1994. *Custom Law, Working Paper*. Wellington: Waitangi Tribunal.

Elder, John Rawson. 1932. *The Letters and Journals of Samuel Marsden, 1765–1838*. Dunedin: Otago University Council and Coulls Somerville Wilke Ltd.

Farmer, Don. 2001. 'A Reflection of Time in the Hot Seat'. *Wairarapa Times Age*.www.times-age.co.nz/weekly/2001/farmer.html. 11 February.

Firth, Raymond. 1929. *Primitive Economics of the New Zealand Maori*. London: George Routledge & Sons.

——. 1959. *Economics of the New Zealand Maori*. Wellington: Government Printer.

Fisheries Task Force. 1992. *Sustainable Fisheries:Tiakina Nga Taonga a Tangaroa*. Report to the Minister of Fisheries. Wellington.

Gardiner, Wira. 1993. *Ngā Kai o Te Moana – Customary Fisheries: Philosophy and Practices, Legislation and Change*. Wellington: Te Puni Kōkiri, Ministry of Māori Development.

Goldman, Irving. 1970. *Ancient Polynesian Society*. Chicago: University of Chicago Press.

Grey, George. 1857. *Ko Nga Waiata Maori*. Capetown: Printed at Pike's Machine Printing Office.

Gudgeon, Thomas Wayth. 1885. *The History and Doings of the Maori*. Auckland: Evening Star.

Halsbury's Laws of England. 1998. 4th ed. Reissue. Vol. 12(1). London: Butterworths.

Hamilton, Augustus. 1901. *Maori Art*. Wellington: The New Zealand Institute.

Handy, E.S. Craighill. 1923. 'The Native Culture in the Marquesas'. *Bernice P. Bishop Museum Bulletin* 9.

——. 1930. 'The History and Culture in the Society Islands'. *Bernice P. Bishop Museum Bulletin* 79.

Law Commission. 2001. *Maori Custom and Values in New Zealand Law*. Study Paper 9. Wellington: Law Commission.

Love, Ngatata. 1996. *Sites of Significance Process: A Step by Step Guide to Protecting Sites of Cultural, Spiritual and Historical Significance to Māori*.Wellington: Te Puni Kōkiri, Ministry of Māori Development.

Mahuika, Api. 1981. 'Leadership: Inherited and Achieved'. In Michael King, ed. *Te Ao Hurihuri*. Auckland: Longman Paul, pp. 64–85.

Mahuta, Robert. 1987. 'Te Whenua, Te Iwi'. In Jock Phillips, ed. *Te Whenua Te Iwi, The Land and the People*. Wellington: Allen & Unwin and Port Nicholson Press, pp. 82–87.

Maning, Frederick E. 1912. *Old New Zealand*. Christchurch: Whitcombe & Tombs.

McLean, Mervyn. 1996. *Maori Music*. Auckland: Auckland University Press.

Mead, Hirini (Sidney) Moko, and Kapua Bargh. 1998. *Understanding the Custom of Aukati*. Whakatane: Ngati Awa Research and Archives Trust.

Mead, Hirini (Sidney) Moko, and Neil Grove. 2001. *Ngā Pēpeha a Ngā Tīpuna: The Sayings of the Ancestors*. Wellington: Victoria University Press.

Mead, Hirini (Sidney) Moko, and Onehou Eliza Phillis. 1982. *The Abundant Earth – Te One Matua : the Centennial of Ruataupare, at Kokohinau Marae, Te Teko, 1882–1982*. Te Teko: Ngati Pahipoto and the Komiti Maori o Kokohinau.

Mead, Hirini (Sidney) Moko, et al. 1984. *Te Maori: Maori Art from New Zealand Collections*. New York: Harry N. Adams.

Mead, Hirini (Sidney) Moko. 1969. *Traditional Maori Clothing*. Wellington: A.H & A.W. Reed.

——. 1984. 'Nga Tikanga Tuku Iho A Te Maori: Customary Concepts of the Maori.' Wellington: Victoria University of Wellington.

——. 1995. *Te Toi Whakairo: The Art of Maori Carving*. Auckland: Reed Publishing.

——. 1996. *Tawhaki: The Deeds of a Demigod*. Auckland: Reed Publishing.

——. 1997. *Landmarks, Bridges and Visions. Aspects of Maori Culture*. Wellington: Victoria University Press.

——. 1997. *Maori Art on the World Scene*. Wellington: Ahua Design and Matau Associates Ltd.

——. 1999. *Taniko Weaving: Technique and Tradition*. Auckland: Reed Publishing.

Meek, James. 2003. 'Dolly the Sheep is Put to Sleep'. *Guardian Unlimited*, www.guardian.co.uk/genes/article/0,2763,895984,00.html. 15 February 2003.

Metge, Joan. 1967. *The Maoris of New Zealand*. London: Routledge and Kegan Paul.

——. 2001. Comments provided to Law Commission in response to draft paper 'Maori Custom and Value in New Zealand Law'.

Ministry of Justice. 2001. *He Hinatore ki te Ao Maori: A Glimpse into the Maori World (Maori Perspectives on Justice)*. Wellington: Ministry of Justice.

Neich Roger. 1977. 'Historical Change in Rotorua Ngati Tarawhai Woodcarving Art'. MA thesis, Victoria University of Wellington.

——. 2001. *Carved Histories: Rotorua Ngati Tarawhai Woodcarving*. Auckland: Auckland University Press.

New Zealand Conservation Authority. 1997. 'Maori Customary Use of Native Birds, Plants and Other Traditional Materials'. New Zealand Conservation Authority. Wellington.

New Zealand Government. 1970. *Reception to her Majesty the Queen, His Royal Highness the Duke of Edinburgh, His Royal Highness the Prince of Wales and Her Royal Highness Princess Anne by the Māori people, Gisborne, 22 March 1970*. Wellington: Government Printer.

Ngata, Apirana. 1959. *Nga Moteatea*. Parts 1 and 2. Wellington: Polynesian Society.

Ngata, Apirana. 1940. 'Maori Arts and Crafts'. In Ivan Sutherland, ed. *The Maori People Today*. Christchurch: Whitcombe & Tombs.

——. 1940. 'Tribal Organisation'. In Ivan Sutherland, ed. *The Maori People Today*. Christchurch: Whitcombe & Tombs Ltd.

——. 1943. *Souvenir of the Ngarimu Victoria Cross Institute Meeting and Reception to his Excellency the Governor General Sir Cyril Newall*. Wellington: Whitcombe & Tombs.

Office of Treaty Settlements. *Waikato-Tainui Deed of Settlement*. 22 May 1995. Enacted as Waikato Raupatu Claims Settlement Act, 1995.

Oliver, Douglas L. 1974. *Ancient Tahitian Society*. Vols 1, 2 and 3. Canberra: Australian National University Press.

Ollivier, Isabel, and Cheryl Hingley, trans. 1982. *Extracts from Journals Relating to the Visit to New Zealand of the French Ship* St Jean Baptiste *in December 1769, under the Command of J.F.M. de Surville*. Wellington: Alexander Turnbull Library Endorsement Trust: National Library of New Zealand.

Orange, Claudia. 1987. *The Treaty of Waitangi*. Wellington: Allen & Unwin.

Pérez de Cuéllar, Javier. 1996. *Our Creative Diversity: Report of the World Commission on Culture and Development*. Paris: UNESCO Publishing.

Polack, Joel S. 1974. *New Zealand: Being a Narrative of Travels and Adventures During a Residence in that Country Between the Years 1831 and 1837*. Christchurch: Capper Press.

Police v Cooper. 1999. *The Maori Law Review*. http://www.bennion.co.nz/mlr/1999/sep.html

Pool, Ian. 1991. *Te Iwi Maori: A New Zealand Population Past, Present & Projected*. Auckland: Auckland University Press.

Porter, Frances, ed. 1974. *The Turanga Journals 1840–1850, Letters and Journals of William and Jane Williams, Missionaries to Poverty Bay*. Wellington: Price Milburn for Victoria University Press.

Puketapu-Hetet, Erenora. 1989. *Maori Weaving with Erenora Puketapu-Hetet*. Auckland: Pitman Publishing.

Salmond, Anne. 1975. *Hui*. Wellington: A.H. & A.W. Reed.

——. 1976. *Amiria: The Story of a Maori Woman*. Wellington: A.H. & A.W. Reed.

——. 1980. *Eruera: The Teachings of a Maori Elder*. Wellington: Oxford University Press.

——. 1991. *Two Worlds: First Meetings Between Maori and European*. Auckland: Viking and Penguin Books.

Savage, Stephen. 1962. *A Dictionary of the Maori Language of Rarotonga*. Wellington: Department of Island Territories and Government of the Cook Islands.

Schwimmer, Eric. 1966. *The World of the Maori*. Wellington: A.H. & A.W. Reed.

Shirres, Michael P. 1982. 'Tapu'. *Journal of the Polynesian Society* 11(1):29–51.

——. 1986. 'An Introduction to Karakia'. Ph.D. diss. in Anthropology. University of Auckland.

——. 1997. *Te Tangata: The Human Person*. Auckland: Accent Publications.

Simmons, David R. 1997. *Te Whare Runanga*. Auckland: Reed Publishing.

Simon, Judith, and Linda Tuhiwai Smith, eds. 2001. *A Civilising Mission: Perceptions and Representations of the New Zealand Native School System*. Auckland: Auckland University Press.

Simon, Judith, ed. 1998. *Nga Kura Maori: The Native School System 1867–1969*. Auckland: Auckland University Press.

Sinclair, Douglas. 1981. 'Land Since The Treaty'. In Michael King, ed. *Te Ao Hurihuri*. Auckland: Longman Paul, pp. 107–128.

——. 1981. 'Land: Maori View and European Response'. In Michael King, ed. *Te Ao Hurihuri*. Auckland: Longman Paul, pp. 86–106.

Smith, Norman. 1942. *Native Custom and Law Affecting Native Land*. Wellington: Maori Purposes Fund Board.

Smith, Stephenson Percy. 1910. *Maori Wars of the Nineteenth Century: The Struggle of the Northern Against the Southern Maori Tribes Prior to the Colonisation of New Zealand in 1840*. Christchurch: Whitcombe & Tombs.

——, trans. 1913. 'The Lore of the Whare-wananga'. *New Zealand Memoirs of the Polynesian Society*. Vol. 3. New Plymouth: T. Avery.

Stafford, Don M. 1967. *Te Arawa: A History of the Arawa People*. Wellington: A.H. & A.W. Reed.

Statistics New Zealand. 1998. *Census 1996: Iwi*. Vols 1 and 2. Wellington: Statistics New Zealand, Te Tari Tatau.

Sutherland, Ivan, and John Pascoe. 1949. *The Ngarimu Hui: V.C. Investiture Meeting, 1943*. Wellington: Polynesian Society.

Swan, L. 'The Man Behind the Moko'. *Panorama*. Air New Zealand Inflight Magazine. August 2001, p. 36.

Taura Whiri i te Reo Māori, Te. 1996. *Te Matatiki*. Rev. ed. Auckland: Oxford University Press.

Taylor, Richard. 1870. *Te Ika A Maui: New Zealand and its Inhabitants*. London: William MacIntosh, and Wanganui: H. Ireson Jones.

Te Kanawa, Diggeress. 1992. *Weaving a Kakahu*. Wellington: Bridget Williams Books.

Te Kuiti, W.B. 1905. *Where The Whiteman Treads: Across the Pathway of the Maori*. Auckland: Wilson and Horton.

Te Puni Kōkiri. 1992. *Nga Toka Tu Moana: Maori Leadership and Decision Making*. Wellington: Te Puni Kōkiri, Ministry of Maori Development.

——. 1996. *Sites of Significance Process: Wahi Tapu*. Wellington: Te Puni Kōkiri, Ministry of Maori Development.

——. 1998. *Progress Towards Closing Social and Economic Gaps Between Maori and Non Maori – A Report to the Minister of Maori Affairs*. Wellington: Te Puni Kōkiri, Ministry of Maori Development.

Te Wananga o Raukawa. 2000. *Studies in Maori Law and Philosophy: Mai i te Ata Hapara Conference Papers*. Otaki: Te Wananga o Raukawa.

Tregear, Edward. 1891. *The Maori–Polynesian Comparative Dictionary*. Wellington: Lyon and Blair.

———. 1926. *The Maori Race*. Wanganui: D. Willis Ltd.

Turbott, Harold B. 1940. 'Health and Social Welfare'. In Ivan Sutherland, ed. *The Maori People Today*. Christchurch: Whitcombe & Tombs Ltd, pp. 229–268.

Vayda, Andrew P. 1960. *Maori Warfare*. Wellington: Polynesian Society.

Waitangi Tribunal. 1986. *Report of the Waitangi Tribunal on the Te Reo Maori Claim (Wai 11)*. Wellington: Government Printer.

———. 1996. The Taranaki Report: Kaupapa Tuatahi. Wellington: GP Publications.

Walker, Ranginui. 1981. 'Marae: A Place to Stand'. In Michael King, ed. *Te Ao Hurihuri*. Auckland: Longman Paul, pp. 21–30.

Walker, Ranginui. 1996. *Ngā Pepa a Ranginui: The Walker Papers*. Auckland: Penguin.

Webster, Steven. 1998. *Patrons of Maori Culture: Power, Theory and Ideology in the Maori Renaissance*. Dunedin: University of Otago Press.

Westra, Ans. 1964. *Washday at the Pa*. Wellington: School Publications Branch, Department of Education.

White, Taylor. 1892. 'Polynesian Society Papers'. MS Papers 1187, Folder 205. Alexander Turnbull Library, Wellington.

———. 1892. 'The Rahui, Extracts from a paper by Taylor White'. *Journal of the Polynesian Society* 1:275–276.

Williams, Herbert W. 1957. *A Dictionary of the Maori Language*. Wellington: Government Printer.

———. 1971. *A Dictionary of the Maori Language*. Wellington: Government Printer.

Williams, Joseph. 1996. 'He Aha te Tikanga?' Unpublished paper for the Law Commission.

———. 2000. 'He Aha te Tikanga Māori?' Paper presented at Mai i te Ata Hapara conference, Te Wananga o Raukawa, Otaki, 11–13 August 2000.

Winiata, Whatarangi. 2001. Address given at Te Herenga Waka Marae, Victoria University of Wellington, 8 September 2001.

Winick, Charles. 1970. *Dictionary of Anthropology*. Westport, CT: Greenwood.

Witherspoon, Gary. 1977. *Language and Art in the Navajo Universe*. Ann Arbor: The University of Michigan Press.

Index

Bold page numbers refer to glossary definitions.

continued over